DEFENDING SAME-SEX MARRIAGE

Defending Same-Sex Marriage

Volume 2

Our Family Values

Same-Sex Marriage and Religion

Edited by Traci C. West

Mark Strasser, General Editor

Praeger Perspectives

Westport, Connecticut
London

Library of Congress Cataloging-in-Publication Data

Defending same-sex marriage / edited by Mark Strasser, et al.
  p. cm.
  Includes bibliographical references and index.
  ISBN 0-275-98772-8 (set : alk. paper)—ISBN 0-275-98773-6 (v. 1 : alk. paper)—ISBN 0-275-98808-2 (v. 2 : alk. paper)—ISBN 0-275-98894-5 (v. 3 : alk. paper) 1. Same-sex marriage—United States. 2. Same-sex marraige—Law and legislation—United States. 3. Gay rights—United States. I. Strasser, Mark Philip, 1955– II. West, Traci C., 1959– III. Dupuis, Martin, 1961– IV. Thompson, William A.
  HQ1034.U5D44 2007
  306.84'80973—dc22   2006031058

British Library Cataloguing in Publication Data is available.

Library of Congress Catalog Card Number: 2006031058
ISBN: 0-275-98772-8 (set)
          0-275-98773-6 (vol. 1)
          0-275-98808-2 (vol. 2)
          0-275-98894-5 (vol. 3)

First published in 2007

Praeger Publishers, 88 Post Road West, Westport, CT 06881
An imprint of Greenwood Publishing Group, Inc.
www.praeger.com

Printed in the United States of America

The paper used in this book complies with the
Permanent Paper Standard issued by the National
Information Standards Organization (Z39.48–1984).

10 9 8 7 6 5 4 3 2 1

CONTENTS

———————————— • ————————————

GENERAL EDITOR'S FOREWORD

———————— • ————————

Lesbian, gay, bisexual, transgender, and intersexual (LGBTI) people, like their heterosexual counterparts, form families; they have children to raise and elderly parents to take care of. LGBTI people wish to marry for many of the same symbolic and practical reasons that most people do. These include love, religious beliefs, security, the ability to make important decisions about education and medical care for family members, and a variety of financial benefits. The latter range from insurance or employment benefits to tax benefits to the ability to make sure that one's estate will go to one's loved ones.

The state benefits when LGBTI individuals marry in the same ways that it does when their heterosexual counterparts marry: the individuals themselves are happier and more productive, children are given an environment in which they can flourish, and the individuals themselves provide services for each other that the state might otherwise have to provide. For example, when an individual is legally recognized as belonging to and being a part of a family, he or she may then have the financial and emotional security to invest time, energy, and effort in taking care of a spouse, a child, or a parent who might otherwise have relied on the state for such services. Further, the state benefits when marriage is viewed as a desirable institution worthy of respect rather than as a political football or as a tool by which undeserved burdens can be imposed on disfavored groups.

Notwithstanding the benefits that would accrue to the individuals themselves and to the state and society as a whole were marriage laws more inclusive, many oppose same-sex unions generally and same-sex marriages in particular. Sometimes such unions are opposed for religious reasons, although there are many misconceptions about the relationship between same-sex unions and religious dictates. For example, some mistakenly believe that no religion permits same-sex marriages to be celebrated, while others mistakenly believe that were the state to recognize same-sex marriages, religious institutions would be forced to perform religious ceremonies for same-sex couples even if such unions were not permitted by that particular denomination.

Other individuals oppose same-sex unions for nonreligious reasons. For instance, they have a mistaken belief about what LGBTI individuals are like, or, perhaps, they worry about what would happen to the institution of marriage were same-sex unions recognized. Still others oppose such unions out of animus toward those with a same-sex orientation. That such marriages are opposed by a substantial portion of the population is made clear by the number of states that have passed constitutional amendments precluding the recognition of same-sex marriages; even more states are expected to do so in the future.

Each volume in this three-volume set addresses the recognition of same-sex unions from a different perspective. The first volume examines some of the legal issues associated with the recognition and nonrecognition of same-sex unions. Examples include the following:

- Whether or not such unions must be recognized in a state where they have been prohibited if they have been validly celebrated elsewhere
- The degree to which federal law has afforded states more flexibility than they might otherwise have had under the United States Constitution
- The similarities and differences between same-sex unions on the one hand and civil unions and domestic partnerships on the other
- The kinds of benefits that are sometimes offered by private employers
- The political effects (and noneffects) of the same-sex marriage debate
- The devastating effects on children that result from a refusal to afford legal recognition to families headed by two individuals of the same sex

The second volume contains chapters that explain why and how same-sex marriage can be understood to be compatible with a variety of religious traditions, including Judaism, Islam, Buddhism, Hinduism, Catholicism, and several Protestant sects. The authors wrote as adherents within their respective faith traditions and were thus better able to address the arguments of opponents of same-sex marriage from the same faith.

The third volume discusses three different areas related to same-sex marriage: advocacy and activism, education and the media, and cultural perspectives. The advocacy and activism chapters were written by individuals who seek to inform the public about these issues through open meetings, public demonstrations, or postings and discussions on the Internet. The chapters on education and the media chapters discuss the ways that same-sex marriage is analyzed by its opponents in college textbooks in particular or in the media more generally. Chapters addressing cultural perspectives convey how same-sex marriage bans affect or are viewed by various minorities. For instance, one chapter addresses same-sex marriage and Native

American traditions, while other chapters reveal attitudes within the African American and Hispanic communities toward same-sex marriage. These latter chapters help clear up misconceptions about who wishes to marry a same-sex partner, explaining that there is a much higher percentage of African American and Hispanic same-sex couples than might be thought and that those families are especially adversely affected by current marriage policies.

The kind of recognition that should be afforded to same-sex couples and their families is likely to be hotly debated for a long time to come, whether the focus of discussion involves recognition by the state, society, or a particular religion. The chapters in this three-volume set provide practical advice to those seeking to convince family, friends, and neighbors about the wisdom of affording recognition to such unions. They also help clarify and correct some of the misconceptions regarding individuals who want to marry a same-sex partner (e.g., what those people are like) and what legal, religious, and social ramifications would occur were such unions recognized and do occur precisely because of the refusal to recognize such unions.

Public attitudes toward recognizing the families of LGBTI individuals are changing, albeit slowly and gradually. There is a growing understanding and acceptance that LGBTI individuals deserve to have their families afforded recognition, not to be subjected to invidious discrimination. The chapters in these volumes are designed to help increase that understanding so that, one day, LGBTI individuals and their families will be able to focus on the kinds of challenges that all families must face. When that happens, the individuals themselves, the state, and society as a whole will be better off.

Mark Strasser

ACKNOWLEDGMENTS

———————— • ————————

I am very thankful to Mary Tolbert, Gary Comstock, Jennifer Wriggins, Aisha Simmons, and Zohorah Simmons for their assistance with resources and ideas as I initially began this project.

For their invaluable help with research, I express my appreciation to Jane Ellen Nickell, who once again tracked down information that I thought was impossible to find, to Susan McRae, as well as to Lynne Darden and the Theological Research Librarian Ernie Rubenstein.

I am also thankful to Joe Busse for much-needed technical assistance.

I offer sincere thanks to the general editor of the series, Mark Strasser, for his patient, encouraging nudges.

I am grateful for the help of the hardworking and talented editorial team at Praeger, especially Hilary Claggett.

For bibliographical and "emergency" editorial assistance as well as loving support and patience with me throughout the ups and downs of completing this challenging project, I offer my deepest gratitude to my life partner, Jerry G. Watts.

INTRODUCTION

——————————— · ———————————

Traci C. West

———————

In most major religious traditions there is an ongoing struggle to enable established religious rituals and traditions of marriage to be conferred upon the union of two people by treating all couples equally, without restrictions related to their sexual orientation and gender identity. It is a struggle that has vital importance for religious beliefs and practices, as well as for the broader society. Each step forward in this struggle offers opportunities to confirm religiously rooted, common moral values of human dignity and equality, as well as the preciousness of all families.

"After the precedent-setting vote, which was one of the first to put a major mainstream American religious group on record in favor of gay marriage, the room broke out in extended applause, cries of joy, and the chanted melody of the traditional Jewish prayer recited at sacred occasions," explained Rabbi Jane Rachel Litman when the Reform movement's Central Conference of American Rabbis voted in 2000 to support rabbis who choose to officiate at same-sex ceremonies.[1] The Conservative movement in Judaism is currently involved in intense debates as they consider lifting their movement's ban on blessing same-sex unions.[2] Among Protestants, fierce legislative battles have taken place at the national meetings of several denominations. For instance, in the Presbyterian Church (USA) the struggle for equality suffered a defeat at its 2000 General Assembly, with the close vote of 268 to 251 in support of banning ministers from performing same-sex marriage ceremonies. The Lutherans (Evangelical Lutheran Church of America) also voted to ban same-sex marriage ceremonies in 2005 (after rejecting the ordination of gays and lesbians by a 51 to 49 percent split vote), but at the same time, they passed a measure that enjoins pastors to provide "faithful pastoral care" to all members, allowing their pastors to support same-sex couples in the same way that they support heterosexual couples.[3] When the United Church of Christ (UCC) 2005 national assembly declared its *support* for equal marriage rights and responsibilities in its churches and in society, General Minister and President John Thomas commented

> I believe the General Synod has acted both out of a concern for justice, demanding that the present discrimination against gay, lesbian, bisexual, and transgender persons be ended, as well as out of a theological conviction that same gender couples are as capable of fulfilling the vocation of marriage as heterosexual couples, a vocation described in our marriage rite as one in which couples offer each other mutual care and companionship, bear witness to God's great gift of joy for them and for others exemplified in the story of Jesus at the wedding at Cana in Galilee, and in the intimacy of their relationship, represent the intimacy of Christ's love for the Church.[4]

In 1995, ten years before this UCC vote, the Soka Gakkai International–USA Buddhists, a community that promotes peace and individual happiness based on the teachings of the Nichiren school of Mahayana Buddhism, embraced the conducting of wedding ceremonies for its couples regardless of sexual orientation.[5] In 1996, the General Assembly of the Unitarian Universalists (UU) of America voted overwhelmingly (97 percent to 3 percent) to support marriage equality for same-sex couples.

In addition to engaging in efforts to change the discriminatory policies of religious groups, some gay couples who desire marriage ceremonies within their religious tradition have claimed their equality without waiting for the sanction of official religious bodies; for example, in Roman Catholicism in which Holy Union Guidelines, Ceremonies, and a National Couples Registry are provided by DignityUSA, a national organization of lesbian, gay, bisexual, and transgender (LGBT) Catholics.[6] Additionally, for religious traditions that have a decentralized organizational structure and widely ranging traditions of belief and practice, individual religious officials often perform marriages on an equal basis based on their own religious discernment. A Hindu priest who conducted a marriage ceremony for two lesbians in 2002 is quoted in the first chapter as commenting that after much thought and on the basis of Hindu scriptures, he concluded, "Marriage is a union of spirits, and the spirit is not male or female."

The struggle for marriage equality within major religious traditions is often overshadowed by the struggle for civil marriage rights that are not attached to sexual orientation or gender identity. For many LGBT members and practitioners of religious traditions, religious ceremonies that celebrate their marital unions are just as important to them as the availability of legal rights for married couples conferred by the state. Religious traditions that surround the ritual of marriage preserve and honor the family values that LGBT religious couples have been taught, in many cases, by their parents and the elders of their communities. Whether their religion was nurtured throughout childhood or chosen later in life through conversion, religious LGBT couples seek religious marriage rituals that reflect the values that they aspire to preserve and honor within the new family units that their unions create.

Marriage rituals, therefore, represent continuity with religious traditions as well as exciting new beginnings for how those traditions will be shaped by, for example, a religiously affirmed Jewish or Buddhist lesbian couple. Religion is transmitted through certain practices in the marriage ritual. The couple and the witnesses conserve its meaning by participating in the ritual. The religious marriage ritual is also a conduit or a means for publicly declaring the love and commitment of the couple, their community's support for them, and the couple's connection to a greater spiritual reality and historic faith community. Religion, at its best, can offer an alternative to the ethos of secular society in the way it values persons by unequivocally affirming their worth, dignity, and mind-body-spirit wholeness. Because LGBT people are subjected to so much hatred, prejudice, and discrimination in broader society, for some, it is all the more important to receive affirmation and support for their families through religious celebrations of their marriages.

The idea that religion could offer such a refuge for gay couples may be met with skepticism. Examples of Christians publicly displaying religious hatred directed at gays and lesbians are all too abundant. There is the unforgettable image of Rev. Fred Phelps's group with "GOD HATES FAGS" signs surrounding Matthew Shepard's grief-stricken family at the funeral shortly after he was brutally tortured and murdered because he was gay. The Christian preachers who call the suffering and deaths of persons with AIDS a gay plague that sinful homosexuals deserve seem impervious to the hatefulness of their message. It is difficult to estimate the damage done to children by parents who expel their gay teenage children from their homes and onto the streets or disown their adult gay children in response to admonitions of their pastors that homosexuality is an abomination. This kind of despicable religious behavior only makes the recognition of alternative religious family values rooted in compassion, justice, and equality all the more urgent.

Even though some secular advocates may argue to the contrary, the struggle for marriage equality in the religious sphere is inextricably linked to marriage equality in secular laws and customs. In seeking to maintain a separation between "church and state," proponents of legal marriage equality sometimes forfeit attention to religion. Some activists for legal marriage equality hold the position that "if religious groups want to discriminate, that's their choice, but U.S. society cannot be governed by religious dictates." I agree that the laws of our broader, religiously pluralistic society must not be bound by the dictates of any religious group. But discrimination within religious traditions should not be tolerated in order to keep homophobic religious activists at bay in the effort to achieve secular forms of marriage equality. A heterosexist interpretation of religious tradition should not be permitted to impose unjust treatment of persons in *either* the secular or the religious arena. A community-wide commitment to religious pluralism compels equality. There are UCC and Reform Jewish same-gender couples, for instance, who wish to be officially married by their clergy, with a clergy-signed marriage license just like heterosexuals in their faith communities are able to do. These same-sex couples should not have their civil (and religious) rights violated because dominant heterosexist religious views in the society demand it.

In major religious traditions, such as Christianity, Judaism, or Islam, the tradition has several subdivisions, each of which include adherents who hold diverse views on many aspects of their traditions encompassing the topics of gender, sexuality, and the interpretation of holy scriptures. Religious understandings that support the equal treatment of marital couples regardless of their sex/gender identity may be a minority viewpoint (or may not, depending on the subdivision of the religious tradition). But, as the chapters in this volume demonstrate, it is a viewpoint that represents an insistent and authentic religious presence that continues to grow and develop.

Because religion is so often used as a weapon in the political arena to oppose legal marriage equality and generally to publicly defame LGBT people, it cannot be ignored. In the current U.S. cultural context, Christianity is not only the dominant religion of the majority of the population but it also carries enormous political currency. It has repeatedly been a primary tool in the opposition to marriage equality expressed by politicians and media pundits. As political scientists David Machacek and Adrienne Fulco observe, on a national level "opponents of same sex marriage are determined to write a religious definition into the Constitution itself."[7]

Thoughtful discussions of religion that take its traditions, history, and cultural contexts seriously, such as those offered in this volume, are crucially needed to correct and expand the representation of religious ideas in contemporary political battles over marriage equality. Perhaps more importantly, these corrective and expanded understandings can add a much-needed public witness to how religious traditions oppose oppressive practices in society, rather than maintain them, and offer respite to socially marginalized people, rather than further scorn. This alternative, egalitarian, and compassionate religious view can perhaps hold out a hopeful communal spirit to fearful heterosexuals as well as despairing, alienated LGBT persons.

The perspectives that this volume brings together are, in a word, traditionalist. They do not, as one might expect of traditionalists, defend religious tradition against any form of change or against the inclusion of multiple vantage points. Instead, the chapters reveal a myriad of ways in which change and multiple vantage points are constant elements of religious tradition. The authors share a presupposition about the merits of religious tradition and delineate certain understandings of faithfulness to the religious traditions they describe. However, the contributors do have diverse locations in relation to religious beliefs and practices. Some are practitioners, others are scholars, and still others are conjointly practitioner/scholars.

In this book, religious traditions are primarily discussed in terms of practices. In its discussions of marriage, sexuality, homosexuality, and religion, this collection emphasizes political realities within history, organized religious groups, and the general society. Community conflicts surrounding issues of race/ethnicity and racism are incorporated into the discussions of several chapters. This collection does not offer a queer theory of religion and same-sex marriage, but a view "from the ground." The voices of religious leaders, the charting of denominational politics, attention to the well-known scripture and traditions most commonly in dispute, and many other details of concern to the ordinary religious adherent are found here. These analytical chapters capture the dynamics of culturally specific practices and institutional experiences of religion. Moreover, the volume provides snapshots of what religious support for same-sex marriage looks and sounds like, but it does not comprehensively represent the varieties of American religious experience or even of all the subdivisions that exist within the religions that are included.

Combined issues of faith, culture, and history inform any account of how the notion of marriage equality across the sex/gender differences of couples is situated within religious tradition. The chapters in the first section of this volume bring distinct and innovative approaches to appreciating the combined role of faith, culture, and history. Ruth Vanita points out incidents of same-sex weddings as well as suicides among Hindus. She also probes premodern Indian history, finding sanctions in some texts forbidding a woman's manual penetration of a virgin, but also locates a few Hindu texts that endorse explicitly sexual same-sex relationships as virtuous. Vanita's chapter illustrates interlinked, global cultural influences. She examines Hindu beliefs and rituals related to same-sex marriage in India and among U.S. Indian immigrants in conjunction with certain practices in their broader societies that affect those beliefs and rituals. In Christian Scharen's chapter, the themes of culture and history are combined somewhat differently. His arguments are centered on Christianity's German Reformation figure, Martin Luther. Scharen makes a case for the applicability of Luther's ideas about marriage in a contemporary Christian theology supportive of same-sex marriage. He enlists the method Luther devised for a new church understanding of marriage in response to the increasing numbers of unconventional unions of couples in his sixteenth-century church context.

J. Terry Todd delves into more recent history by exploring Christian voices in the movement for same-sex marriage in the 1970s in the United States. He also demonstrates how oppositional contemporary Christian rhetoric, claiming that same-sex marriage equality poses a threat to the nation and the family, parallels previous objections to interracial marriage. Todd notes that this parallel to racist objections to interracial marriage provides evidence of past Christian disagreements about who should have access to marriage and what God has to say about it. In her examination of the roots of homophobia in black churches and communities, Kelly Brown Douglas offers a case study in the shaping of religious understandings of sexuality, especially religious opposition to same-sex marriage, by racist cultural and historical influences. She uses a literary reference point, Alice Walker's novel *The Color Purple*, which portrays early-twentieth-century black southern life. In her chapter, Douglas depicts the lives of blues-singing black women as sites not only for understanding the effects of white racist cultural stereotyping and repressive Christian theology about sexuality but also for recognizing possibilities for transgressive, self-affirming sexuality.

On the one hand, religious legacies received from the past may hold resources of faith that can be supportive of religious marriage equality, as in the case of Luther's Christian theological method and of certain medieval Indian Hindu traditions. On the other hand, such legacies may hold meaningful clues about the evolution of dominant cultural and religious perspectives opposing equality, such as the impact on Hinduism when homophobic British colonial law in India was instituted or the capacity for fueling Christian homophobia fostered by traditional white racist Christian rhetoric concerning interracial marriage and the sexual stereotyping of blacks. Either way, as these chapters persuasively illustrate, attention must be paid to the historical and cultural legacies that set the context and terms of the religious struggle for marriage equality.

The next section of the volume continues to explore the legacies of religious traditions but also focuses on the details of specific understandings of faith and practice that offer support for same-sex marriage. Patricia Beattie Jung identifies Catholic insights for a Christian theology of marriage and family that includes same-sex marriage. Jung crafts the faithful analysis needed for a reconstruction of tradition. She provides point-by-point responses to official Roman Catholic teaching that opposes the blessing of same-sex marriages, such as its concern about the devaluation of the institution of marriage and harm to children. Similarly, Peter S. Knobel offers a Reform Jewish affirmation of gay and lesbian sacred relationships as having the same sanctity as heterosexual sacred relationships. He maintains a perspective that is rooted in the reading of sacred texts and in the movement's ethical and theological understanding of marriage. Knobel carefully considers texts from Genesis, Leviticus, and Song of Songs, and he addresses rabbinic concerns about procreation for the biological preservation of the Jewish people, as well as the unnaturalness of celibacy.

In a more personal account, Herbert Chilstrom, a former bishop of the Evangelical Lutheran Church of America, puts forth a Christian basis for welcoming LGBT persons and blessing same-sex couples that follows the path of his own faith journey. His story about the transformation of his views includes serious engagement of the Bible, Luther's *Augsburg Confession*, and his own emotionally and spiritually demanding conversations with gay and lesbian Christians and their parents. With the same thoughtfulness that Chilstrom applies to the Lutheran heritage that he treasures, Roger Corless delineates Buddhist ideas and practices related to sexuality and relationships. Corless explains that marriage is not a central concern of Buddhism, and same-sex unions are not addressed in canonical Buddhist texts. Therefore, it is not possible to represent one Buddhist point of view as authoritative on this topic. Corless does find support, however, for same-sex unions in Buddhist practices emphasizing the central importance of interdependent relationships and in those that de-emphasize dualisms in their view of sexuality.

For United Methodist Tex Sample, the strongest Christian support for homosexual marriage can be claimed when Christian biblical passages concerned with same-sex practice are directly addressed, especially the passages in Paul's letter to the Romans. Sample also considers texts concerned with heterosexual unions in Genesis and ancient church traditions on marriage established by the influential ancient church bishop Augustine. Integrating contributions from other religious scholars in this study of scripture and tradition, Sample advances a detailed confirmation of homosexual marriage as neither a violation of Christian scripture nor of traditional understandings of the goods of Christian marriage. With a contrasting approach to Sample, Mel White insists that there is not a Bible-based apologetic for same-sex marriage that fundamentalist Christians would find convincing. White speaks out of his own experience as an evangelical Christian and a gay man who awaits legal marriage to his beloved partner of over twenty-five years. He poses several pointed questions about how Jesus would respond to current concerns about same-sex marriage. As White explores these questions, he reviews several heart-wrenching lessons about Christian antigay prejudice in today's society.

An Islamic approach to religious tradition, presented by Muslim Imam and scholar Daayiee Abdullah, concludes this section of the volume. His gentle, comforting message affirms marriage for same-sex Muslim couples with a concise exploration of some of the teachings in the Holy Quran and stories of the Prophet Muhammed in the Islamic tradition. Daayiee Abdullah reassures lesbian, gay, bisexual, transgender, and queer (LGBTQ) Muslims of Allah's concern for their well-being and their right to a healthy relationship with a spouse.

Avoiding the opposition, problems, and obstacles within religious tradition does little to advance an understanding of the religious foundations of marriage equality. Far from avoidance, the contributors in this second section of the volume offer a variety of models for locating support. They offer responses to Catholic papal teachings condemning the treatment of same-sex partnerships as equal to heterosexual marriage; rabbinic concerns about homosexuality as nonprocreative in Reform Judaism; interpretations of the crimes of the men of Sodom in the Holy Quran in Islam; Christian scripture opposing women exchanging natural intercourse for unnatural; and mean-spirited claims of current Christian fundamentalist leaders like those of James Dobson asserting the impending fall of Western civilization due to "homosexual activism." This section also demonstrates how support for religious marriage equality includes admitting the absence of positive Buddhist teachings on sexuality as well as an author more personally confessing previous obliviousness and insensitivity to church condemnations of homosexuals while serving as a Lutheran minister. The authors exhibit an unflinching engagement of problematic religious ideas and practices.

The third section of the volume provides more information about religious support for marriage equality, shifting from the content of the religious traditions passed down to contemporary believers to political practices in the religious struggle for equality. Christian Protestant groups and their unique role as the dominant religious tradition in this society are the principal focus of this section. The chapters explore the practices of religious bodies and leaders, starting out with the more general landscape of public debates about marriage equality and then moving to discussions of particular accounts of denominational upheaval and activism.

Marvin Ellison's chapter maps varying moral perspectives in the public debates about marriage equality and then outlines a Reform Protestant ethical approach. Ellison incisively criticizes not only opponents, such as Christian marriage traditionalists seeking to preserve patriarchal marriage and negative views of sex and passion, but also proponents of marriage equality who insist that same-sex couples are not interested in altering marriage. His Christian ethical support for same-sex marriage upholds a nonapologetic defense of healthy eroticism, including gay sex. Like Ellison's chapter, my chapter, which follows his, concentrates on public debates about marriage equality. I focus on the politics of religion and race. Looking mainly at examples of national news media coverage, I make suggestions about why it is that so much attention has been given to the views of black Christian leaders opposing same-sex marriage and, conversely, about why black church leaders in several parts of the nation appear to be taking so much interest in addressing this issue publicly.

With a spotlight on public practices *within* the church, Norman Kansfield narrates the story of some of the policy struggles related to "active homosexuality" and same-sex marriage in the Reformed Church of America (RCA). He describes the emergence of RCA denominational policies labeling a "practicing homosexual lifestyle" as problematic, but the major focus of Kansfield's chapter includes the confrontation that occurred between himself and the RCA. He was removed from the office of Professor of Theology at New Brunswick Theological Seminary, and his ordination was suspended by the General Synod of the RCA because he presided at the wedding of his daughter Ann and her partner Jennifer. Renee Hill, an ordained Episcopal priest, begins her chapter by describing the first time she officiated at a wedding/commitment ceremony of a lesbian couple over thirteen years ago. She, like Kansfield, offers an insider's view of denominational turmoil. Hill analyzes resistance and struggle within the Anglican Communion, especially in the Episcopal Church USA. Her reflections place the debates surrounding homosexuality and the blessing of same-sex unions in the context of a broader, complex struggle for power and authority related to racism, sexism, ethnocentrism, global poverty, and neocolonialism.

Keith Kron has written a history of the Unitarian Universalist (UU) journey of denominational support for marriage equality that also highlights the leadership of ministers and churches in several statewide movements for legal marriage equality. Kron describes the painstaking education and advocacy work spearheaded by staff within the denomination and reveals several beneficial links between the struggle for racial justice and the struggle for marriage equality. He also chronicles UU activist support and celebrations of legal victories, including the Unitarian lead plaintiffs in the Massachusetts lawsuit enabling same-sex couples to receive marriage licenses. The final chapter in this section, by Joseph Tolton, an Elder in the Pentecostal tradition, also makes a constructive connection between past justice struggles for equality and the current one for marriage equality, particularly urging African American Pentecostals to make this connection. Tolton's chapter extends this invitation to church members by citing the Pentecostal (USA Holiness movement) history of supporting just causes, such as the abolition of slavery. He also points to the particular character of Pentecostal faith, which embraces ecstatic spirituality and new revelations from God, as a unique building block they can contribute to the movement.

The authors in this third section of the volume document the dynamic expression of religious tradition. As the authors state, to create religious marriage equality requires all of the vitality found in religious practices ranging from urban ministry with black gay Pentecostals to the activism of UU ministers who announced from their pulpits that they refused to sign marriage licenses until all couples could be legally married. In local and global Anglican denominational tumult, there is a need to recognize a systemic reaction to the extension of power and authority to women, people of color, and LGBT persons. There is also a need to take notice of individual courageous acts that remind the church, as Norman J. Kansfield declared at his trial, "You may depose and suspend me, but the terrible plight of the children of the Reform Church who are gay and lesbian will remain before you." Also, there is a yearning here for the inclusion of certain Christian views that are currently underrepresented in public discourse surrounding marriage equality, such as a Christian gay-sex-affirming ethic and the perspectives of black LGBT Christian communities as standard bearers representing "the black church."

The final section of the volume encapsulates the religious practice of marriage equality in three ways. The descriptions of the authors present this commitment as embodied in religious tradition, religious leadership, and a religious group's communal decision-making process.

Rebecca Alpert explains that, for Reconstructionist Judaism, same-sex marriage is understood as a religious value because it provides economic justice, creates stable committed relationships, and fosters support for child rearing. As Alpert proves, Reconstructionist Jewish tradition always includes an egalitarian approach to marriage, defining the marriage ceremony as a transaction of interdependence between equal, and removing any assumption that those equals must have different genders. Similar to Alpert's discussion of Reconstructionist Judaism, Karen Oliveto assumes that the equal treatment of persons is the standard of religious practice that must be manifested in her ministry as pastor of a local church in San Francisco. Unfortunately, this understanding is not shared by Oliveto's United Methodist (UMC) denomination. Her chapter gives an exhilarating account of her fielding telephone calls from her parishioners who asked her to join them at San Francisco City Hall where they were standing in a long line of same-sex couples waiting for marriage licenses. Arriving at City Hall where it was swarming with local and national media, Oliveto was clothed in clergy shirt and clutching the UMC *Book of Worship*; she faithfully responded to her congregants' requests, marrying several couples, only to have official charges of "disobedience to the Order and Discipline" of her denomination filed against her later.

In the last chapter, Ruth Garwood describes the moment when her UCC denomination's 2005 General Synod meeting decided to affirm equal marriage rights for LGBT people. Garwood outlines the decision-making process, describing the facilitated discussions about the meaning of marriage and ministry before resolutions were considered, the reflections of the moderator of the plenary session who ensured that no conversation was shortened or vote rushed, and the speeches of several delegates. Of her own elation after the vote was taken, Garwood comments, "The United Church of Christ had felt welcoming to me, a lesbian, and now I feel that welcoming embrace even stronger, as if the arms of the church had been thrown open wider than ever. It felt like my church was reaching out to me as enthusiastically as God reaches out."

The volume cumulatively shows a range of historical, cultural, political, and tradition-bound ideas and practices. Consideration of this wide spectrum is necessary to understand the complicated dynamics that are involved in the struggle to achieve equal regard for couples participating in religious marriage traditions and practices, across differences in their sex/gender identities. As the contributors point out, this kind of religious commitment uproots several cherished norms that maintain the superiority of some persons over others, but it creates wonderful possibilities for a genuine spiritual, material, and social valuing of families.

NOTES

1. Rabbi Jane Rachel Litman, "A Historic Moment," Beliefnet, http://beliefnet.com/story/17/story_1770.html (accessed October 11, 2006). Also see Gustav Niebuhr, "Reform Rabbis Back Blessing of Gay Unions," *New York Times*, March 30, 2000.

2. Laurie Goodstein, "Jewish Panel Delays a Vote On Gay Issues," *New York Times*, March 9, 2006.

3. Laurie Goodstein, "Lutherans Reject Plan to Allow Gay Clerics," *New York Times*, August 13, 2005.

4. "John Thomas: Press Statement after Marriage Equality Vote," United Church of Christ News, July 13, 2005, http://news.ucc.org/index.php?option=com_content&task=view&id=273&Itemid=54 (accessed October 11, 2006).

5. See Brief of *Amici Curiae* in the Court of Appeal of the State of California, First App. Dist., Div. 3, *Coordination Proceeding Special Title* (Rule 1550[b]) *Marriage Cases*, December 1, 2005 (No. A110449). See also testimony supporting same-sex marriage by Zen

Buddhist leader Robert Aiken, http://www.flex.com/~aitken/roshi/writings/pages/marriage.html (accessed October 11, 2006).

6. See http://www.dignityusa.org/couples/index.html (accessed October 11, 2006).

7. David W. Machacek and Adrienne Fulco, "The Courts and Public Discourse: The Case of Gay Marriage," *Journal of Church and State* 46, no. 4 (Autumn 2004): 785.

Part I

FAITH, CULTURE, AND HISTORY

1

TOGETHER IN LIFE AFTER LIFE: SAME-SEX MARRIAGE AND HINDU TRADITIONS

Ruth Vanita

In June 2002, I attended the wedding of two Indian women, Vegavahini Subramaniam and Vaijayanthimala Nagarajan, in Seattle. After the Hindu ceremony, in which several of their family members and friends participated, I talked to the Hindu priest who conducted the ceremony; he is from an important priestly lineage in India. He told me that other priests might disapprove, but after much thought, he had concluded, on the basis of Hindu scriptures, that "marriage is a union of spirits, and the spirit is not male or female."

I was amazed by the similarity of this response to those by other Hindus in different contexts. In her 1977 book, *The World of Homosexuals,* mathematician Shakuntala Devi recorded her interview with Srinivasa Raghavachariar, Sanskrit scholar and priest of the major Hindu Vaishnava temple at Srirangam in south India. He said that same-sex lovers must have been cross-sex lovers in a former life. The sex may change but the soul remains the same in subsequent incarnations, hence the power of love impels these souls to seek one another.[1] Even more interestingly, when two policewomen, Leela Namdeo and Urmila Srivastava, got married according to Hindu rites in 1987, their neighbor, a village schoolteacher, remarked to journalists, "After all, what is marriage? It is a wedding of two souls. Where in the scriptures is it said that it has to be between a man and a woman?"[2]

Underlying these responses is the Hindu doctrine of rebirth, wherein the individual spirit (an expression of the universal spirit) retains its attachments from one birth to the next but not such characteristics as class, caste, species or gender. A possibly conflicting doctrine, differently interpreted by different Hindu traditions, is that one should adhere to *dharma* (variously translatable as duty, righteousness, or the law of one's being), which pertains to one's status as a human being. If one has not renounced the world, dharma also pertains to one's status as defined by age, family position, gender, occupation, and other social relationships including *jati*. A *jati* is a birth-based group, and Portuguese missionaries translated this word as "caste" (from the Latin *casta* or pure). Because Hinduism, one of the oldest continuously practiced religions in the world, has many priestly hierarchies, a very large number of holy books (written in Sanskrit and several other languages over a period of more than two millennia), and many philosophical and devotional traditions, Hindus differ on many questions, including that of same-sex relations. However, certain doctrines, such as those of rebirth and of the ultimate oneness of all things, are accepted by most Hindus.

Hindus constitute about one-sixth of the world's population today, and most of them live in India and Nepal, although there are old communities in parts of Southeast Asia, such as Bali, and also immigrant Hindu communities in almost every part of the world today, including a vibrant and prosperous community in the United States. Even though Hindus in the United States have built their own traditions here, establishing temples, Ashrams, schools and other institutions, the ties between Hindus and India remain very strong.[3] Even American Hindus of non-Indian origin, such as Christopher Isherwood, tend to spend time in India, visit pilgrimage sites in India, and maintain ongoing dialogue with Hindu communities in India. For American Hindus of Indian origin, these ties are even stronger, reinforced by kinship and marriage. Lesbian, gay, bisexual, and transgender (LGBT) Indians in America also tend to maintain many ties with India, hence my many references in this chapter to same-sex marriage and Hinduism in India.

DIVERSE APPROACHES

The diversity of present-day Hindu teachers' attitudes to same-sex marriage emerged in interviews conducted at a major pilgrimage destination, the Kumbha Mela, north India, in 2004, by Rajiv Malik, a journalist from the U.S.-based magazine *Hinduism Today*. Several teachers condemned same-sex marriage—for example, Swami Avdheshananda called it "unnatural, uncommon and unusual"[4]—but others presented remarkable arguments in favor of it. Mahant Ram Puri, who belongs to the same lineage as Swami Avdheshananda, said, "There is a principle in all Hindu law that local always has precedence. In other words, the general rules and the general laws are always overruled by a local situation. I do not think that this is something that is decided on a theoretical level. We do not have a rule book in Hinduism. We have a hundred million authorities."[5]

Equally thoughtfully, Pandit Shailendra Shri Sheshnarayan Ji Vaidyaka pointed out that definitions change over time: "Whatever is done in a hidden manner becomes a wrong act and is treated as a sin. Whatever is done openly does invite criticism for some time but ultimately gains acceptance. Why not give them the liberty to live in their own way, if they are going to do it anyway? After all, we have *kinnars*, eunuchs, who have been accepted by the society. Similarly, these people can also be accepted. Like we have a *kinnarsamaj*, eunuch society, we can have a gay *samaj*."[6]

These three facts—that in Hindu law, local custom always takes precedence over written texts, that Hindus revere a wide range of sacred texts, and that Hindu communities define their own identities that evolve over time—help explain the diversity of family and community responses to the same-sex Hindu weddings that have been reported in India during the last two decades. In my book, *Love's Rite: Same-Sex Marriage in India and the West*, I examine the two most starkly contrasting phenomena that embody this diversity—same-sex weddings and same-sex couple suicides; I also look at unions that are marriage-like; for example, partnership contracts and live-in relationships accepted by local communities as marriages.[7]

WEDDINGS AND SUICIDES

There is a long tradition of joint suicide by lovers in India, as in most cultures. The tradition is celebrated in Hindu and Islamic literature and also in modern Indian cinema. Reports of joint suicide by heterosexual as well as homosexual lovers, generally impelled by parental attempts to separate lovers and force them into unwanted marriages to others, continue to appear in the Indian press. Couples generally leave behind letters, avowing their refusal to be separated, their hopes of union in the next life, and sometimes their wish to be jointly cremated, thus rendering their deaths a form of marriage, or public statement of union.

The first joint suicide attempt of a same-sex couple, on which I have a press report, is that of Mallika, twenty, and Lalithambika, seventeen, who attempted to drown themselves in Kerala, south India, in 1980.[8] They left behind letters stating that they could not bear imminent separation. They were rescued, and their families separated them.

Hindu young people in the United States too often face family pressure to marry. *Trikone*, the South Asian LGBT magazine published in San Francisco, and many South Asian LGBT chat lists and Listservs regularly carry personal advertisements placed by lesbians and gay men looking for a cross-sex marriage of convenience.[9] Some of these are children of first-generation immigrants who have grown up in the United States; others are professionals who migrated as adults but still feel the need to marry to please their parents in India. Conversely, many lesbian and gay couples migrate to the United States to escape family pressure. In an early anthology about South Asian LGBT people, a Bengali lesbian couple narrated the story of their struggle, which culminated in migration to the United States.[10] Of course, because the United States does not honor same-sex unions for purposes of immigration, such migration has to be undertaken individually by each member of the couple.

Same-sex marriage is only one disapproved type of marriage; interreligious, cross-caste, cross-class, and international marriages are equally, if not more, disapproved of in many Indian communities. Nevertheless, all of these types of marriages do take place, and many win some degree of family approval and participation. Perhaps the first widely reported Hindu same-sex wedding was that of two policewomen, Leela Namdeo, a widow, and Urmila Srivastava, a divorcee, which took place in December 1987 and made national headlines in early 1988 after the two were suspended from the police force.

Journalists visited Urmila's family home in the village of Bhamora in central India, where the women were staying as a married couple, and interviewed them.[11] The marriage had taken place in a temple and, after the women were suspended from

their jobs, Urmila's family held a reception in their village home to console the dis-
traught couple. Later in the same year, the women, under pressure from police
authorities, denied they were lovers or had gotten married.

In subsequent years, newspapers have reported a number of such same-sex
marriages. Among the most recent is that of Raju, twenty-four, and her childhood
friend, Mala, twenty-two, who eloped to Delhi from Amritsar, in December 2004,
and married in a temple according to Hindu rites. Their families tried to have them
arrested, but when they were produced in court, local magistrate Sanjeev Joshi said
they "enjoyed the constitutional right to live according to their wishes and no one
had the right to interfere in their lives."[12] Several judges in different parts of India
have similarly declared adult couples' right to live together, despite the antisodomy
law introduced by the British in 1860, which still remains on the books and is used
to harass such couples.[13]

Most of the couples who marry or commit suicide are young women from
lower income groups, generally with some education; most are Hindus, although
some are Muslims or Christians. Reports of such unions come from both rural and
urban areas and most parts of the country. In the last few years, LGBT and human
rights organizations in big cities have begun to come to their aid and have sent fact-
finding teams to investigate suicides.[14]

This preponderance of women, especially poorer and less educated ones, points
to the difficulties such women face in living independently outside of family sur-
veillance, in a society where the family is the main form of support available to
most people because the state does not provide unemployment benefits. Getting
married or committing suicide are ways to compel the family to acknowledge a
same-sex union.

Conversely, middle- and upper-middle-class couples, both male and female,
who are better educated and able to obtain high-paid employment, resist family
pressure and live together, often with the help of LGBT organizations. Several
Hindu same-sex weddings, between people self-identified as gay or lesbian, have
taken place, both in India and other countries; some of them are international marriages. Among the earliest was the marriage of Aditya Advani to his American partner, Michael Tarr, in 1993. They live in the United States but were married
according to Hindu rites in India. Aditya's parents hosted the wedding in their family home in New Delhi, and the family's spiritual preceptor conducted the Hindu
ceremony. In a private conversation with me, the officiant remarked, "My attitude
was, 'Here are two people who want to live together so it has to have the blessings
of God, parents and elders.' I chanted a mantra from the Upanishads for their prosperity, for their love." Many friends and relatives attended. In 2004, a representative
of Lakshya Trust in Baroda stated that this gay organization has facilitated fifteen
same-sex marriages.[15]

HINDU ATTITUDES TOWARD SEXUAL RELATIONS

This range of Hindu attitudes toward same-sex relationships is symptomatic of the
range of Hindu attitudes, present and past, to sexual relations in general. Ancient
Hindu ascetic traditions, like ascetic traditions worldwide, tend to view all sexual

acts with some distaste. This distaste arises in part from the mistrust of physical pleasure as binding one to the phenomenal world and in part from rules of purity and pollution. Although carefully regulated, procreative sex is enjoined on the householder, nonprocreative sex is viewed with disfavor. As in most ascetic traditions, women are stereotyped as more lustful than men and as temptresses of men.

These ideas influence householder life, which is structured as a set of obligations—to ancestors and to society. Many Hindu texts insist that everyone has a duty to marry and have children. If one renounces the world, one may be freed of this duty, but not otherwise.

However, these anxieties are countered in devotional practice and also in philosophy and literature, where Gods and Goddesses are represented as erotic beings, who are often married and/or engaged in erotic relationships. These are living deities, worshiped today by millions; their images can be seen in most Hindu homes and shops everywhere in the world. One of the Gods is Kama (desire), a deity similar to the Greek Eros. In the earliest texts, he is a creative force inspiring desire and animation in the universe, but from the first millennium onward, he is a beautiful young man who shoots flower-tipped arrows that induce love. An eleventh-century sandstone sculpture from Orissa shows Kama, a blissful smile on his face, shooting an arrow at two embracing women, who also smile blissfully.[16] Kama (desire) is also one of the four normative aims of human life.

In Hindu philosophy, good and evil are relative, not absolute, because all things are ultimately manifestations of divine energy. The Gods and Goddesses are present everywhere, in every plant, animal, and element; in every part of the body; and in every movement, thought, and feeling. Eulogies to Gods and Goddesses often praise them as the best in every category (the best of trees, the best of snakes, the best of mountains) and as male, female, and neuter. It is in this spirit that the priest who married two women in Seattle in 2002 told me that he gives all the donations he receives for performing rites to the temple in his village in India, thus offering whatever merit or demerit the rites may accrue to Shiva, who absorbs it all.

AYONI (NONVAGINAL) SEX AND SAME-SEX RELATIONS

Ascetic, devotional, and philosophical traditions are intertwined both in texts and in practice; hence the often contradictory approach to sex within the same text. Prescriptive texts (such as legal and medical treatises) tend to take a censorious approach to sexual activities that narrative sacred texts describe nonjudgmentally or even celebrate. For example, ancient Hindu law books, which are permeated by purity and pollution concerns, declare *ayoni* (nonvaginal) intercourse impure and punishable. But narrative sacred texts, including the epics, often show heroic children and even deities springing from nonvaginal sex.[17] Often, the same text—for example, the epic *Mahabharata* and several *Puranas* (medieval compendia of stories about the Gods)—contains both narrative and precepts and contradicts itself on the question of whether nonvaginal sex is impure or sacred.[18] An explanation for this may partly pertain to the fact that what is normally taboo or polluted may be sacred in special or ritual contexts.

The category of *ayoni* sex is wide—it encompasses, among other things, oral sex, manual sex, anal sex, sex with animals, and masturbation in the water or in a pot or other aperture. Yet the penalties prescribed are very light compared to the penances, such as torture and death, imposed for certain kinds of heterosexual adultery and rape. The ancient legal treatise the *Manusmriti* exhorts a man who has sex with "a man or a woman in a cart pulled by a cow, or in water or by day" to "bathe with his clothes on" (11.174). The penalty for a man who has *ayoni* sex is a minor fine, also prescribed for "stealing articles of little value" (11.165).[19]

Modern commentators wrongly read the *Manusmriti*'s severe punishment for a woman's manual penetration of a virgin (8.369–70) as revelatory of that text's antilesbian bias. In fact, the punishment (chopping off two fingers and shaving the head) is exactly the same for either a man (8.367) or a woman who does this act and is related not to the partners' genders but to the virgin's loss of virginity and hence of marriageable status. The *Manusmriti* does not mention a woman penetrating a nonvirgin woman, and the *Arthashastra* prescribes a negligible fine for this act.

At first glance, *ayoni* sex as a catchall category appears comparable to the category of "sodomy" developed in medieval European Christendom. But the two categories are in fact very different. First, sodomy came to be constructed in Christendom as a horrific sin, almost the worst of all sins, "a favored synecdoche for sin itself."[20] Conversely, *ayoni* sex was a minor infraction of Hindu law. Second, sodomy came to be considered unspeakable, the sin not to be named among Christians, whereas no similar prohibition on mentioning *ayoni* sex developed among Hindus. Third, from the Renaissance until the nineteenth century in England and many other European countries, sodomy became not just a sin to be atoned for with religious penance but a legal crime to be punished with disenfranchisement, torture, and even death. No such development took place in the case of *ayoni* sex.

HINDU IDEAS OF LOVE

The debate about same-sex marriage is in many ways a debate about the value of erotic love that is not linked to procreation. In same-sex marriage, society confronts its deepest fears about the dangers of erotic love. Hence the paranoid questions constantly voiced by some opponents of same-sex marriage: if same-sex marriage is allowed today, can incestuous, polygamous, and bestial marriages be far behind? Such fears explain these opponents' obsessive focus on sexual acts, to the exclusion of loving relationships.

To borrow philosopher Martha Nussbaum's argument, developed in another context, erotic love tends to be viewed as socially and morally inappropriate insofar as lovers' extreme valuation of one another is private, not public, and no one else can participate in its excess.[21] Perhaps the strongest component of many cultures' ambivalence toward erotic pleasure is the fear that it makes individuals selfish and indifferent to the welfare of others. Same-sex sexual relationships, being biologically infertile, are tainted with the suspicion of being entirely selfish and based on sexual pleasure alone.

However, not procreation alone but love too, in its larger, more universal sense, may render erotic love between two individuals less threatening. The defining

myths about love in many cultures, including the Hindu, suggest that love is perceived as unquestionably good only when it enables the welfare of others in addition to the two partners. Lovers who suffer and make sacrifices only for one another
generally end up dead, but those who struggle also for the well-being of the community become heroes.

The most significant difference in this regard between premodern Indian and
European texts concerns sexual intercourse. Alan Bray has demonstrated that long-
term same-sex relationships were celebrated in public spaces from the fourteenth to
the nineteenth centuries in Western Europe.[22] Same-sex friends whose relationship
was seen as contributing to societal welfare were even buried in joint tombs in
churches. But Bray finds that these relationships were always represented as non-
sexual. Even in the case of early-nineteenth-century British heiress Anne Lister,
whom we know, from her diaries, to have had sexual relationships with women,
Bray argues that society, including her family and the local church, which blessed
one of these relationships as a spiritual union, was not aware of its sexual nature.

Conversely, a few Hindu texts endorse explicitly sexual same-sex relationships
as virtuous and contributing to the greater good. Hindu texts do not distinguish
desirable relationships from undesirable ones solely on the basis of the partners'
gender or the sexual acts performed by them. Rather, relationships, including same-
sex sexual relationships, that contribute to the general good are represented as desirable, whereas selfish relationships, including otherwise approved cross-sex
relationships, are represented as undesirable.

SAME-SEX UNION BLESSED WITH OFFSPRING

The most explicit endorsement of same-sex unions that I have is in a cluster of devotional texts composed in fourteenth-century Bengal in eastern India.[23] These texts
tell the story of a royal child miraculously born of intervaginal sex between two co-
widows; the birth continues an important lineage whose survival is seen as essential
to communal well-being. The child, named Bhagiratha, grows up to perform the
heroic feat of bringing the sacred river Ganges down from heaven to earth.

The two queens suffer embarrassment and grief as a result of the pregnancy and
childbirth, and this suffering helps legitimize their relationship, whose outcome is
beneficial to the community; however, they also enjoy the pleasures of romantic
intimacy. Their relationship is a marriage-like union because it is a committed, loving, and long-term relationship, planned and blessed by the Gods; it is not purely
selfish because they suffer for the good of others, and it results in a child perceived
as legitimate, who is heir to the kingdom. In a Bengal recension of the *Padma Purana*,
a Sanskrit devotional text, the family preceptor, a famous sage, instructs the two
women to have intercourse and performs a sacrificial ritual (*putreshti*) for them to
obtain a son.[24] This type of ritual is still performed today for married couples.

One version of the Bengali *Krittivasa Ramayana* describes the relationship
between these two women in terms that are highly conventional in Indic narrative:

> The sky was overcast with clouds,
> the swans sang and the peacocks danced.

The skies darkened and a stormy rain followed.
Burning with desire induced by Madan [another name of Kama, God
      of love], Chandra and Mala
took each other in embrace,
and each kissed the other....
The two women dallied and made love
[*Dui nari mono ronge rongo krira kori*].
God's blessing had enabled the two women to play the game of love
and the energy [*tej*] of Madan entered the womb of Malavati.
This is how Malavati became pregnant.[25]

In all three versions that I examined, the child is named Bhagiratha, and they provide a folk etymology for his name, construing it as a reference to his birth from
intercourse between two vaginas (*bhaga*).

SAME-SEX UNIONS IN THE *KAMASUTRA*

A much earlier sacred text, the *Kamasutra*, a fourth-century treatise on eroticism,
describes same-sex union that is not linked to procreation. This text categorizes
humans into three groups—men, women, and those of the third nature. It further
classifies men of the third nature into those who are masculine-appearing and desire
other men, and those who are feminine-appearing and also desire men. It describes
the lives and activities of men of the third nature (the occupations of hairdresser,
masseur, and flower seller are recommended to them as ways of meeting men), and
gives a detailed and sensuous account of oral sex between men. It also mentions oral
and manual sex between women. Several ancient texts, including Sanskrit plays,
Hindu medical texts, and Jain texts, develop a taxonomy of those who are inclined
to same-sex desire.

In a series of textual cruxes, the *Kamasutra* describes women's manly behavior
during sex, which has been read by some translators as describing only female-male
interaction, and by others as describing both female-male and female-female interaction.[26] In another important crux, the *Kamasutra* states that two men friends who
have complete trust in each other may "unite" (II 9.36). The term used for the action
of uniting, which translators have variously translated as "marry," "have sex," and
"mutually service one another" is *parasparaparigraham. Paraspara* means "mutual,"
and *parigraha* has many meanings, including "take in marriage," "have sexual intercourse," "take," "accept," or "seize."[27] Danielou translates the phrase as "get married
together," two Hindi translators as "have oral sex together," and Doniger and Kakar
as "do this service" for one another.[28]

I examined other uses of *parigraha* and its variants throughout the *Kamasutra* and found that it is used eight times to refer to marriage; five times to mean
"seize," "accept," "take" or "obtain" (as in seizing lips with lips, penis with vulva,
or obtaining money); and six times to refer to copulation. Apart from the reference to male-male union, there is only one other use of *parigraha* along with
paraspara (mutual). *Parasparaparigrahayoha* (V.4: 41) refers to a man establishing a mutual bond with another man's wife. *Paraspara* (mutual) is also used along

with "enjoyment"—*parasparamranjayeyuhuhu* (V.6:1), referring to mutual sexual enjoyment between secluded women. Both of these verses, like the reference to two men uniting, refer to unconventional types of union.

Most interesting are several uses of the words that refer to a woman who acts like a wife, *parigraham cha charet* and *parigrahamkalpam* (VI.5: 36 and VI.5: 4). These verses refer to a courtesan who behaves like a wife to a man who rewards her well. A courtesan's daughter whose hand is taken by a man acts as his wife for a year (VII.1: 21–22), and the ceremony of taking her hand is termed *panigrahanavidhi*, which is also used in other texts and even today to refer to a marriage ritual.

Parigraha, then, unlike *vivaha* (which is a fully sanctified marriage), can be used to refer to different types of marriage, including a type of marriage that has a lower status in society. Cross-class and cross-caste marriages and widow and divorcee remarriages are treated by many communities as lower-status marriages. A modern equivalent in the United States might be a third or fourth remarriage, which, though legally a marriage, nevertheless usually has a lower social status than a first marriage. *Parigraha* also refers to lasting bonds outside traditional marriage, such as those between a man and another man's wife or those between a courtesan and her long-term lover. So, to return to the verse that describes two men mutually uniting, the term *parigraha* there refers to mutual intercourse but also carries the connotation of a union or bond of mutual acceptance, such as taking someone in a lower-status marriage.

It is important that this verse refers to the two men as *nagaraka*; that is, they are definitely not persons of the third sex but are men of the type the text constructs as normative urban males. Hindu texts recognize many types of union as higher- and lower-status forms of marriage. I argue that some same-sex marriages today are accepted as a type of lower-status marriage. Civil unions, such as those legalized in several European countries and in the state of Vermont, and domestic partnerships, recognized by many cities in the United States, are also lower-status marriages, insofar as they confer some but not all of the rights of marriage.

MODERN HOMOPHOBIA

In *Same-Sex Love in India: Readings from Literature and History* (2000), our collection of translations and analyses of texts about same-sex relationships in fifteen Indian languages, composed over a period of two thousand years, Saleem Kidwai and I find that same-sex love and romantic friendship flourished in ancient and medieval India in various forms, without any extended history of persecution.[29] We demonstrate the existence in precolonial India of complex discourses around same-sex love and also the use, in more than one language, of names, terms, and codes to distinguish homoerotic love and those inclined to it. This research confirms Sweet and Zwilling's argument in their work on ancient Hindu and Jain medical texts, Brooten's recent findings from Western antiquity, and Boswell's earlier argument that same-sex desire as a category was not the invention of nineteenth-century European sexologists, as Foucault claims it was.[30] Like the erotic sculptures at the Hindu temples of Khajuraho and Konarak, ancient and medieval texts like the *Kamasutra* and the *Krittivasa Ramayana* constitute irrefutable evidence that the whole range of sexual behavior was known, represented, and discussed in precolonial and even pre-Islamic India.

Kidwai and I argue that a major shift occurred with the establishment of British colonial rule, whereby homophobic trends that were marginal in premodern India but dominant in nineteenth-century England became dominant in modern India.[31] The British inscribed this homophobia into modern Indian law, and many national-ist social reformers, both Hindu and Muslim, embraced it as a sign of progress. Most modern educated Hindus, however, are unaware of this history and claim that homosexuality is a foreign import, unknown in ancient Hindu society and alien to Hindu culture.

Present-day Hinduism bears the traces of all these pasts—older, more diverse traditions coexist with modern homophobia. Some Hindu right-wing organizations vigorously espouse nationalist and xenophobic sex-phobia and homophobia, mani-fested perhaps most dramatically in annual violent agitations against urban Indian celebrations of Valentine's Day and in attacks on theaters showing the lesbian film *Fire* in 1998.[32] In contrast, many Hindu groups and teachers, both in India and in the United States, also quietly continue to practice more accepting traditions.[33]

For example, in 1996, Arvind Kumar and Ashok Jethanandani, who are pio-neering activists in the South Asian LGBT community in the United States and among the founders of *Trikone* magazine, got married according to Hindu rites on their tenth anniversary of being together. They are both engineers, who were raised in Bihar, India, but met in California, where they have lived together since 1986. Arvind's mother, Ma Yogashakti, is a Hindu teacher who renounced the world in 1960, when Arvind was a small boy, and now has Ashrams in the United States, as well as in India. She initially disapproved of Arvind's being gay and thought he would never be happy. But eight years after he got together with Ashok, it was she who suggested that they marry, and she offered to perform the ceremony. The wedding took place in Toronto, with Arvind's entire family present. Arvind says, "I finally entered the family circle."[34]

Ashok's family were not present at the wedding because it had not been planned sufficiently ahead of time to enable them to make it. Ashok's father was ini-tially very disapproving although his mother had always been very accepting; over time, Ashok's father has changed his attitude. Both parents migrated to the United States and now live with Ashok and Arvind.

HINDU CONCEPTS OF MARRIAGE

As in Catholicism, traditional Hindu marriage is a sacrament, not a contract, and is not dissoluble. However, modern Hindu marriage, regulated by the Hindu Marriage Act that was passed by the government of independent India in 1955, is both a sacrament and a contract and is dissoluble. Many Indian immigrants to the United States were married in India by Hindu law, and their marriages are recognized in the United States. Many U.S. citizens also return to India to marry there by Hindu rites.

Most ancient Hindu texts recognize eight types of marriage.[35] One of them is the *gandharva vivaha* or marriage by mutual consent; it requires no parental con-sent, no ritual, no officiant, and no witnesses. Although some ancient legal texts disapprove of this type of marriage, ancient and medieval narrative literature, both sacred and secular, often describe it nonjudgmentally or even celebrates it as the best form of marriage because it is based on choice.

One article on the marriage of policewomen Leela and Urmila describes their union as a *"gandharva vivaha."*[36] Most Indians today understand this Sanskrit term as the equivalent of what today in Indian English is called a "love-marriage," as distinct from the more conventional and more prevalent family-arranged marriage.

Although most Hindu marriages today are family arranged, marriage by individual choice is also described in premodern texts and is widely prevalent in modern India. Such marriages often lead to violent conflict, social isolation of the couple, and even to suicide and murder, especially when regional, caste, class, and other boundaries are crossed by the two people coming together in marriage. However, many families also happily accept such marriages of choice. A traditional way for Hindu communities to understand and accommodate such unions involves viewing them in the perspective of rebirth. Any strong and spontaneous, apparently inexplicable, attraction between persons, or even between a person and a place or object, is often understood to be the consequence of an attachment in a former life.

I have found evidence in ancient texts of parents deciding to accept their children's cross-caste and cross-class marriages on the basis that these young people must have been spouses of the same caste and class in a former lifetime.[37] In the same way, these texts also explain same-sex attachments that last a lifetime. For example, in the eleventh-century Sanskrit story cycle the *Kathasaritsagara* when Pulindaka, a bandit chief, first sees the merchant Vasudatta, he immediately feels intensely drawn to him. The narrator comments: *"Vakti janmaantarapritim manah snihyadakaaranam."* (Affection [that arises] in the heart without a cause speaks of love [persisting] from a former birth.)[38] When Vasudatta later falls in love with the woman who becomes his wife, exactly the same explanation is given for their love. All three spend their lives together, and when Vasudatta kills himself, having remembered his identity from a former birth, his wife and his male friend kill themselves along with him.

Hindu marriage ceremonies emphasize friendship as the basis of marriage—in the important Vedic *saptapadi* ritual (seven steps taken together and seven verses recited together), the final step represents friendship between the spouses. This rite derives its name from the idea, reiterated in many ancient and medieval Hindu texts, from epics to fables, that seven steps taken together or seven verses recited together constitute friendship (*saptopadam hi mitram*).[39]

Similarly, the term *swayamvara* (literally, self-chosen), commonly used to signify the ceremony in which Hindu women of warrior classes choose a bridegroom, is also used in the *Kathasaritsagara* as an epithet for a special self-chosen same-sex friend, whether male (*sakha*) or female (*sakhi*). Such a friendship is referred to as *janamantara* (continuing from birth to birth), a term also used for marriage. Like a marriage, it is based on reciprocity, selfless devotion, and sacrifice; as in ideal marriage, the partners live and die together. When a heavenly female Somaprabha sees Princess Kalingasena and is spontaneously attracted to her, she decides that they must have been linked in a former birth and that she should therefore make Kalingasena her *swayamvara sakhi* (self-chosen friend).

In 2001, a Hindu priest in the Srivaishnava lineage conducted a friendship ceremony for two Hindu women in Sydney, Australia. A gay man wrote to ask him if a same-sex couple could have a *gandharva* marriage. The priest replied,

> Marriage (*vivaha*) by definition is between male and female, the purpose being reproduction and the performance of one's duties as householders. There is a commitment ceremony for friendship as described in the *Ramayana* between Rama and Sugriva—it is not the same as a "marriage" but has some of the same ritual elements —holding hands, exchanging garlands and walking around the sacred fire—taking seven steps together etc., the purpose being to confirm and validate one's commitment to the friendship-relationship. So the question of *gandharva* or any other form of "marriage" cannot arise within the Hindu context between members of the same sex.[40]

As we have seen, several Hindu priests disagree with him and do perform wedding ceremonies for same-sex couples. But the fact that the friendship ceremony and wedding ceremony share many ritual elements points to the overlapping and inextricable nature of marriage and friendship in many traditional societies.

THE RIGHT TO MARRY AND CUSTOMARY HINDU LAW

The lawsuit that led to the legalization of same-sex marriage in Canada was based on the fact that, even in modern Western democracies, customary marriage still retains some type of social and even state recognition. Under the Ontario Marriage Act, any couple may be granted a marriage license if a church, following ancient tradition, reads the marriage banns for three consecutive Sundays prior to the wedding. In 2001, the Metropolitan Community Church in Toronto read the banns and married two men, Kevin Bourassa and Joe Varnell, and two women, the Vautours. The couples filed a lawsuit, asking the state to register their marriages. The Court of Appeal ordered the province to register the marriages, and the rest is history. Similarly, under Hindu law, any marriage performed by rites customary in one partner's community is a legally valid marriage.

A few female couples, after getting married by customary Hindu rites, have tried to obtain the Indian state's sanction for their marriages and have been refused. For example, on April 27, 2001, two nurses, Jaya Varma, twenty-five, and Tanuja Chouhan, thirty-two, got married in a Hindu ceremony at Mahamaya temple in Ambikapur, Bihar, in eastern India. "The couple took the traditional vows as a priest chanted the *mantras*. They went seven times round the sacred fire to solemnize their marriage."[41]

At the same ceremony, Jaya's sister was also married, to a man. Although Jaya's sister's marriage is validated by the Indian state and Jaya's is not, Jaya's family and community and the Hindu priest validated both equally. About a hundred people were present at the reception, including Jaya's entire family.

A week after the ceremony, the same-sex couple attempted to register their marriage. Maninder Kaur Dwivedi, the registrar, who happens to be a woman, listened to their arguments but refused to register the marriage. The president of the Bar Council said, "The Hindu Marriage Act of 1955 will not recognise this as a marriage. This is illegal. However, this is not a crime." The situation is ripe for the filing of a lawsuit similar to the one filed by the two couples in Toronto.

This paradox within Hindu marriage law makes clear what is sometimes obscured in the United States—the fact that however many rights a government may confer or withhold, marriage is ultimately defined by people themselves, not by governments. A few decades ago, interracial marriages were illegal in the United States, and many Americans considered them unnatural; in the nineteenth century, many Hindus considered intercaste marriage and widow remarriage illegal, immoral, and unnatural. Nevertheless, such marriages did take place and they were real marriages in the eyes of "enlightened people" and some religious communities.[42] The same is true of same-sex marriage today, everywhere in the world. The battle around same-sex marriage in India is being fought not so much at the level of the courts and the state but in communities and families.

Nevertheless, in the next decade, the battle for state recognition of same-sex marriage is bound to heat up in India. Several LGBT and some civil rights organizations there have already raised the demand. In the United States too, lesbian and gay Indians, including Hindus, are involved in the struggle for marriage rights. After their marriage in 2002, Vaijayanthimala Nagarajan and Vegavahini Subramaniam joined five other couples in a marriage equality lawsuit, demanding that the state of Washington accord their marriage legal recognition. They won the suit in two lower courts, and it is now before the state of Washington's Supreme Court. *Trikone*, the South Asian LGBT magazine based in San Francisco, has brought out a special issue on Hinduism, as well as one on same-sex marriage and one on adoption by same-sex couples. The fact that the U.S.-based *Hinduism Today* journalist asked Hindu teachers in India about same-sex marriage and received such a range of interesting replies, suggests that the centuries-long traditions of debate within Hinduism around many questions, including that of same-sex unions, continue to flourish.

NOTES

1. Shakuntala Devi, *The World of Homosexuals* (Delhi: Vikas, 1977), 146–47.

2. Chinu Panchal, "Wedded Women Cops to Challenge Sack," *Times of India*, February 23, 1988.

3. For studies of these connections, see Diana Eck, *A New Religious America: How a "Christian Country" has become the World's Most Religiously Diverse Nation* (San Francisco: Harper Collins, 2001); and Nancy Auer Falk, *Living Hinduisms: An Explorer's Guide* (Belmont, CA: Thomson Wadsworth, 2005), 295–317.

4. Rajiv Malik, "Discussions on Dharma," *Hinduism Today*, October–December 2004, 30–31.

5. Ibid.

6. Ibid.

7. Ruth Vanita, *Love's Rite: Same-Sex Marriage in India and the West* (New York: Palgrave/St. Martin's, 2005).

8. Victor Lenous, "'Girlfriends' in Suicide Pact," *Blitz*, July 11, 1980.

9. See Ruth Vanita, "All in the Family: Same-Sex Relationships in Traditional Families,"in *Love's Rite* (see note 7). Here, I examine personals for marriages of convenience between gay men and lesbians in twenty issues of *Trikone* magazine from 1998 to 2003.

10. See Meera [pseud.], "Finding Community," in *A Lotus of Another Color: An Unfolding of the South Asian Gay and Lesbian Experience*, ed. Rakesh Ratti (Boston: Alyson Publications, 1993), 234–45. In June 2005, while I was staying in Delhi, a lesbian couple from Mumbai contacted me and other activists, who helped them move to Delhi to escape harassment by their families. They are now considering migrating to another country.

11. Nirjhar Dixit, "Bride Grooms Bride," *Savvy*, February 21, 1988.

12. "Legal Seal on Lesbian Marriage," *Statesman*, December 13, 2004.

13. Section 377 ot the Indian Penal Code makes "unnatural intercourse" (generally interpreted as homosexual, particularly male-male intercourse) a crime punishable by up to ten years of rigorous imprisonment. On August 11, 1992, AIDS Bhedbhav Virodhi Andolan (AIDS Anti-Discrimination Movement), known as ABVA, held the first-ever protest in India condemning the police use of Section 377. In March 1994, after prison authorities, citing Section 377, refused to make condoms available to prisoners, ABVA filed a public interest petition in the Delhi high court, asking for repeal of Section 377 on the grounds that it violates constitutional rights to life, liberty, and nondiscrimination and obstructs AIDS prevention. The petition came up for hearing in March 2001 and was dismissed without arguments because ABVA failed to appear. In December 2001, Naz Foundation (India) Trust, an anti-AIDS organization, and Lawyers Collective (whose HIV/AIDS unit was set up in 1998) jointly filed a petition in the Delhi high court, asking that Section 377 be read down to apply only to sexual assault on children. In September 2004, the court dismissed the petition on technical grounds. An appeal of this decision is now pending before the Supreme Court. For more details, see Ruth Vanita, "2002: India Considers Abolishing Sodomy Laws," in *GLBT History* (Pasadena, CA: Salem Press, 2005).

14. See, for example, the report on the 1998 suicide attempt by Mamata and Monalisa in Orissa, eastern India, *For People Like Us* (New Delhi: Aids Bhedbhav Virodhi Andolan, 1999).

15. Prathima Nandakumar, "Gay Marriages Groom Anti-AIDS Battle," *Times News Network*, August 28, 2004, http://www1.timesofindia.indiatimes.com/articleshow/830976.cms (accessed October 11, 2006).

16. Kama, God of Love, shooting an arrow at two women. Sandstone sculpture, Orissa, eastern India, circa eleventh century. Seattle Art Museum, Accession no. 74.17. A photograph of this sculpture by Paul Macapia appears as the frontispiece of Ruth Vanita, *Love's Rite* (see note 7).

17. Both the preceptors in the *Mahabharata*, Dronacharya and Kripacharya, are born in this way. A divine variant occurs when Shiva, interrupted during intercourse with his wife, ejaculates into the fire god Agni's hands or mouth (in different versions), an ejaculation from which the god Kartikeya later springs. For further details on these and other such texts, see Ruth Vanita and Saleem Kidwai, *Same-Sex Love in India: Readings from Literature and History* (New York: Palgrave/St. Martin's, 2000), 1–106.

18. Between a third and a half of the *Manusmriti* appears also in the *Mahabharata*.

19. See Manu, *The Laws of Manu*, trans. Wendy Doniger and Brian K. Smith (Delhi: Penguin, 1991). In 11:174 (267), the penance prescribed for a man who ejaculates in something other than a vagina is a minor one, also prescribed for "stealing articles of little value" (2.165).

20. Mark D. Jordan, *The Invention of Sodomy in Christian Theology* (Chicago: University of Chicago Press, 1997), 17.

21. Martha Nussbaum, "Steerforth's Arm: Love and the Moral Point of View," in *Love's Knowledge* (New York: Oxford University Press, 1990), 335–64.

22. Alan Bray, *The Friend* (Chicago: University of Chicago Press, 2003).

23. For translations and analysis of three of these texts, see Ruth Vanita, "Born of Two Vaginas: Love and Reproduction between Co-Wives in Some Medieval Indian Texts," *GLQ*

11, no.4 (2005): 547–77. These materials also appear in somewhat different form in Ruth Vanita, "Monstrous to Miraculous: Same-Sex Reproduction and Parenting," in *Love's Rite* (see note 7).

24. *The Swarga Khanda of the Padma Purana*, ed. Asoke Chatterjee Sastri (Varanasi: All-India Kashiraj Trust, 1972), 43–46.

25. *Nalinikanta Bhattasali*, ed. Ramayana-Adikanda (Dacca: P. C. Lahiri, Secretary, Oriental Texts Publication Committee, University of Dacca, 1936), 90–92. These extracts are translated into English by Anannya Dasgupta. A full translation appears in Ruth Vanita, *Love's Rite*, 147–49 (see note 7). See Bhattasali's introduction for an account of the many different versions of the *Krittivasa Ramayana*, which is still an extremely popular text among Bengali Hindus.

26. See my essay, "Vatsyayana's *Kamasutra*," in *Same-Sex Love in India*, 46–53 (see note 17).

27. Vaman Shivram Apte, *The Student's Sanskrit-English Dictionary* (Delhi: Motilal Banarsidass, 2000), 319.

28. Alain Danielou, *The Complete Kama Sutra* (Rochester, VT: Park Street Press, 1994); Devdutta Sastri, *Kamasutram* (Varanasi: Chowkhamba Sanskrit Series, 1964); Parasnath Dwivedi, *Kamasutram* (Varanasi: Chowkhamba Surbharati, 1999); Wendy Doniger and Sudhir Kakar, *Kamasutra* (Oxford: Oxford University Press, 2002).

29. Vanita and Kidwai, eds., *Same-Sex Love in India* (see note 17).

30. Michael J. Sweet and Leonard Zwilling, "The First Medicalization: The Taxonomy and Etiology of Queers in Classical Indian Medicine," *Journal of the History of Sexuality* 3, no. 4 (1993): 590–607; Michael J. Sweet, "'Like a City Ablaze': The Third Sex and the Creation of Sexuality in Jain Religious Literature," *Journal of the History of Sexuality* 6, no. 3 (1996): 359–84; John Boswell, *Christianity, Social Tolerance and Homosexuality* (Chicago: University of Chicago Press, 1980); Bernadette J. Brooten, *Love between Women: Early Christian Responses to Female Homoeroticism* (Chicago: University of Chicago Press, 1996); and Michel Foucault, *The History of Sexuality*, vol. 1, trans. Robert Hurley (1976; English repr., New York: Random House, 1978).

31. Vanita and Kidwai, eds., *Same-Sex Love in India*, 194–97, 200–201 (see note 17).

32. See Associated Press, "India Set for Anti-Valentine Demos," *CNN.com*, February 11, 2003, http://edition.cnn.com/2003/WORLD/asiapcf/south/02/11/india.valentines.ap/ (accessed October 11, 2006); "Call for Valentine's Ban in India," People's Daily Online, February, 13, 2001, http://english.peopledaily.com.cn/english/200102/13/eng20010213 _62250.html (accessed October 26, 2006). For an account of right-wing and left-wing responses to *Fire* in India and the United States, see Geeta Patel, "Sexuality and Its Incitements" and Monica Bachmann, "After the Fire," in *Queering India: Same-Sex Love and Eroticism in Indian Culture and Society*, ed. Ruth Vanita (New York: Routledge, 2002), 222–33, 234–44.

33. See Amara Das Wilhelm, *Tritiya-Prakriti: People of the Third Sex* (Philadelphia: Xlibris, 2003); "Hinduism and Homosexuality," *Trikone* special issue, 11, no. 3 (July 1996); and Vanita, *Love's Rite*, 29–30 and chapter 10 (see note 7). See also Arvind Sharma, "Homosexuality and Hinduism," in *Homosexuality and World Religions*, ed. Arlene Swidler (Valley Forge, PA: Trinity Press, 1993), 47–80.

34. Arvind Kumar in conversation with the author, September 13, 2004.

35. S. K. Mitra, *Hindu Law* (Delhi: Orient Publishing Co., 2000), 516–17.

36. See, for example, Anu [pseud.], The Mahabharata of Krishna Dwaipayana and Giti [pseud.], "Inverting Tradition: The Marriage of Lila and Urmila," in *A Lotus of Another Color*, 81–84 (see note 10).

37. See the section titled "Rebirth; The Justification of Impossible Loves," in Vanita, "Introduction to Ancient Indian Materials," in *Same-Sex Love in India, 28–30* (see note 17).

For a more detailed exposition, see Ruth Vanita, "Love-Death and Rebirth," in *Love's Rite*, chap. 4 (see note 7).

38. Pandit Durgaprasad and Kasinath Pandurang Parab, eds., *The Kathasaritsagara of Somadevabhatta*, 4th ed. (1930; repr., Bombay: Nirnaya Sagara Press, 1852), 86. Extract translated by author.

39. See, for example, *The Mahabharata of Krishna Dwaipayana Vyasa*, trans. Kisari Mohan Ganguly (1883–1896; New Delhi: Munshiram Manoharlal, 1970, 3rd edn. 1973), vol. VII, 105; Karna Parva, section XLII, vol. VIII, 295; Shanti Parva, part I; Apadharmanusasana Parva, section CXXXVIII.

40. Reported on the Gay Bombay list, gaybombay@yahoogroups.com, June 13, 2001.

41. Suchandana Gupta, "Husband at Home, in Sari at Work," *Telegraph* (Calcutta), May 29, 2001.

42. The phrase is that of the rabbi who conducted the Jewish part of my wedding ceremony in June 2000 in New York; a Hindu ceremony was also conducted.

2

"MARRIED IN THE SIGHT OF GOD": MARTIN LUTHER, THEOLOGY, AND SAME-SEX UNIONS

Christian Scharen

As theologian Mark Jordan has written, "The weight of tradition that now stands against blessing same-sex unions once stood, as the Protestant reformers well knew, and still stands in part, as any 'traditional Catholic' can tell you, against the choice of marriage itself as a Christian vocation."[1] This chapter takes as its central thesis that Martin Luther's innovative effort to recover a vibrant theology of marriage in contrast to this traditional rejection of marriage can be of considerable help in constructing a theology of same-sex unions for the church today, even in the face of the traditional rejection of such unions. Therefore, in this chapter I show how attending to Martin Luther's method along with his theological conclusions provides the basis for an inclusive theology that is faithful to scripture and tradition while also making room for openness to blessing same-sex unions and allowing those living in such unions to accept the call to pastoral office.

The crux of the issue here is this: can one say that certain traditional Christian purposes of marriage are fulfilled in same-sex unions? Raising this question suggests its corollary—to what extent do traditional heterosexual marriages fulfill these same Christian purposes? In this short chapter, I offer suggestive lines of argument that could facilitate the development of a full relational theology open to all persons who make promises of fidelity, one to another.

Constructive theological efforts would fail at the outset if one were to turn to what Luther said explicitly about "homosexuality" or, better, same-sex sexual encounters, because very likely he was not aware of what we today consider a "sexual orientation." Luther mentioned same-sex relations only once in his comments on the story of Sodom:

> Moses proceeds with a terrible sin. I for my part do not like dealing with this pas-
> sage, because so far the ears of the Germans are innocent of and uncontaminated

by this monstrous depravity; for even though this disgrace, like other sins, has crept
in through an ungodly soldier and a lewd merchant, still the rest of the people are
unaware of what is being done in secret.[2]

Clearly, an ethic for same-sex relationships goes nowhere with this view as its
foundation.

As I show below, however, Lutherans must not fall into the trap of simplisti-
cally retrieving the theological ideas of a previous generation for application in their
own time. Thus the fact that Luther came to a negative conclusion regarding what
he understood of same-sex attraction does not weigh as heavily as it may first
appear. The point is *not* to discover exactly which ethical prescriptions were developed in the Germany of 1520 based on theological conclusions. Rather, careful
attention to the fundamental theological grounds and the method for deriving ethical prescriptions from those grounds bears most directly on the work of today's
Christians. Faithful action in response to the work of a living God requires new theological work that is willing to speak clearly about methods of engaging both traditional sources and contemporary social situations.

After a brief description of the way I intend to use resources from various points
in Luther's theological work, I look specifically at Luther's writings on marriage and
especially on creation and the "first marriage" in his commentary on Genesis. These
writings yield surprising results that can be brought to bear on a theological position
that could speak with integrity to the present. I turn now to some brief comments on
the use of a tradition before turning to Luther's theology proper.

REFLECTIONS ON THE USE OF A TRADITION

Theology, as well as science, regularly presumes that new research begins by closely
examining the tradition of reflection on a specific issue. Theologians have, on the
whole, a greater reverence for the received traditions than their counterparts in
the sciences and thus often attend to certain scriptural texts or figures in the Christian
tradition with devoted and sometimes uncritical care. Nonetheless, both theology and
science develop in response to new historical circumstances, new methodological or
technological tools, and new insights into God and the world. In theology new views
develop, James M. Gustafson argues, "in part by abandoning aspects of what is
received including what is received in the charter document, the Bible."[3] One can
give examples of this sort of change: decisive new views have been developed on
such issues as slavery, religious liberty, and the equality between men and women.[4]
In developing such positions, prior interpretations and emphases have been left aside,
and fresh work with scripture and the tradition has taken a central place.[5]

Given the reality that changes in prescriptive ethics often entail the abandonment of aspects of the received tradition, I examine the question of change and prescriptive sexual ethics with some care. Abandoning certain scriptural or other
traditional resources rightly evokes caution in many faithful Christians as the community tries to discern what God is doing today and how the community should
respond. We begin by recognizing that interpretation and choice must accompany the
use of Christian scripture and tradition, just as they accompany philosophy, science,
and experience. Although many contemporary Lutherans in the United States claim

that scripture is divinely inspired, few wish to completely deny its fundamental historical character and thereby be required to follow such chilling directives as stoning to death rebellious children in Deuteronomy 21:18–21. Similarly, many wish to hold Luther's work in the highest esteem, but few would affirm his encouragement of the slaughter of the peasants in 1525 or his diatribes against the Jews late in his life.

In explicating an ethic for marriage and sexuality, I wish to find a middle path that avoids not only such untenable prescriptions within scripture and tradition but also similarly unattractive concessions to the whims of contemporary society. This middle path requires attention to human experience, including what is known both through the sciences and everyday life, held in tension with the witness of scripture and tradition. After an explication of this view, I then turn to how Luther worked when making a change in his time. That is, I highlight the method guiding Luther's effort to bring the resources of tradition to bear on what God was doing in his day. These methodological moves focus our attention on a certain theological underpinning provided by the tradition that is fundamental to any revision of ethical relational theology.

A METHOD FOR REVISION IN THEOLOGY

Sexual morality exists to give shape to biological drives in ways that limit harmful actions and encourage beneficial ones.[6] Although in some societies and in some historical eras, moral strictures regarding sex remain tacit, the last two generations in most North Atlantic nations experienced rapid and radical changes in the formerly tacit sexual moralities. Among the challenges were the advent of mass-marketed contraceptive drugs, a relaxing of the social and religious condemnation of divorce, changes in gender roles, the emergence of gay and lesbian communities, the legalization of abortion, and cohabitation as an alternative to marriage. Challenges from society make contemporary Christians painfully aware of how out of step traditional Christian regulations regarding sex appear. Indeed, the strictness of Christian sexual morality has also been criticized by Christians themselves as profoundly antihuman, antibody, and antiwoman.[7]

That is, Christian sexual morality has come under attack in places where it is contrary to human experience. Today many Christians find goodness in sexuality. Sexual experience offers some of life's most profound pleasures and delights. These pleasures can of course refer to the physical responsiveness of one to another. Yet, such pleasures also include the wonder of learning about the intricacies of our bodies as God has created them, the mutuality and trust that can accompany such physical intimacy, and certainly, for many, the process of bearing and raising children. A caution: an increased incidence of certain sexual ideals or practices that can be documented statistically does not constitute a valid warrant for a change in the moral rules that Christians embrace. For example, one could argue that violence against women is statistically "normal," yet it is incredibly damaging for the victim, the perpetrator, and society as a whole. Still, statistical "normalcy" can be an indication of a gap between human experience and ethical prescriptions. When moral rules are deemed quite contrary to human experience they are ignored. Thus, at least on a descriptive level, the plurality of human experience provides one key test for the continuing validity of ethical prescriptions.

There are certain aspects of human experience that echo the deepest insights of the Christian tradition on sexuality and marriage. It is these insights that must be recovered if revisions in Christian ethics are to honor traditional sources while aiming to speak to the needs of the current historical moment. Gustafson identifies three aspects of human sexual experience that should inform Christian ethics:

> First, sexuality is part of our biological and personal natures. About the first there can be no dispute; by personal, I mean to suggest that our sexuality relates to our sense of identity, of human worth and fulfillment, and so forth. Second, our experience of sin, of human moral fault, is deeply related to our sexuality.... Third, sexuality is related to our experience as social beings, and particularly to our need for covenants.[8]

These three aspects provide a descriptive lens on the wisdom of traditional Christian ethics as well as some insight about how and why arguments for change have met with some success. Emphasis on procreation in Christian sexual ethics required primary emphasis on the biological, reproductive aspect of human life. However, this emphasis was never completely convincing to modern Christians as an understanding of sexuality, because it does not do justice to the personal nature of humans. Revisions of the procreative prescription have centered on this argument. Yet, these revisions, sometimes in the name of "sexual liberation," neglected the second aspect necessary for Christian ethics: sin. Tacit trust necessarily goes along with sexual expression and intimacy that lead to some sort of bond or commitment, an insight at least as old as St. Paul (1 Corinthians 6:12–16). Using another person for the careless pursuit of self-fulfillment is only one of the many forms that sexual exploitation can take. Thus revisions in Christian sexual ethics need to attend to the power of the human propensity to sin. The difficulties of human sin raise the need for attention to the third aspect: covenants aimed at fostering an environment in which trust and confidence can flourish. Such explicit commitments to one another serve as traditional a purpose as one can find in Christianity. They protect against the negative effects of sin. Just as surely, they express and reinforce fidelity and mutual love. These three aspects—nature, sin, and covenant—offer a foundation for entertaining changes in prescriptive ethics so that, although some resources from scripture and tradition are necessarily left aside, fundamental insights are drawn on nonetheless.

To embrace a more relational Christian theology that speaks faithfully from the tradition of Christian thought to contemporary experience, careful and generous listening to the present is required to avoid hasty judgments against those arguing for change. Also required is serious attention to the wisdom of one's tradition. Experience must be honored as a primary way by which Christians know God and God's world; yet, experiences and the truths known from them must also be tested by the fundamental wisdom found in scripture and tradition.[9] I now turn to Martin Luther showing how he, also, adhered to something like this method in what he wrote regarding sexuality and marriage during his lifetime.

MARTIN LUTHER

Martin Luther's mature views on sexuality and marriage represent three related reversals in traditional Christian teaching on marriage. Luther reversed a tradition that (1) devalued sex and marriage while uplifting celibacy, (2) made marriage a sacramental rather than a civil affair, and (3) viewed the work of marriage as necessary but not properly Christian work.[10] Reformation historian Kristen Kvam argues that the church today has the most to learn from Luther's unconventional views. She writes, "Luther must think it important to counter traditional ways of thinking about sexuality, especially the traditions that uphold the propriety of celibacy vows and that minimize the significance of embodiment and sexual activity."[11]

Luther built both his criticisms of late medieval ideals and practices and his new theological view on a two-fold attention to his own pastoral observations and the study of scripture. One of Luther's first major public works, *Address to the Christian Nobility of the German Nation* (1520), advocated drastic changes in many spheres of churchly life, including sexuality and marriage. Luther wrote this work not out of an interest in self-promotion nor mere academic debate but rather out of a priest's moral outrage over the situation of Christians "oppressed by distress and affliction." Such distress and affliction stemmed at least in part from the burden of vows of celibacy taken without the gift of keeping chaste—something Luther thought to be a very rare gift, indeed, and at any rate not something the church could require.[12] Two years later, in the introduction to his treatise, *The Estate of Marriage*, Luther comments that the current state of marriage

> has give rise to so many dreadful abuses and false situations, that I would much prefer neither to look into the matter nor to hear of it. But timidity is no help in an emergency; I must proceed. I must try to instruct poor bewildered consciences, and take up the matter boldly.[13]

These sorts of statements are common in Luther's writings, leading the reader to remember that Luther not only served as professor but also as pastor. His experiences of the problems and his motivations for action were rooted in moral outrage, to be sure, but just as much in deep compassion for the plight of the people.

Luther's unconventional arguments against monastic vows and compulsory celibacy for all who wished to really serve God aright can serve to summarize both Luther's method and the fundamental theological grounds upon which he built his constructive views. On the issue of priests and celibacy, Luther spoke from experience: "We also see how the priesthood has fallen, and how many a poor priest is overburdened with wife and child, his conscience troubled."[14] Luther took issue with the legal prohibition of clerical marriage, arguing from scripture that marriage is neither precluded nor required; rather, he was convinced that because scripture did not preclude it, evangelical freedom should supersede the strictures of canon law: "my advice is restore freedom to everybody and leave every [person] free to marry or not to marry."[15] Astutely, Luther recognized that such a shift would require an alteration in church policy as well as the elimination of certain elements of the church's Canon Law.

Although his actions carried dramatic ramifications for the status quo in church and society, Luther steadily worked on behalf of priests who were already living with spouses and children. Finding resources in Pauline literature to the effect that a bishop should be the husband of but one wife, Luther proclaimed that ministers should be "given liberty by a Christian council to marry to avoid temptation and sin."[16] In moving prose, Luther claimed that, despite the condemnation of canon law,

if "from the bottom of their hearts both are of a mind to live together in lawful wedded love...the two are certainly married in the sight of God."[17] His authority for
offering this pronouncement was not based upon his clerical office nor his profes-
sorial appointment but rather his simple claim to "the authority of a Christian to
advise and help my neighbor against sins and temptations."[18]

Over time, Luther elaborated his defense of sexuality and marriage while following the basic method of bringing personal experience to the careful study of
scripture. Increasingly, a theology of creation dominated his writing on sexuality
and marriage. First, Luther derived from Genesis 1:27 ("God created them male and
female") the claim that each of us are and can only be exactly what God created us
to be and moreover that we should honor God's delightful handiwork. One should
not deride the other, but honor their bodily distinctiveness.[19] For Luther, the body in
all its physicality and wholeness should be seen "as a divine and good creation that
is well-pleasing unto God himself."[20] Luther used this argument about the goodness
of embodied human life to encourage monks and nuns to forsake monastic vows for
marriage. Additionally, he underscored the goodness of marriage both as a general
civil estate intended for all people and specifically appropriate for Christians.

Second, drawing from Genesis 1:28 ("Be fruitful and multiply"), Luther claimed
that sexual desire is as natural as sleeping and drinking and moving the bowels;
whenever one tries to resist this desire, "it remains irresistible nonetheless and goes
its way through fornication, adultery, and secret sins, for this is a matter of nature
and not of choice."[21] Writing on the sixth commandment, Luther commented that
where "nature has its way, as God implanted it, it is not possible to remain chaste
outside of marriage; for flesh and blood remain flesh and blood, and the natural
inclinations and stimulations have their way without let or hindrance, as everyone's
observation and experience testify."[22] Kristen Kvam notes that Augustine and other
early church fathers regarded sexual desire as clear evidence of the corruption of
humanity: it was neither present in the original creation nor will it be in the coming Reign of God. In this context, Luther's affirmation of the sex drive and sexual
relationship as a fundamental aspect of God's good creation marks a bold turn in
his theology.[23]

Luther understood sin to be profoundly deforming of this good creation, however. In the original state of creation, Luther could say of sexual intercourse that

> in Paradise that union would have taken place without any bashfulness, as an activ-
> ity created and blessed by God. It would have been accompanied by a noble delight,
> such as there was at the time in eating and drinking. Now, alas, it is so hideous and
> frightful a pleasure that physicians compare it with epilepsy or falling sickness.[24]

Sin distorts the original goodness of the body and thus causes humans to regard neither God, humanity, nor the world with proper faith, trust, and love. Under the conditions of sin, Luther suggested that marriage is proper in order to bear children, to
provide companionship, and to serve as an "antidote against sin," by which he
meant that committing to one sexual partner enables one's lust to be guided away
from many sinful behaviors. Basing his arguments on the existence of natural sexual desires, Luther not only opposed compulsory celibacy and supported marriage
but also defended marriage as a place where Christians can be certain that they are
doing God's will. "They can therefore," Luther wrote, "also be certain that the estate

of marriage and everything that goes with it in the way of conduct, works, and suffering is pleasing to God."[25]

It may be striking to see Luther speak of the lustful corruption of sexual desire in one breath and in the next praise all aspects of Christian conduct, works, and suffering in marriage. Luther firmly believed that, through the gift of grace, forgiveness, and new life in Christ, one takes on a new righteousness. Luther spoke of this new righteousness as "alien," given by Christ as a cloak to cover human sinfulness. Nonetheless, under this cloak, and prior to its giving, union with Christ through the dying and rising of baptism begins to restore the original righteousness, a process that finds completion in the coming Reign of God.[26] Ordinary household duties, even the father changing dirty diapers, are properly good works—not because they achieve goodness in God's eyes but because they serve the neighbor. The simple tasks required in a relationship "are pleasing to God who has so ordained them, and thereby graciously cares for us like a kind and loving mother."[27]

Lastly, Luther drew on Genesis 2:22 ("And God brought her to Adam") to show God's original intention that humans are not meant to live alone but to have someone with whom to share the joys and burdens of life. God intends marriage as an equal relationship of shared intimacy and commitment. Luther wrote of Adam and Eve that whatever "the husband has, this wife has and possesses in its entirety. Their partnership involves not only their means but children, food, bed, and dwelling; their purposes, too, are the same."[28] Though sin also corrupts this original equality, still Luther expected each person "to love and cherish the wife or husband whom God has given. For marital chastity it is above all things essential that husband and wife live together in love and harmony, cherishing each other wholeheartedly and with perfect fidelity."[29]

Thus in reenvisioning the theology of creation, Luther comes full circle from his experience of Christians in distress caused by untenable sexual prescriptions to a reexamination of scripture for a renewed theology of sexuality and marriage. Luther, at his best, expressed an earthy and often colorful embrace of bodily life. His proposal for reenvisioning sexual ethics combined the three levels of human experience mentioned earlier: nature (biological and personal); sin; and covenant. Luther saw the importance of sexuality in both its biological and personal aspects. He took care to warn about sinful temptations and the harm that can accompany the expression of one's sexuality. He also affirmed the importance of marriage as a covenant that protects against temptations to sin while also offering a context for loving, cherishing, and serving one's family as the nearest of neighbors.

Luther's theological method and the fundamental presuppositions undergirding it can be of great service to contemporary Christians. First, Luther's outrage over people's suffering due to the unjust imposition of compulsory celibacy led him to a reexamination of scripture in order to assist those under distress. His concern about canon law and church structure came later, and though he attended to it, he first attended to the individuals who were unjustly burdened by it. Any reasonable person, once having heard the witness of queer Christians, would no doubt recognize a similar situation today among church communities in the United States.

In the Evangelical Lutheran Church in America, the largest Lutheran body in the United States, queer clergy and candidates for ministry are forced to accept options that cause pain and suffering, including the constant threat of being found out or being rejected. According to official documents, they choose among three unappealing options: work in the ministry and remain celibate; leave the ministry in order to have the companionship, joy, and physical intimacy a partnership affords (although the church does not sanction such unions for any persons, lay or clergy); or, as in Luther's time, keep their partner a secret while remaining in the ministry. There is a fourth option, though it exists in defiance of the official church structure: the Extraordinary Candidacy Project works to pair queer candidates who are qualified in every other way with congregations that will call them. These extraordinary ministries consider a contemporary version of Peter's question found in Acts 15 about how we can "continue to exclude those God has poured out the Holy Spirit upon" and the other apostles' active response, "We can't."[30]

It does not take much imagination to recognize parallels between compulsory celibacy for sexual minority candidates today and its imposition for all candidates in Luther's time. There is also a parallel between Luther's turn to scripture and his experience as grounds for a revised theological and ethical position on marriage and contemporary grounds for supporting same-sex marriage. Regardless of one's subsequent interpretation, scriptural references to sex between men or between women contain no direct affirmation of same-sex marriage and sexuality. However, given the fact that biblical (and Reformation) writers did not understand people to be constitutionally oriented toward heterosexuality or homosexuality, the biblical condemnations of same-sex desires and behaviors cannot adequately answer questions raised by same-sex committed relationships today.[31]

Several scriptural texts (especially Genesis 1, Matthew 19, and 1 Corinthians 7) are often used today as part of a "confessional" reading of the scriptural witness on the issue of marriage. The "confessional" view of a "heterosexual order of creation" entered Lutheran debates in the 1950s as a way to reinforce traditional gender roles.[32] Today, it provides those against same-sex marriage a blanket interpretation of scripture and tradition and therefore, they believe, clear insight into the mind of God.[33]

But the Genesis texts need not be used defensively to keep in their place women, queers, or any other group deemed threatening to the status quo. If one examines scriptural texts using Luther's approach, keeping contemporary problems of exclusion and compulsory celibacy for sexual minority persons in mind, different conclusions are possible for Christians. First, Luther was not a simple literalist with regard to scripture; he saw the ways it can be twisted "like a wax nose, into whatever shape you want."[34] Luther distinguished between the Word (who is Jesus Christ) and Scripture (through which he is revealed). While admitting the normative place of the living Word of God in shaping the life of Christian community, Luther did not worship scripture as such. Luther was willing to exclude the books of James and Revelation because he did not feel that they showed forth Christ. Luther argued that

> one must deal openly with the Scriptures. From the very beginning the word has come to us in various ways. It is not enough simply to look and see whether this is God's word, whether God has said it; rather we must look and see to whom it has been spoken, whether it fits us. That makes all the difference between night and day.[35]

Luther found scripture's center in the Word that is Jesus Christ, but he advised that one must also be discerning so as to hear the Word of God "for you." This means one must avoid the mistake of blindly following interpretations of scripture made in previous generations. Referring to the interpretations of the early church fathers, Luther wrote that they "often speak as a result of an emotion and of a particular mood which we do not have and cannot have, since we do not have similar situations."[36]

Therefore, as Luther turned to scripture for a fresh interpretation that spoke to his day, so the church today ought to look to scripture for the foundational sources of God's good will. First, if Christians turn to the classic texts that Luther drew upon, such as Genesis 1:27 ("God created them male and female"), it could lead to an affirmation that the text says what Luther said it did—we are each created to be what we are, no more. Just as Luther asserted that women and men should not belittle each other, so today, we should not belittle those whose identities are queer.[37] Perhaps the major divide in Christian discussions of same-sex unions centers upon this question of whether queer identities represent an intentional variation within God's good creation or a defect in God's good creation resulting from the presence of sin in the world.[38] If one claims the former, Luther's proclamation that we should delight in God's handiwork can be read as theological support for queer pride in themselves as wholly pleasing to God, countering the historic claim that they are an "abomination"[39] or are "abidingly defective."[40]

Of course this interpretation of Luther assumes that sexual orientation is natural, good, and God's intention in creation. Such an argument cannot be made in any simple way based on scriptural evidence that presupposes a heterosexual norm and condemns same-sex acts. Various branches of science are searching for conclusive evidence to support this claim of natural or biological origins of sexual orientation. At this time, the findings are not conclusive, and much of the research and its reporting suffer from the overriding polemical climate of debates about sexuality in the United States.[41] However, from admittedly anecdotal evidence based upon my experience, the reflections by queer people that I have heard consistently report that "choice" about sexual orientation was never an option. They have from an early age understood themselves to be oriented as they are. They have, in some cases, contemplated suicide in response to the condemnation they have received from the church. Unable to believe that the God of Jesus Christ would condemn a whole class of persons to such a fate, I join Patricia Jung and Ralph Smith when they affirm

> homosexuality as a part of God's original blessing for profoundly theological reasons. Given what we know about the centrality of sexuality to human personhood and about sexual orientation, to contend that homosexuality is an expression of the fallenness of the world entails the conclusion that God is against homosexual people in the very fabric of their existence as human beings.[42]

Jung and Smith invoke Peter's words in Acts 10:15b in support of their position: "What God has made clean, you must not call profane."

Drawing from Genesis 1:28 ("Be fruitful and multiply"), Christians could also affirm with Luther that, indeed, God has created a basic sexual desire that is as natural and healthy as sleeping and drinking and moving the bowels. Good passion, which serves to draw humans into relation with one another, needs to be held distinct from sinful lust. These are conflated in some unhelpful ways by Luther. He came close to breaking away from the unfortunate notion that all aspects of human sexuality as well as any experience of pleasure equal sin, but Luther still spoke quite disparagingly about lust and sex, even within such "a blessed and God-pleasing estate" as marriage.[43] However, knowledge of human physiology and psychology informs our contemporary sense of healthy human experiences of sexuality; we know that passion brings joy and for some constitutes a way to know the wonder and love of God.[44]

Yet, paradoxically, Luther's worry about lust and the dangers inherent in the sphere of sexuality help make the case for encouraging same-sex unions as a matter of church teaching. Sexual desire is a powerful force and can destroy trust, self-esteem, and even lives. Furthermore, sexualized power and violence pervade our culture in which women are attacked and raped with horrifying frequency, children are abused, marriages are broken through betrayal and adultery, and pain and distrust are created when one person is used for the sake of another's sexual pleasure. Sin distorts the original goodness of the body. It distorts human relationships, as well. The strong influence of sin, according to Luther, impacts the interpretation of God's intention that marriage serves as an "antidote" against sin. Although the language may seem antiquated, the concept is not. A person's marital commitment to another should provide a context in which the trust and intimacy inherent in sexuality are honored and strengthened, as well as a context that avoids many of the harms possible when lust drives one's choices.

Lastly, Luther drew from Genesis 2:22 ("And God brought her to Adam") as a way to show that God is the author of marriage. This fact meant that in some form or another, in every culture, men and women form kinship systems that allow the sharing of daily tasks and the raising of families. Marriage may produce other social goods necessary for society, including the bearing and raising of children. These other goods might indeed be part of God's design for the temporal good of human life in this world. But the primary good in such coupling, from God's perspective as witnessed to in scripture, is the imitation of an unconditional choosing and being chosen, an experience of unity and fidelity that is at the same time radical self-giving and fullness of being. It is, in short, an experience of the divine life, the abundant and fulfilled life, for which God made us.[45]

Although this covenantal promise making is often symbolized in scripture through heterosexual images (Christ and his bride, the Church), it is not always portrayed this way (see Ruth 1:16–17 or Matthew 23:37). At any rate, the key factor is not sexual orientation (God's or ours), but the promise making and practice of fidelity. To experience love and self-giving and to receive the fullness of unconditional promise in return are not heterosexual hopes or homosexual hopes. They are human hopes. They are, fundamentally, responses to Adam's lonely plight in the Garden of Eden, reflecting a concern that the human not be alone, that this new creature have companionship of its own kind. God has made marriage that we might learn something of God's own Trinitarian life: a perfect community of mutual self-giving and love. And thus, what God wants from marriage is to provide for the most basic of human hopes. Consider this eloquent testimony of British theologian and priest Jeffery John speaking of "homosexual" Christians he has known:

What they hoped for was precisely the same as their heterosexual friends: finding someone to love and be wholly given to, someone to grow together with, someone to be there at the end of the day and to the end of their life. It seems to me inhumane and un-Christian (in a profound, not trivial sense) to deny that hope to so many men and women whom God has created for fulfillment—yes—but a fulfillment which will only be reached through our learning in this life to love one another in God's way. That is why I believe we have an absolute duty in the Church to offer homosexual couples, clerical and lay, not merely a grudging admission, but a positive theological understanding of their relationships, just as we do for heterosexual couples in marriage: to help them realize the same hope, the same ideal, of secure, faithful, lifelong love.[46]

CONCLUSION

I began this chapter by proposing that Martin Luther's innovative recovery of a vibrant theology of marriage in contrast to a medieval bias against marriage as sin ought to be a positive resource for our work on developing a theology of same-sex unions today. It is important to engage traditional resources like Luther so that the church may build a theological and ethical position on marriage and sexuality that both welcomes queer Christians fully and upholds the fundamental aspects of church teachings on marriage and sexuality. Martin Luther's theology points to the fundamental promise of lifelong fidelity between a man and a woman as the foundation of the church's understanding of marriage. Why, then, could individuals in a same-sex couple not also voluntarily take each other and promise lifelong fidelity? Or, to bring the question up to date and sharpen it a bit, when individuals in same-sex couples do indeed voluntarily take each other and promise lifelong fidelity, why does the church not recognize and bless the marriage in the sight of God?[47] If today, guided by pastoral concern and scripture, we were to discern the Spirit leading us to affirm that the church should support, encourage, and bless such covenantal unions, then Martin Luther's theology helps us see how we might speak of these unions as authentic embodiments of our best teaching on sexuality and marriage.

Such an affirmation should not be seen as denigrating the church's support for the traditional pattern of male-female marriage and family. That pattern is and shall remain normative for Christians. Rather, it simply means that marriage cannot be seen as exclusively the domain of male-female couples. Theologically, the exclusive reservation of marriage for male-female couples is neither justified nor truthful to contemporary experience: most fundamentally, marriage recognizes natural human needs, sexual and personal; the need for protections against abuse; and the need for structures of commitment that foster trust and fidelity. These fundamental affirmations are supported by Luther's work and do not, in their essence, depend on male-female patterns for marriage.[48]

Because I believe God has created queer people "clean"—that is, good in their fundamental being—then I must affirm as Luther did the goodness of human bodily nature. Further, on this basis, those ministers who are wrongly kept under a false vow of celibacy should consider themselves free to find a partner or not as they see fit in their life. Those who suffer under the secrecy of a committed relationship while serving a congregation should turn again to their consciences, consider themselves married in God's sight, and formalize their commitment with friends and clergy who will support them.

Not only within the church but also in civil society, the created goodness of queer people supports a struggle for marriage as a legitimate option, a true and general civil estate intended for all people who wish it, as well as for liturgies of the church with which to offer witness to God's blessing.

NOTES

1. Mark D. Jordan, *Blessing Same-Sex Unions: The Perils of Queer Romance and the Confusions of Christian Marriage* (Chicago: University of Chicago Press, 2005), 12.

2. Martin Luther, "Lectures on Genesis 15–20, 1535–1545," in *Luther's Works*, American ed., vol. 3, trans. George V. Schick (St. Louis: Concordia Publishing House, 1986), 251–52.

3. James M. Gustafson, *Ethics from a Theocentric Perspective*, vol. 1, *Theology and Ethics* (Chicago: University of Chicago Press, 1981), 144. This section of Gustafson's book is a rich and challenging reflection on the use of tradition in constructive theological work.

4. Gregory Baum, "Homosexuality and the Natural Law," *The Ecumenist* (January–February 1994): 35.

5. See here a set of examples drawn from Roman Catholic scholars: Charles Curran, ed. *Change in Official Catholic Moral Teaching* (Mahwah, NJ: Paulist Press, 2003).

6. In the following paragraphs I depend on James M. Gustafson, "Nature, Sin, and Covenant: Three Bases for Sexual Ethics," *Perspectives in Biology and Medicine* (Spring 1981): 483ff.

7. This point is a staple component of progressive sexual ethics over the last thirty years. See the influential statement by James B. Nelson, *Embodiment: An Approach to Sexuality and Christian Theology* (Minneapolis: Augsburg, 1978), 19ff.; A more recent work that consciously builds and extends Nelson's work is Marvin M. Ellison, *Erotic Justice: A Liberating Ethic of Sexuality* (Louisville: Westminster/John Knox 1996). Yet even more conservative theologians such as Max Stackhouse argue that "forms of dualism adopted by some Christians have been antisensual." See his recent *Covenant and Commitments: Faith, Family, and Economic Life* (Louisville: Westminster/John Knox, 1997), 34.

8. Gustafson, "Nature, Sin, and Covenant," 487 (see note 6).

9. For more on the role of experience in theology, especially in relation to issues raised by same-sex unions, see Christian Scharen, "Experiencing the Body: Sexuality and Conflict in American Denominations," *The Union Seminary Quarterly Review* 57 (2003): 94–109.

10. For more here, see Christian Scharen, *Married in the Sight of God: Theology, Ethics, and Church Debates Over Homosexuality* (Landham, MD: University Press of America, 2000), chap. 2.

11. Kristen E. Kvam, "'Honoring God's Handiwork': Challenges of Luther's Doctrine of Creation," in *A Reforming Church...Gift and Task: Essays from a Free Conference*, ed. Charles Lutz (Minneapolis: Kirk House, 1995), 183.

12. Luther, "To the Christian Nobility of the German Nation Concerning the Reform of the Christian Estate, 1520," in *Luther's Works*, American ed., vol. 44, trans. Charles M. Jacobs, revised by James Atkinson (Philadelphia: Fortress Press, 1965), 124–25.

13. Luther, "The Estate of Marriage, 1522," *Luther's Works*, American ed., vol. 45, trans. Walther I. Brandt (Philadelphia: Fortress Press, 1965), 17.

14. Luther, "To the Christian Nobility of the German Nation Concerning the Reform of the Christian Estate, 1520," 176 (see note 12). Luther's commitment to uphold Christian freedom whenever it was warranted led him to bold views on canon law. He found dependence

on the letter of the law to be confounding in the effort to do what love and justice require. He remarked at table, "The stupid canon lawyers want to apply laws that were framed in other times and for other reasons. They say, 'Thus it is written in the book,' and they don't see that the times have changed and that former circumstances and laws have passed away." Martin Luther, "Marriage Laws Must Be Adapted to the Times, 1539," *Luther's Works*, American ed., vol. 54, trans. Theodore G. Tappert (Philadelphia: Fortress Press, 1965), 349.

15. Luther, "To the Christian Nobility of the German Nation Concerning the Reform of the Christian Estate, 1520," 176 (see note 12).

16. Ibid., 177.

17. Ibid.

18. Ibid.

19. For more on this denigration of sex and marriage at the time of the Reformation, see Steven Osment, *When Fathers Ruled: Family Life in Reformation Europe* (Cambridge: Harvard University Press, 2004).

20. Luther, "The Estate of Marriage, 1522," 17 (see note 13).

21. Ibid., 18.

22. Luther, "The Large Catechism," in Theodore G. Tappert, ed. *The Book of Concord*, (Philadelphia: Fortress Press), 393–94.

23. Kvam, "'Honoring God's Handiwork'," 179–80 (see note 11).

24. Luther, "Lectures on Genesis 1–5, 1535–1545," *Luther's Works*, American ed., vol. 1, trans. George V. Schick (St. Louis: Concordia Publishing House, 1954), 119. This is one among many places where it becomes clear how different Luther's understanding of science was from ours today. We simply work with a completely different understanding of human anatomy and physiology than did Luther and therefore have evidence that affects our theological understandings of sexuality in ways he could not have foreseen. See Thomas Laqueur, *Making Sex: Body and Gender from the Greeks to Freud* (Cambridge: Harvard University Press, 1992).

25. Luther, "The Estate of Marriage, 1522,", 38 (see note 13).

26. Tuomo Mannermaa, *Christ Present in Faith: Luther's View of Justification* (Minneapolis: Fortress Press, 2005); See also William H. Lazareth, *Christians in Society: Luther, the Bible, and Social Ethics* (Minneapolis: Fortress Press, 2001).

27. Luther, "The Estate of Marriage, 1522," 43 (see note 13).

28. Luther, "Lectures on Genesis 1–5, 1535–1545," 137 (see note 24).

29. Luther, "The Large Catechism," 394 (see note 22).

30. Of the many examples, one might point to the just-concluded ministry of Ruth Frost and Phyllis Zillhart, a lesbian couple who were ordained in 1990 and have served for fifteen years of vibrant ministry at St. Francis Lutheran, San Francisco, http://www.st-francis-lutheran.org (accessed October 26, 2006).

31. As Mark Jordan notes, the question of whether homosexual relations are permissible to Christians, and the question specifically of "the Bible and homosexuality," marks for the church "an obsessive distraction from thinking about same-sex unions." Such distractions set aside all sorts of difficult questions beginning with how such a nonbiblical term like "homosexuality" fits with canonical texts, as well as basic questions of interpretation and the authority of scripture in the Christian life, not to mention questions raised when the church asks about "the bible and heterosexuality" (e.g., rates of divorce, adultery, pornography, rape, prostitution, and on and on). See Jordan, *Blessing Same-Sex Unions*, 12–13 (see note 1). At the very least, one can say that biblical scholarship conducted during the last fifty years on the so-called homosexuality texts in the Bible has raised serious questions about their direct applicability. In some cases, as in the story of Sodom in Genesis 19:1–29, no serious person any longer connects the story to contemporary same-sex relationships. Those who wish to write, as Robert Gagnon has, that "there is clear, strong, and credible evidence that the Bible

unequivocally defines same-sex intercourse as sin" now cannot assume common acceptance of their view (as might have been the case one hundred years ago) and must write a 500-page defense. See Robert Gagnon, *The Bible and Homosexual Practice: Texts and Hermeneutics* (Nashville: Abingdon, 2001).

32. For a more detailed discussion of this history, see Scharen, *Married in the Sight of God*, 60–66 (see note 10).

33. Robert Benne, *Ordinary Saints: An Introduction to the Christian Life*, 2nd ed. (Minneapolis: Fortress Press, 2003), especially Chapter 7. The point is put succinctly by Leonard R. Klein: "The relevant loci are the creation story, the Sixth Commandment, Ephesians 5 with its meditation on marriage as a sacramental sign of the union of Christ and his Church, the end of Revelation with its depiction of the marriage of the Lamb, and the whole narrative stream of holy scripture that assumes the heterosexual monogamous norm, despite the fact of royal and patriarchal polygamy." See "Lutherans in Sexual Commotion," *First Things* 43 (May 1994): 31–38.

34. Martin Luther quoted in Douglas John Hall, "The Theology of the Cross for Our Day," *The Lutheran* (March 2004): 23.

35. Luther, "How Christians Should Regard Moses," in *Martin Luther's Basic Theological Writings*, ed. Timothy F. Lull (Minneapolis: Fortress Press, 1989), 145.

36. Luther, "Lectures on Genesis 1–5, 1535–1545," 61 (see note 24).

37. Mark Jordan writes, "I do not use the acronym LGBT (Lesbian Gay Bisexual Transgender). It implies that the most general description is gotten by summing four particular identities. I use queer as a term that leaves the number and fixity of identities unspecified just in order to emphasize that they have in common some deviation from majority norms for sex, gender, and bodily pleasures." I share Jordan's general sense of the issues and his practice in generally using queer in this way. See Jordan, *Blessing Same-Sex Unions*, 212 n. 39 (see note 1).

38. The ELCA's monthly magazine, *The Lutheran*, published two articles on this exact question in 2003. I argued yes, and Merton Strommen argued no. See Christian Scharen, "Gay Christians: Symbols of God's New Creation," *The Lutheran* (March 2003): 22–23; and Merton Strommen, "Not Part of God's Intention," *The Lutheran* (March 2003): 24–25.

39. Leviticus 18:22.

40. Paul R. Hinlicky, "Recognition, Not Blessing," *Journal of Lutheran Ethics* (August 2005). http://www.elca.org/scriptlib/dcs/jle (accessed October 26, 2006).

41. An obvious example within debates in the ELCA is Merton Strommen's *The Church and Homosexuality: Searching for a Middle Ground* (Minneapolis: Kirk House, 2001). Strommen's training is in psychology, and he cites many studies in this book to bolster his claim that homosexuality is abnormal and therefore not only theologically objectionable but also so unhealthy for persons that he encourages change therapy for them.

42. Patricia Beattie Jung and Ralph F. Smith, *Heterosexism: An Ethical Challenge* (New York: SUNY, 1993), 88.

43. Luther, "The Large Catechism," 394 (see note 22).

44. For a remarkable and provocative contemporary exploration of the question of bodily experience in sexual ethics written by a Lutheran woman, see Mary D. Pellauer, "The Moral Significance of Female Orgasm: Toward Sexual Ethics That Celebrates Women's Sexuality," *Journal of Feminist Studies in Religion* 9 (Spring/Fall 1993): 161–82; see also Christine Gudorf, *Body, Sex, and Pleasure: Reconstructing Christian Sexual Ethics* (Cleveland: Pilgrim Press, 1994).

45. I take this to be the main point of the complex and highly significant book by Eugene Rodgers, *Sexuality and the Christian Body* (New York: Blackwell, 1999).

46. Jeffery John, *Permanent, Faithful, Stable: Christian Same-Sex Partnerships* (London: Darton, Longman, and Todd, 2000), 54.

47. Even Paul Hinlicky, whose confessional Lutheran credentials are widely respected, argues persuasively for church recognition of same-sex unions as a less bad option than promiscuity. See Hinlicky, "Recognition, Not Blessing" (see note 40). The question of blessing, however, depends on the single issue of one's evaluation of the status of queer identity vis-à-vis creation—is it a fact of variation within a good creation or a defect resulting from sin? Blessing sin is out of the question for me, just as much as for Hinlicky. But because of this foundational split on interpretation the rest of our commitments biblically and theologically follow.

48. Jung and Smith make a similar argument in *Heterosexism*, 140–51 (see note 42).

3

RELIGION AND THE FREEDOM TO MARRY: HISTORICAL REFLECTIONS ON MARRIAGE EQUALITY IN AMERICA

J. Terry Todd

I can't go that far. That's the year 2000. Negroes—OK; but that's too far.
—President Nixon commenting on same-gender marriage, 1970,
not long after the decriminalization of interracial marriage[1]

Say the word "marriage," and what is conjured in the minds of most Americans is the white clapboard church where family and friends are gathered in the presence of a minister, to be joined in something called "holy matrimony." The groom stands at the altar, awaiting the bride, who glides down the aisle, clasping the arm of her father. After the couple exchange vows and rings, the minister pronounces them "husband and wife." The scene has many variations, of course. Maybe the minister is a Catholic priest or a rabbi. Perhaps it's not a clapboard church after all but a temple or a catering hall or a seaside garden or even a Las Vegas "chapel."

In the imagination of many Americans, the sacred setting and the presence of a religious leader compound the confusion about what marriage really means. Is it a religious rite? A civil ceremony? A private contract? Recently, the question of whether same-gender couples can rightfully marry has complicated matters even further, occasioning a great deal of commentary, much of it focused on legal matters. The chapters in this volume present forceful arguments for marriage equality from a number of religious perspectives, demonstrating that same-gender marriage is a religious concern as well. Although it is important to recall that legal marriage is a civil affair in the United States, religious organizations are free to set their own requirements for which marriages they will bless and which they will not. Ministers have a dual role; many preside at marriages as licensed agents of the state, while at other times they preside solely in their ritual capacity as religious figures, invoking no civil powers. Most of the time they act in both capacities. Yet what matters in law is not the marriage *ceremony*, but the marriage *license*, and that comes from the state.

It is still the case, however, that religious ideas, practices, and institutions have contributed mightily to defining (and redefining) legal marriage in America. That is especially true with Christianity given the cultural and political power that Christians have exercised in the United States. In this chapter I review some aspects of an immensely complicated story, focusing especially on Christian responses to the insistence that people should be free to choose their marriage partners. Sometimes religious people have supported that freedom, while at other times they have been complicit in denying equal access to marriage.

I begin this chapter by reviewing the rise of the early movement for same-gender marriage in the United States, showing how some religious voices insisted on the freedom to marry for same-gender couples. I also show how that advocacy created a furious backlash that helped fuel the rise of the Christian Right in the 1970s and later. I move on to compare the movement for same-gender marriage to earlier struggles for the right to marry. For most of U.S. history, the color line was a barrier to marriage freedom. After all, it took a Supreme Court ruling to decriminalize interracial marriage in the United States, and that finally happened only in 1967.

Many reject attempts to compare the struggle for black civil rights with the quest for lesbian and gay equality and for very good reason. Through slavery, lynchings, Jim Crow laws, and violent white resistance to the African American freedom struggle, black people have faced ferocious brutality throughout the entire span of U.S. history. These are different struggles indeed, with very different histories, and any facile comparison must be rejected. The historical parallels I trace in this chapter have to do specifically with discourses about marriage—interracial marriage and same-gender marriage. As calls for gender equality in marriage grew more insistent after 1970, opponents of marriage equality—many of whom had also opposed freedom to marry for interracial couples—drew arrows from the same rhetorical quiver. Opponents of marriage freedom appealed to a natural order of things, sounding alarms about the transgression of supposedly God-given roles and warning that change would signal civilization's imminent demise. It all seemed so familiar. In this case, however, objections to marriage freedom were based on God's plan as it related to gender, not race. The point I wish to make in this chapter is that Christians, and other religious people too, have disagreed with each over just what marriage means, who should have access to it, and what God has to say on the matter.

RISE OF THE EARLY MOVEMENT FOR SAME-GENDER MARRIAGE

Same-gender marriage seemed to explode into public consciousness only in the 1990s, yet securing the freedom to marry had been a concern for some lesbians and gay men long before that. By the 1950s homophile civil rights organizations like the Mattachine Society and the Daughters of Bilitis already had begun to debate the merits and meanings of marriage. The June 1963 edition of *ONE*, the Mattachine Society's monthly magazine, featured an article praising marriage as a ticket into the mainstream. The author, Randy Lloyd, had been surprised by "hetero" friends who treated Lloyd and his lover as married, even though the couple's homosexuality remained the love that dared not speak its name. "My real eye opener occurred when these heteros, with a cool nonchalance that made me feel woefully unsophisticated, [began] introducing us to other homophile married couples." Like Lloyd and his partner, these same-gender couples also thought of themselves as married and were accepted as such by their friends. Lloyd was certain that marriage was not for everyone —straight or gay—but his experience taught him that marriage just might be the path to social acceptance. "When society finally accepts homophiles as a valid minority with minority rights," Lloyd argued, looking into the future, "it is going first of all to accept the married homophiles. We are, after all, the closest to their ideals."[2]

As the debate heated up in subsequent decades, hopes for assimilation would compete with liberationist impulses among many in lesbian and gay communities, including religious advocates of same-gender marriage. The assimilation imperative was at work in one of the first books on religion and homosexuality published in the United States. In *Christ and the Homosexual* (1960), the Reverend Robert Wood, a Congregationalist minister from New York, presented a sometimes sensationalist but also sympathetic investigation of gay life. Wood represented homosexuals as unhappy outcasts, whose relationships were furtive and inevitably disappointing. (Such a condescending tone was common for Wood's time and remains so even today in some circles.) Yet Wood's call for Christian recognition of same-gender marriage surely put him ahead of his time. If a same-gender couple wanted his blessing, Wood said, he would require premarital counseling, just as he did of every other couple. And if Wood judged a same-gender couple prepared and committed, he would not hesitate to bless their union. Marriage stabilized lives, Wood believed, and marriage also would lead to greater social acceptance of homosexuals. "One of my main tenets is that the homosexual needs to adjust to the established conventions of society as nearly as he can," Wood declared. For him marriage was the most direct path into the mainstream. Yet there was also a theological mystery at work. God becomes a third partner in every marriage, Wood claimed, working to bless and strengthen the union. Wouldn't God do the same for two men or two women?[3]

Although some advocates, from the mid-1960s into our own time, continued to promote marriage as the ticket to assimilation and social acceptance, other voices denounced marriage as a patriarchal, oppressive institution that held no promise for same-gender couples. In 1969, for example, the Marxist-inspired Gay Liberation Front (GLF) attacked marriage as "one of the most insidious and basic sustainers of the system" and called the family "the microcosm of oppression."[4] Some gay and lesbian Christians, particularly in the 1970s, questioned whether marriage was a goal they wanted to achieve. Mark Jordan highlighted that ambivalence in a quotation he found in *Agape and Action*, a Berkeley-based Protestant ecumenical magazine:

> It may be that the tendency of many homosexuals to be promiscuous is simply a symptom of their despair: an easy way to feel real, visible, and touchable, sex as a deadening escape from pain instead of a constant and growing revelation. Or the opposite may be true; that homosexuals who seek endlessly for that faithful marriage are just trying to play bourgeois heterosexuals. Or it may be that homosexual love is bound to be, as it was in more open times, a band of men, a brotherhood, and that the commune and group marriage scene is the sane and "normal" way for homosexuals.[5]

Was marriage something to be fought for? That was an open question, at least for *Agape and Action*'s anonymous Christian writer whose mixture of romanticism and liberationist sentiment made him wonder whether marriage might spell an end to the revolutionary sexual (and spiritual) possibilities of same-gender—or at least, male-on-male—relationships. "Indeed," as George Chauncey has written, "the long and contentious gay and lesbian debate over the wisdom—and even the desirability—of pursuing marriage rights should disabuse anyone of the idea that there has ever been a single 'gay agenda.'"[6]

As the push for gay and lesbian civil rights continued to grow throughout the 1970s and into the 1980s, marriage equality was never a priority for movement leaders at either the local or national levels, many of whom seemed to share an ambivalence about the wisdom of demanding equal access to a social institution that seemed anchored in patriarchal oppression. Only a small number of community voices called for the freedom to marry, and many of them were religious. The Reverend Troy Perry organized what was no doubt the earliest faith-based campaign for same-gender marriage in the United States, and he did so with a liberationist insistence that same-gender couples should have the same marriage rights as heterosexuals.

Perry, a Pentecostal minister defrocked because of his homosexuality, had founded the Metropolitan Community Church (MCC) in 1968 as a gay-friendly church in the living room of his West Hollywood home. The church grew rapidly, attracting gay and lesbian Christians weary of the hostility they faced from their own churches. The MCC began blessing same-gender marriages, or "holy unions," soon after Perry founded the church in 1968. An early case, in 1970, took the issue out of the church and into the public square, raising questions about whether same-gender marriages might have legal status after all.

Perry had married a lesbian couple, Neva Joy Heckman and Judith Ann Belew, under a California law allowing clergy to issue a marriage certificate to couples who had lived together in a common-law marriage for at least two years. It was described by a gay publication, *The Advocate*, as "the first marriage in the nation designed to legally bind two persons of the same sex." But when Heckman and Belew attempted to record the marriage, their request was refused. Perry sued in an attempt to force the state of California to recognize the same-gender marriages he performed as a licensed minister, but the case was dismissed.[7] Perry was undeterred. He and his church continued the practice of blessing holy unions while also fighting for legal recognition in California and other states. By the year 2005, an estimated eighty-five thousand holy unions have taken place in MCC churches, and Perry himself claims to have presided over one thousand of them. Perry and the MCC insisted that these couples were joined in the sight of God even if the law refused to recognize their marriages.

Other instances of clergy participation in legally ambiguous same-gender marriages surfaced during the early 1970s. One highly visible case involved James Michael McConnell and Richard John Baker, a Minnesota couple whose very public battle to obtain a state marriage certificate landed them in *Look* magazine's feature article on "The American Family." Jack Baker was a law student at the University of Minnesota and also president of the university's Student Government Association. His partner, Mike, was a librarian who had lost his job because of his civil rights activism on behalf of lesbians and gay men. After Baker and McConnell managed to obtain a valid marriage certificate through a loophole in Minnesota law, they asked a personal friend, United Methodist minister Roger Lynn, to marry them. And he agreed. The ceremony was arranged in haste before anyone could mount a legal challenge.

On September 3, 1971, with friends and family in attendance, Rev. Lynn asked Michael, "Will you live with Jack in this marriage? Will you respect him? Will you love him?" The minister then asked Mike the same questions, and after each answered affirmatively, the Reverend Lynn pronounced them "joined in marriage, in the Name of the Father, and the Son, and the Holy Spirit. Amen." Predictably, uproar ensued. Rev. Lynn was censured by his bishop and threatened with indictment by the Hennepin County District Attorney on the dubious charges of violating Minnesota marriage laws. Although the marriage was voided after a protracted court battle, Rev. Lynn had presided over the first recognized same-gender marriage ever performed in the United States.[8]

In those early years, there were other legally ambiguous cases that included clergy participation. In 1975, for example, the Reverend Freda Smith—the first woman ordained as a minister in the Metropolitan Community Church—performed a wedding at Denver's First Unitarian Church, marrying Richard Adams and Anthony Sullivan, two men who had managed to obtain a valid marriage license from a sympathetic county clerk in Boulder. Soon after the wedding, the Colorado Attorney General voided the Adams-Sullivan marriage.[9] Despite barriers to legal same-gender marriage, sympathetic priests, rabbis, and ministers continued the practice of blessing same-sex unions that looked much like heterosexual marriages. In churches and synagogues and in private homes and catering halls, same-gender couples "tied the knot," often with clergy presiding, even though the ceremony had no legal effect.

Christian groups like the MCC were not the only religious advocates of "holy union." During the 1970s some newly formed gay-friendly synagogues in Los Angeles, New York, Washington, D.C., and other major cities began offering *kiddushin* ceremonies, using a Hebrew term that is typically translated as marriage. And in 1984, the Unitarian-Universalist Association became the second denominational body—after the Metropolitan Community Church—to affirm the practice of same-sex unions and to encourage its churches to support ministers who decided to perform them.[10]

After a promising beginning in the 1970s, religious advocacy for same-gender marriage became less of a priority in the following decade. Many gay men and lesbians refocused their activist energies to deal with the challenges posed to their communities by the HIV/AIDS crisis. Yet as George Chauncey has argued, it was that very crisis—along with a boom in lesbian parenting—that led to a resurgence of marriage equality activism by the late 1980s. Especially during the early years of the AIDS epidemic, many gay men discovered that the lack of legal recognition of their partnerships became a major liability while dealing with a partner's illness and death. After all, who was next of kin, the biological family or one's long-term partner? Many of the privileges that married heterosexual couples took for granted, such as the right to make medical care decisions and the responsibility to make funeral arrangements, were often denied to gay men. So were insurance benefits and bereavement leave. The history of the AIDS epidemic in the United States is marked by many instances of glaring injustice, of same-sex partners whose love had no legal recognition either in life or in death.

In the very same decade, as it happened, there was an unprecedented boom in lesbian parenting. Of course there had always been gay men and lesbians with children, most of them from previous heterosexual marriages, yet in the decade of the 1980s, there were increasing opportunities to become parents through adoption and reproductive technologies. What a number of heart-wrenching court decisions proved at the time was that same-gender parents were nothing but strangers under the law. "The mass experience of child-rearing and death in the 1980s pushed lesbian and gay politics and culture in new directions," Chauncey has observed. "These experiences made people realize that no matter how accepted they were by their families, friends, and workmates, their relationships were still dangerously vulnerable."[11] Unabashed discrimination by insurance companies, employers, government agencies, and the courts also politicized more lesbians and gay men, leading to demands for domestic partnership arrangements that delivered at least some of the rights and responsibilities of legal marriage. Others pushed further, demanding the freedom to marry.

Religious advocacy for same-gender marriage took on new visibility in the 1990s thanks in part to the continued efforts of Troy Perry and the Metropolitan Community Church. On April 24, 1993, the day before hundreds of thousands jammed the nation's capital for the National March on Washington for Lesbian, Gay, and Bi Equal Rights and Liberation, Perry presided over an event called "The Wedding," a frothy brew of political theater, religious ritual, and romantic sentimentalism designed to draw attention to demands for marriage equality. Perry had staged a similar spectacle in Washington, D.C. during an earlier lesbian and gay rights demonstration in 1987, but the much larger 1993 event was a marker of how much interest in same-gender marriage had blossomed since then. The Wedding brought an estimated twenty-five hundred couples to the plaza of the Internal Revenue Service building, a location Perry had chosen for its symbolic value to underscore the injustice of denying the financial and legal benefits of marriage to same-gender couples.

"Dearly beloved," Perry thundered in an invocation, deploying the words of a traditional Christian marriage liturgy and giving it a liberationist spin. "We stand before our nation and our friends because we wish to proclaim our right to love one another. We stand here knowing that love makes a family—nothing else, nothing less!" Perry went on to recall the Hebrew Bible stories of Ruth and Naomi and Jonathan and David as exemplars of same-gender love and devotion. Next was a public exchange of vows written by Perry and a bestowal of tokens symbolizing love and mutual commitment. Then Perry drove home the political message of The Wedding: "We proclaim together our rights as couples in hope that the day will come when not only our community will recognize our relationships, but the laws of our country will also. Couples, you may kiss." In April 2000 Perry returned to Washington once again along with tens of thousands of other demonstrators for the Millennium March for Equality. This time he chose the Lincoln Memorial as the site to stage The Wedding, recognizing the memorial's power to evoke deep associations with American freedom and liberty.[12]

Throughout the 1990s and into the new millennium the divisions in American religious life on the subject of marriage equality grew deeper and more unsettling. In no other corner of the Christian community did the debate rage as heatedly as in the United Methodist Church (UMC), the second-largest U.S. Protestant denomination. UMC minister Jimmy Creech presided over a holy union service for two lesbians in Nebraska in 1997 and was hauled before a church court for violating a 1996 church ban that declared, "Ceremonies that celebrate homosexual unions shall not be conducted in our churches." Although acquitted in the first trial, when Creech performed another service for two men in Chapel Hill, North Carolina, in 1998, he was tried in another ecclesiastical court, convicted, and stripped of his clergy credentials. One year later, in defiance of church law, ninety-two United Methodist clergy, joined by ministers from other denominations, gathered in Sacramento to bless the union of a lesbian couple, Ellie Charlton and Jeanne Barnett. Participating ministers were investigated, but charges were never filed.

However, even when religious leaders did not affirm religious marriage for same-gender couples, some supported marriage equality under civil laws. Such was the case in the Episcopal Diocese of Massachusetts during debates over marriage equality in the months leading up to the 2004 *Goodridge* decision that legalized civil marriage for same-gender couples in Massachusetts. Episcopal Bishop Thomas Shaw gave his support to equality in civil marriage, yet forbade priests in his diocese from presiding over civil marriages and from using the word "marriage" to describe the church's blessing of same-gender relationships. Holy unions were offered to same-gender couples in the Episcopal Diocese of Massachusetts but civil marriage was not.[13]

At the very same time a political backlash continued to mount. In 1977, fifteen states had passed legislation restricting marriage to heterosexual couples. That number had doubled by the late 1990s. In 1996 the U.S. Congress passed—and President Clinton signed into law—the Defense of Marriage Act (DOMA), codifying the exclusion of same-gender couples from the federal definition of marriage. The act declared, "The word 'marriage' means only a legal union between one man and one woman as husband and wife, and the word 'spouse' refers only to a person of the opposite sex who is a husband or a wife." After Massachusetts became the first state to legalize same-gender marriage in 2004, President Bush urged Congress to pass the proposed Federal Marriage Amendment to the U.S. Constitution. If passed, the amendment would mean a restrictive definition of marriage in all of the states. "Marriage in the United States shall consist only of a union between a man and a woman," the proposed amendment reads. Its second clause would also seek to roll back gains made on domestic partnership over the last two decades. "Neither this constitution or the constitution of any state, nor state or federal law, shall be construed to require that marital status or the legal incidents thereof be conferred upon unmarried couples or groups."[14] Such were the conflicts over the meanings of marriage—civil and religious—in the United States at the beginning of the twenty-first century.

Religious opposition to same-gender marriage had been increasing steadily for nearly thirty years, in direct proportion to strides made toward marriage equality. In 1970, the same year that the Reverend Troy Perry attempted to legalize the marriage of Heckman and Belew in the state of California, a high-ranking Catholic moral theologian writing in the Vatican newspaper *L'Osservatore Romano* called marriages between two men or two women "moral aberrations that cannot be supported by human conscience, much less Christian conscience." The Vatican official, the Reverend Gino Concetti, warned that same-gender marriage was a "totally and radically revolutionary concept outside all laws, all social systems and all ethical customs." He called on Catholics and others to resist any recognition of such marriages.[15]

Meanwhile, many Protestant denominations began to respond negatively to the increasing public visibility of the lesbian and gay movement and to demands for equality in marriage. In 1972, the United Methodist General Conference, the governing body of the Reverend Roger Lynn's church and America's second-largest Protestant denomination, adopted a resolution declaring homosexuality "incompatible with Christian faith" and forbidding its ministers to participate in blessing same-gender marriages or unions. The Southern Baptist Convention (SBC), the nation's largest Protestant group, issued a declaration at its 1976 meeting calling for a reaffirmation of "biblical truth regarding the practice of homosexuality and sin." The resolution also urged Southern Baptist churches "not to afford the practice of homosexuality any degree of approval through ordination, employment, or other designations of normal lifestyle." The very next year, SBC delegates overwhelmingly approved a resolution condemning homosexuality and its "devastating consequences for family life in general and children in particular" and denouncing "the radical scheme to subvert the sacred pattern of marriage in America."[16]

In the decade of the 1970s, fears about homosexuality, gender, marriage, and the family became increasingly prominent, and also increasingly conflated, in the discourse of politically engaged conservative Christian leaders—what I call the Christian Right.[17] Complex economic and international questions failed to motivate the right's possible constituencies in its political juggernaut, sociologist Sara Diamond has argued, so the leadership of the Christian Right turned its attention to concerns closer to hearth and home. "It was in the realm of reproductive and family policy," Diamond writes, "where issues could resonate both at the most personal, even visceral level of gender relations."[18]

The proposed Equal Rights Amendment (ERA) to the U.S. Constitution is an excellent case in point. By March 1972, Congress had passed a Constitutional amendment guaranteeing that "[e]quality of rights under the law shall not be denied or abridged by the United States or by any state on account of sex." President Nixon had declared his support for the ERA, and New York and several other state legislatures moved quickly to ratify it. Yet elsewhere anti-ERA forces began to organize opposition, and the amendment failed when its 1979 time limit for ratification passed.

Opponents of the ERA argued that passage would not only lead to unisex bathrooms and military conscription of women but, even more menacingly, to the legalization of marriage between two men or two women. The issue had already arisen during Senate hearings, when Sen. Sam Ervin of North Carolina, a prominent ERA opponent, warned that judges might interpret the amendment to allow homosexuals to marry and thus be enabled to claim the same rights as heterosexual couples.

Ervin's dire warning was repeated time and again by antiamendment opponents, including Phyllis Schlafly, founder of STOP-ERA and its succeeding organization, the Eagle Forum. Although it is unclear to what degree the specter of same-gender marriage led to the amendment's defeat, researcher Ruth Murray Brown discovered in interviews with local activists in Oklahoma that homosexuality and same-gender marriage were major concerns that mobilized their campaign against the ERA. "Homosexuality," replied Bunny Chambers, director of Oklahoma Women Who Want to Be Women, when asked what social issue had been her most effective organizing tool. "I really do believe the ERA will legalize homosexual marriages, and that upsets people."[19]

The claim that homosexuality was the foremost threat to the American family characterized the 1977 Save Our Children campaign, which sought to block anti-discrimination legislation protecting gay men and lesbians in Dade County, Florida. The Save Our Children crusade, led by Anita Bryant, a radio and television personality and former Miss Oklahoma, was one of the most important early political mobilizations of the Christian Right. It demonstrated the extent to which Christian Right leaders would go in their efforts to roll back the tenuous political gains and legal protections that lesbians and gay men had managed to achieve by the late 1970s.

As the campaign's title suggests, Save Our Children trotted out the old fiction that equated homosexuality with pedophilia. Bryant and her associates hurled charges that homosexuals needed to "recruit" children because they themselves could not reproduce and warned that the ultimate aim of homosexuals was the utter destruction of family life. They also warned—falsely of course—that Christian schools would be forced to hire "known" homosexuals as teachers.

Bryant's own minister, Brother Bill Chapman of Miami's Northwest Baptist Church, declared on a television broadcast that he would "burn down the school rather than to let a known homosexual be a role model for children." Largely ignoring lesbian life, the campaign's leaders focused their attacks on gay men, warning that politically engaged homosexuals were "militant in nature, involved in sadistic sexual rituals, and abominable practices." Save Our Children campaigners also warned that homosexuality was the most prominent sign of society's rot and that "our civilization—like Rome—is headed for destruction unless we change our present course."[20]

The Save Our Children campaign succeeded in defeating anti-discrimination protections in Dade County, but even more notably it gave the Christian Right a rhetorical arsenal that would define its antigay agenda for the next three decades. In subsequent years charges of pedophilia and sexual decadence, although never too far in the background, would be soft-pedaled somewhat in favor of amplifying the charge that homosexuality—and same-gender marriage—presented the ultimate threat to the divinely ordained order of American family life. "We would not be having the present moral crisis regarding the homosexual movement if men and women accepted their proper roles as designated by God," Jerry Falwell declared in 1979, exposing the rigid understanding of gender roles that lay at the heart of the Christian Right's opposition to homosexuality and to same-gender marriage.[21]

Falwell and the leadership of the Christian Right seemed to share the belief that greater strides toward equitable social roles for men and women had opened up a cultural space for homosexuality to flourish. At the same time they believed that homosexual expression permitted men and women to question their God-given gender roles. God had created men to be in positions of leadership, with women in submission to men, and all in submission to God. Same-gender marriage allowed for a visible expression of equitable roles, and that in part is what made it so dangerous.

The charge of gender-role transgression appeared in somewhat subtler ways in later Christian Right literature, usually as a somewhat amorphous "threat to God's plan." "Why is this battle so important?" asked Alan Sears and Craig Olsten in their diatribe, *The Homosexual Agenda*. "Because it goes to the very heart of God's plan for marriage and the family. When anyone tinkers with that plan, the emotional, physical, and spiritual well-being of future generations is put at risk."[22]

As demands for marriage equality began to grow more insistent during the 1990s, same-gender marriage was cast as the greatest menace to a system of social order that its proponents claimed was rooted in the very mind of God. Nowhere is the sense of panic more evident than in the current campaign against same-gender marriage headed by psychologist Dr. James Dobson, founder of Focus on the Family and the Family Research Council, two of the most powerful and effective antigay organizations in the United States.

In Dobson's 2004 book, *Marriage under Fire: Why We Must Win This Battle*, he deploys apocalyptic language in the crusade to block the freedom to marry. One passage in particular is worth quoting at length, especially because it conveys Dobson's sense that this is a cosmic battle with deep historical roots and the very highest of stakes:

> For nearly sixty years, the homosexual activist movement and related entities have been working to implement a master plan that has had as its centerpiece the utter destruction of the family. Now the final battle is at hand: The institution of marriage and the Christian church are all that stand in the way of the movement's achievement of every coveted aspiration. Those goals include universal acceptance of the gay lifestyle, the discrediting of Scriptures that condemn homosexuality, muzzling of the clergy and Christian media, granting of special privileges and rights in law, overturning laws prohibiting pedophilia, indoctrination of children and future generations through public education, and securing all the legal benefits of marriage for any two or more people who claim to have homosexual tendencies. It is a perfect storm.[23]

The rhetorical components of the 1977 Save Our Children Campaign are all present in this passage from Dobson's book—the specter of pedophilia, the perils of outlaw sexuality (here, "the gay lifestyle"), the ominous indoctrination of the innocent, the wrecking of a divinely ordained order of family life, and finally the ruin of civilization as we have known it. The Christian church and heterosexual marriage are the only possible defenses to save society from "the perfect storm." Of course Dr. Dobson has taken exclusive claim to the Christian mantle, erasing—or at least trying to erase—the memory of four decades of advocacy some Christians have mounted on behalf of marriage equality.

Appeals to a natural order of things, alarms sounded of God-ordained roles transgressed, premonitions of civilization's end: we have heard all this before in the not-too-distant past and also over the subject of marriage. For most of U.S. history the panic was focused on marriage across the color line, which was illegal in some states until 1967.

THE CIVIL RIGHTS STRUGGLE AND THE
STRUGGLE FOR MARRIAGE RIGHTS

Many people have resisted calls to compare efforts to win marriage rights for same-gender couples with the struggle to end the criminalization of interracial marriage. "As an African American, I find it highly offensive to associate homosexuality with civil rights," the Reverend Stephen Craft has said. "People have been trying to run on that civil rights banner and to use this whole idea of homosexual marriage to say it's the next wave of the movement. But race and sexuality have nothing to do with each other."[24] Although it is true that the struggle for civil rights for African Americans is a different movement and indeed has its own unique history, arguments supporting the denial of marriage rights across the color line and the denial of marriage rights to same-gender couples are often quite similar. A brief survey of these arguments shows that race and sexuality are not only intimately intertwined in the American psyche but also tellingly so on the subject of marriage.

Although Christians have never been of one mind on the matter, bans of interracial heterosexual marriage have a long history in North America, dating to the colonial period. The first law prohibiting marriage across the color line was adopted in colonial Maryland in 1664. As Nancy Cott has shown, the statute seemed to assume a particular kind of coupling because it targeted "freeborn English women" who made "shamefull Matches" with "Negro slaves."[25] This particular race- and sex-based assumption, that the law must prevent the pairing of white women and black men, set up a dynamic that kindled fears about interracial marriage for a very long time. Many states in the early national period adopted laws prohibiting marriage across the color line, and slavery continued to muddle the matter even more in the years leading up to the Civil War. Slaves had no rights to marriage, a fact that abolitionists held out as yet another reason that slavery must end. Slaveholders and their clerical defenders, on the other hand, rooted the denial of marriage rights in a divinely ordered pattern of life that linked the destiny of the church and nation to the model slave-holding family.

The Reverend Joseph Wilson of the First Presbyterian Church of Augusta, Georgia, claimed that God "included slavery as an organizing element of that family order that lies at the very foundation of Church and State."[26] Slavery was essential to God's natural law that placed the patriarch at the apex of a family pyramid with relationships extending downward from there. Everyone else in the household was subordinate—women and children and slaves too. In this divine scheme slaves, as property, had no right to marry. The Christian church and America itself depended on the maintenance of this God-given—*natural*—order of things.

With the end of the Civil War and the passage of the Fourteenth Amendment to the U.S. Constitution, the United States extended equal protection, including the freedom to marry, to former slaves. But racial prejudice continued to shape attitudes toward—and laws against—interracial marriage for a century after the Civil War. Esther Hawks, a white woman who had served as a missionary among African American soldiers and who then went on to teach black children in South Carolina just after the war, recalled a quarrel she had with a Union army chaplain who refused to marry a black soldier and a white woman. "I took the ground that he had no right to refuse to perform the ceremony simply on account of color," she explained, and as the argument grew heated, Hawks defended the couple's freedom to marry: "If a white woman chooses to marry a black man who can say her nay?"[27]

A future white Methodist bishop, Gilbert Haven, called for an end to the common Christian belief that racial segregation was "divinely intended to separate members of the same human family, who are and must ever be one in blood and destiny, in sin and salvation, in Adam and in Christ." Yet Haven even went beyond affirming the freedom of interracial couples to marry. For him, as for a minority of other Christians, interracial marriage carried some kind of spiritual power that might transform the nation in the Radical Reconstruction period. "The hour is not far off when the white hued husband shall boast of the dusky beauty of his wife," Haven declared in 1869, "and the Caucasian wife shall admire the sun-kissed countenance of her husband as deeply and as unconsciously of the present ruling abhorrence as is his admiration for her lighter tint."[28]

Despite the utopian sentiments of Haven, after the collapse of Reconstruction, the freedom to marry was restricted by new and even tougher laws prohibiting marriage across racial lines—and not just in the South. As Peggy Pascoe tells us, "It was not until after the demise of slavery that [laws] began to function as the ultimate sanction of the American system of white supremacy."[29] Young white women, as potential mothers, were believed to be especially in need of protection from that old bogey—the sexually voracious black man. Nowhere is the fear more pronounced than in the rhetoric of U.S. Representative Seaborn Roddenbury, Democrat of Georgia, who in 1912 introduced a constitutional amendment requiring that marriage between "persons of color and Caucasians…[be] forever prohibited" in order "to uproot and exterminate now this debasing, ultrademoralizing, un-American, and inhuman leprosy." Roddenbury warned of another civil war if his amendment was not adopted. "No more voracious parasite ever sucked at the heart of pure society, innocent girlhood, or Caucasian motherhood than the one which welcomes and recognizes the sacred ties of wedlock between Africa and America."[30]

Anxieties about intermarriage extended beyond the union of black and white. In the western region of the United States especially, fears of "mongrelization" were exacerbated by anxieties about the economic success of immigrants from Asia. A growing number of states, particularly in the West, forbade marriage between whites and Japanese, Chinese, Koreans, or Filipinos. Pascoe tells us that a 1901 Arizona law forbade marriage between white people and "negroes, Mongolians, or Indians." In 1931, those bans were extended to include "Malays" and "Hindus."[31]

California's ban on interracial marriage was voided by the state's Supreme Court in 1948 in *Perez v. Sharp*, a case that involved a rather novel argument about freedom of religion. When Andrea Perez and Sylvester Davis applied for a marriage license from the Los Angeles County Clerk in 1947, it was denied on the grounds that Perez was classified as white, whereas Davis was a "Negro male." Perez and Davis sued the state. Legal counsel for Perez claimed that because Perez and Davis were both Catholics—and because the Catholic Church did not forbid interracial marriage—then state law represented an unreasonable burden on the couple's religious expression. Although the religious freedom argument convinced only one of seven judges, a 4–3 majority nonetheless ruled the state's law banning interracial marriage unconstitutional. The court recognized a right to marry under the California constitution, declaring, "The essence of a right to marry is freedom to join in marriage with the person of one's choice."[32]

Early twentieth-century attempts to protect the fiction of white racial purity resulted in what Pascoe calls "the most draconian miscegenation law in American history," an act passed by the Virginia legislature in 1924, the same year in which Congress enacted new limits on immigration. Although the federal measure relied on racialist arguments to severely restrict immigration into the United States from southern and eastern Europe and from South and East Asia, the Virginia statue tackled the question of marriage between the races by tightening the definition of who was to be considered white by law.

Since the colonial era Virginia had prohibited marriage between whites and persons of African descent, defined as anyone who had one-sixteenth "negro blood." But with the passage of the 1924 law, entitled "an Act to preserve racial integrity," Virginia codified a severely restrictive definition of what it was to be white. It also made intermarriage a felony. The act is worth quoting at length in order to give a sense of the Virginia legislature's increasing panic over the perceived dilution of white racial purity:

> It shall hereafter be unlawful for any white person in this State to marry any save a white person, or a person with no other admixture of blood than white and American Indian. For the purpose of this act, the term "'white' person" shall apply only to the person who has no trace whatsoever of any blood other than Caucasian; but persons who have one-sixteenth or less of the blood of the American Indian and have no other non-Caucasian blood shall be deemed to be white persons.

The act specified the racial categories that the legislators had in mind: "Caucasian, Negro, Mongolian, American Indian, Asiatic Indian, Malay, or any mixture thereof, or any other non-Caucasian strains." Perhaps it was a nod to the state's colonial-era Pocahontas legend that allowed a person to qualify as white with no more than one-sixteenth American Indian blood. But any amount of other admixture would make a person unfit for marrying a genuinely "white" person. The point was to preserve what Virginia legislators sensed was fragile and in need of protection—the fiction of white racial purity. Yet they were not the only Americans to feel that interracial love would challenge white supremacy. Within a decade, Pascoe tells us, Virginia's "racial integrity act" was copied by Georgia, and an adapted version was passed in the state of Alabama.[33]

In a well-known case, the U.S. Supreme Court dealt a crushing blow to legal barriers to interracial marriage in its aptly named *Loving v. Virginia* case of 1967. The Loving case began in 1958 with the story of two Virginia residents, Richard Loving and Mildred Jeter, who married in the District of Columbia because their home state denied them the freedom to marry. Loving was white, and Jeter was a woman of African descent. The Lovings returned to Virginia with a valid Washington, D.C., marriage license, which they framed and posted on a wall at home. Late one night in July 1958, a county sheriff and two deputies walked into the Lovings' house through an unlocked door and arrested the husband and wife in their bedroom, charging them with violating the 1924 state law banning interracial marriage.

At their trial the Lovings pleaded guilty and were slapped with a one-year jail term, a sentence the judge suspended on the condition that the couple agree to leave the state for a period of twenty-five years. The Lovings appealed, setting in motion a series of legal challenges that would culminate in a ringing declaration of the freedom to marry. "The freedom to marry has long been recognized as one of the vital personal rights essential to the orderly pursuit of happiness by free men," Chief Justice Earl Warren declared, and "Marriage is one of the 'basic civil rights of man,' fundamental to our very existence and survival.... Under our Constitution, the freedom to marry, or not to marry, a person of another race resides with the individual and cannot be infringed by the State."[34]

What is less well known about the *Loving* case is that the Virginia trial judge who convicted the couple held that the Lovings had violated not only man's law but divine law as well. "Almighty God created the races white, black, yellow, malay and red, and he placed them on separate continents," Federal Circuit Court Judge Leon A. Bazile wrote. "And, but for the interference with his arrangement, there would be no cause for such marriage. The fact that he separated the races shows that he did not intend for the races to mix."[35]

Judge Bazile embraced a form of what historian Jane Dailey has called "segregationist theology," the pious conviction that God demanded the segregation of the races. This was not a marginal view in the mid-twentieth-century South, as Dailey has proven. It had wide support, "articulated across a broad spectrum of education and respectability, by senators and Ku Klux Klansmen, by housewives, sorority sisters, and Rotarians, and, not least of all, by mainstream Protestant clergymen." Such theological convictions led to the insistence that it was wrong to send children to mixed-race schools, not just because it was wrong for the races to associate but because integration would inevitably lead to the greatest sin in segregationist theology—"miscegenation," the mixing of the races through sex and marriage. "In integrating the races in the schools, we foster miscegenation," declared the congregation of Cameron Baptist Church in Cameron, South Carolina, during debates in the wake of the Supreme Court's *Brown v. Board of Education* ruling in 1954, "thereby changing God's plan and destroying His handiwork."[36]

A young white minister in Virginia expressed similar fears. Integration, according to the Reverend Jerry Falwell in 1957, would lead to the destruction of "our race." "If we mix the races in schools, in churches, the ultimate end will be the social mixing which can only lead to marital relationships." Although Falwell later repudiated those words, the apocalyptic warnings of ruin and destruction so common among Southern whites would resurface later in Falwell's campaigns against same-gender marriage.[37]

In one of the more revealing parallels between the old discourse of segregation and our own current discussions of homosexuality and same-gender marriage, some white clergy and laity identified sex across the color line as the sin of Sodom and Gomorrah and warned that America faced imminent destruction if racial integration progressed further. "Anyone familiar with the Biblical history of those cities during that period can readily understand why we here in the South are determined to maintain segregation," declared Texas Baptist minister Carey Daniel.

In yet another disturbing parallel, Christian opponents of integration demonized civil rights workers with charges of sexual perversion. According to some Southern newspapers and rumor mills, interracial sexual orgies marked the 1965 Selma-to-Montgomery March, as marchers were promised "$15 a day, 3 meals a day, and all the sex [they] could handle."[38]

In the generation since *Loving v. Virginia* ended the criminalization of interracial marriage, there have been remarkable changes in the attitudes of many Christians toward marriage across the color line. Segregationist theology has been discredited and even repented of, the link between sex and race almost willfully forgotten. However, in our historical moment, long after the legal battle for the freedom to marry across racial and ethnic boundaries has been won, the realities of fear and discrimination remain.

An article in the flagship evangelical magazine *Christianity Today* underscores the point. "The church must repent not only of bad theology but also failing to protest racist laws in the past," Harold Myra wrote in 1994, "We must face up to the studies pointing to evangelicals as very prejudiced in this area." In defense of interracial couplings, Myra went on to appeal to biblical warrant, "Our theology says that Christ came to make all things new, where there is 'neither Jew nor Greek.'"[39] Interestingly, he omitted the rest of St. Paul's admonition, which reads, "nor male nor female, but we are all one in Christ Jesus" (Galatians 3:28).

In this chapter I have presented a glimpse into how historical trends in the United States have supported an enlargement of the freedom to choose one's own marriage partner while also showing that such freedom does not come without conflict and struggle. Over the years some religious people have worked to promote the freedom to marry, yet many others have justified human prejudice by appeals to an unchanging and divinely inspired social order. A virulent segregationist theology that identified marriage across the color line as a threat both to the family and the nation contributed mightily to the criminalization of interracial marriage and also to the demonization of people of color. It was only in 1967 that the freedom to marry triumphed with *Loving v. Virginia*, a case that inevitably influenced demands for marriage equality for same-gender couples. In today's debates, as we have seen, antigay activists deploy rhetoric that is remarkably similar to that offered up by earlier opponents of interracial marriage. One difference is that today it is no longer race but gender that opponents of the freedom to marry emphasize in their claims to know the mind and heart of God.

By insisting that divinely decreed but biologically rooted characteristics dictate the roles that human beings should play in marriage, self-styled "defenders of marriage" and prophets of apocalypse like James Dobson turn to arguments that are as deterministic and yet as crude as those held by some of their spiritual forebears who insisted that God required the submission of women and the segregation of the races. Perhaps they should take note of the witness of another Christian, the Reverend Robert Wood, who was whistling a different tune as early as 1960. "Those who say that a man-woman marriage is the only natural and morally approved sexual outlet must remember that biology does not necessarily provide the best basis for theology," Wood declared in his pioneering book *Christ and the Homosexual*. "The marriage ceremony speaks of lasting fidelity, of genuine love, of full commitment one to the other. At times, these can be as readily manifested between two men or two women as between a man and a woman."[40] It's as simple—and as complex—as that.

NOTES

1. Quoted in Peter Wallenstein, *Tell the Court I Love My Wife: Race, Marriage and Law, An American History* (New York: Palgrave), 240.

2. George Chauncey, *Why Marriage? The History Shaping Today's Debate over Gay Equality* (New York: Basic Books, 2004), 87–88. Instead of the word "homosexual," many early advocates used the term "homophile" for lesbian and gay equality, in part to shift the emphasis away from sex. For a history of the homophile movement, see John D'Emilio, *Sexual Politics, Sexual Communities: The Making of a Homosexual Minority in the United States, 1940–1970*, 2nd ed. (Chicago: University of Chicago Press, 1998), especially 57–107.

3. Robert W. Wood, *Christ and the Homosexual* (New York: Vantage Press, 1960), 198–200. Wood made it clear that his advocacy was not a call for legal marriage. He wrote instead to change the minds of church people.

4. Quoted in William N. Eskridge Jr., *The Case For Same-Sex Marriage: From Sexual Liberty to Civilized Commitment* (New York: Free Press, 1996), 53.

5. Mark Jordan, *Blessing Same-Sex Unions: The Perils of Queer Romance and the Confusions of Christian Marriage* (Chicago: University of Chicago Press, 2005), 71.

6. Chauncey, *Why Marriage?*, 88 (see note 2).

7. Ellen Lewin, *Recognizing Ourselves: Ceremonies of Lesbian and Gay Commitment* (New York: Columbia University Press, 1998), 7. For Perry's own reflections on the early history of MCC holy unions, see Troy Perry, *The Lord is My Shepherd and He Knows I'm Gay*, with Charles L. Lucas(Los Angeles: Nash Publishing, 1972), 186–88.

8. For an excellent account of the relationship between Baker and McConnell and the Reverend Lynn's involvement in their marriage, see Ken Brownson, "A Quest for Full Equality," May 18, 2004, http://www.may-18-1970.org/Quest.pdf (accessed October 27, 2006), especially pages 24–25 and 67. For more on Baker and McConnell, see Kay Tobin and Randy Wicker, eds., *The Gay Crusaders* (New York: Arno Press, 1975), 135–55.

9. The marriage record of Adams and Sullivan is available on the Web site of the Colorado Department of Health and Environment, http://www.sctc.state.co.us/marriages (accessed October 27, 2006). The license, dated April 21, 1975, lists Adams as groom and Sullivan as bride.

10. See Eskridge, *The Case For Same-Sex Marriage*, 46–47 (see note 4). For a text of the original Unitarian-Universalist resolution, see the UUA Social Justice Statements page, http://www.uua.org/actions/bglt/84union.html (accessed October 27, 2006).

11. Chauncey, *Why Marriage?*, 95 (see note 2).

12. Lewin, *Recognizing Ourselves*, 1–3, 24–28 (see note 7). The text of Perry's ritual is reproduced in Kittredge Cherry and Zalmon Sherwood, eds., *Equal Rites: Lesbian and Gay Worship, Ceremonies, and Celebrations* (Louisville: Westminster/John Knox Press, 1995), 106–9.

13. Alan Cooperman, "Massachusetts Clergy Are Divided on Eve of Historic Same-Sex Unions," *Washington Post*, May 16, 2004, http://www.washingtonpost.com/wp-dyn/articles/A29987-2004May15.html (accessed October 11, 2006).

14. The full text of DOMA and the proposed Federal Marriage Amendment can be accessed at the Library of Congress site, http://thomas.loc.gov (accessed October 27, 2006).

15. "Vatican Aide Condemns Homosexual Marriages," *New York Times*, 8, July 26, 1970.

16. Ruben Herring, "Southern Baptist Convention Resolutions on the Family," *Baptist History and Heritage* 17 (January 1982): 39.

17. I follow the definition of the Christian Right offered by sociologist Didi Herman: "a broad coalition of pro-family organizations and individuals who have come together to struggle for a conservative Christian vision in the political world." See Herman's *The Antigay Agenda: Orthodox Vision and the Christian Right* (Chicago: University of Chicago Press, 1997), 9.

18. Sara Diamond, *Roads to Dominion* (New York: Guilford Press, 1995), 165.

19. See also Ruth Murray Brown, *For a "Christian America": A History of the Religious Right* (Amherst, NY: Prometheus Books, 2002), 85–87. See also ibid., 165–72.

20. Anita Bryant, *The Anita Bryant Story: The Survival of Our Nation's Families and the Threat of Militant Homosexuality* (Old Tappan, NJ: Fleming Revel, 1977), 62, 68, 87.

21. Jerry Falwell, *Listen, America!* (Garden City, NY: Doubleday, 1980), 183.

22. Alan Sears and Craig Osten, *The Homosexual Agenda: Exposing the Principal Threat to Religious Freedom Today* (Nashville: Broadman and Holman Publishers, 2003), 94.

23. James Dobson, *Marriage under Fire: Why We Must Win This Battle* (Sisters, OR: Multonmah Publishers, 2004), 19.

24. Quoted in Evan Wolfson, *Why Marriage Matters: America, Equality, and Gay People's Right to Marry* (New York: Simon and Schuster, 2004), 165.

25. Nancy F. Cott, *Public Vows: A History of Marriage and the Nation* (Cambridge: Harvard University Press, 2000), 44.

26. Mitchell Snay, *Gospel of Disunion: Religion and Separatism in the Antebellum South* (New York: Cambridge University Press, 1993), 71.

27. Quoted in Edward J. Blum, *Reforging the White Republic: Race, Religion, and American Nationalism, 1865–1898* (Baton Rouge: Louisiana State University Press, 2005), 73.

28. Ibid., 61, 73.

29. Peggy Pascoe, "Miscegenation, Law, Court Cases, and the Ideologies of 'Race,'" in *Interracialism*, ed. Werner Sollors (New York: Oxford University Press, 2000), 178–209.

30. Randall Kennedy, *Interracial Intimacies: Sex, Marriage, Identity, and Adoption* (New York: Vintage Books, 2004), 83–85.

31. Peggy Pascoe, "Miscegenation, Law, Court Cases, and the Ideologies of 'Race,'" in *Interracialism*, 183 (see note 29).

32. Ibid., 196. *Perez v. Sharp*, 32 Cal. 2d 711, 717 (1948). The full decision can be accessed at http://online.ceb.com/calcases/C2/32C2d711.htm (accessed October 11, 2006).

33. Peggy Pascoe, "Miscegenation, Law, Court Cases, and the Ideologies of 'Race,'" in *Interracialism*, 194 (see note 29). On the link between miscegenation laws and their relation to fears about immigration, see Gary Gerstle, *American Crucible: Race and Nation in the Twentieth Century* (Princeton: Princeton University Press, 2001), 114.

34. *Loving v. Virginia*, 388 U.S. 1, 12 (1967). The full decision can be accessed at http://www.law.cornell.edu/supct/html/historics/USSC_CR_0388_0001_ZO.html (accessed October 11, 2006).

35. Quoted in Kennedy, *Interracial Intimacies*, 274 (see note 30).

36. Jane Dailey, "Sex, Segregation, and the Sacred after *Brown*," *Journal of American History* (June 2004): 125.

37. Quoted in Chauncey, *Why Marriage?*, 158 (see note 2). This section of my chapter draws heavily from Chauncey's convincing and highly nuanced discussion of the links among civil rights, segregationist theology, and the struggle for lesbian and gay equality.

38. Dailey, "Sex, Segregation, and the Sacred after *Brown*," 141 (see note 36).

39. Harold Myra, "Love in Black and White," *Christianity Today* (March 7, 1994): 18–19. Sociologist Sara Diamond has questioned the newfound enthusiasm for interracial marriage among white evangelicals. While applauding what she calls "the project of racial reconciliation," Diamond believes that, for most white evangelicals, the embrace of interracial marriage allows them to elide other boundary questions "between believers and the 'unsaved' and between men and women." See Sara Diamond, *Not By Politics Alone: The Enduring Influence of the Religious Right* (New York: Guilford Press, 2000), 224.

40. Wood, *Christ and the Homosexual*, 199 (see note 3).

4

TESTIFYING TO THE BLUES:
SEXUALITY AND THE BLACK CHURCH

Kelly Brown Douglas

Sexuality is a complex matter within the Black Church community. There is, perhaps, no issue that causes more consternation within this community than that of sexuality, especially nonhetero expressions of sexuality. Even with all of their diversity, Black Church people are regarded as strikingly similar in their attitudes toward nonhetero expressions of sexuality. They are viewed not simply as homophobic but as more homophobic than other segments of society. Recent polls suggest that, although various constituencies of American society are becoming more supportive of gay and lesbian rights, African Americans are not. In fact, the African American community seems to be moving in the opposite direction.[1]

There is probably no issue that better highlights Black Church views toward nonhetero sexuality than that of same-sex marriages. A recent Pew study indicated that the Black Church community was more opposed to these marriages than other communities. The study cited 64 percent of African Americans opposing same-sex marriages, a percentage that has held steady for several years, whereas the overall population has become less opposed to these marriages (from 41 percent in 1996 to 30 percent in 2003).[2] Moreover, predominantly black and all-black denominations, such as the Church of God and Christ and the African Methodist Episcopal Church, respectively, have issued proclamations making clear not only that same-sex marriage is unacceptable but also that homosexuality itself is a "sin" and a "violation of the law of God."[3]

The Black Church community's obstinate stance in regard to issues surrounding gay and lesbian sexuality and rights is most striking when one considers the historical black struggle for social equality and the Black Church's prominent role within that struggle. It appears inconsistent, if not hypocritical, for the Black Church to be in the forefront of racial justice concerns yet resistant if not repressive when it comes to the rights of nonheterosexual persons. How are we to account for this "close-mindedness" when it comes to nonhetero expressions of sexuality? Is it possible to move the Black Church community toward more progressive and even equitable views on matters of sexuality? If so, how? These are the questions that I address in this chapter. Before doing so, however, two things must be established.

First, it is important to clarify what is meant by the "Black Church." The Black Church is not a singular or monolithic institution. Rather, it is a disparate collective of churches that reflect the diversity of the black community itself. These churches vary by origin, denomination, doctrine, worshiping culture, spiritual ethos, class, size, and other less obvious factors. They may be within white denominational systems or independent of them. They can reflect congregational, connectional, or epis-copal polities. They can be urban, suburban, or rural. They can range in size and structure from storefronts to megachurches. Yet, as disparate as black churches are, they share a common history and play a unique role in black life, both of which attest to their collective identity as the Black Church. In short, black churches emerged as a central part of a black culture of resistance to dehumanizing white racist oppression, that is slavery, and have consistently played a pivotal role in black people's continuous struggle for life and freedom. In this regard, W. E. B. DuBois's description of the Black Church as both the "religious and social center" of the black community remains apt.[4]

Furthermore, although the impetus for this chapter is the pervasive homopho-bic sentiment and heterosexist privileging within the Black Church community, it is important to note that there are various black churches with more liberating and pro-gressive views toward sexual issues including same-sex marriages.

The second thing that I must note before proceeding in this discussion is the vantage point from which I speak. I am an Episcopal priest who claims my voice as a womanist theologian. Thus, I represent that part of the Black Church community that is a part of a white denominational system. As a black Episcopalian, however, my story of faith is inextricably linked to the story of Absalom Jones, former slave, cofounder of the Free African Society, coinitiator of the independent Black Church movement (along with African Methodist Episcopal founder Richard Allen), and the first black Episcopal priest. Jones signifies the persistent black presence within the Episcopal Church community, which has constantly advocated for racial justice within the denomination and whose primary identification is with the wider black community in the struggle against white racism.

Moreover, even though the denomination of which I am a part might be con-sidered more progressive in its views toward nonheterosexuals, as it permits the ordination of openly gay and lesbian persons and the blessings of same-sex unions and has consecrated a self-identified gay bishop (this last action has created much dissension within the wider Anglican communion), the black Episcopal community with which I identify tends to mirror the prevailing attitudes of the wider Black Church community.[5] Although there are black Episcopal voices that are supportive of gay and lesbian rights within the church, there are also significant black voices that are not.[6] Interestingly, the most strident opposition to the 2003 consecration of Gene Robinson has been from the African continent, suggesting perhaps a consis-tency of passion throughout the African diaspora when it comes to nonhetero sexu-alities. For instance, during a recent address to a national gathering of Black

Episcopal clergy, those who were most strident in responding to my talk on sexuality were several clergymen from the African continent. They were quite clear in stating that homoerotism was something that the "African" continent simply could not tolerate. Perhaps even more telling, however, were the responses from the African American clergy—they were conspicuously silent as if refusing to even consider such a topic.[7] Nonetheless, it is from out of and to the wider Black Church community, of which black Episcopalians are a part, that I speak.

Denominational affiliation notwithstanding, my womanist identity further compels me to speak about matters of sexual injustice. As a womanist theologian I am "committed to the survival and wholeness of entire people, male and female."[8] I am therefore obliged to speak to any form of injustice, whether it is present within the black community or in the wider society. More specifically, as a womanist theologian I feel compelled by my very womanist identity to interrogate homophobic attitudes and heterosexist systems and structures as they exist within the Black Church community in an effort to "debunk" and dismantle them.[9] These very attitudes and systems have infringed upon the lives of many black women and men. They have most notably contributed to the Black Church's delayed response to the HIV/AIDS crisis that now ravages the black community.[10] Thus, if for no other reason, the womanist commitment to "survival and wholeness" requires a discerning theological response to issues of sexuality. As a womanist theologian I cannot ignore that aspect of the womanist definition that states that a "womanist loves other women sexually and/or non-sexually."[11] It is the inherent task of those of us who claim our voices as womanist theologians to work toward creating a church and community where nonheterosexual persons are able to love themselves and those whom they chose to love without social, political, or ecclesiastical penalty so that they along with all black men and women may enjoy life and "wholeness." It is out of my commitment as a womanist theologian that I address this issue of the Black Church's views toward sexuality in general and nonheterosexuality in particular. Let me now turn to the complex matter of sexuality within the Black Church community.

THE BLACK CHURCH'S ATTITUDE TOWARD SEXUALITY

Why is the Black Church so repressive when it comes to matters of nonheterosexuality? Why does this community appear more opposed to same-sex marriages than other communities? The answers to these questions must begin with an understanding of the black community's responses to sexuality in general. For it is the case that in the main the Black Church's view toward nonheterosexuality flows from its attitudes toward matters of sexuality in general. And so, we must first ask the question, what is it about sexuality when it comes to the Black Church community? I believe that an appreciation for the "testifyin'" tradition of the women singing is key to answering this question, even as it is central to moving the black community to a new understanding of sexuality. Let me now explore how this is the case. Alice Walker's novel, *The Color Purple* (which some have dubbed a womanist novel), provides the framework for this exploration.

There is perhaps no novel that does more to expose the complex reality of black sexuality than *The Color Purple*. In this novel Walker provides a piercingly accurate glimpse into the sociohistorical reality of black women. Through her black female characters' interactions with themselves, with black men, and with white society, Walker exposes how throughout history black women have been defined according to their sexual bodies by the racially coded patriarchal society of which they are a part. Essentially, *The Color Purple* lays bare the experience of black women as they have struggled to claim their voice in worlds, black and white, in which their bodies have been put upon by sexual abuse and/or racially sexualized commodification in a way reminiscent of slavery. There is, however, one black female character in the novel, Shug Avery, who attempts to break this cycle of racially sexualized victimization. It is as Shug seeks to claim agency over her own body sexual and thus to resist the sexually oppressive reality of black womanhood that we are best able to gain insight into why sexuality has become such a complicated matter for the Black Church community and what that has to do with the blues. It is through the description of Shug Avery's reputation within the community by Celie, the main protagonist, that we gain this insight. Celie writes,

> Even the preacher got his mouth on Shug Avery, now she down. He take her condition for his text. He don't call no name, but he don't have to. Everybody know who he mean. He talk bout a strumpet in short skirts, smoking cigarettes, drinking gin. Singing for money and taking other women mens. Talk about slut, hussy, heifer and streetcleaner.[12]

Why is Shug Avery the object of disparaging gossip? To answer this question is to bring us closer to understanding the Black Church community's troubling responses to sexuality, especially nonhetero sexualities.

A Hyper-Proper Sexuality

"Slut, hussy, heifer and streetcleaner"; this is what everybody seems to think of Shug Avery.[13] Celie believes that "somebody got to stand up for Shug."[14] But nobody in the community does. Certainly not the preacher and not even the good black churchwomen. The question becomes why?

The answer begins with an understanding of the way in which white culture has caricatured black people and how black people have responded to that caricature. Briefly stated, white culture depicts black men and women as oversexualized, lascivious beings. Sexualized ideology has undergirded and sustained white racist oppression of black people, as initially manifest in the slavocracy. This ideology projects black women and men as hypersexualized beasts controlled by lust (i.e., the urgings of their genitalia). Black men and women are thereby characterized as immoral animals driven by abnormal sexual proclivities. Specifically, black men are characterized as rapacious predatory bucks and black women as promiscuous seductresses. Black men have been portrayed as mandigos and black women as Jezebels. Such caricatures allowed for black people to be seen as beasts suitable for breeding, not human beings capable of loving relationships. Moreover, these sexualized caricatures have provided throughout history ample justification for terrorizing attacks on black bodies, such as the lynching of black men and the rape of black women. White lynchers often deceitfully posited black men's predatory behavior in regard to white women as a reason for lynching them. At the same time, white males were considered hapless victims of black women's seductive wiles and thus permitted to rape black women with impunity.[15] It has been black people's persistent history of racially sexualized oppression that has helped shape their responses to various social issues, especially sexual matters.

In an effort to offset the white racist hypersexual caricature of blacks, the black community has projected a standard of "acceptable" behavior governed by a norm of *hyper-proper sexuality*. This has been done in an effort to mitigate if not sever the link between blackness and "abnormal" sexuality. This hyper-proper sexuality is characterized by a strident determination to engage sexuality in a "proper" manner and to present the black community as an exemplar of proper sexuality, if not "acceptable" behavior. What it means to be proper is shaped by what is deemed acceptable in society and is therefore defined by sociocultural narratives of power. Proper sexuality is thus discerned according to white heterosexist, patriarchal notions of sexual propriety. In this regard, this notion of hyper-proper sexuality is not without class implications. For indeed, it is very much shaped by black middle-class aspirations to be deemed acceptable to white mainstream society. It then becomes the task of the black middle class not only to display a "hyper-proper sexuality" but also to induce the members of the black working class to do the same.

A historically significant example of the institutionalization of hyper-proper sexuality, especially as it regarded black women, was the Negro Women's Club movement, later to become the National Association of Colored Women (NACW).

The NACW in many respects mirrored the values of the white women's club movements that had preceded it, particularly when it came to sexual matters. Negro club women, such as Mary Church Terrell, Anna Julia Cooper, Fannie Barrier Williams, and even Ida Wells Barnett, adopted the white non-working-class Victorian notion of sexual purity when it came to women's sexuality. They believed that black women were to be paragons of sexual purity. They considered black women to be the purveyors of morals if not the gatekeepers of morality within the black community. Hence, Anna Julia Cooper proclaimed, "When and where I enter, in the quiet, undisputed dignity of my womanhood…then and there the whole *Negro race enters with me.*"[16]

Of course the troubling implication of this "moral centering" of black women was that black women were held accountable for the downfall of the black community. Inasmuch as black women were seen as "wanton," then the black community was considered vulnerable to degeneracy. Therefore, the key to the success of the race, club woman believed, was the "uplift" of black women. And to reiterate, this uplift meant refraining from what Ida B. Wells called bodily excesses like "drunkedness, gambling and fornication." It was not lost on the club women that if black people were ever going to be accepted within white society, then as Wells said, they had "to refute" charges of black people's lascivious nature by leading a "stainless life."[17]

The Negro club women, therefore, not only worked tirelessly in their antiracism and antilynching efforts but also in their advocacy for standards of sexual propriety; that is, a hyper-proper sexuality. Reflective of the class- and gender-biased assumptions about this hyper-proper sexuality, most of the club women's efforts in promoting a hyper-proper sexuality were waged among working-class black women. It is worth pointing out that, although the Negro club women did not believe that sexual impropriety was a matter of race, they did believe that it was an

effect of class, given the disadvantaged circumstances and impoverished living conditions that most working-class black people endured. Such circumstances, in their
minds, fostered unrestrained sexual behavior. Thus, during the turn-of-the-century
migrations of black people from the South to the urban centers of the North, Negro
club women were especially active in advocating for better working and living conditions for black female migrants. Better life circumstances, they believed, would
foster a hyper-proper sexuality.

In sum, the National Association of Colored Women's agenda reveals the institu-
tionalized reality of a hyper-proper sexuality as it functioned within the black community. In this instance, it served to promote a standard of behavior—that is nonsexualized
behavior—for working-class black women. The members of NACW believed that such
a way of behaving was key to dispelling the myth of black hypersexuality and hence
key to black people's progress in society. The significance of a hyper-proper sexuality
for black people, particularly for black women, provides the context for understanding
why Shug Avery was castigated within her community and thus for our understanding
of the Black Church community's responses to matters of sexuality.

Shug Avery was a blues-singing woman. Through the fictionalized Shug, Alice
Walker captures the reality of what the "classic" blues-singing women represented
in regard to women's sexuality and thus how they were an affront to the black community's notion of a hyper-proper sexuality.

The classic blues, even as they are contested as not being "pure" blues like that
sung by the "wandering lone wandering male," but rather a more commercialized ren-
dition if not "aberration" of the blues, were that which brought the blues (as a mixture
of southern work songs, folk songs, and vaudeville) to the urban centers of the North
during the period of the Great Migrations.[18] With the 1920 release of Mamie Smith's
"*Crazy Blues*," the booming musical "race market" of the 1920s and 1930s began, a
market that was defined by the classic blues. The classic blues tradition was dominated
by women, such as Ma Rainey, Bessie Smith, Ida Cox, Sippie Wallace, Victoria Spivey,
and others. Although these women did not write all of the songs that they sang and
recorded, the blues they sang and interpreted reflected the realities of black women's
lives, especially those of working-class women of the North. In many instances, this
was a reality shared by the blues-singing woman herself. Sippie Wallace noted, "Most
of my [blues] is about myself."[19] Essentially, the classic blues tradition was "about the
facts of life" for black women. In this regard, as blues historian Daphne Duval Harrison
points out, "Through the blues, [Ma Rainey, Bessie Smith and others blues-singing
women] became the principal spokespersons for black women in the North and the
South."[20] The problem, in regard to the black community's notion of a hyper-proper
sexuality, was the message proclaimed by these blues-singing women.

As these women sang the blues of black women's experience, they placed in
the foreground the intimate sexuality of black women. The discourse of the classic
blues was dominated by themes of anguished love and explicit sensual relationality
between women and their male and/or female lovers. Blues-singing women testified
unabashedly and proudly to black women as agents of their own sexual body and thus
represented black women as sensual, passionate beings for whom sexual fulfillment
was an important aspect of intimate relationships and of life in general. The blues-
singing women, as Hazel Carby notes, "had no respect for sexual taboos."[21] Carby further describes the classic blues as a "privileged space" through which blues women

have taken black women's "sensuality and sexuality out of the private and into the public sphere."[22] This is exemplified in the lyrics of a song sang by Ida Cox entitled "One-Hour Mama" in which she sings of a women's sexual prowess and of the kind of man required to satisfy her sexual needs. The lyrics go like this:

> I'm a one-hour mama, so no one-minute papa
> Ain't the kind of man for me.
> Set your alarm clock papa, one hour that's proper.
> I may want love for one hour,
> Then decide to make it two.
> Takes an hour fore I get started,
> Maybe three fore I'm through.
> I'm a one-hour mama, so no one-minute papa
> Ain't the kind of man for me.[23]

Needless to say, blues-singing women through the songs they sang, if not in the lives they lived, betrayed the notion of a hyper-proper sexuality. If the Negro club women attempted to confront the white cultural connotation of black people as hypersexual by promoting a hyper-proper sexual norm, then blues women dealt with this racist connotation by ignoring it. They refused to be restrained either by white cultural stereotypes or by the black community's prudish responses to them. These women, in essence, were not as concerned about the appearance of fulfilling a stereotype as they were concerned to rescue their sexuality from the limitations of such a stereotype. And so it was that blues women provided a way for black women, if not also black men, to take control of their own body sexual without having to adopt a hyper-proper sexuality.

With this understanding one can now appreciate why Shug was rejected by her community and hence can come closer to discerning the reasons for the Black Church community's troubling responses to sexual issues. Through her singing of the blues, songs that in the words of Celie "sound low down and dirty" and "are a sin to hear"[24] (about which I say more below), Shug does indeed claim agency over her body. She makes clear that her body is her own—to be used the way she wants, when she wants. Shug does not hide from her sensual/sexual self. In fact, she revels in it. In so doing, she accentuates the power of her sexuality as she unabashedly employs it to navigate her place in a hostile world while also providing a means for Celie to discover her own sexual body. Unfortunately, by doing so Shug Avery seemingly gives into the white cultural stereotype of oversexualized black people and thereby subverts her community's efforts to project a standard of hyper-proper sexuality. Hence, as Celie recounts, "nobody stands up for her."

It is not simply, however, the fact that Shug betrays a standard of hyper-proper sexuality that causes her to be castigated within her community. For it is important to note that it is "the preacher that got his mouth on [Shug]" and makes her condition the subject of his sermon. What is it that Walker is pointing to by placing the derision of Shug within the particular context of the Black Church? Perhaps what Walker is attempting to make clear is that the black community's sense of sexual propriety is not driven solely by sociohistorical narratives of power. In fact, it is driven most significantly by a platonized Christian theology. In other words, that Shug could so easily become the text of the preacher's sermon is suggestive of a platonized theological influence upon the Black Church community. Given the importance of this influence I briefly examine what precisely I mean by a platonized theology.[25]

A Platonized Christianity

Platonized theology shapes an influential strand of the Christian tradition. This theology, and thus the platonized Christian tradition that it gives way to, emerged as early Christian thinkers and apologists integrated into their Christian theologies the most prominent Greek philosophies of their day. In so doing, they established within mainstream Christian thinking a platonic and stoic-influenced view of the body sexual. Specifically, the platonic belief in the world of forms as being different and superior to the world of the senses coalesced in Christian thought with the stoic regard for reason and disregard for passion. In so doing, a significant strand of Christian thinking adopted a theology that esteemed the immaterial world (which came to be regarded as the opposite of the world of passion/flesh/body). This split between two realms of being eventuated into a body devaluing theology and tradition, namely, platonized Christianity.

Platonized Christianity invariably places the body in an antagonistic relationship with the soul. The soul is divinized, whereas the body is demonized. The soul is revered as the key to salvation; the body is condemned as a source of sin. The locus of bodily sin is human passion, that is, sexual pleasure or lust. This "sacred" disdain for the sexual body pervades the Christian theological tradition, particularly as it has given way to a definite sexual ethic. The writings of the Apostle Paul, especially as they are refracted through an Augustinian reading, are perhaps most responsible for this body-denouncing, theo-ethical tradition.

Specifically, platonized Christianity advocates a dualistic sexual ethic. That is, it suggests there are only two ways in which to engage in sexual activity: one is tolerable and not inherently sinful, and the other is intolerable and sinful. Procreative sexuality is tolerably good; nonprocreative/pleasurable engagement is intolerably evil. Furthermore, platonized Christianity does not permit a third possibility. A platonized sexual ethic does not allow for sexual activity to be an expression of an intimate—that is, loving—relationship.

Platonized Christianity became an influential part of the black faith tradition during the religious revivals of the eighteenth century. During these revivals a significant number of black men and women were converted to Evangelical Protestant thought, the principal conduit of platonized Christianity in America. Black Church people most affected by this evangelical—that is, platonized—tradition tended to affirm the assertions of Paul that one should "make no provision for flesh," but if one must engage in sexual behavior, "it is better to marry than to burn."[26] Given this understanding of platonized theology, its concomitant sexual ethic, and its significance in the Black Church, the reason that Shug would become the target of the preacher's sermon is clear: she makes provision for the flesh. Hence, she is as sinful as the blues she sings. Indeed the blues have been traditionally regarded within the black community as the "devil's music."

Although various blues women developed their singing talents in the church and considered themselves Christian women, they also recognized that singing the blues placed them outside of the church. This was clear to blues singer Ida Goodson at an early age as her parents admonished her that the blues were the "Devil's work"; "therefore Goodson hid her penchant for playing the blues on her piano from her parents.[27] Again, blues-singing women knew that they were looked down on not only because they violated the black community's sense of a hyper-proper sexuality but more significantly because they brazenly betrayed the platonized Christian imperative of the Black Church to "make no provision for the flesh." Indeed it is the case that the Black Church's platonized sexual ethic essentially provides a sacred canopy for the community's hyper-proper sexuality, thus making violation of this norm not simply a social violation but also a sin. Consequently, blues women were often viewed as those who not only simply lived according to white cultural stereotypes but also "made a pact" with the devil. As Angela Davis observes, "Blues singers were (and to some extent still are) associated with the Devil because they celebrated those dimensions of human existence considered evil to the tenets of Christianity...blues singers are unmitigated sinners and the creativity they demonstrate and the worldview they advocate are in flagrant defiance of the...prevailing religious beliefs."[28] Thus it is no wonder that it would be the preacher that "had his mouth on Shug," for the blues Shug sung were "a sin to hear."

With this recognition of the role that a hyper-proper sexuality and platonized sexual ethic play within the Black Church community, it is now possible to understand one aspect of why the blues are significant to understanding Black Church responses to sexuality. For, the blues signify a particular response to white cultural sexualization of black people. They testify to black women's freedom from both the racially sexualized oppression imposed on their sexual bodies and the black community's responses to that oppression. Viewed in this way, the classic blues—as well as the women who sing them—represent the most profound opposition to the standard of hyper-proper sexuality adopted by the black community and given sacred legitimation by a platonized black faith tradition. Again, Angela Davis puts it best when she writes, "The church played a pivotal role in valorizing that aspect of racist ideology that sexualized the ascription of intellectual and spiritual inferiority to black people."[29]

In effect, two narratives come together to shape the Black Church community's attitudes toward sexuality: a cultural-historical narrative (that is, white cultural hypersexualization of black people) and a theo-religious narrative (that is, platonized theology), thus giving way to a sanctified hyper-proper sexuality. The classic blues tradition reveals how these narratives inexorably lead to trouble and/or castigation of certain persons within the Black Church community. Blues women thereby symbolize those persons who are marginalized within the Black Church because of the way they express their sexuality. I now look briefly at how this is the case in regard to women and nonheterosexuals. Again, Alice Walker's blues-singing woman, Shug, is helpful to this analysis.

In *The Color Purple*, Shug is unlike any other black female character (with perhaps the exception of Sophie) in the sense that she takes control of her relationships with men. It is Shug who defines the nature of her male relationships, not the men. She does not allow herself to be defined as the keeper of their homes or the breeder of their children. Moreover, she determines the parameters of their sexual intimacy. Once again the fictionalized Shug points to the reality of the classic blues tradition.

The classic blues songs often reflected black women's independence, sexually and otherwise, from men—even as they may have mirrored the independence of the women who sang them. The blues songs can thus be interpreted, as noted by Angela Davis, as "a bold, perhaps implicitly feminist contestation of patriarchal rule,"[30] just as the women who sang them "did not typically affirm female resignation and power-lessness, nor did they accept the relegation of women to private and interior spaces."[31] This can be seen in lyrics from Bessie Smith's song "Down Hearted Blues":

> I got the world in a jug, the stopper's in my hand.
> I got the world in a jug, the stopper's in my hand
> I'm gonna hold it until you men come under my command.[32]

Clearly then, the portrait of independent black womanhood upheld in the classic blues tradition violates the standard of sexual propriety defined by white, heterosexist, patriarchal, and platonized theological narratives. Both the narratives of this blues tradition and of platonized theology ostensibly deny black women the possibility of nonprocreative and hence non-male-centered sexual expression. In other words, they both uphold the center of patriarchal power: a heterosexual male-centered family in which women's primary role is to be of service to the man and to engage in sexual activity only as it fosters the bearing of children. To assume any other role is to transgress the sanctified sense of hyper-proper sexuality.

Nonheterosexual persons violate the sexual norm of the black faith community in a similar way. In short, as long as homoerotism is maligned in the wider heterosexist society, and inasmuch as it is considered nonprocreative (therefore exemplary of lustful sex), then nonheterosexual expressions of sexuality are deemed unacceptable and in fact are sinful. And hence, it is no wonder that same-sex unions are profoundly denounced within the Black Church community, for they are wrongly considered nonprocreative relationships and thus bastions of sinful sexuality.

Again, it is worth noting that just as Walker portrays blues-singing woman Shug as engaging freely in homoerotic sexuality, so too did the blues women explore the themes of homoerotic sexuality in their songs. Some were even involved in lesbian relationships.[33] There is no stronger attestation to homoerotism than Ma Rainey's song, "Prove It on Me Blues" (which is not considered technically to be a blues song). The song includes lyrics such as the following:

> They said I do it, ain't nobody caught me
> Sure got to prove it on me
> Went out last night with a crowd of my friends
> They must've been women, 'cause I don't like no men.[34]

To reiterate, the blues represent a reality in contempt of the standard of hyper-proper sexuality upheld by the black community and sanctioned by a platonized black faith tradition. In this regard, the Black Church community's views toward sexuality reflect the thrust of a theo-historical dynamic. That is, platonized theology and a hyper-proper sexuality come together with such force in the lives of Black Church women and men that they generate an almost impregnable standard of sexual propriety that does not allow them to accept the blues reality. Yet, it is the blues and their testimony that can help the Black Church community move toward more liberating and equitable views of sexuality.

TESTIFYIN' TO THE BLUES

In the Hollywood big-screen version of Alice Walker's *The Color Purple*, the story moves toward its end as Shug is seen leading a group of people from the jook joint where they were reveling all night in Shug's singing of the blues into the black church of her minister father. As contrived as such a scene may be (it is not a part of the novel), it is suggestive of the way in which the Black Church community might move beyond its repressively oppressive views toward sexuality: by listening to the testimony of the blues. This is not to romanticize the blues, for to be sure they point to and sometimes affirm troubling aspects of black women's experiences that need to be denounced, such as domestic violence. Nevertheless, the blues suggest the acceptance of the black sexual body in a way that foils the impact of racially sexualized caricatures of black people without resorting to a constricting, and invariably oppressive, standard of sexuality.

Moreover, the blues defy any notion of the body as evil. In this regard, the blues most decidedly point toward a black faith tradition that consistently affirmed the sanctity of the black body. It is this tradition that pulsates through the sung testimony of the enslaved: the spirituals. We see this, for instance, as the spirituals maintained in their coded language the connection between heavenly salvation and earthly freedom. That is, enslaved men and women testified in song to the urgency to save their souls while simultaneously singing about the urgent need to free their bodies. Again, the blues resonate with the spirituals' refusal to diminish the sacred worth of the body sexual. Recognizing the intrinsic relationship between the spirituals and the blues, James Cone calls the blues "secular spirituals" because they reflect the "bodily expression of black soul" and "are impelled by the same search [as the spirituals] for the truth of the black experience."[35]

One of the ways in which the blues differ from the spirituals, as implied in Cone's description, is that they explore the sexual implications of the acceptance of the body. Specifically, they reveal that the refusal to devalue the body and hence to demonize sexuality allows for an acceptance of intimate sexuality as not solely an object of procreation or lust but as an expression of a loving relationship—thus opening the way to affirming same-sex loving sexuality. Such is what the blues women testified so passionately to as they sang of "love," regardless of how that love was gendered.

In sum, an essential step toward the Black Church community moving beyond its insular views on sexuality is its ability to see the blues not as the "devil's music" but as sacred discourse. To be sure, not until the Black Church community is able to testify to the blues will it be able to live into its justice-affirming tradition and thus accept the rich and varied expressions of human sexuality.

NOTES

1. A 2004 Pew Forum University poll indicated that while support for gay and lesbian rights had grown in American society from 35 percent to 45 percent since 1993, this was not the case within the African American community. A plurality of African Americans opposed

gay and lesbian rights, whereas four years prior 56 percent of African Americans favored those same rights, http://pewforum.org/gay-marriage (accessed May 5, 2005).

2. This Pew Forum on Religion and Public Life study is cited at "Longitudinal U.S. Public Opinion Polls: Same-Sex Marriage (SSM)," http://www.religioustolerance.org/hom_poll5.htm (accessed June 28, 2005). It should be noted that various polls are being constantly conducted with varying results. Some suggest that the gap in opinion between the overall population and that of African Americans is closing, with opposition in the wider society growing. See for instance, The Pew Research Center for the People and Press, *Religious Beliefs Undergird Opposition to Homosexuality*, November 2003, http://people-press.org/reports (accessed June 28, 2005).

3. See Presiding Bishop, General Board and Board of Bishops, Church of God in Christ, "Marriage: A Proclamation to the Church of God in Christ Worldwide," http://www.cogic.org/marriageproclamation.htm, reprinted by *The Human Rights Campaign*, http://www.hrc.org (accessed May 31, 2005). See also Human Rights Campaign, "African American Episcopal Church," news release, http://www.hrc.org/ (accessed May 31, 2005).

4. W. E. B. DuBois, *Souls of Black Folk* (1903; repr., New York: Alfred A. Knopf, 1993), 153.

5. In November 2003 Gene Robinson, a self-identified gay priest, was consecrated as ninth Episcopal Diocesan Bishop of New Hampshire.

6. It should be noted that at the Third International Conference on Afro-Anglicanism held in Toronto Canada, July 20–27, 2005, an accord was agreed upon that addressed, among several issues, the topic of human sexuality. In regard to sexuality the accord states: "We have wrestled with deep sincerity with the complex issues of human sexuality…. The vast differences of approach have been evident in our dialogue. Nevertheless, we have not departed from the sacred truths of our common humanity. We have all been created in God's image. God's compassion and love are extended to all whom God has created…. We yearn together for the day when the human body will become the symbol and source and sacrament of unity among us and no longer a cause of division or an instrument of strife." Third International Conference on Afro-Anglicanism, "The Toronto Accord," 3, http://afroanglican.com/TorontoAccord/default.htm (accessed April 3, 2006).

7. The conference to which I am referring is the Seventh Triennial Black Clergy Conference and the First Convocation for the Recently Ordained, sponsored by the Episcopal Church Office of Black Ministries. The conference was held in Atlanta, Georgia, October 23–26, 2005.

8. Alice Walker, *In Search of Our Mothers' Gardens* (New York: Harcourt Brace Javanovich, 1983), xi.

9. Womanist ethicist Katie G. Cannon coined this term "debunk" as she has spoken on numerous occasions of the womanist task to "debunk" the methods and notions of white patriarchal ethical and theological systems.

10. See my discussion in *Sexuality and the Black Church: A Womanist Perspective* (Maryknoll, NY: Orbis Books; 1999).

11. Walker, *In Search of Our Mothers' Gardens*, xi (see note 8).

12. Alice Walker, *The Color Purple*, 10th anniversary ed. (New York: Harcourt, Inc., 1982), 41.

13. Ibid., 40.

14. Ibid.

15. See for instance Phillips Dray's discussion of Lynching in *At the Hands of Persons Unknown: The Lynching of Black America* (New York: Random House, 2002); See also Ida B. Wells discussion of lynching in *Crusade for Justice: The Autobiography of Ida B. Wells*, ed. Alfreda M. Duster (Chicago: University of Chicago Press, 1970).

16. Anna Julia Cooper, *A Voice from the South* (1892; repr., New York: Oxford University Press, 1988), 31.

17. See Miriam DeCosta-Wills, ed., *The Memphis Diary of Ida B. Wells: An Intimate Portrait of the Activist as a Young Woman* (Boston: Beacon Press, 1995); see particularly her letter written under the pen name Iola.

18. Quoted in Dray, *At The Hands of Persons Unknown*, 55 (see note 15).

19. Quoted in Daphne Duval Harrison, *Black Pearls: Blues Queens of the 1920s* (New Brunswick, NJ : Rutgers University Press, 1988), 114.

20. Ibid., 9.

21. Hazel Carby, *Cultures in Babylon: Black Britain and African America* (London/New York: Verso, 1999), 18; see also ibid., chap. 4, "They Put a Spell on You."

22. Ibid.

23. Lyrics cited in ibid., 19.

24. Walker, *The Color Purple*, 53 (see note 12).

25. I have written about this concept of a platonized Christianity in many places. My most developed discussion of this is found in Kelly Brown Douglas, *What's Faith Got to Do With It? Black Bodies/Christian Souls* (Maryknoll, NY: Orbis Books, 2006).

26. See Paul's First Letter to the Corinthians 7:9.

27. Story recounted in Carby, *Cultures in Babylon*, 53 (see note 21).

28. Angela Y. Davis, *Blues Legacies and Black Feminism: Gertrude "Ma" Rainey, Bessie Smith, and Billie Holiday* (New York: Pantheon Books, 1998), 124.

29. Ibid., 133.

30. Ibid., 21.

31. Ibid., 20.

32. Lyrics cited in ibid., 274.

33. It is widely assumed that Ma Rainey and Bessie Smith were from time to time lovers. To be sure, Ma Rainey's bisexuality was a fairly well-known fact.

34. Lyrics cited in Davis, *Blues Legacies and Black Feminism*, 238 (see note 28).

35. James Cone, *The Spirituals and the Blues: An Interpretation* (New York: Seabury, 1972), 112.

Part II

Faith and Practice

5

SAME-SEX MARRIAGE AND ROMAN CATHOLICISM

Patricia Beattie Jung

My aim in this chapter is to sketch a distinctively Roman Catholic argument that is supportive of ecclesial blessing for and the civil licensing of same-sex marriages. However, because official Roman Catholic Church teaching condemns such efforts so vehemently, this argument needs to be developed in three distinct stages. The first part entails the faithful study of current official Catholic teaching on same-sex marriage. The second step involves the critical analysis of the rationale given for this teaching. Faithful analysis requires the reconstruction of all those elements within the tradition related to marriage and family that are not flawed. My ultimate goal is to suggest how distinctively Catholic insights into the Christian theology of marriage and family might be reconfigured so that same-sex, as well as heterosexual, couples whose relationships are just and loving might be encouraged to marry.

OFFICIAL TEACHING ON SAME-SEX MARRIAGE

Officially the Roman Catholic Church opposes both the civil licensing of same-sex marriages and their ecclesial blessing. "Rome has spoken" in recent years quite decisively in this regard. The first Vatican statement that addressed explicitly the practice of same-sex marriage came as a response to the dramatic increase in rates of (sexual) cohabitation in recent decades and to various legislative efforts in the European Union not to privilege (heterosexual) marriage over other forms of de facto sexual union. In its statement issued in 2000 on "Family, Marriage and *De Facto* Unions" (FMU), the Pontifical Council for the Family (PCF) argued that no form of sexual cohabitation—even those same-sex partnerships that are voluntary, steadfast, and sexually exclusive—should be treated in a manner equal to (hetero-sexual) marriage.

In 2003 the Congregation for the Doctrine of the Faith (CDF) reached a similar conclusion. Its letter—"Considerations Regarding Proposals to Give Legal Recognition to Unions Between Homosexual Persons" (LRU)—was issued precisely in response to such legislative and judicial developments not only in Northern Europe but also in North America. Here the CDF explicitly condemned efforts to civilly license same-sex marriage.

On the one hand, the Catholic Church clearly condemns at least some forms of discrimination based on sexual orientation. The 1994 *Catechism of the Catholic Church* (CCC) teaches that gay and lesbian persons "must be accepted with respect, compassion and sensitivity. Every sign of unjust discrimination in their regard should be avoided."[1] The CDF concludes that the "whole moral truth" of its teaching on homosexuality is contradicted by every instance of "unjust discrimination against homosexual persons."[2]

On the other hand, the Catholic Church endorses at least some discriminatory practices based on sexual orientation, arguing that they are not only just but also morally required for the sake of the common good. In 1992 the CDF spoke to this issue in a set of observations titled "Some Considerations Concerning Catholic Response to Legislative Proposals on the Non-Discrimination of Homosexual Persons" (SCC). In this document, the CDF pointed out that the church has always taught that some nonarbitrary, differential treatment can be justified by the state's obligation to restrict even basic human rights, "for example, in the case of contagious or mentally ill persons, in order to protect the common good."[3]

The Catholic Church recognizes that the legal approval of same-sex marriage is quite distinct from its decriminalization or mere toleration of homosexual relationships. Thus the church teaches that the "legal recognition of homosexual unions would obscure certain basic moral values and cause a devaluation of the institution of marriage."[4] The Catholic Church forbids consent to and active participation in the enactment and application of such legislation. Various forms of material cooperation are discouraged as well.

However, the Catholic Church recognizes that even though civil laws are morally formative of both social institutions and personal attitudes, it is imprudent to attempt to encode the entire natural moral law in civil law. In some circumstances it is morally wiser to tolerate an immoral behavior as a "lesser evil" than to enact a law against it that proves unenforceable. So, the legislative strategies regarding same-sex marriage that the church commends to the faithful are of two basic types.

In political contexts in which homosexual relationships are merely tolerated, generally the Catholic Church encourages discretion and a prudent, nonaggressive course of action. Such action might include "unmasking the way in which such tolerance might be exploited or used in the service of ideology; stating clearly the immoral nature of these unions; reminding the government of the need to contain the phenomenon within certain limits so as to safeguard public morality and, above all, to avoid exposing young people to erroneous ideas about sexuality and marriage that would deprive them of their necessary defenses and contribute to the spread of the phenomenon."[5]

In political contexts where same-sex unions have already been recognized in various ways, the church teaches that opposition to "such gravely unjust laws" is a moral duty for all Catholics because of the harm such laws pose to the "common good." The right to conscientious objection in such circumstances is upheld.[6] When the full repeal and total abrogation of such legislation are not possible, the church teaches that a Catholic may support proposed legislation that would limit the harm thought to accompany the recognition of same-sex marriage.[7] For instance, in a country in which same-sex marriage is legal, a Catholic may lobby for a bill that would restrict the adoption rights of same-sex spouses.

The heart of these Vatican judgments received unequivocal papal support when in 2005, not long before his death, Pope John Paul II gave his "state of the world" address to the Vatican diplomatic corps. Charging them repeatedly to "overcome evil with good" by facing the challenges before humanity, the pope identified the safeguarding and promotion of human life as the first and most significant of these challenges. He argued that human life is being particularly challenged in two specific arenas. Not surprisingly he argued that life is threatened in its early embryonic stage. Pope John Paul II argued that the integrity and dignity of human life are being violated by "abortion, assisted procreation, the use of human embryonic stem cells for scientific research and cloning."[8]

It is the second arena that is of interest here. Pope John Paul II also argued that life itself is under siege because the sanctuary of life—*the family*—is threatened. In some countries, he declared, legislation sometimes directly attacks the family's "natural structure, which is and must necessarily be that of a union between a man and a woman founded on marriage."[9] In this address Pope John Paul II gave more priority to combating same-sex marriage than to the other challenges he subsequently identified, which included the distribution of food, peace building, and the protection of basic human rights, especially the fostering of religious freedom. It is noteworthy as well that he identified current challenges to the heterosexual form of marriage and family as constitutive of a challenge to life itself.

Pope Benedict XVI confirmed this papal teaching officially on June 6, 2005, in an address he gave to participants in the Ecclesial Convention of Rome. Among other practices that he argued contribute to the erosion of marriage, "pseudo-marriages between people of the same sex" do not lead to true human liberation because they are "based on a trivialization of the body" and "dualism."[10]

THE FAITHFUL DISCERNMENT OF TRUTH

Though "Rome has spoken" quite consistently and publicly about this issue in the past few years, like Christians everywhere, Roman Catholics disagree about how to evaluate same-sex marriage. Many moral theologians, pastors, ordinary lay Catholics, and even a few bishops are engaged in an open and lively debate about the Vatican's teachings on this matter.

Catholics believe that fidelity to the church's living Tradition requires serious engagement with official Roman Catholic Church teachings. They understand such teachings to be authoritative. Yet the weight of this authority can vary. Generally speaking, teachings like the ones reviewed here, which come from

Vatican congregations and papal addresses, are viewed as part of the ordinary teaching magisterium.

What this means precisely is itself a matter of considerable debate. All faithful Catholics concur that such teachings warrant their respect and should be morally formative. For some, this means that such teachings warrant their humble submission and silent obedience. For others (including myself), this means that all such teachings carry the presumption of truth. However, if after faithful study it is determined that particular teachings lack sufficient grounding in faith and reason, Catholics may in good conscience disagree with them and engage in further respectful public conversations about these matters aimed to foster a fuller discernment of the truth.

CRITICAL EXAMINATION OF THE OFFICIAL ARGUMENTS

The Vatican condemns the practice of licensing and/or blessing same-sex marriages for five major reasons. The church teaches that the endorsement of same-sex marriage will (1) have a negative impact on Christian sexual values, (2) harm the (heterosexual) institution of marriage, and (3) harm children nurtured in or near such unions, and that all same-sex unions lack both (4) the (heterosexual) complementarity requisite for "true" spousal and parental love and (5) procreative potential.

Whether or not the endorsement of same-sex marriage has the impacts specified above, the Catholic Church also teaches that it needs to be resisted because such affirmation will inevitably institutionalize—that is, sanction—sexual behaviors that the church views as "intrinsically evil." In its 1975 "Declaration on Certain Questions Concerning Sexual Ethics" (PH for its Latin title *Persona humana*), the CDF declared that all "homosexual acts are intrinsically disordered."[11] In a subsequent (1986) "Letter to Bishops on the Pastoral Care of Homosexual Persons" (PCHP), the CDF reiterated that "a person engaging in homosexual behavior therefore acts immorally."[12]

Because human sexuality is so central to who we are as persons, the Catholic Church teaches that there is no parvity of matter regarding genital activities.[13] Thus the church teaches that objectively homosexual behavior is always grievously immoral. According to the *Catechism of the Catholic Church,* "homosexual practices are 'sins gravely contrary to chastity.'"[14] Chastity requires total, lifelong sexual abstinence of gay and lesbian persons. The church recognizes that this counsel to complete sexual self-denial is difficult. Gay and lesbian believers are therefore encouraged to recognize the will of God in this trial and to associate the suffering they are called to bear with the Cross of Christ.[15]

All same-sex relationships, Rome contends, are immoral for two closely interrelated reasons. As mentioned above, they all lack both the (heterosexual) complementarity requisite for "true" spousal and parental love and procreative potential, the emphasis on which is central to several dimensions of the Vatican's account of good sex. The church claims deep roots in the biblical witness for its negative judgments against same-sex relationships. Genesis 19:1–11, Leviticus 18:22 and 20:13, I Corinthians 6:9, Romans 1:18–32, and I Timothy 10 are cited as confirming this view. New interpretations of these texts, which do not confirm these conclusions and which raise serious questions about the church's interpretation of them, are described as "gravely erroneous" and "causes of confusion."[16] Exegetes are reminded that when properly interpreted sacred scripture will not contradict but rather will be in substantial accord with the church's living Tradition. (It is taken as axiomatic that the church's current teaching is in accord with that living Tradition.) Theologians are warned of the biblical condemnation found in 1 Timothy 10 against all "those who spread wrong doctrine."[17]

The question of what precisely is revealed about human sexuality in the Bible is examined later in this chapter. At this juncture, it is important to note that according to Rome, the Bible is not the only source of moral wisdom that testifies to the naturally heterosexual design of human sexuality. In its millennial declaration, the Pontifical Council for the Family noted that the Catholic Church's sexual norms are rooted in and "determined by the structure of the human being, the woman and man: mutual self-giving and the transmission of life."[18] Thus it is appropriate to analyze each of these five reasons, including the final "foundational" two, in light of the canons of reason. To that task, I now turn.

Will Same-Sex Marriage Prove Corrosive of Human (Hetero)Sexual Values?

Rome believes that the licensing of same-sex marriages will prove morally confusing. As the CDF put it, such a "scandalous" practice will give young people and others "erroneous ideas about sexuality and marriage that would deprive them of their necessary defenses and contribute to the spread of the phenomenon."[19] However, it is not clear precisely who these "young people and others" are. The Catholic Church teaches that the number of men and women "who experience an exclusive or predominant sexual attraction toward persons of the same sex"[20] is "not negligible" and that these tendencies are for the most part "deep-seated," "not chosen," and "a trial."[21]

Because the *Catechism* recognizes that homosexuality is not usually a choice, it is highly unlikely that even Rome worries that definitively heterosexual people would be "drawn" or "seduced" into same-sex relationships by their affirmation. Given its context, it is reasonable to presume that here the Vatican is concerned about those whose sense of sexual identity might be in some significant sense "transitory." Rome is worried most probably that a change in policy regarding same-sex marriage might lead bisexual and/or transgender people to view same-sex relationships as morally acceptable. Certainly, the CDF is worried that the recognition of same-sex marriage would "modify the younger generation's perception and evaluation of forms of behavior."[22]

Undoubtedly the social and religious approval of same-sex marriage would have a tremendous social impact and prove to be morally transformative. But here Rome has begged the very real question of whether these changes would be good or bad. Far from being morally corrosive, it can be argued that the celebration of same-sex marriages will trigger much-needed moral reforms. Consider some of the good consequences that might come from such a change in public policy.

Gay and lesbian adolescents would no longer feel pressured to deny their attractions to persons of the same sex or be tempted to closet themselves in heterosexual marriages. All our children would be safer from hate crimes. All people would also be encouraged to form sexual bonds that are mutually enriching, exclusive, and steadfast. The prospect of such developments can be presumed morally harmful or confusing only if one takes it to be axiomatic that same-sex relationships per se are disordered. That assumption begs precisely the question under examination.

Will Same-Sex Marriages Prove Harmful to Heterosexual Marriages?

The CDF predicts that the celebration of same-sex love will "cause a devaluation of the institution of marriage,"[23] because "such unions are not able to contribute in a proper way to the procreation and survival of the human race."[24] The Vatican asserts that only sexual relationships that "express and promote the mutual assistance of the sexes in marriage and are open to the transmission of new life" are genuinely humanizing.[25] Thus heterosexual relationships alone are worthy of social promotion. In the final section of this chapter I demonstrate that there are many ways that same-sex relationships can serve both life and love.

Will Same-Sex Marriage Prove Harmful to Children?

Perhaps as many as one out of four same-sex couples are already raising children. Yet, according to Rome, they are not contributing to the common good, at least not "properly." According to the CDF, "the absence of sexual complementarity in these unions creates an obstacle in the normal development of children," and such an environment "is not conducive to their full human development."[26] Indeed, the CDF concluded the following: "allowing children to be adopted by persons living in such unions would actually mean doing violence to these children."[27]

Were these assertions about the malformation of children true, this would indeed be a grave cause for concern. However, despite the Vatican's assertion that experience has proven these claims, they are far from self-evident. Studies confirm that some of the children of single parents and children raised in orphanages are statistically "at risk." But there is no evidence to support the claim that the millions of children already living today in households headed by same-sex couples face significant developmental obstacles. Indeed, in her 1999 review of the literature, social scientist Bridget Fitzgerald argues that an admittedly small but growing number of studies give evidence to the contrary.[28]

Can Same-Sex Relationships Be Genuinely Complementary?

Most couples—whether same-sex or not—experience their relationship as enriching; that is, as sexually, intellectually, emotionally, and parentally enhancing. That is why they are drawn to and remain in partnership with each other. According to Rome, however, same-sex couples cannot genuinely love each other. Instead, such relationships confirm an "essentially self-indulgent" inclination, because partners of the same sex do not draw each other into a love that is sufficiently other regarding.[29] The basic elements of this biblical vision of the (heterosexual) "spousal significance" of the human person were summarized in 2004 by the CDF in its "Letter to the Bishops of the Catholic Church on the Collaboration of Men and Women in the Church and in the World." Here heterosexual differentiation is linked not only to reproduction but also to the human capacity to love and thereby image God.[30]

Social scientists, however, have established that apart from reproductive matters the range of difference among men and among women is greater than the range of difference between men and women. Thus it is far from evident that same-sex relationships cannot be significantly other regarding. The Vatican, however, continues to attribute the potential for such conjugal enrichment exclusively to heterosexual relationships. Why? The church concludes that heterosexual partnerships alone have the potential to be genuinely complementary at all levels because they alone can be reproductively complementary.[31] The official Roman Catholic case against the endorsement of same-sex marriage rests decisively on the importance given to procreativity in Catholic sexual ethics.

Should the Human Potential for Procreativity Be So Emphasized?

The place of procreativity in Catholic sexual ethics has deep roots. Until modern times, the desire to make love by sharing pleasure was not really understood as a justification for sexual activity even in marriage. Even then, pleasure sharing and love making could be justified only so long as the couple also intended their sexual activity to be baby making. The Catholic Church still teaches that openness to love is inseparable from openness to life. Even though the church no longer teaches that this "finality" is the exclusive or primary purpose of the human sexual "faculty," openness to the possibility of procreativity is still deemed an "essential and indispensable" ingredient to all well-ordered sexual activities.[32] The PCF summarized the matter in the following way: same-sex unions should not be treated as equivalent to marriage because such partnerships cannot be "fruitful through the transmission of life according to the plan inscribed by God in the very structure of human being."[33] So, no matter how otherwise just, merciful, faithful, or life serving a same-sex relationship might be, it is not open to procreativity, and hence, from Rome's point of view, it can be neither genuinely loving nor life serving. Thus it should not be celebrated.

Ultimately, for Catholics the question of same-sex marriage hinges decisively on whether or not the Vatican's understanding of and emphasis on the moral significance of procreativity and heterosexual (reproductive) complementarity are correct. Does this emphasis on procreativity make good sense? Is this in fact what is revealed in the Bible as God's design for human sexuality?

REASON AND PROCREATIVITY

The canons of reason require minimally that the Catholic Church's emphasis on procreativity be upheld consistently and that it be comprehensive of human sexual experience. Only then could one say it makes good sense.

The fact is, however, that even the Vatican no longer consistently upholds its traditional emphasis on reproductive procreativity. The coital activities of pregnant and postmenopausal married women are not in any real sense open to procreativity (except perhaps iconically). Yet, the church no longer teaches that these sexual activities are "unnatural." Today, many faithful heterosexual Catholic spouses enjoy manual and oral sexual activities, even to the point of orgasm. They experience such genital activities as lovemaking, despite their lack of procreative potential. The church has not spoken out against such activities, except when engaged in by same-sex couples.

The gradual acceptance by the Catholic Church in the twentieth century of "natural" forms of family planning suggests that marital activity can be sanctifying, even when for all practical purposes there is almost no possibility of it proving pro-creative. Many gay and lesbian Catholics argue that they are as open to the possi-bility of their sexual activity proving procreative as are sterile, pregnant, and/or elderly heterosexual wives. If the possibility of procreativity is in fact not necessary for the sanctification of sexual activity, why should the iconic representation of such a possibility be required of all Christian spouses?

Finally, though the Vatican continues to proscribe so-called "artificial" forms of contraception, it no longer lobbies against their distribution and sale in North Atlantic countries. Confessors no longer deny absolution or refuse to give commun-ion to heterosexual spouses who in good conscience practice birth control. There is clearly a double standard in church teaching: one for heterosexual spouses and another for everyone else.

The traditional emphasis on procreativity can also be judged unreasonable because it is not comprehensive of (a) women's sexual physiology, (b) heterosexual experi-ence, (c) homosexual experience, and (d) the intrinsic value of sharing sexual pleas-ure. In men's experience of their sexuality, an orgasm is usually linked to ejaculation. But for women the processes of ovulation, fertilization, and implantation are not linked to female orgasm. As a matter of fact, the connection between coital activity and reproduction in women's experience is periodic at most and lasts only for a sea-son of a woman's life. Male sexual physiology alone should not define what is nor-mative for human sexuality. Overall, even from a purely physiological perspective, the link between human sexual desire and reproduction is naturally quite diverse.

The traditional emphasis on procreativity does not take adequate account of the fact that most heterosexual spouses find no necessary or exclusive connection between their being open to the possibility of procreation and their being fully self-giving and other regarding. Furthermore, many heterosexual couples do not experi-ence traditional conventions about gender differences and roles as foundational to their experience of their partner as enriching. Likewise, this emphasis on procreativ-ity does not do justice to the experience of many faithful same-sex couples. Despite stereotypes to the contrary, social studies show that they are just as emotionally inti-mate as their straight counterparts. In fact, some studies suggest that same-sex cou-ples are less deceitful overall with one another than many straight couples. Given the lack of religious and civil support for their sexual commitments, same-sex rela-tionships are remarkably faithful. Finally, this emphasis on procreative potential does not adequately account for the ability of shared pleasure to engender love and further the bonding among queer and straight couples alike.

THE BIBLE, PROCREATIVITY, AND
HETEROSEXUAL COMPLEMENTARITY

Like virtually all other Christians, Catholics recognize the Bible as an essential source of moral wisdom. The debate among Christians about how to interpret properly the texts cited earlier, which deal directly with same-sex erotic activity, has been raging for nearly two decades now without resolution. Why? The texts themselves—though clear in their condemnation of at least some sorts of same-sex erotic activity—do not speak directly to several other morally relevant questions. Consequently, liberals conclude on the basis of the study of their historical context that these texts condemn *only some* types of same-sex activity (such as pederasty or same-sex activity associated with sexual slavery, prostitution, and/or idolatry). Conservatives conclude these texts condemn *all* types of same-sex activity, including that which we might associate with just, loving, monogamous, and steadfast relationships.

Much hinges on what frames the interpretative process, particularly the assumptions about human sexual diversity that interpreters bring to the Bible. Conservatives are apt to find that biblical texts confirm the assumptions they bring: presuming a "heterosexual structure of God's design for sexuality," it follows that God would forbid *all* same-sex erotic activity. Similarly, liberals are apt to find that these texts confirm the assumptions they bring: presuming God's sexual order is diverse, *only some* same-sex activities, just like some other-sex activities, are forbidden by God in the Bible.

Christians who are party to these debates grow increasingly self-conscious of this hermeneutical circle. Quite some time ago James P. Hanigan described these convictions about reproductive and gender complementarity as the symbolic framework for all debates about sexuality.[34] The "big picture" about human sexuality that informs much of official Catholic biblical interpretations is often articulated in reference to the opening chapters of Genesis.

In several respects the traditional interpretations of Genesis 1–3 are being contested. For centuries they have been understood to reveal that sexual relationships should be patriarchal, either by God's original design or as a deserved punishment for sin. With regard to this understanding, the Catholic Church has recently reinterpreted these texts. The church now officially teaches that all structures of male domination and female submission, whether violent or not, are far from God's original plan; that is, they are a tragic consequence of, not a deserved punishment for, "the Fall." Rome has officially identified both patriarchy and sexism as sin.

The conclusion at the heart of the conservative position on same-sex marriage is that Genesis reveals the Creator's design for human sexuality to be uniformly heterosexual and essentially for reproductive purposes. No one who is party to this debate doubts that in Genesis 1 sexual differentiation is associated with fecundity. What is at issue in the debate is the precise nature of this link. Though English translations of Genesis carry imperative connotations, progressives argue that in the original Hebrew "be fruitful" may be understood as a blessing rather than a command.

Also central to the debate about same-sex marriage is the issue of complementarity. Does Genesis 2 reveal the Creator's design for sexual companionship to be exclusively heterosexual? According to standard interpretations, men and women are given different natures, designed by God to complement each other. Thus the Catholic Church teaches that diversity in sexual orientation is not part of God's original plan but a "disorder."

It must be noted, however, that this interpretation is not necessitated by the silence about same-sex desire or the celebration of other-sex marriage in Genesis 2.

In fact there are at least three reasons to question this conclusion: (1) Genesis 2 does not specify why Adam is lonely. Human solitude was a problem whose solution is associated with sexual differentiation, but nothing in the text suggests it was *caused* by the absence of a differently gendered complement. Indeed, the Hebrew terms that specify male and female do not occur in the text until after the Creator puts Adam to sleep. Only then does the text suggest that humankind was sexually differentiated. (2) The only creatures specified in the text as unfit life partners are from different species. They are unsuitable because they are not human. Nowhere is gender explicitly identified as a necessary criterion for authentic complementarity. (3) The text does explicitly identify Eve as suitable for partnership with Adam, but not specifically because she is sexually "other" (though obviously she is). The text suggests she is fit partner because she is human. Adam does not cry out *"Vive la différence!"* but exclaims instead "bone of my bone, flesh of my flesh." The story emphasizes the similarities between these two partners at least as much, if not more, than their differences.

It is reasonable to conclude that the creation accounts found in Genesis do not reveal the order of creation to be exclusively heterosexual and/or that same-sex partnerships are incongruent with God's design for human sexuality. Consequently it is reasonable to conclude that the biblical texts prohibiting at least some same-sex activity might well be referring to *only some* forms of such behavior.

Yet, nowhere in the Christian scriptures does one find an explicit endorsement of same-sex erotic covenants like those given to male-female unions in Genesis 1 and 2 and later in the Song of Songs. Catholics have long recognized that biblical silence about a practice or tradition does not mean necessarily that it is incompatible with the church's living tradition. What must be tested is the coherence of same-sex marriage with other, biblically inspired traditions about marriage. I now turn to the constructive task of exploring the compatibility of same-sex marriage with broader Catholic assumptions about Christian discipleship, sexuality, and marriage. Though by now it should be obvious, I want to note that such arguments as the ones that follow that minimize the theological and moral significance of sexual differentiation and that "make homosexuality and heterosexuality virtually equivalent" within a "polymorphous" model of human sexuality, have been explicitly rejected by Rome as misguided theories based on dualistic attempts to escape the implications of biological conditioning.[35]

CONSTRUCTIVE RETRIEVAL OF TRADITIONAL INSIGHTS

In the end, all judgments about the form(s) marriage should take hinge decisively on foundational judgments about the purpose(s) of marriage. For all Christians, such normative claims about the purpose(s) of marriage are deeply embedded in faith convictions about God's designs for and work in the world.

Basically, all Christians believe that God is drawing all creation away from sin and death and toward the fullness of life. Christians believe that in Christ God inaugurated a "new creation." Just as God is actively sanctifying all of creation, so Christ's disciples are called to join in and work toward the holy transformation of all their relationships. Jesus suggested that friendship is an important paradigm for our vocation to embrace one another: "This is my commandment, that you love one another as I have loved you. No one has greater love than this, to lay down one's life for one's friends" (John 15:12–13). Such friendships certainly make of life a delightful dance, but they are not without their demands. Such affections tie us to each other's agendas and concerns. Although the need for total physical self-sacrifice may be comparatively rare, in fact genuine friends lay down their lives for one another every day. Quite literally, friends spend their lives—their time, energy, and resources—on behalf of one another.

The realities of sin and grace make the human existential experience of embodiment and sexuality ambiguous. The Christian tradition is ambivalent about the body in general and sexual desire in particular. Thus it makes sense to talk about sanctifying the sexual dimensions of our friendships.

Marriage and Chastity

Roman Catholics see marriage as but one of three lifestyles wherein Christians might express their discipleship. Like the decision either to remain single (whether lay or ordained) or the decision to enter into communal life as a vowed religious, *the choice to marry is seen by Catholics as one way of embodying the general Christian vocation to love.*

The Catholic Church rightly commends sexual responsibility (known in the tradition as chastity) to all people, regardless of gender or sexual orientation, whether married or celibate. Despite its connotations to the contrary, chastity is not exclusively, or even primarily, about sexual suppression or the denial of desire. Rather, chastity is about the cultivation of sexual passion. Of course, whether we are married or not, sometimes living chastely requires that a person practice sexual restraint. But this virtue inclines us to do far more. Chastity forms our sexual desires so that they promote human flourishing. For example, in its letter, "Always Our Children," the U.S. National Conference of Catholic Bishops explains that chastity invites us all to integrate our "thoughts, feelings and actions in the area of human sexuality in a way that values and respects one's own dignity and that of others" as children of God.[36] Whether married, vowed, or single or whether queer or straight, chastity requires that we be sexually authentic. This is as much a matter of personal integrity as it is of interpersonal honesty.

Obviously in other respects the way we live chastely differs, depending upon whether we have been called to wed or not. Marriage is but one way of homemaking through which God calls us to lay down our lives for one another. Like the paths associated with communal and single ways of life, the basic paradigm for marriage is friendship. But Christian marriage is distinguished from other friendships by spousal promises to be both steadfast and sexually exclusive.

Marriage can be a tremendously powerful expression of God's love here and now, giving us a taste of the interpersonal communion we will enjoy in the life of the world to come. A distinctively Catholic case in support of same-sex marriage must demonstrate that faithful same-sex relationships have the same potential to serve both life and love as committed heterosexual relationships.

The Catholic Church blesses marriage because fidelity serves love. Given the stunning rates of divorce and family violence, it is clear that such promise making does not guarantee that marriages will be loving or that conjugal love will last. And obviously, genuine love exists apart from such promises. So the question is, why does the tradition teach that such commitments serve sexual love? Why does the church encourage marriage?

Sexual desire draws us toward one another, and when we are honest with ourselves, we find that we want to know *all* about the other. In wanting to know about the other, we want them emotionally and intellectually as well as physically. In turn, we want to be wanted completely. We want to be touched in the same way. We want the full and undivided attention of our lover. Genuinely great sex is integrative. It sparks in us a desire to throw our whole selves into the other's arms with abandon. Passion's flame may be fleeting, but it heats us from head to toe.

The experience of desiring and being desired physically fires our desire to know and be known emotionally and intellectually as well. Ideally, our hearts, minds, and bodies will speak the same language; they will be in sync. To the degree that we lack integrity, our relationships may prove to be disingenuous. In general, our hearts harden as we keep distant from one another; this is especially true when we keep our sexual encounters anonymous or "purely" recreational.

From a theological point of view, the whole-hearted nature of passion is what makes it graceful. However, it is also the root of our sexual vulnerability and viciousness as well. The relational structure of sexual desire sets up the very real threat of rejection and abandonment. Far from being romantic idealists, Christians are very realistic about the ways that sexual desire wanders and wanes. Christians are very hard-nosed about the human capacity for betrayal. This is one reason why the contemporary church encourages those who feel they are "in love" to marry each other, to promise to remain steadfast and exclusive. The Catholic Church encourages such promises in order to provide lovers with some protection in the midst of what is a very risky business.

In most North Atlantic cultures, weddings are often celebrations of how much a couple already loves each other. When Christians wed, we also celebrate the willingness of the couple to promise to learn how to love each other over the course of their life together. Even if we think we have found our "soul-mate," we promise to be or become "the one" for each other.

In and through such a steadfast partnership, Christians embody for each other and the world the enduring character of God's love for all that is. Next to their relationship to God, spouses promise to give each other "second" place in their lives. The promise of sexual exclusivity, which symbolizes this affective priority, is a largely practical rule necessitated by human finitude. The central problem with adultery, so-called open marriages, and other forms of polygamy is that they shortchange everyone. Even when we are monogamous, we are not able to give our spouses the full and complete attention they deserve as God's beloved children. Catholic couples seek to marry in the hope that such promise making will help them become better lovers. This is just as true for Catholic homosexual couples.

Marriage is most assuredly about love. Intimate companionship is a central purpose for which our desire to become "one flesh" was created. Love matches are personally gratifying and individually edifying. In a good marriage we can be schooled in a variety of virtues: justice, kindness, courtesy, generosity, self-care, dutifulness, mercy, respect, and loyalty. Couples help each other cope with life's economic ups and downs, take care of themselves, accept the loss of a beloved family member or friend, survive accidents or life-threatening illnesses, live with a chronic disease, learn together to accept disability or growing diminishment, age gracefully, enjoy retirement, and (in the case of one spouse) die well. Recently, scientific studies have confirmed what the tradition has long taught: marriage is good for most adults most of the time. It is on average a healthier, happier, and safer way of life than being single.

But Catholics are quite clear that these are not the only reasons why civil society promotes and the church blesses marriage. Marriage is not simply a matter of interpersonal affection and mutual assistance. For this reason questions about the form or forms marriage should take are not purely private; marriage is both a personal vocation and a social concern.

The church blesses marriage because fidelity serves life in a variety of ways. It is important to understand that society extends to those who marry many legal and economic benefits because marriage serves not only the individual spouses involved but also the community as a whole.[37]

First, the mutual assistance that spouses offer one another in times of trouble contributes to the commonwealth. Marriage serves the common good as well as the couple. Such companionship helps stabilize lives, which otherwise might be shattered by crisis. The lifeline that is marriage strengthens the community as a whole. This is true for same-sex marriage as well.

Second, because they have covenanted to take on one another's "business," spouses contribute as couples to society through their work and volunteer commitments. Consider the examples of the spouse who supports his partner while she finishes her formal education, or the spouse who watches their children while her partner volunteers at a Catholic Worker house. This is true for same-sex marriage as well.

Third, marriage also weaves a couple into a network that extends beyond the biological ties established by their own extended families of origin. Humans are unique among animal species in their construction of that class of kin known as "in-laws." Spouses often provide the lion's share of the daily care that their parents-in-law need in their twilight years. There is nothing exclusively heterosexual about generosity to "in-laws" that springs from conjugal forms of love. One gay man I know spent his entire annual vacation helping the elderly parents of his partner of nearly thirty years to sell their house and dispose meaningfully of most of their belongings before moving into an assisted living facility. A bisexual friend cosigned the loan for the retirement home in which her partner's parents live.

Marriage can bind spouses to "in-laws" of all sorts: their partner's grandparents, parents, aunts, uncles, siblings, cousins, nieces, nephews, etc. These ties are often sustained beyond the marriage itself. Consider what one widowed daughter-in-law said to her former mother-in-law long ago: "Do not press me to leave you or to turn back from following you! Where you go, I will lodge; your people shall be my people, and your God my God. Where you die, I will die" (Ruth 1:16–17).[38]

Fourth, though there are many notable exceptions, scientific studies suggest that on average married parents are better able to create a stable environment for the nurturance of children. Married parents can "spell" each other on an "everyday" basis when the demands of childrearing become overwhelming, and each brings different, mutually enriching skills to the process. The nurture of children—whether through foster care, adoption, or reproduction—is a very important way in which married couples can contribute to the well being of society. It is a wondrous privilege to cooperate in this way with God in the nurturing of new life. Again, as I noted earlier in this chapter, social scientific studies suggest same-sex parents can create a stable environment for the nurture of children, and therefore they can enjoy this wondrous privilege of cooperating with God as well.

But it is crucial to note that creating a stable environment for nurturing and raising children is not the only way in which marriage strengthens society. The promise to welcome children that is part of the traditional Catholic wedding has never been understood to require that the couple have and/or raise children. This is not the only or even an essential reason for celebrating marriage. The church's blessing has never been conditional on a couple's fertility or willingness to adopt. Although physical infertility is described as an evil to be patiently endured, the church teaches that heterosexual spouses who are childless "can give expression to their generosity by adopting abandoned children or performing demanding services for others."[39] Certainly same-sex couples can give expression to the fecundity of their love in these same ways.

The Catholic Church has always recognized that marriage serves both the call to love and the common good in a variety of ways. Its purpose has never been reduced to the transmission of new life. Pair bonding itself and the extension of kinship ties to "in-laws" are but two of these other ways in which marriage serves both life and love.[40] Any distinctively Roman Catholic argument in support of same-sex marriage must hinge on the fact that same-sex relationships can likewise serve both life and love.

NOTES

1. *Catechism of the Catholic Church* (Washington, DC: United States Catholic Conference, Inc.—Libreria Editrice Vaticana, 1994), 2358.

2. Congregation for the Doctrine of the Faith, "Considerations Regarding Proposals to Give Legal Recognition to Unions Between Homosexual Persons" (2003), http://www.vatican.va/roman_curia/congregations/cfaith/documents/rc_con_cfaith_doc_20030731_homosexual-unions_en.html (accessed October 30, 2006). Also see the National Conference of Catholic Bishops Committee on Marriage and Family, "Always Our Children: A Pastoral Message to Parents of Homosexual Children and Suggestions for Pastoral Ministries" (1997), http://www.usccb.org/laity/always.shtml (accessed October 30, 2006).

3. Congregation for the Doctrine of the Faith, "Some Considerations Concerning the Catholic Response to Legislative Proposals on the Non-Discrimination of Homosexual Persons" (1992), http://dignitycanada.org/rights.html (accessed October 30, 2006).

4. Congregation for the Doctrine of the Faith, "Considerations Regarding Proposals to Give Legal Recognition to Unions Between Homosexual Persons" (see note 2).

5. Ibid., 5.

6. Ibid.

7. Ibid., 10.

8. Pope John Paul II, "Address of His Holiness Pope John Paul II to the Diplomatic Corps Accredited to the Holy See for the Traditional Exchange of New Year Greetings" (January 10, 2005), 5.

9. Ibid.

10. Pope Benedict XVI, "Address to the Participants in the Ecclesial Diocesan Convention of Rome" (June 6, 2005).

11. Congregation for the Doctrine of the Faith, "Declaration on Certain Questions Concerning Sexual Ethics" (1975), http://www.vatican.va/roman_curia/congregations/cfaith/documents/rccon_cfaith_doc_19751229_persona-humana_en.html (accessed October 30, 2006).

12. Congregation for the Doctrine of the Faith, "Letter to Bishops on the Pastoral Care of Homosexual Persons" (1986), http://www.vatican.va/roman_curia/congregations/cfaith/documents/rc_con_cfaith_doc_19861001_homosexual-persons_en.html (accessed October 30, 2006).

13. This expression "parvity of matter" stems from the traditional teaching that sexual sin always concerns "grave matter" and hence always has the potential to serve as matter for mortal sin.

14. *Catechism of the Catholic Church*, 2358 (see note 1).

15. Congregation for the Doctrine of the Faith, "Letter to Bishops on the Pastoral Care of Homosexual Persons" (see note 12).

16. Ibid., 4.

17. Ibid., 6.

18. Pontifical Council for the Family, "Family, Marriage and *De Facto* Unions" (2000), http://www.vatican.va/roman_curia/pontifical_councils/family/documents/rc_pc_family_doc_20001109_de-facto-unions_en.html (accessed October 30, 2006).

19. Congregation for the Doctrine of the Faith, "Considerations Regarding Proposals to Give Legal Recognition to Unions Between Homosexual Persons" (see note 2).

20. *Catechism of the Catholic Church*, 2357 (see note 1).

21. Ibid., 2358.

22. Congregation for the Doctrine of the Faith, "Considerations Regarding Proposals to Give Legal Recognition to Unions Between Homosexual Persons" (see note 2).

23. Ibid.

24. Ibid., 7.

25. Ibid.

26. Ibid.

27. Ibid. Also see Congregation for the Doctrine of the Faith, "Some Considerations Concerning the Catholic Response to Legislative Proposals on the Non-Discrimination of Homosexual Persons" (see note 3).

28. Fitzgerald, Bridget, "Children of Lesbian and Gay Parents: A Review of the Literature," *Marriage and Family Review* 29 (1999): 57–75. Furthermore, the Vatican's hypothesis about the welfare of these children is reasonable only if heterosexual parenting alone is presumed morally normative for child rearing. Historically and cross-culturally, the nurturance of children has taken many forms, involving as the primary caregivers grandparents and other members of extended families, wet nurses, nannies, religious women and men, schools, etc. In its wisdom the Roman Catholic Church has never pronounced as natural in the normative sense only one way of raising children.

29. Congregation for the Doctrine of the Faith, "Letter to Bishops on the Pastoral Care of Homosexual Persons" (see note 12).

30. Congregation for the Doctrine of the Faith, "Letter to the Bishops of the Catholic Church on the Collaboration of Men and Women in the Church and in the World" (2004), http://www.vatican.va/roman_curia/congregations/cfaith/documents/rc_con_cfaith_doc_200 40731_collaboration_en.html (accessed October 30, 2006).

31. Congregation for the Doctrine of the Faith, "Considerations Regarding Proposals to Give Legal Recognition to Unions Between Homosexual Persons" (see note 2).

32. Congregation for the Doctrine of the Faith, "Letter to Bishops on the Pastoral Care of Homosexual Persons" (see note 12).

33. Pontifical Council for the Family, "Family, Marriage and *De Facto* Unions" (see note 18).

34. James P. Hanigan, "Unitive and Procreative Meaning: The Inseparable Link," in *Sexual Diversity and Catholicism: Toward the Development of Moral Theology*, ed. Patricia Beattie Jung and Joseph A. Coray (Collegeville, MN: Liturgical Press, 2001).

35. Congregation for the Doctrine of the Faith, "Letter to the Bishops of the Catholic Church on the Collaboration of Men and Women in the Church and in the World" (see note 30).

36. National Conference of Catholic Bishops Committee on Marriage and Family, "Always Our Children: A Pastoral Message to Parents of Homosexual Children and Suggestions for Pastoral Ministries" (see note 2).

37. To some extent the civil privileging of marriage is fair. When spouses marry, they take on many responsibilities and burdens not routinely carried by those who remain de jure single. For example, married couples are responsible for each other's debts and, as divorce law makes clear, in some cases even for the their divorced partner's ongoing economic welfare. Though spouses cannot be criminally prosecuted for their partner's crimes, their (joint) estate can be civilly sued. This is not to say that the current socioeconomic and political system that de facto ties many basic human rights to marriage is fair. It is unjust that many who are single, widowed, or divorced often have no access to food, shelter, health insurance, and/or a decent pension. It is vitally important to recognize that if our society continues to make access to such basic human goods a "benefit" linked to marriage, then marriage is not only civilly promoted. It is made "compulsory," and this is wrong.

38. So powerful are such alliances that royal marriages have been known to tie the welfare of whole countries together, so that their respective rulers saw the maintenance of peace between their nations to be in their own best interest.

39. *Catechism of the Catholic Church*, 2379 (see note 1).

40. The claim here is not that only married couples can serve the commonwealth. Obviously, both singles and people living in community can contribute greatly to society. Rather, the point is to identify a few of the characteristic, though not unique, ways in which marriage serves the common good.

6

KIDDUSHIN:
AN EQUAL OPPORTUNITY COVENANT,
NOT ONLY FOR HETEROSEXUALS

———————————— • ————————————

Peter S. Knobel

The international debate on same-sex marriage requires an authentic Jewish response from the Reform Movement.[1] It should be in keeping with the criteria set out by Prof. Mark Washofsky:

> We are Jews. We are the latest generation of that national, cultural and religious enterprise known as *yisrael*. Our religion is therefore inextricably bound up with the historical religious experience of the Jewish people. We, too, stood at Sinai. We do not and cannot understand ourselves as separate and distinct from the ongoing tradition that, for millennia, we have called Torah. Yes, we are modern, able to look critically at our imperfect tradition. But we are not radically separated *from* tradition. We hold it, not at arm's length, but in a powerful embrace close to our heart. Thus, we seek to explain ourselves by constant recourse to our sacred sources; we justify our religious choices by means of argument that is constructed from, expressed through and energized by the texts of our tradition. Our discourse is not chiefly the discourse of science and philosophy, but rather that of Torah and text. We strive to build a religious life that, though it speaks to us as moderns, is unmistakably Jewish in form and content.[2]

For Reform Judaism, our position on same-gender marriage must be rooted in a reading of sacred texts to be authentic. All readings of sacred literature are selective. The texts we lift up as central determine our understanding of the nature of humankind and of our intimate relationships.

A primary ethical and meta-*halachic* principle in Reform Judaism is the egalitarian principle. It is rooted in the first creation narrative in Genesis, in which *adam* (humankind) is created in the image of God; both male and female are identified as *adam*.[3] The same verse from Genesis upholds the uniqueness and preciousness of each person, regardless of sexual orientation.

If there is one agreed upon principle in Reform Judaism that is beyond compromise, it is the egalitarian principle. In marriage it means that husband and wife have equal worth and equal responsibility and at least in theory there are no predetermined role expectations or limitations.[4] The *halachah* must be changed to reflect this commitment to male-female equality.[5] In Judaism, sanctification is an act of separation that causes one to be in God's presence and/or to live in relationship to God. *Imitateo dei* (the imitation of God) is a major mode of sanctification. It is a reciprocal process.

> You shall sanctify yourselves and be holy for I am the Eternal your God. You shall faithfully observe My laws. I the Eternal make you holy.[6]

In Reform Judaism, *kedushah* (holiness) is primarily but not exclusively an ethical category.[7] For example, in Genesis 2:2–3, God rests, blesses, and hallows the seventh day, thereby creating Shabbat. Each week the Jew follows God's example in order to create Shabbat. Without human action Shabbat does not come. The time remains in the category of *chol* (ordinary), rather than *kodesh* (holy). If the Jew does not do what God does, Shabbat does not come, but remains only *in potentia* (unrealized). The Torah provides that the primary rationale for Shabbat observance is to serve as a reminder of creation and redemption. These theological concepts have important ethical implications, and in relationship to marriage, creation and redemption are the basic themes of the *Sheva Berachot* (Seven Wedding Blessings).

Leviticus 19:1ff. describes in great detail how our imitation of God serves as the means of achieving holiness. An analysis of this passage demonstrates that the emphasis is overwhelmingly on ethical behavior, but there are also acts that distinguish a Jewish society from others. The hermeneutic of Reform Judaism is an ethical critique understanding of *kedushah* (holiness). But to identify the holy only with the ethical is a grievous error. Holiness means living a life in relationship to and in the presence of God. Marriage is the sanctified relationship par excellence that sets the parameters of all other relationships, "*Kedushah* is acquired through fulfilling the *mitzvot* [commandments]."[8]

Reform Judaism, in its quasi-*halachic* guide to Jewish living, *Gates of Mitzvah*,[9] asserts that marriage is a *mitzvah* incumbent upon every Jew.

> It is a *mitzvah* for a Jew to marry and to live together with his/her spouse in a manner worthy of the traditional Hebrew designation for marriage, *kiddushin*.[10]

It is the meaning of the term *kiddushin* that is essential to our understanding of Jewish marriage. Only when we understand the values that define the word will we be able to ask the appropriate *halachic* questions. One of the best descriptions of the meaning of marriage as *kiddushin* in Reform Judaism is found in an essay by Rabbi Herbert Bronstein in *Gates of Mitzvah*. The essay is both definitional and emblematic. It does not define the *halachah* of marriage, but it describes the theology and ethics that must be represented by the *halachah*.[11]

Nothing clarifies the Jewish attitude toward marriage quite as well as the traditional name for the wedding ceremony, *kiddushin,* derived from the Hebrew *kadosh*. As we come to understand the deeper meaning of *kadosh*, we may begin to appreciate why Jewish tradition reserved the word *kiddushin* for marriage.

In the outlook of Judaism, all existence is derived originally from God and is, therefore, potentially holy. Time and space, God given, are sacred, but can also be desecrated by idolatry—the worship of things or of self. In consequence, we set special times and places aside for respect, for reverence, so that they may be kept apart from the realm of the profane, from exploitation for material gain and utilitarian usage.

Humanity lives, however, not only in the dimensions of time and space but also, from birth, in the dimension of relationships. And while all relationships, like all time and space, should be considered essentially sacred, certain relationships are especially exalted. In Judaism, the Holy of Holies of all relationships, to which the poetic genius of the Hebraic spirit turned most often for the paradigm of the covenant between God and Israel, was and is the covenant between husband and wife (see, for example, Hosea 1 and 2). A sacred entity comes into being in Jewish marriage. As in the Kiddush of Shabbat, we set apart a period of time as holy, in *kiddushin* husband and wife set each other apart. Jewish tradition considered the woman who married as *mekudeshet* made holy, set aside and apart for her husband, consecrated and thus inviolate. In the view of Reform, this "setting aside" is mutual; both husband and wife are consecrated to each other.[12] They create a sacred entity in the act of *kiddushin*, consecration.

In the Jewish marriage service, in the very act of consecrating a particular relationship as holy, the potential sanctity of all relationships is asserted. Husband and wife represent the bond between God and humanity, the ideal toward which all human relationships should strive. *Kiddushin* is the rooting of the human in the realm of the sacred, with the goal that all our relationships become holy, bearing the blossom and fruit of life.[13]

The word *Kiddushin* is derived from the Hebrew root *q-d-sh*, meaning to set apart as distinct, unique, sacred. Midrashically, *matan Torah* (the gift of Torah) is understood as a marriage ceremony between God and the Jewish people, in which God the groom presents Israel the bride with a *ketubah* (marriage contract), namely, the Torah. Each Jewish marriage is a replication of this moment. Jewish marriage is undergirded by a sacred contract, a *brit*. The text is read and studied and lived. Although this description must be adjusted for our current understanding of the equality of men and women and to eliminate its inherent heterosexism, the concept of a sacred contractual partnership between two people is a good starting point. Rooting *kiddushin* in partnership law rather than in property law reflects the new reality of a world that strives for gender equality. Sanctity involves both separateness and morality. Acts and objects possess holiness when they relate humans to God. The purpose of *kiddushin* is to define family beyond the biological parameters of descent. Its goal is the perpetuation of the human species as well as the Jewish people. It is rooted in the universal, the story of Adam and Eve, and in the particular, for example, the story of Abraham and Sarah.

Maurice Lamm, in his book, *The Jewish Way in Love and Marriage*,[14] offers seven axioms for sexual conduct in Judaism: (1) The human being is not an animal, (2) the human being is not an angel, (3) human sexuality is clean and neutral, (4) sexuality cannot be separated from character, (5) human sexuality has meaning only in the context of relationships, (6) sexuality has value only in a permanent relationship, and (7) sexuality needs to be sanctified. Although Lamm would be scandalized by my use of these criteria to justify same-sex marriage, he sets forth a description of sexual conduct that can describe both heterosexual and homosexual relationships.

REREADING THE BIBLICAL TEXT

Steven Greenberg, in his book, *Wrestling with God and Man: Homosexuality and Jewish Tradition*, offers a very interesting and, as far as I can tell, novel interpretation of Leviticus 18:22.

Ve'et zakhar	And a male
Lo tishkav	you shall not bed (sexually penetrate
Mishkeve ishah	engulfing one's penis) as in the lyings of a woman
Toevah hi	it is abhorrent.[15]

He points out that the word *mishkeve* is used once more in the Bible, in Jacob's curse of Reuven for raping Bilhah. He therefore concludes that what is prohibited in Leviticus 18:22 is sexual intercourse that is violent or humiliating:

> Sex for conquest, for shoring up the ego, for self-aggrandizement, or worse, for the perverse pleasure of demeaning another man is prohibited—this is an abomination. The verse now reads as follows:

Ve'et zakhar	And a male
Lo tshkav	shall not sexually penetrate
Mishkeve ishah	to humiliate
Toevah hi	it is abhorrent.

This reading of Leviticus 18:22 is a law against sexual domination and appropriation, and is a rather radical approach to the biblical verse. It is a reading that offers gay people a way to reconnect to God, Torah, and the Jewish people. While sources under girded this interpretation as traditional, talmudic, and biblical, have never before been used together in concert toward this end.[16]

Rabbi Greenberg then proceeds to describe a particular way of interpreting a text in which the particle *et* offers the rabbis an opportunity to open up a text to new meaning—to say what was left unsaid.

> There is only one prohibition in Leviticus 18 that begins with the word *et*.

Ve'et zakhar	And (et) a male
Lo tshkav	you shall not sexually penetrate
Mishkeve ishah	to humiliate
Toevah hi	it is abhorrent.

> The *et* adds a missing element—then the verse should be read: "You shall not penetrate either a ? or a male, to humiliate it is abhorrent." The *et* adds an unspoken element of the text. There is an obvious candidate to suggest—a woman!

V(nekeva o) zakhar	And either (a female or) a male
Lo tshkav	shall not sexually penetrate
Mishkeve ishah	to humiliate
Toevah hi	it is abhorrent.

> Until very recently only the sexual humiliation of men could be understood as important. However, as women become their own agents, as they approach equality

with man, the verse cries out to be applied to women too. It could be argued that the superfluous word was ready and waiting for the moment when human equality would be fully extended to women, when as a culture we would be ready to interpret the verse to mean that the fusion of sex and power into a single act is abhorrent between any two people.[17]

Rabbi Greenberg's interpretation is especially important from a progressive perspective, because it argues that the text is not about a sex act per se but about the use of the sex act as a form of humiliation. To now interpret it as rejecting the sexual humiliation of women is a great stride forward and promotes the concept that all intimate relationships worthy of the designation *kiddushin* must be egalitarian and nonexploitative.

Reform Judaism takes theology seriously, and when its liturgical formulae and ritual actions do not accurately reflect its ethico-theological underpinnings, the formulas and ritual actions are changed or reinterpreted.[18]

MARRIAGE AS COVENANT

The primary metaphor for marriage, which dominates Jewish theology, is *brit*. The marriage metaphor is used to describe the covenant between God and the Jewish people. The wedding took place at Sinai with the Torah as the *ketubah*. It is this theme of covenant that dominates the thinking of Eugene Borowitz as Reform Judaism's leading contemporary thinker. He has described marriage as the most appropriate ethical context for sexual relations because it is the best vehicle for expressing intimacy and perpetuating the Jewish people and because every Jewish marriage is a reflection of the covenantal marriage between God and the Jewish people.[19]

> The Jewish community has found no more central and significant form for the individual Jew to live in...than the personal covenant of marriage. In its exclusiveness and fidelity it has been the chief analogy to the oneness of the relationship with God as the source of personal worth and development. In marriage's intermixture of love and obligation the Jew has seen the model of faith in God permeating the heart and thence all one's actions. Through children, Jews have found the greatest personal joy while carrying out the ancient Jewish pledge to endure through history for God's sake.[20]

Contemporary Jewish marriage is ideally an I-Thou relationship between the lovers. For Buber the Eternal Thou (God) is present in every I-Thou relationship, and the rabbis believed that God was present in proper moments of sexual intimacy between wife and husband. Theologically, Borowitz struggles with an understanding of the relationship with God, who is superior and more powerful than humankind, and how the relationship to that deity is modeled in marriage. Ultimately, Borowitz maintains that human dignity depends on autonomy and freedom.[21] He writes,

> We have an old-new model for such open, unsettled but mutually dignifying relations, namely "covenant" now less a contract spelled from on high than a loving effort to live in reciprocal respect. As the pain of trying to create egalitarian marriages indicates we cannot know early on what forms and processes most people

will find appropriate to such relationships. We can, however, accept covenantal relationship as a central ethical challenge of our time and pragmatically learn how we might sanctify ourselves by living it.[22]

It is important to note that Borowitz realizes that marriage is undergoing significant change. Central to the covenant of marriage as Borowitz describes it is its egalitarian nature. This, he indicates, represents a substantial shift from the past.

The relationship's intimacy and egalitarianism are reflected in contemporary readings of Song of Songs. One of the most frequently invoked wedding texts—*Ani ledodi v'dodi li* (I am my beloved's and my beloved is mine)—is from this book of the Bible. The book, seen as a whole, is a description of an ideal mutual loving relationship in which both lovers initiate sex. The woman's voice in the relationship is as prominent as the man's voice. The rabbinic interpretation of Song of Songs, as an allegory about the relationship between God and Israel, only heightens the religious meaning of sexual intimacy. Love is the dominant emotion. The lovers freely choose one another. Feminist readings suggest that the book provides a model for a loving relationship in which neither partner is dominant.

The relationships between Jonathan and David and Ruth and Naomi are marked by covenantal promises.[23] Jonathan and David's relationship is described as *brit* and is marked by a ceremonial gift. Although neither relationship is a marriage, both are illustrative of the transfer of primary loyalty from the family of origin to another family. Both have elements of risk and sacrifice. Fidelity is their primary characteristic. Although the lack of a sexual component distinguishes them from marriage, the love and friendship that they represent are paradigmatic for the ideal marriage. Human love is also the love of God. Proper marriage has a deep spiritual dimension. The *shekinah* (feminine spirit of God) is present in the partners' sexual intercourse. This is further reflected in Hosea 2:21–22:[24] "I will espouse you forever. I will espouse you with righteousness and justice and loving kindness and compassion. I will espouse you in faithfulness and you shall know God."[25]

It is the *Sheva Berachot*, the Seven Wedding Blessings, that express the essence of marriage and it is to this text that we must look if we are to understand marriage. As Adler says, "it is these blessings which make it 'respectable' and reframe *kiddushin* as acquisition as an archetype of redemptive union."[26] God is creator, and humankind shares the divine image with God and, like God, is capable of creation. The couple's love participates in the perfection of the Garden of Eden and the first marriage of Adam and Eve, whose *m'sader kiddushin* (arranger of the wedding) was God, and its joy anticipates the messianic fulfillment promised by the prophets. Its symbols are a cup of blessing and the *chuppah*, the marital chamber, which is symbolic of the intimacy they will share and the sanctuary they will build. For the home is the replacement for the sanctuary. It is *mikdash me-at*, the Temple writ small.

ATTITUDES TOWARD SEXUALITY

Rabbinic teaching considers celibacy unnatural. "It is not he who marries who sins. The sinner is the unmarried man who 'spends all his days in sinful thoughts.'"[27]

The great revolution of the Torah in the realm of sexuality is to insist that sexual expression is legitimate only within the confines of a commitment to the sexual partner as a complete person. Sexuality outside of these bounds devolves into a form of objectification, in which a human being—a reflection of the image of God—is reduced to a useful (even if voluntary) object for sexual release. The Torah and subsequent rabbinic tradition, in defiance of the devaluation of the human being so prevalent in the world, insist that sexuality ought to further human dignity by embracing the entire person, not take advantage of their willingness or their utility. From the perspective of the Jewish tradition sexual intercourse is an expression of and an outcome of commitment and responsibility toward another person.[28]

The major concern of the rabbis seems to be that homosexual activity will be nonprocreative, and it will prevent men and women from marrying and producing children. Some of the most tragic family circumstances created by forcing gays or lesbians to live straight lives and marry have been the pain caused to spouses and children when gays and lesbians can no longer pretend to be heterosexual. In a society that accepts gays and lesbians, they will not feel compelled to be what they are not. The *mitzvah* of *p'ru ur'vu* (procreation) is considered extremely important. In the Talmud, the failure to propagate is compared to murder.[29] In rabbinic tradition the *mitzvah* is limited to men,[30] although in Reform Judaism the mitzvah is equally applicable to men and women. The movement has also come to recognize that some people ought not to be parents and, therefore, we have limited the *mitzvah* of procreation to those who are physically and psychologically capable of performing it.

The issue of procreation is complex. The biological preservation of the Jewish people remains an obligation. However, new reproductive techniques are being used with increasing success to overcome the problems of infertility. Artificial insemination has become a relatively common technique. For men, surrogate motherhood[31] and adoption are possibilities to fulfill the *mitzvah* of procreation. We might also consider mentoring of children or children's advocacy as substitutes to procreation. There are also issues of gestational, genetic, patrilineal, and matrilineal parenthood.[32] They are complex but not insurmountable issues.

The Central Conference of American Rabbis (CCAR) Ad Hoc Committee on Homosexuality asserted, "In Jewish tradition heterosexual, monogamous, procreative marriage is the ideal human relationship for the propagation of the species, covenantal fulfillment, and the preservation of the Jewish people." It then acknowledged that the ideal was not possible for some individuals either because they were homosexual or because they were unsuited psychologically, physically, or situationally to fulfill all the elements of the ideal, but that such people still could have valuable and important relationships. It would not occur to us to refuse to marry a heterosexual couple that was nonprocreative.[33] The committee further asserted, "While acknowledging that there are other human relationships that possess ethical and spiritual value and that there are some people for whom heterosexual, monogamous, procreative marriage is not a viable option or possibility, the majority of the committee reaffirms unequivocally the centrality of this ideal and its special status as *kiddushin*."[34]

Gay and lesbian relationships potentially lack only one characteristic of the ideal as set out in the report of the Ad Hoc Committee, namely, heterosexuality. Because homosexuality is neither a sin nor an illness it should not be considered to be in the category of *to'eivah* (abomination). The new information that we possess justifies our understanding that we are warranted by the concept *shinui ha-itim* (changed reality). to say that same-gender sex for individuals who are gay or lesbian is permitted under the same circumstances as heterosexual intercourse. Homosexuals are bound by the same *mitzvot, asei* and *lo ta-asei* (positive and negative commandments) that are obligatory for heterosexuals.

IS GAY AND LESBIAN MARRIAGE *KIDDUSHIN*?

I have argued in my paper "Love and Marriage Reform Judaism and Qiddushin"[35] that Reform Judaism has changed its understanding of marriage so radically that it fits into a different *halachic* paradigm called *Brit Ahavah*. In spite of what I believe is a cogent *halachic* argument by Rachel Adler, we are unprepared to give up the term *kiddushin* for many reasons, the most important one being that we believe Reform Jewish marriages possess the same sanctity as marriages performed by other Jewish streams, and we own the tradition equally with them. However, gay and lesbian relationships give us a unique opportunity to indicate our changed understanding of marriage by adopting a new ceremony that symbolizes the partnership aspects of marriage, rather than the property transfer aspects of marriage, and encouraging all couples to use it.[36] I prefer the term *Kiddush Brit Ahava* to *Kiddushin* because it better reflects our concept of an egalitarian relationship that is rooted in partnership. It better mirrors our understanding of Israel's relationship to God.

The wedding ceremony is that moment of magical transformation when two individuals become a *bayit beyisrael*. These layers of meaning do not disappear when the individuals are homosexual.

The ritual format by which Jewish tradition affirms this transformation is the wedding. Since we know that sexual orientation is both unalterable and irrelevant to the capacity of an individual to form a loving and stable relationship with another, and since it is our business and our calling to promote the formation of Jewish households that affirm Jewish values, we should offer wedding ceremonies to gay and lesbian Jewish couples. Some Reform rabbis will call these ceremonies *kiddushin*, while others may prefer a different term that carries less historical baggage. Some will structure a ceremony filled with the rituals and choreography of the traditional Jewish wedding (*chupah*, wine, the breaking of a glass, the reading of a *ketubah*, and so forth), others may prefer to create new ceremonies whose imagery does not so obviously mirror that of the traditional wedding of bride and groom. But in either case, we will be fulfilling our rabbinic responsibilities to Jewish people in our time, in the world, and in the culture in which we live.[37]

Depriving gays and lesbians of the opportunity for Jewish marriage forces them to live in what are, at best, second-class relationships Jewishly. Given what we know about human beings as sexual beings and their need to express intimacy physically, celibacy is not a viable option. A serious *halachic* approach will require that we establish a table of consanguinity that defines adultery and incest for gay and lesbian relationships. In removing homosexual relationships from the category of *ervah* (sexual transgression) we do not eliminate the category, we extend its boundaries.[38]

Rabbi Bradley Artson writes,

By developing a public ceremony to mark the beginning and termination of an exclusive committed homosexual relationship, the traditional Jewish standards would be clear and enforceable. In fact by extending these standards to include responsible gay and lesbian love, we would simultaneously strengthen our resolve to place sexual expression within the confines of commitment and fidelity for heterosexuals as well—applying one clear and moral standard to all.[39]

Marriage is the primary institution for the perpetuation of Judaism. It must reflect our highest values. Judaism is an ethico-legal tradition that uses the best of the new and the best of the old to determine God's will. In my view, the time has come to unequivocally declare that gay and lesbian sacred relationships have the same sanctity as heterosexual sacred relationships. *Kiddushin* is a *brit* between two loving persons, each of whom is created *b'tzelem Elohim* (in the image of God), and this *brit* is sanctified through the words and symbols of Jewish tradition.

NOTES

Previously published in *CCAR Journal, A Reform Jewish Quarterly*, Volume 11/4, Fall 2005 and used by permission.

1. This chapter draws heavily on my previously published works on marriage and same-sex marriage: "Love and Reform Marriage and Qiddushin," in *Marriage and Its Obstacles in Jewish Law*, ed. Walter Jacob and Moshe Zemer (Pittsburgh: Solomon B. Freehof Institute of Progressive Halacha, 1999), 27–56; and "Reform Judaism and Same-Sex Marriage: A Halakhic Inquiry," in *Gender Issues in Jewish Law*, ed. Walter Jacob and Moshe Zemer (New York: Berghah Books, 2001), 169–83.

2. Mark Washofsky, "Reinforcing Our Jewish Identity: Issues of Personal Status," *Central Conference of American Rabbis Yearbook* (1994): 54. Although I am quoting him accurately, I am quoting him out of context and intend to use the citation to defend same-sex marriage, whereas in his original paper he uses it for the opposite purpose.

3. Genesis 1:27; 5:1–2.

4. I say "in theory" because women still carry a disproportionate share of familial responsibilities. Marriage as an institution is still in a state of flux.

5. Societal change constitutes *shinui ha-itim* (change in the times). New information justifies a change in the halachah.

6. Leviticus 20:7–8.

7. We do not believe that God commands the unethical. Therefore, if a particular law is deemed unjust, we exercise our authority using the principle, *Ein lo la-dayyan ella mah she-einav ro'ot*. See Joel Roth, *Halakhic Process: A Systemic Analysis* (New York: Jewish Theological Seminary, 1986), 85. We also would apply the concept attached to some of the laws in Leviticus and Deuteronomy that anything that oppresses or exploits another is prohibited because we were strangers and slaves in Egypt. A hermeneutic of justice strictly and carefully applied is part of the Reform halachic process.

8. See Max Kadushin, *Worship and Ethics* (Evanston: Northwestern University Press, 1964), 223.

9. Simeon J. Maslin, ed., *Gates of Mitzvah* (New York: Central Conference of American Rabbis, 1979), 123. This slim but important volume is a guide to Reform Jewish religious living. It is designed to list and briefly describe the essential deeds, *mitzvot*, that constitute an observant Jewish life. The footnotes and essays were written to clarify the meaning of the *mitzvot* in a Reform context. In Reform Judaism, *taamei hamitzvot* (providing the rationale for a *mitzvah*) is an important aspect of the halachic process. It is used to defend or refine the

meaning of an ancient practice or as a means to change that practice so that it conforms to contemporary understanding. In addressing an essentially minimally observant community, the rationale becomes part of the deed. This is especially important when societal changes or new knowledge requires a break with the past. Rabbi Maslin, the editor of *Gates of the Mitzvah*, reminds us that the burden of proof remains on the one who wishes to change a practice, rather than on the one who wishes to maintain a practice. This is a fundamental principle of Reform Judaism's approach to the *halachah* for those in the Reform movement who claim that Reform Judaism is a halachic movement.

10. Ibid., 123–24. The concept that marriage is the norm is problematic for those who are concerned about our sensitivity to single people and also for those who believe marriage is an outmoded or incorrigible patriarchal institution. Marriage is understood as a *mitzvah* only for those who are physically and psychologically able. Reform Judaism reaffirms, even in the face of criticism and the high divorce rate, that marriage is a Jewish norm. In a similar vein, it affirms that procreation is a *mitzvah*. The assertion of norms or ideals that some cannot or will not abide by may cause pain, but this in and of itself is insufficient to cause us to abandon them.

11. Halachah is the crystallization of *aggadah*. This is most clear in Reform Judaism in which the tradition of *taamei mitzvah* is taken for granted as providing the rationale for observance. Reform Judaism has tended to reject or reformulate that which it cannot justify ethically, psychologically, or aesthetically.

12. The issue of mutual *kinyan* (acquisition) is discussed in detail below.

13. Maslin, ed., *Gates of Mitzvah*, 124 (see note 9).

14. Maurice Lamm, *The Jewish Way in Love and Marriage* (New York: Harper and Row, 1982), 3.

15. Steven Greenberg, *Wrestling with God and Man: Homosexuality and Jewish Tradition* (Madison: University of Wisconsin Press, 2004), 203.

16. Ibid., 206.

17. Ibid., 208.

18. The double-ring ceremony and substitution of either a marriage certificate or an egalitarian ketubah for the traditional are among the most obvious examples in the wedding ceremony.

19. Maslin, ed., *Gates of Mitzvah*, 129 (see note 9).

20. Eugene Borowitz, *Exploring Jewish Ethics* (Detroit: Wayne State University Press, 1990), 256.

21. Laura Levitt, *Jews and Feminism: The Ambivalent Search for Home* (New York: Routledge, 1997), 79.

22. Eugene Borowitz, *Renewing the Covenant* (Philadelphia: The Jewish Publication Society, 1991).

23. See Ruth 1 and 1 Samuel 18.

24. For discussion of this text, see Rachel Adler, *Engendering Judaism: An Inclusive Theology* (Philadelphia: Jewish Publication Society, 1998), 156–67. The culmination of the passage, according to Adler, is nothing less than a prophecy of "a time when marriage will not be a relationship of master to subordinate, owner to property or omnipotent giver to extractive dependent. In a striking parallel to the hopes of contemporary ecofeminists, the prophesied resolution of the war between the sexes is to usher in a new covenant of universal harmony" (165–66).

25. This text is often added or substituted for *Harei at mekedushet li be taba'at zo kedat Moshe ve Yisrael*. See David Polish, ed., *Maaglei Tzedek Rabbi's Manual* (New York: Central Conference of American Rabbis, 1988), 54. See also ibid., 165–66.

26. Ibid., 181.

27. BT Kid. 29b.

28. Bradley Shavit Artson, "Enfranchising the Monogamous Homosexual," *S'vara: A Journal of Philosophy, Law, and Judaism* 3, no. 1 (1993): 24. For a complete discussion of marriage as the most appropriate Jewish context for sexual expression, see Eugene Borowitz, *Choosing a Sex Ethic—A Jewish Inquiry* (New York: Schocken, 1969), 83–98.

29. It was taught: R. Eliezer stated, "He who does not engage in propagation of the race is as though he sheds blood; for it is said, 'Whoso sheddeth man's blood by man shall his blood be shed,' and this is immediately followed by the text, 'And you, be ye fruitful and multiply.'" R. Jacob said: "As though he has diminished the Divine Image; since it is said, 'For in the image of God made he man,' and this is immediately followed by, 'And you, be ye fruitful etc.'" Ben 'Azzai said: "As though he sheds blood and diminishes the Divine Image; since it is said, 'And you, be ye fruitful and multiply.'" BT Yevamot 63b.

30. BT Yevamot 65b; Qiddushin 34b–35a.

31. I have certain reservations about how women are recruited to be surrogate mothers, because these practices may lead to the exploitation of poor women. See "Surrogate Mother," in *American Reform Responsa*, ed. Walter Jacob (New York: CCAR, 1980), 505–7.

32. Noam J. Zohar, *Alternatives in Jewish Bioethics* (New York: SUNY Press, 1997), 69–84.

33. A more difficult case is the couple who on principle rejects the mitzvah of *peru urevu* (procreation).

34. Quoted in CCAR Responsa Committee, "On Homosexual Marriage," No. 5756.8, *CCAR Journal: A Jewish Reform Quarterly* (Winter 1998), 15.

35. See note 1.

36. I am aware that there is a debate among those who perform same-sex commitment or marriage ceremonies as to whether the ceremony ought to be the same or different from the standard Reform marriage ceremony.

37. CCAR Responsa Committee, "On Homosexual Marriage," 25–26 (see note 34). This represents the minority view.

38. "Given that the function of *qiddushin* has always been to draw lines that separate us (i.e., 'sanctify us') from the *arayot*, it is implausible to suggest that this legal act can actually permit a sexual relationship which the Torah and all of tradition so define. Moreover, as we have noted, *qiddushin* effects a change in the legal status of the parties by making them subject to the laws of adultery and divorce and by expanding the range of the prohibited incestual *arayot*. Whatever the potential of homosexual couples to establish loving and stable relationships, these laws do not apply to them. The partners in a homosexual union cannot legally commit incest with each other's relatives; they cannot legally commit adultery; and neither requires a divorce should he or she desire to enter into a Jewish marriage. It therefore makes little sense to use the term *qiddushin* to describe a union which involves none of these matters and does not alter the legal status of its participants" (Ibid., 26). The basic premise of my argument is that the same strictures that apply to heterosexual relationships apply to homosexual relationships. Therefore, I disagree with the statement of the Responsa Committee.

39. Artson, "Enfranchising the Monogamous Homosexual," 25 (see note 28).

7

SPEAKING OF LUTHERANS: THE JOURNEY OF AN ODD ADVOCATE

Herbert W. Chilstrom

Garrison Keillor notwithstanding, all Lutherans are not alike. Moreover, the vast majority of them live in communities that bear not even a remote resemblance to Lake Wobegon. There are more than twenty separate Lutheran church bodies in the United States, ranging in size from the Evangelical Lutheran Church in America with nearly five million members to some that embrace only a few hundred members in a small handful of congregations. Like most Christians, Lutherans are divided on most any issue one can name—divorce, ordination of women, abortion, war, ecumenical relations, and many others. None, however, has challenged us as much as the sexuality issues.

For this reason, it needs to be stated at the outset that though I am the former presiding bishop of one of the Lutheran churches in this country—the Evangelical Lutheran Church in America (ELCA)—there is no way that I can speak for Lutherans as a whole or even for the ELCA. Even as I write these words the ELCA is engaged in an intense debate regarding sexuality issues. It is clear from the discussion that there is no consensus on what the ELCA should do about the common questions now before the major Protestant churches: How should lesbian, gay, bisexual, and transgender (LGBT) persons be welcomed? Should we bless the relationships of same-gender couples? Should we open the ranks of the ordained ministry to persons in faithful, committed same-gender relationships, who are fully qualified on all other grounds?

Thus, what follows in this chapter is a very personal statement. I write not *for* Lutherans, but *of* them and out of my own personal experience. It is the expression of how one Lutheran who treasures his heritage has come to grips with these issues and how he has tried to do so as one who seeks to be faithful to his roots in the Lutheran expression of the Christian faith.

AN ODD ADVOCATE

Had you known me thirty years ago, you would never have guessed that I would become known in my church and beyond as a strong and very public advocate for justice for LGBT persons, nor would I have expected my life to have taken such a turn.

I spent my childhood and youth in a typical Midwestern farm community. Sex education in the schools was unheard of, and sex was never discussed in our family except in the format of humor. The only thing said about sex in our church was that we should not be intimate until we married and that divorce was wrong. At Bible camp we were all scheduled for a personal interview with one of the pastors. The only thing said to me about sex was that masturbation was wrong. "If you feel the urge," the counselor said, "go chop a pile of wood. The desire will go away." All other sex education was learned from male friends, and most of that was not healthy.

As for homosexuality, the subject was completely off my radar screen. I knew no LGBT individuals. More correctly, I should say that I did not think that I knew any such persons. It turns out that one of my closest friends during my youth and well into adulthood was in fact gay. But we never discussed his sexuality, and I did not know he was gay until after he died in his mid-sixties.

The same pattern of silence continued throughout my years of college, seminary, and the early part of my ministry. In my years as a parish pastor no one ever came to me to discuss homosexuality. No parent expressed concern about a child who was gay or lesbian. There were no church-sponsored workshops on sexuality. It simply was not an issue. Again, more accurately, I should say that it *was* an issue, but not one about which I had any great concern.

My first conversation with a homosexual person came when I was in my midthirties and serving as dean of men at a Lutheran college in the East. A young man came to me one day and announced that he was gay. He did not necessarily express any desire to change; he simply wanted me to know his story. Assuming he needed to change, I did what I thought was best for him. I suggested he keep coming for conversation and prayer and that he make an appointment with the college's clinical psychologist. I assured him that if he did as I prescribed he would soon change and become "normal" like the rest of us. Within a few weeks he disappeared from campus. Had you asked for my opinion at that time, I would have said that he made an unfortunate decision, rebuffed my offer to help, and would surely have changed had he followed my suggested regimen.

A LONG JOURNEY OF GROWING UNDERSTANDING

When I was in my mid-forties, I was elected bishop of the Minnesota Synod of the Lutheran Church in America, one of the churches that merged into the Evangelical Lutheran Church in America in 1988. I had little idea what assuming this position would mean. I soon learned, however, that one of its primary requirements was to be prepared for surprises. The first surprise came just a few days after I assumed office. Someone came to me and asked for my stance on the referendum in St. Paul, Minnesota, that called for granting civil rights to gay and lesbian persons. I begged for time to consider my response. In the next few days I contacted other religious leaders to talk with them about their views and then decided that it was proper to support the referendum.

In the next several weeks I learned that this referendum would be an incendiary issue. Responses came from both sides. There were those who were keenly disappointed and angered that I would affirm even the most minimal rights for gay and lesbian persons. The issue had nothing to do with what we are discussing today—blessing same-gender unions and ordaining persons in such relationships. The only question was civil rights—equal opportunity in housing and work.

My support for the referendum signaled those favoring its passage that I might be a religious leader who would be open to dialogue. One day a young man called and identified himself as part of a group of Lutheran men in St. Paul who met regularly for fellowship. He wondered if my wife and I would be open to an invitation to meet with them. Had I followed my first instinct I would have said, "I'm sorry, but I've done all I'm going to do about this issue. I don't have time to meet with your group. I have more important things to think about." When he went on to suggest a possible meeting date, I felt relieved to tell him that I was busy that evening. He persisted and suggested other dates until we finally settled on a day that was open on my schedule. I hung up, wondering if I should have let my name go forward in the election to the bishop's office.

On the appointed evening for our meeting, my wife Corinne and I were filled with trepidation. We felt we were about to enter an alien world. Our session was to be held in a stately old mansion in one of St. Paul's regentrified neighborhoods. As we came into a large, wood-veneered parlor we found a group of about twenty-five men sitting in a circle. They were very quiet, tense, and apprehensive. For them, this was a time of "coming out," and the fact that they were coming out to the bishop of their church only intensified their anxiety. There was a shared tension in the air. They were as fearful as we were.

What followed in the next two hours turned into one of life's "defining moments" for my wife and for me. They told their stories. Some had tried marriage, only to realize that they were not only ruining the life of their partner but also that it did not change their attraction to persons of their own gender. Some had spent considerable sums seeking medical and psychological resolution to their sexual orientation, only to come to the conclusion that any change was temporary and illusionary. Some spoke of coming from large families and being the only one among their siblings to be homosexual. Most important, all shared a common conviction that they loved Christ, they loved the church—the Lutheran church—and they wanted to be accepted as whole and complete persons. Among those in the circle that evening were the sons of two of the most prominent and respected pastors in our Synod. We left the gathering that evening with a strong sense that this would not be our last discussion of homosexuality or our last meeting with homosexual persons. We had no idea where this journey would take us. We only knew that there was no turning back.

It took many years for me to change my mind about how the church should respond to homosexual persons. Those years included study of literature across the spectrum, from those who wrote books based on the certainty that homosexual persons could change to those who were just as certain that change was impossible. I have met with those who are convinced that they have changed from gay to straight. I have had conversations with parents who have agonized over how to deal with the news that they have a homosexual child. I have attended retreats and conferences with homosexual persons, including accepting an invitation to speak to more than one thousand attendees at the first ecumenical assembly for homosexual persons. At the end of that long and arduous process of reflection, prayer, study, and reaching out, I came to fully support the call for our Evangelical Lutheran Church in America to bless same-gender unions and open the door for ordination to those who live in faithful partnership with a same-gender partner and are fully qualified on all other grounds.

How did I come to this position? Because of my deep roots in the Lutheran heritage, I did not change my mind without looking carefully at four elements: the Bible, Lutheran theology, reason, and experience. These four elements are at play in every aspect of my personal reflections, no matter what the subject might be, and they have been especially significant as I was changing my mind on something with as much importance as this issue.

THE BIBLE

For all of my more than seventy years of life, the Bible has played a central role. I grew up in a home where family devotions were a part of our daily routine. When I was fourteen the faith I received as a gift in infant baptism was awakened at a church camp. As a result of that experience I began to read my Bible daily. Before finishing high school I had read it from cover to cover (including every "begat" in Leviticus and every "selah" in the Psalms!). After high school and before enrolling in college, I spent a year at a Bible institute concentrating on acquiring a basic knowledge of the Bible, and once enrolled in college I took courses on the Bible and minored in Greek, the language of the New Testament. At seminary, I continued with biblical studies, including courses in biblical Greek and Hebrew, and was introduced to the importance of studying the historical context in which the Bible was written. Several years after I was ordained, I pursued a second master's degree at Princeton Seminary, specializing in New Testament studies, and my doctoral studies in religious education at New York University included a thesis in the area of biblical studies.

In addition to the formal study of the Bible, I have always found it important to read the Bible for the purpose of enriching my walk as a follower of Christ. For all of our married life my wife and I have followed the discipline of reading scripture daily, a practice that continues now in retirement. Each morning we read three separate scripture lessons for the day. In my twenty years as a Lutheran synod and churchwide bishop, I deliberately carved out time in my schedule to teach the Bible to pastors and laity. In my final year as presiding bishop I traveled to every corner of the country to gather together pastors and lay leaders to reflect on the importance of the message of the book of Acts for today.

Why do I dwell on my personal experience with the Bible? I do so to underscore for the reader that studying and teaching the Bible have not been an ivory tower pursuit for me. The Bible has been at the core of my life, both professionally and personally. The difficulty Christians face when discussing human sexuality is not a matter of whether we read, study, and love the Bible, but of *hermeneutics*—how we *interpret* the Bible. To help focus Christian discussions about human sexuality, we must answer these critical questions: What is the purpose of the Bible? How should we use the Bible when dealing with difficult issues?

We live in a culture where there is a growing tendency to use the Bible in a manner that is alien to the traditions of the church of which I am a member—the Evangelical Lutheran Church in America—as well as many others that trace their roots to the Protestant Reformation. The recent rise of Protestant fundamentalism has brought with it the assumption that every verse of the Bible is of equal importance and that all one needs to do in resolving any difficult issue one faces in life is to find the right Bible verses and apply them. When this approach is accepted, the Bible becomes a fetish, an object of worship that must be regarded with unthinking reverence.

Because it challenged such fetishism, when Joseph Sittler, professor of theology at the Divinity School of the University of Chicago, wrote his book *The Doctrine of the Word* more than a half century ago, it caused quite an uproar in Lutheran circles and beyond.[1] As Sittler himself said to me one day when speaking about the reaction to his book, "I didn't know the gun was loaded!" What did he say that was so unsettling? His book argued that the Bible must be read from its center and its witness to Jesus Christ, not from its edges in an attempt to use it for purposes for which the Bible was not intended. In reflecting on Luther's understanding of the Bible, Sittler wrote that it arose out of Luther's wrestling with sin and alienation from God and his discovery of "the measureless and shocking love of God." Sittler described that love of God as "the whole context of mighty works, prophetic declarations and pleadings, the cries and moans and lyrical songs of the Psalter through which that message moves to its fulfillment in Jesus Christ—*that*, for Luther is the Word of God."[2] Having established the distinction between Christ as the living word and the Bible as the written word, Sittler pointed out that Luther was able to move among problems of textual criticism with extraordinary freedom.

In our Lutheran tradition we often speak of the Bible as the source and norm for the Christian faith. This does not mean, however, that we take every verse and apply it literally to every issue we encounter. Rather, it means that Christians take the Bible seriously and then wrestle with how to apply its word to our contemporary situation. First and foremost, the Word of God is a word of judgment and mercy, of law and gospel, of sin and grace. That revelation—that Word—has been with us from the beginning. It was there in creation, in the history of Israel, and in the specific, particular event of the incarnation of Jesus Christ, the Living Word of God. Christians thank God that the story of those events was written down and exists as our holy scriptures. Yet, if a single word had never been written, we would still have the "Word of God"—the Good News that God comes to us in every age, but especially in the life, death, and resurrection of Jesus Christ. People would still be converted by the preaching of Christ, just as they were on the Day of Pentecost.

It would be most unfortunate if this sounds like an attempt to diminish the importance of the Bible for Christians. On the contrary, what I am saying is that the Bible will come to have an even more important role in the life of the church if we make certain it is used in the proper way.

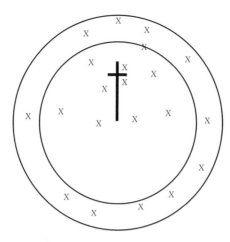

Figure 7.1

Many theologians also address this question by differentiating between the "canon" of the Bible—every verse from the beginning of Genesis to the end of Revelation—and the "canon within the canon," those parts of the Bible that speak more directly to the Good News about Jesus Christ.

In Figure 7.1, the outer circle represents the canon, and the inner circle represents the canon within the canon. Some parts of the Bible, like the "Xs" in the outer circle, may be interesting, but no longer applicable to life today. Other verses, like the "Xs" in the inner circle, are relevant for every age. The sacrificial laws from Leviticus belong in the outer circle. They are very engaging and certainly lay the groundwork for the great sacrifice of Christ on the cross, but would not be placed side by side with, for example, a verse like John 3:16, which belongs in the inner circle. The Song of Solomon is a lovely story of sexual passion, but we would not say it is central to the story of salvation. Galatians, in contrast, goes to the heart of the Gospel.

The Bible and Homosexuality

What I have written thus far would probably meet with nods of approval from most Christian readers. Now comes the hard part. What *is* the proper way to use the Bible in the church, especially when we are faced with trying to apply it to such complex and potentially divisive issues as homosexuality? Given this view of the Bible, how should we employ the holy scriptures as "the source and norm of the Christian faith"?

During the early part of my journey in dealing with this issue I spent much time and effort studying what some call the "clobber texts"—that handful of references in the Bible that are commonly considered to be addressing homosexuality. It became clear to me that all of these references are negative regarding same-gender activity, condemning of such behavior. That should have settled the matter. After all, if the Bible says homosexual activity is sinful, what more is there to say? The question is settled.

However, I soon learned that respected biblical scholars are in serious disagreement on *how one should apply these texts* to our contemporary world. Even at the same Lutheran seminary, colleagues of equal competence in reading the Bible in its original languages have strong differences of opinion. Some, taking Adam and Eve as their model, insist that there is only one pattern in scripture for a sexual relationship— a male and a female. They point out that both Jesus and Paul reaffirm this basis for sexual partnerships in the human family. Therefore, this is the only sexual relationship we can recognize and bless.

Others point out that homosexuality *as a sexual orientation* was not understood until quite recently and that therefore one cannot assume or even expect that the biblical authors were laying down a rule for all times and all places.

All of these efforts to wrestle with the question of how to apply the Bible to the issue of homosexuality brought me back to the question I raised earlier: *Do these texts belong in the canon within the canon or simply in the canon?* It became apparent to me that, yes, even though they are a part of the canon, part of the text of the Bible, these verses do not belong in the canon within the canon; they are not a part of the Good News that leads to faith in Jesus Christ.

For those who believe that every verse must be applied equally to all moral questions, this methodology may seem questionable. Yet, throughout the Bible itself and certainly in the history of the church we see this distinction being made. For example, in the New Testament, the church was faced at its outset with the question of what to do about those who were not considered "pure" and with those who had not been circumcised.

In Acts 8, Philip the evangelist meets the man from Ethiopia, who is a eunuch. The sacred writings we now call the Old Testament forbid eunuchs from certain privileges that others took for granted. They were not pure enough to mingle with the rest of the people of God or to enjoy the same privileges. But in Acts, when the Ethiopian comes to understand and accept that Jesus is the Messiah, Philip brings him without reservation or qualification into the water to be baptized. There is no conversation about change or becoming pure. He is completely acceptable as he is. He is a full member of the Christian church and a beneficiary of all of its rights and privileges. Now let's suppose that Philip had said: "I'm glad you've come to understand the faith. But before I baptize you and give you full status as a fellow believer, we've got to deal with a small problem—this eunuch business. You see, the sacred writings of my people forbid eunuchs to mingle freely with the people of God. If only you could change and become 'normal' like the rest of us, it would be no problem. Until then, you must remain outside the gate." We can't even imagine such a scenario.

In Acts 10, Peter is convinced that he must accept Cornelius, an uncircumcised Roman, as his full brother in Christ. It had to be an excruciating decision for Peter to give up a long-standing tradition based on the sacred texts of his people, the "Law of Moses." It is not surprising that the vision had to be repeated *three times* before Peter "got it."

This same pattern can be seen in the history of the church. Luther and other reformers abandoned celibacy as a rule for ordained clergy, in spite of several centuries of tradition based on what was believed to be scripturally prescribed practices for the church. When freely chosen, celibacy was legitimate and good, but supposed Scriptural requirements of clergy celibacy were no longer regarded as part of the canon within the canon. Moreover, after more than eighteen hundred years of a tradition that most white Christians believed was based on scripture, the legitimacy of slavery started to be questioned. In the United States, a hard struggle and division ensued among believers and churches. Ultimately, slavery was outlawed and abolished. It was decided that slavery did not belong in the canon within the canon.

When I was ordained fifty years ago I believed, based on the Bible and tradition, that the Lutheran church should not ordain women. But I had to examine my stance carefully and eventually abandon it. Biblical verses prohibiting leadership roles for women, including ordination, did not belong in "the canon within the canon."

A LUTHERAN PERSPECTIVE

As I continue to offer my personal testimony of how my background as a Lutheran has shaped the way I deal with the issues of homosexuality, I want to reiterate that I cannot speak for other Lutherans. My deepest roots are in Swedish Lutheranism. For the first thirty years of my life I was part of what was called the Augustana Lutheran Church. The church took its name from the Latin word for the Augsburg Confession. My seminary training laid heavy emphasis on studying the confessional writings of the Lutheran church. As I do with my Bible, I read the Book of Concord from cover to cover, underlining key passages.

Most Lutherans call themselves *confessional*. That means that, like me, they view the Christian life not only through the pages of the Bible but also through the lens of those confessional writings that are part of the Book of Concord. Included in this volume are the Augsburg Confession, the Smalcald Articles, Luther's Small and Large Catechism, and the Formula of Concord.

As with the Bible, Lutherans have asked the question, do all parts of the confessional writings apply equally? No, of course they do not. As with the Bible, we identify the meaning of these confessional texts in the context in which they were written and then apply them with modifications that are in accord with the context in which we are currently living. Thus, for example, it would be hard to find a Lutheran, even in the most conservative ranks, who still regards the pope, as suggested in the confessions, as the Antichrist. Similarly, in spite of its strong recommendation in the confessions, few Lutheran congregations celebrate the Lord's Supper every week. Nor do they go to weekly confession, as is also recommended in the confessional material.

Is there a core, a "canon within the canon" in the Lutheran Confessions? Most would agree that the Augsburg Confession, particularly certain articles within it, is at the heart of our understanding of the Christian faith, as the following examples demonstrate.

Article One: There are three persons in this one divine essence: God the
    Father, God the Son, God the Holy Spirit.
Article Two: All…are unable by nature to have the fear of God and true
    faith in God.
Article Three: God the Son became man, born of the virgin Mary.
Article Four: We cannot obtain forgiveness of sin and righteousness
    before God by our own merit, works, or satisfactions, but…we
    receive forgiveness of sin and become righteous before God by

grace, for Christ's sake, through faith, when we believe that Christ
suffered for us and that for his sake our sin is forgiven and righteousness and eternal life are given to us.

Article Five: To obtain such faith God instituted the office of the ministry.... For through the Word and Sacraments…the Holy Spirit is
given, and the Holy Spirit produces faith, where and when it pleases
God, in those who hear the Gospel.

Article Six: This faith is bound to bring forth good fruits.

Articles Seven and Eight: The church is the assembly of saints in which
the Gospel is taught purely and the sacraments are administered
rightly…the sacraments are efficacious even if the priests who
administer them are wicked.

Article Nine: Baptism is necessary and…grace is offered through it.

Article Ten: The true body and blood of Christ are really present in the
Supper of our Lord.[3]

There are twenty-eight articles in the Augsburg Confession. I have included
excerpts from the first ten because they are the essence of our Lutheran understanding of the Christian faith.

If you ask me whether there is anything in these articles that would forbid the
blessing of same-gender unions or that would forbid someone in a faithful, same-
gender relationship from being an ordained minister, my response would be that I
find nothing. I hear some in our church raging against any change in our current
position on gay blessings, arguing that it flies in the face of the Lutheran
Confessions. One could only make such arguments by induction; that is, by insert-
ing into the confessions something that its authors never intended. We should not
expect to find any specific references to the blessing of gay couples or the ordination of those in gay relationships. These questions were no more on the agenda at
the time of the Reformation than they were on the agenda of my church when I was
ordained in the 1950s.

It should also be noted that among the key articles of the Augsburg Confession
nothing is mentioned about the Bible. A description of the Bible as "infallible" and
"inerrant" grew out of the later period of rationalism in European intellectual history. For Luther and other reformers of his time, the key to understanding and using
the Bible was to recognize that its heart was Law and Gospel, Sin and Grace,
Judgment and Mercy. Thus, to take a few scattered verses about homosexuality and
isolate them from the larger body of scripture is completely inconsistent with our
historic Lutheran approach to the Bible. To put it another way, the Bible has a core,
but the boundaries are open—not to live irresponsibly, but to live with love of God
and our neighbor as our chief aim. Straight and gay, this is what we are called to do
in marriage.

Baptism and Homosexuality

In my struggle to align my convictions as a Lutheran pastor and leader with the teachings of my church, it was a letter from a farm couple in Montana that gave me as
much insight as anything else that I have received from those in structured, formal

settings for education and training. With their permission, I share some of the most relevant parts of that letter:

Dear Bishop Chilstrom:

We have been blessed with three sons—Peter, Andy, and Ben—all sensitive, intelligent, kind, and decent boys, each baptized as little babies and received as fellow members of the body of Christ. We could be any family in the ELCA, except that last summer, as we sat around the supper table after our meal…our seventeen-year-old son Ben told us that during the past four years he had come to realize…that he was gay. In the next breath he tearfully added, "I know that in the Bible it talks against homosexuals, but I know that God made me and I know that I am not bad." After many questions and much discussion we assured Ben that our love for him…was absolutely unconditional.

…About this same time there appeared in *The Lutheran Magazine* many hate-filled letters which said, in essence, that homosexual people have no place in our church. These letters were like physical blows to us, for they were directed toward our child—not a nameless faceless person—but our son, Benjamin Philip…whom we trustingly brought to the baptismal font…on December 28, 1975, hearing…our pastor give God thanks for granting Ben the new birth in Holy Baptism and for receiving him as His child and heir to His kingdom. We suddenly realized that in the eyes of our church, our beloved child did not after all meet the requirements to be accepted as he had been told when he was baptized.

On page 125 of the Lutheran Book of Worship we as a congregation say to the newly baptized persons: "We welcome you into the Lord's family. We receive you as a fellow member of the body of Christ, a child of the same heavenly Father, and a worker with us in the Kingdom of God." There is no fine print at the bottom of the page that says, "But if you discover as you grow up that your sexual orientation is homosexual rather than heterosexual your membership in the body of Christ is null and void—that Jesus's words in John 10:10, "I came that they may have life and have it abundantly," are not meant for you.

Sincerely,
Sylvia and Richard[4]

The letter shook me up because these humble members of one of our congregations were telling me what I already knew: sexual orientation was not a choice. Of the hundreds of LGBT persons I had met, not a single one of them said that they had made a choice. Instead, they all spoke of their sexual orientation as a discovery, which for some was made very early in life and, for others, later in their lives. The letter from this couple made me wonder how I could be so blindly obstinate and unwilling to see these matters from the perspective of what is so central to our Lutheran heritage—Holy Baptism. Then I began to see the ways in which our whole church was hypocritical. We were saying to the homosexual community,

Welcome to our churches. We want you to worship with us. Welcome to our choirs and organ lofts. We need good musicians. Welcome to our classrooms. Good teachers are always in short supply—so long as you don't say anything about your sexuality. If you have a pet, welcome to our service of blessing on the commemoration day for St. Francis of Assisi. We will gladly bless your dog or cat. But there, we draw the line, we build a wall: this far, but no farther.

The Church says to a baptized child of God:

> If you have a same-gender partner whom you love and respect and with whom you share a deep commitment to be faithful to each other for life, don't expect us to recognize your relationship or bless it. This would be out of keeping with our understanding of the Bible and with the traditions of our church. If you feel called by God to be an ordained minister and if you qualify in all the ways expected by our church—competence in scripture, excellence in preaching, skill in administration, ability in teaching, sensitivity in interpersonal relations—you cannot be ordained if you have a same-gender partner. Even if you have been with your partner for many years and pledge lifelong fidelity, you cannot be ordained.

I can no longer draw such lines or maintain these walls. They must go. When I hear of churches that regard homosexual persons as "disordered" and "imperfect" I wonder how they can justify it biblically or theologically. We are all imperfect and disordered, in need of God's unmerited grace. How can we single out a whole category of persons who are homosexual through no choice of their own and declare them to be more sinful or more in need of change or more unworthy of the blessings and offices that are wide open to those of us who are straight? In the Lutheran church, our understanding of Baptism will not allow for us to go on acting this way.

REASON AND EXPERIENCE

We like to think that we decide all religious and moral questions on the basis of the Bible. But even a moment of reflection reveals the fallacy of that position. I've just pointed to Holy Baptism as a core doctrine for Lutherans. It is clear to us in the Lutheran churches that we should baptize infants so that they might receive the full benefits of the death and resurrection of Christ (Romans 6:4). But, regardless of the depth of my conviction, I have to come to terms with the fact that tens of millions of fellow Christian believers do not agree with us Lutherans on this issue of baptism. Is their knowledge of the Bible inferior? Are they lacking in competent biblical scholarship? Don't they care about the eternal welfare of their youngest members? Obviously, they are not lacking in any of these gifts or in concern for their children. We simply disagree on what the Bible teaches on this important subject.

When we cannot resolve an issue on the basis of the Bible alone, we turn to tradition. Tradition is the accumulated wisdom of the church that comes down to us through centuries of religious reflection. *Tradition* gives balance to the way we interpret the Bible. Yet, as I have pointed out above, even long-standing tradition must give way at times.

This is where reason and experience come into play. In his book, *The Lutheran People*, Martin Marty speaks well for us by asserting, "While Luther and Lutherans have reverent and even awesome regard for biblical authority, they have never been *mindless* (emphasis added) in their reading of Scripture."[5] In addition, the insights of colleagues in other churches have deepened my articulation of the relationship between these aspects of faith. For example, Henry May, in writing about Presbyterian tradition, explains that the church's process of arriving at decisions on moral issues includes "a sober coalescence of biblical authority, doxological science, a vigorous intellectual tradition, and a common sense employment of human reasoning."[6]

As I met more and more homosexual persons who share my faith in Christ and my love for the church—the Lutheran church—I found it unreasonable to exclude them from all the rights and privileges of *our* church. Peter Gomes, Harvard University chaplain, asks, "When we speak of the authority of scripture...does that mean that we suspend all those faculties of mind and intelligence which we apply to all other books and all other instances of our life?"[7] Likewise, Christians can ask about experience. If the Spirit of God is alive and at work in the church in every age, should we not expect that there will be new insights to be discovered from the experience of believers in the world?

I hear many of my friends in the Lutheran church using the same phrase I once employed: *"Hate the sin, but love the sinner."* Because of my experience with homosexual brothers and sisters in Christ I now grieve over ever having used those words, as well as when I hear them used by others. I now know, based on my *experience* with homosexual persons, how it hurts them to be judged in that way. How can we separate ourselves from our sexuality?

Is it not possible, in the case of homosexuality, that we have greater understanding of its nature than did our ancestors? Has our world changed in a way that calls on Christians to adapt the church's traditional understandings and practices related to sexuality, just as it has done in other centuries (e.g., clergy celibacy) and just as it has done in other areas (e.g., ordination of women)?

Christians often speak of the ministry of proclamation. But there is also a ministry of listening, of being willing to hear the stories and experiences of other believers. That has been true for me.

Let me conclude with just a few examples of the hundreds of letters I have received that offer testimonies of some of my sisters and brothers in Christ.

Dear Dr. Chilstrom:

I am a mostly closeted lesbian. I, too, believe in the Spirit-led life...now in my seventies I am more keenly aware of the presence of God in my life than ever before. Two years ago, after the deaths of my two best friends, I told the Lord, "I'm alone now, but I'm yours, and you may use me as you wish." My path led unexpectedly into the charismatic movement. There I discovered much antigay sentiment, which led me into a deeper study of homosexuality than I ever anticipated at my age. I had previously accepted my state as something that I would simply have to endure for my remaining years in this world.

...My prayer partner suggested that I change my position and see if I had peace with it. I did take the opposite view. But I did not have peace with it. I thought of the thousands of sufferings gays—especially the young who are facing years and years of what I lived through, but now in a world obsessed with sex. I can understand their temptations to suicide and drugs. I was fortunate to have a strong religious faith; but I, too, prayed for death. When death didn't come, I was overwhelmed with the thought that God must want me to live.

...All of my adult life I have longed for someone special whose hand I could hold, someone whose waist I could embrace. In fact, during the last two years when I have encountered the cruelty of some of the antigay expectations, I have wished for a loving shoulder on which I could lean and cry my heart out. But my church doesn't allow any of that. I have sometimes thought that when I get to heaven I would like to be held in the Lord's arms for a long time to make up for what I have been denied. A lifetime is a long time to wait for something we crave as much as love.

But even though the church is harsh, I know that our Lord is not. And when I need that loving shoulder, I hear the words, "Jesus wept," and "He was despised and rejected of men, a man of sorrows, familiar with suffering," and because I know He is sharing my pain, I can let Him use it to try to make it better for someone else.

Sincerely,

Borghild[8]

Dear Bishop Chilstrom:

I knew at a very early age—as early as eight—that I was different. It was not until I was twelve that I realized that my attraction to males was wrong by everyone else's standards. I became a pro in the art of hiding who I was. I went to college and learned to hide even better. Then I went into the Air Force and my hiding became even more proficient.

I was married for twenty-two years. Though they weren't all bad, I knew that I never could be the husband that I needed to be. There were times, two in particular, when I reached the point that I didn't want to live any longer....

As much as I loved God I could not understand why He was not taking my homosexuality away. I wanted to be rid of it. I wanted to be "cured." I would go to church during the week, sit and pray in front of the cross, begging and crying to God to change me. I even became the new director for Lutheran Lay Renewal of the Carolinas. Yet, I was still miserable in a marriage that was not centered in love and could not understand why God was not changing me.

Then I met a stranger and it changed my life. I was on my way to a meeting at another Lutheran church. I took a shortcut but began to run late. I stopped at an old gas station to see if there was a better route. As I pulled up this man walked out. He was unkempt and very grizzled looking. I rolled down my window and asked him if he knew a better way. He looked at me for a minute and then said, "You know Jesus Christ, don't you?" I looked at him and assumed he was going to ask for a handout because of his appearance. But I answered him with, "Yes, I do know him." I was waiting for the request for money. Instead, he said to me, "I know. I could see it in your eyes and just want to shake your hand." He took my hand, smiled, and walked away.

To this day I wonder if he was an angel. As I drove away, for whatever reason, I suddenly realized that I was truly a child of God and that He loved me no matter who and what I was, and that He didn't need or want to change me because I was the person He had made. For the first time in my life I felt a boulder roll off my shoulders and it was the first time I ever accepted that I was gay and that I was loved by God, the Creator of us all. I had hit rock bottom in the days before this and suddenly I was at the top of the mountain.

Telling my wife was not easy, but I got through it. Telling my family and friends was not easy, but I made it. I lost my best friend of twenty-eight years, but though it still hurts I am dealing with it. My life with my partner Ron is centered in our love for God and for the first time in my life I am IN love. We are partners in all ways. We share a love for doing church work, worshiping together.... We work side by side and we give each other comfort and strength when it is needed the most. We will soon be celebrating our sixth year together. We had a simple blessing of union by a Unitarian pastor because we wanted to bind our lives together. But we long for the time when we can stand before a Lutheran pastor with our friends and family and celebrate our love and togetherness.

Yes, I am gay and proud of it. I am a Christian. I love God with all my heart. I would much rather talk about my faith than about being gay. I just happen to be gay. I don't want to lead a parade. I don't want to be militant. I simply want to be accepted.

Love through Christ,
Dean[9]

Dear Dr. Chilstrom,

Both of us thank you for speaking out on the issue of gay marriage. My partner...and I have been together for thirty-seven years. We both have strong connections with our families and attend reunions every year. Both of our families treat us as a couple. We are active in our neighborhood and are treated as a couple.

Thank you again.
David[10]

Because of persons such as these and hundreds of others I have come to know over the years, I continue to advocate for justice and full acceptance in church and society for every homosexual person.

HERE I STAND

I often introduce myself as "an evangelical conservative with a radical social conscience." Judging by the looks on the faces in the audience, some wonder how one can be both a *conservative* and a *radical* at the same time. I see no conflict whatsoever. I am an *evangelical* because my life is centered in the Good News that Jesus Christ is my hope for this life and the life to come. I am a *conservative* because I confess the ancient creeds when I gather for worship with fellow believers. I am a *radical* because I believe that those whose lives are centered in Christ and in the historic faith of the church must speak up and speak out when they see others being treated unjustly. In those good Lutheran words: *Here I Stand!*

NOTES

1. Joseph Sittler, *The Doctrine of the Word in the Structure of Lutheran Theology* (Philadelphia: Muhlenberg Press, 1948).

2. Ibid., 16.

3. Martin Luther, *Augsburg Confession: A Confession of Faith Presented in Augsburg by Certain Princes and Cities to His Imperial Majesty Charles V in the Year 1530*, trans. and ed. Theodore G. Tappert (Philadelphia: Fortress Press, 1980), 23–24.

4. Personal correspondence, June 14, 1994.

5. Martin Marty, *The Lutheran People* (Royal Oak, MI: Cathedral, 1973), 25.

6. *Princeton Seminary Bulletin* (Summer 2002): 233.

7. Peter J. Gomes, *The Good Book* (New York: William Morrow, 1996), 10.

8. Personal correspondence, May 30, 1987.

9. Personal correspondence, November 9, 2003.

10. Personal correspondence, July 6, 2005.

8

A BUDDHIST ARGUMENT
FOR SAME-SEX UNIONS

Roger J. Corless

In Buddhism, love and marriage do not go together like a horse and carriage. This is not because love is unimportant in Buddhism, for indeed developing unconditional love for all living beings is a primary goal of Buddhist practice, but because marriage is not a central concern for traditional Buddhism. The Buddha was a monk, and even though the majority of his followers have always been lay men and women, the ethical focus, especially in regard to sexual matters, is monastic. Because the monk or nun is vowed to celibacy, the discussion of sex in the monastic rule (known as the *Vinaya*) is all about what *not* to do. We need to realize this in order to interpret the remarks of some prominent Buddhist leaders who have spoken against sexual activity in general, and homosexual activity in particular. In regard to same-sex unions, the topic is never, as far as I am aware, raised in a canonical Buddhist text, so no matter how learned the Buddhist leader may be, he or she has no clear guidelines in the tradition and can respond only with a personal opinion. The statements should be received with respect, but they cannot be set in stone as "the Buddhist viewpoint."

Buddhism is, in any case, not a matter of doctrine so much as of practice. In some ways it is more helpful to call Buddhism a therapy rather than a religion. The Buddhist goal is not the conversion of everyone to Buddhism but to bring about the complete end of all suffering for all living beings throughout the universe. This is an ambitious goal, and because there are so many suffering beings, there are many Buddhist lineages with different, sometimes contradictory, practices suitable for different beings at different places and times. The Buddha compared himself to a physician who diagnoses a person's problem and prescribes a customized cure. A physician who has a wide knowledge of disease, a sharp eye for symptoms, and an encyclopedic grasp of treatments and their possible side effects is more trustworthy than one who says, "Take two aspirin and call me in the morning," no matter what the problem is. Similarly, the rich variety of Buddhist teachings and practices is regarded as a strength, not a weakness. Buddhism does not derive its unity from doctrinal consistency but from therapeutic effectiveness. Buddhism does not become corrupt when it adds to or modifies the teachings of the Buddha; it becomes corrupt when it no longer helps beings move toward peace of mind and the end of suffering.

Buddhism is, therefore, always changing. When it enters a new culture it adapts to it, and as it becomes accepted, the culture also adapts to Buddhism. Buddhism has come to the West and is putting down strong roots in the United States. It makes sense, at this time and place, to take the ethical focus off the Buddhist monastic and allow Buddhism to adapt to a democratic society serving the needs of lay men and women. To achieve this change in focus, Buddhists will need to develop an ethic of sexuality that is appropriate to the new situation but that does not violate the established therapeutic principles of the Dharma (the teaching of the Buddha). A tree grows downward as well as upward. The Buddhist experiment, in what Thomas Jefferson called the great experiment of America, must look to the past as it moves into the future. If it is successful, it can come up with an understanding of love, marriage, and same-sex unions that will be helpful to all Americans, whether they consider themselves Buddhist or not.

So, first let us look backward, at the ancient Buddhist tradition, and see what it has to say about sex and relationships.

TRADITIONAL BUDDHISM AND SEX

Because of their concentration on monastic celibacy, traditional Buddhist attitudes toward sex are almost unrelievedly negative. Even when addressing lay men and women, Buddhism has little to say about any positive value to sex and sexual relations.

Buddhist ethics are founded on the Five Precepts, five vows or commitments that may be taken by anyone who wishes to practice Buddhism in daily life. The precepts are couched in negative terms because they are advice on how to turn away from unskillful activities that have brought suffering to ourselves and others. The first and most important precept is to refrain from killing or otherwise harming living beings. The other four—to refrain from stealing, sexual misconduct, hurtful and deceitful speech, and intoxicating beverages—are, in a sense, elaborations of different ways of not harming beings. Refraining from intoxicating beverages is included because a drunken person is liable to kill, steal, engage in sexual misconduct, and speak untruthfully or harmfully.

The third precept can be translated literally from the Pali[2] as "I undertake the rule of training to abstain from wrongdoing in sensual and sexual matters." The word *kama* is used, meaning sensuality in general and sex in particular. In the word I translated as wrongdoing the prefix *miccha* has the nuance of falsity or deceit and is similar to the English prefix *mis-* as in misconduct.

We can see that this precept is not simply about sex, and it does not tell us that sex is bad. It warns us to be mindful when we notice the arising of passion. Sensual delights can trap us; they can be like a drug. The well-known Vietnamese teacher

Thich Nhat Hanh emphasizes this aspect by broadening the precept to include all forms of addictive consumerism.

But when we ask, "what specifically is sexual misconduct" according to the Buddhist tradition, we find very little in the texts to help us, and what little we find is often quite curious. The Tibetan Master Gampopa (1079–1173) gives the following list in *The Jewel Ornament of Liberation*:

> There are three types of sexual misconduct: protected by the family, protected by the owner, and protected by the Dharma. The first one means sexual misconduct with one's mother, sister, and so forth. The second one means sexual misconduct with someone owned by a husband or king, and so forth. The third one has five subcategories: even with one's own wife, sexual misconduct refers to improper parts of the body, improper place, improper time, improper number, and improper behavior. Improper parts of the body are the mouth and anus. Improper places are close to the spiritual master, monastery, or stupa, or in a gathering of people. Improper times are during a special retreat, when pregnant, while nursing a child, or when there is light. An improper number is more than five times. Improper behavior refers to beating or having intercourse with a male or hermaphrodite in the mouth or anus.[3]

Gampopa does not justify the inclusion of any of these activities in his list, and he reproduces it as if it were already well known and accepted. It does not seem to go back to the sutras (the teachings of the Buddha), and its origin and meaning are, at present, as far as I am aware, mysterious. It seems to characterize sexual misconduct as similar to stealing, as harmful to the partner, as abhorrent to established custom, and as addictive. It may also be influenced by what the medical lore of the time regarded as sexual dysfunction. These considerations may be addressed briefly as follows:

- Sexual misconduct as stealing: The wording makes it clear that the partner is assumed to be a woman who is the property of another man. In a society where the equality of the sexes is recognized fully, it does not apply.
- Sexual misconduct as harming the partner: Rape is, we now realize, more about power than sexual pleasure. Its condemnation is not culturally specific and is thoroughly Buddhist.
- Sexual misconduct as abhorrent to established custom: The intent seems to be to protect the good name of Buddhists and Buddhism. In cultures such as the United States, which encourage individualism and innovation, this issue is of minimal importance.
- Sexual misconduct as addictive: The image presented by Gampopa is that of a man who sees women as sexual objects and little more and who cannot restrain himself from copulating again and again. Such a person would today be referred to a psychotherapist.
- Sexual misconduct as sexual dysfunction: The identification of "improper parts of the body" and even the inclusion of "male" and "hermaphrodite" may derive from medical models that were compelling at the time of the Buddha (or of Gampopa) but that no longer seem credible.[4]

Generally, lay sexual misconduct is not dealt with in detail and is chiefly confined to the condemnation of adultery. The case of modern Thailand is typical:

> In Thailand lay sexual misconduct (*kamesu micchacara*) has traditionally been glossed as *phit mia khon eun*, "violating another person's wife," or as *phit phua-mia khon eun*, "violating another person's spouse (husband or wife)."[5]

Tantric Sex

If there is little to say about sex and the Buddhist lay person, there is, popular rumors to the contrary, practically nothing useful for our purposes in the tradition of tantric sex. The Orientalist imagination filled the monasteries in the Land of Snows with randy mystics who were constantly, as the British phrase has it, "on the job." Their approach to sex, we were told, was positive, reversing the body-negating practices of early Buddhism. This blessed lasciviousness has recently broken out of the fancied cloister to become a growth industry. Certain glossy magazines of new age spirituality advertise that, for a not inconsiderable fee, one can enjoy one's partner in a weekend of so-called tantric ecstasy on Maui.

The reality on which this lucrative fiction is based is not only more interesting but also considerably more obscure. It is more powerful than its modern proponents realize because it is not (merely) a palliative; rather, it effects full liberation from suffering. It is more obscure because of the Tantric Secret. The Tantric Secret is kept for a reason. The preliminary and intermediate practices of tantric Buddhism, known as Hinayana and Mahayana, transform the consciousness of the practitioner by encouraging it to mix with the Buddhist teachings at the level of concepts and reason.[6] Vajrayana (Buddhist tantra) interacts with the practitioner's consciousness directly, at the level of deep mind, by means of powerful energies manifesting as symbols, colors, sounds, and anthropomorphic and theriomorphic figures. Its purpose is to put a sudden end to the misperception of reality as suffering in cyclic existence (*samsara*) and allow reality to manifest as bliss and nirvana. During the meditation session the tantric practitioner self-visualizes as, and acts as, a powerful deity who transcends *samsara*. At the completion of the session the practitioner dissolves the visualization and returns to ordinary consciousness.[7]

As any psychotherapist knows, deep mind should not be entered alone or without proper preparation, for the process arouses the demons within, negative forces that C. G. Jung called the Shadow. The most powerful demon is sex, the basic energy (as Freud began to realize) of the human rebirth. Sexual symbolism is found in tantra, but it is, as far as an outsider can determine, sexual *symbolism*, not real sex.[8] The male practitioner visualizes himself in sexual union with a powerful goddess, who also transcends samsara, and concentrates on a circulation of energy between them. The details of this practice are only made available by direct oral transmission from master to disciple. Published accounts, even those in the tantric section of the Tibetan Buddhist canon, are purposely incomplete, preventing their use by unsuitable persons.

However, it seems clear that tantric sexual yoga is a method of realizing enlightened attitude or pure perspective so that the practitioner can go out from the session to teach and transform beings with renewed wisdom and compassion. It is not recreational sex, and it is not about establishing and nurturing a committed relationship with a human partner. Some tantric teachers are married, but the marriage itself does not seem to be the focus of their tantric practice.

Summary

When traditional Buddhism deals with sex explicitly, it does not give the lay person many helpful guidelines. Marriage, same-sex unions, or indeed any sexual activity is at best permitted as a weakness that the Buddhist hopes to overcome in a subsequent life by building stronger roots of merit in this life. Sexuality is reduced to the physical activity of the genitals fueled by passionate desire (*raga*) for sensual pleasure (*kama*), which can never be sated and so is addictive. The focus of attention is the male, with the sexual activity of the female being treated, if at all, by analogy with that of the male.[9] Its heterosexism supports a dualism between subject and object despite a rhetoric of nonduality. This discordance is especially poignant in tantra, where the symbolism of nonduality is entirely patriarchal. The absence of any discussion of sexuality as relationship, in a tradition that bases itself on the teaching of interdependence, is startling. To this question we now turn.

SEX AND RELATIONSHIP

To put it crudely, the view of sexuality in traditional Buddhism, centering on the Vinaya, is a celibate's wet dream: it concentrates on lust and genital activity. But a marriage or a committed relationship is just that, a relationship, and if the focus is not on the connection between the partners the relationship dies.

Christianity, perhaps surprisingly, can help Buddhism develop an ethic of sexuality, marriage, and same-sex unions. Christianity has, like Buddhism, a strong tradition of celibacy, but unlike Buddhism, it also manages to honor, rather than merely tolerate, marriage and sexuality. The Christian witness is indeed not all positive—the ascetical writings are often pathological in their fear of sex, their hatred of women, and their homophobia—but, leaving that aside, we find marriage being, literally, celebrated. Before the Reformation, and after it in the unreformed churches, celibacy had a higher ranking than marriage, but the liturgical books nevertheless provide a Christian context for marriage, and the Roman Catholic Church regards it as a sacrament; that is, an occasion for a ritual hierophany (celebration of sacred mystery). The union of the man and woman in holy matrimony is regarded as a symbol of, and a participation in, the union of Christ and the Church.

This conception raises sexuality to the level of a relationship between two persons and places it in the context of love, rather than the mechanism of genital interaction. Christianity often falls away from the ideal of sex as relationship, but that is not our concern. It gives us the clue where to look for a Buddhist ethic of sexuality. Is there anything in Buddhism that supports the primacy of relationship? The question is rhetorical and is almost foolish. It is a secret hidden in plain sight. All that we need to do is apply the teachings to marriage and committed relationships.

The teaching that reality is interdependent arising (*pratityasamutpada*) is so central that it is sometimes said that fully awakening to this reality is what constitutes perfect enlightenment. When a Buddhist is with a partner, whether intimately or socially, bringing the knowledge of interdependent arising into awareness will assist the relationship and, if the partner is also Buddhist, further the spiritual practice of both partners.

We can find a basis for a Buddhist ethic of sex as relationship in both the Theravada and Mahayana scriptures.

Theravada, the form of Buddhism dominant in Southeast Asia, has preserved a canon of scripture in Pali.[10] The teachings in the Pali Canon were systematized by Buddhaghosa (fl. fifth century CE) in the Pure Path (*Visuddhimagga*, variously interpreted as the Path of Purity or the Path of Purification). In Chapter nine, Buddhaghosa gives an extensive and detailed teaching on the four pure abidings (*brahma-vihara*): friendliness (*metta*), compassion (*karuna*), sympathetic joy (*mudita*), and equanimity (*upekkha*). He catalogues them, describes them, and explains how to develop and nurture them, supporting his argument with many references to the *suttas* (the sermons of the Buddha in the Pali Canon). He recommends the following:

> The student who wishes to begin with the development of the Four Pure Abidings
> …should first…reflect on the disadvantages of hate and the advantages of patience.
> Why? Truly by means of this practice hate is put away and patience is acquired.[11]

Buddhaghosa is addressing monastics, but his teaching can be readily adapted to lay life. Couples may not have as much time for meditating on the pure abidings "in a secluded spot" as Buddhaghosa recommends, but they will have more opportunities to develop these virtues in the vicissitudes of daily life.

Mahayana, the Buddhism of Inner and East Asia, is richer than Theravada in teachings that explicitly address interconnection. The most elaborate teaching is in the Flower Garland Sutra (*Huayan Jing*), a text that runs to more than fifteen hundred pages in English translation.[12] Its core teaching is helpfully summarized by Fazang (643–712 CE) in his *Essay on the Golden Lion*.[13] Pointing to a golden statue of a lion and using it as a metaphor of reality, he distinguished between the gold, as a symbol of essence, and the lion form, as a symbol of manifestation, going on to describe in detail the various ways in which essence, or Buddha Nature, and manifestation, or everyday experience, interact and interpenetrate. His final teaching is the mutual interpenetration of manifestation with manifestation; that is, the mutual enfolding (coinherence) of everyday reality, which he has already said is coinherent with Buddha Nature, with itself. This grand vision, which unifies everyday reality and Buddha Nature while preserving the distinction between them, is so popular in East Asian Buddhism that it is almost a cliché (Japanese: *jijimuge*). When this vision is applied to interpersonal relationships, each partner sees himself or herself in the other and the other in himself or herself, fully and completely. It is a profoundly intimate understanding of the Golden Rule, to treat others as oneself.

In Tibetan Buddhism there is a practice of the Golden Rule called taking and sending or exchanging self for other (*tonglen*). In meditation, one concentrates on the breath and visualizes that one takes away the sufferings of others on the in breath and sends them joy on the out breath. One may be taught to visualize the in breath as a black cloud and the out breath as a white cloud. In the meditation, one is not actually removing the sufferings of others and replacing them with joy; rather, one is changing one's attitude from a habitual "me first" to a more compassionate "others first." As a consequence, when one rises from the meditation to meet others in daily life, one's actions will be less self-centered. Couples who practice *tonglen* should find their relationship improved.

In the light of the above I suggest that we reinterpret the third precept as *inauthentic* sexual conduct. Sexual conduct that does not take account of the interdependent arising of all phenomena, of their interpenetration, and of the supreme value or Buddha Nature of the other person is not authentically Buddhist.

OVERCOMING DUALISTIC THINKING

Buddhism teaches that the untrained mind divides the interconnectedness of reality into discrete units, such as person, place, or thing, and assigns an essence or "own-being" (*svabhava*) to each unit. The effect of this is to close up the basic openness of reality, to deny change, and, most important, to block the door to freedom by assuming that the sufferings of our present existence are inescapable, imposed by fate or some other outside force over which we have no control. But when these supposed essences are subjected to penetrating analysis in concentrated meditation, they are found to be illusory and the basic openness and transparency (*shunyata*, often translated as emptiness) of the world are seen to be the case.

This has implications for the way we approach, and think about, interpersonal relationships. If the definition of marriage is restricted to the union between a man and a woman, and men and women are assumed to be not just different but intrinsically and unalterably different, there is an unbridgeable gulf between the partners and true intimacy is impossible. Buddhism asks us to look closely at these assumptions and see that they are false. The identification of men and women as male or female *in their essence* is recognized as a misperception made by the untrained mind. When we really examine ourselves, where do we find our maleness or femaleness? We can point to certain bodily organs and to what are called secondary sex characteristic, but when we "play doctor" with a person of the opposite sex we find that we are not as different as we supposed. This is true even if our sexual characteristics are unambiguous. It is more than obvious to the large minority of humans who find themselves somewhere in between male and female, or who feel strongly that their gender was misidentified at birth and wish to live as a person of another gender. The famous research of Masters and Johnson established that human sexual activity is not simply heterosexual or homosexual, but can be plotted along a spectrum between these two extremes.[14]

To put it simply, human sexuality is a matter not of fixed opposites but rather a constantly changing flow of interaction. Science has come to agree with Buddhism on this conclusion. This agreement arises in both cases from observation: they are not arbitrary doctrinal statements.

In the United States, society at large is starting to wake up to this conception of human sexuality. Persons are identifying themselves not only as homosexual rather than heterosexual, but as lesbian, gay, bisexual, transgender, and intersexual (LGBTI). Sometimes the word "queer" is used to refer to all LGBTI persons, and queer is coming to be used by heterosexual persons who enjoy sexual activities that differ from cultural norms. All such persons challenge us to realize that sexual relationships are about relationship as much as or indeed more than they are about sex narrowly defined as male-female genital performance.

Feminists have made the case that it is men who have set up the dichotomy between "real men" and "real women" and defined the roles of each. This dichotomy has led, they say, to a fixed way of viewing the world as inherently divided between object and subject. The rational, dispassionate man observes reality as if it were external, passive, and irrational—the despised female Other. When reality is seen from a feminist perspective the dichotomy does not disappear but it becomes fluid, and the interconnections between things, and between persons, comes into focus.[15]

The importance of interconnection rather than dichotomy in sexual relationships is even clearer when the world is viewed from a gay or lesbian perspective. Harry Hay, who is regarded as the founder of the modern gay movement,[16] has proposed that gays[17] see reality differently. When a gay man falls in love with another man, the relationship is not that of subject to object, as it might be for a man and a woman, but of subject to another subject; it is not of "me" to another ("an-other") but of me to "another me":

> The Hetero monogamous relationship is one in which the participants, through bio-cultural inheritance, traditionally perceive each other as OBJECT. To the Hetero male, woman is primarily perceived as sex-*object* and then, only with increasing sophistication, as person-*object*. The Gay monogamous relationship is one in which the participants, through non-competitive instinctual inclinations, *and contrary to cultural inheritances*, perceive each other as Equals and learn, usually through deeply painful trials-and-errors, to experience each other, to continuously grow, and to develop *with* each other, *empathically*—as SUBJECT.[18]

Hay calls this gay consciousness *subject-subject* consciousness or *analogue consciousness* and proposes it as a solution to the problems brought about through the unthinking acceptance of Hetero male consciousness, what the feminists would later call patriarchal consciousness. Hay regards the gay male as neither male nor female at the level of consciousness, but as something else. In an address to gay men, he reminds them that when they were young the other boys told them that they threw a ball like a girl. Had they asked a girl about this, however, she would have told them they did not throw a ball like a girl, but like something other. Harry states that gay men were not feminine boys; they were *other*.[19]

Hay goes on to describe how gays are "other": they live in what he calls a "new planet of Fairy-vision"[20] that, as his friend and collaborator Mitch Walker claims, overturns culturally conditioned views of reality: "Imagine, for instance, that the tops of the trees are really the roots."[21] Hay states, "Subject-SUBJECT consciousness is a multi-dimensional consciousness which may never be readily conveyable in the Hetero-male-evolved two-dimensional, or Binary, language to which we are primarily confined."[22]

Gay or queer consciousness, then, challenges dualistic thinking and replaces it with nondual or interdependent thinking. It overturns, inverts, and turns inside out our perception of consensus reality. This is also a stated goal of Buddhism. Ordinary, deluded views about reality are called "upside down" views. One school of Mahayana Buddhism, Yogachara, teaches that wisdom is nothing other than the radical inverting of the deepest level of ordinary, deluded consciousness.

BUDDHISM AND SAME-SEX UNIONS

Harry Hay's paean to gay consciousness is exhilarating and thought provoking, but taken as it stands, it is somewhat idealistic and it tends to classify people into good gays and bad heterosexuals. In real life, we find many gay men, lesbians, and queer persons in general who are anything but loving and egalitarian: if they have gay consciousness, they do not manifest it. On the other hand, there are many heterosexual men and women who have gay consciousness and are comfortable manifesting it. Locating gay consciousness in nonheterosexuals and denying it to heterosexuals escapes from one form of dualistic thinking only to fall into another.

Gay consciousness is not really about sex, although sex is a part of it. It is about relationships. When gay consciousness is recognized and allowed to show itself, it moves our attention away from sex as genital interaction and the mechanics of reproduction between men and women and transforms lust into the pure abidings. It creates an environment in which Buddhism can revisit sexual relationships and see them as noble, rather than as an obstacle on the Path.

As Buddhism has become a familiar part of the American scene, people have started to call themselves Buddhists, and when they prepare for marriage, they want a Buddhist wedding ceremony. Because there is no tradition of Buddhist weddings, these ceremonies have to be invented, usually by the partners in consultation with their Buddhist teacher or the staff of a Buddhist center.

This development is the result of the interaction between Buddhism and American culture. It will be instructive to digress briefly from our main argument to take a closer look at this development: doing so will help us understand why marriage and same-sex unions are hot topics in American society and politics.

It is only a slight exaggeration to say that there were no Buddhists, and there was no Buddhism, until the teaching of the Buddha came to the West. "Buddhism" and "Buddhist" are Western words that have emerged in a Western context. There were no direct equivalents, as far as I am aware, in any Asian language until recent times, when Asian languages attempted translations of these imported Western words. In traditional Asia, people would engage in Buddhist practices and follow Buddhist customs without the slightest notion that doing so prevented them in any way from engaging in other practices or following other customs. Generally, the line between Buddhism and the rest of the culture was vague, although it was not entirely absent, and a person's identification was cultural rather than religious. Organizationally, traditional Buddhism has a center but no periphery. Like a planet, it could be located, but its influence (its gravitational force) spreads outward indefinitely.

Christianity, on the other hand, is organizationally more like a city or a house. Its boundaries are (in theory though not always in practice) clearly drawn. From very early times, tests were imposed to determine who was inside the church and who was outside. During the Reformation of the western church around the sixteenth century, this issue took center stage, and some people who belonged to a branch of Christianity that had fallen out of official favor escaped persecution by coming to the New World. In the United States, these Christians established themselves on the basis of their different church memberships, and to prevent a repeat of the persecution they had experienced in the Old World, the categories "church" and "state" were enshrined in the Constitution and declared to be forever separate.

Religion in the United States thus became a social, cultural, and legal entity in a way that was novel to Asian immigrants. Asian immigrants were asked to declare their religion, and at first they were at a loss how to answer, but they soon learned to use words like "Hindu," "Buddhist," "Confucian," or "Shinto" and found that these words gave legal protection to important elements of their cultures of origin.

In contrast, it came naturally to those non-Asians in the United States who began to practice Buddha Dharma to self-identify as Buddhists.[23] Because Christianity, which self-identifies as a religion, had developed a tradition of wedding ceremonies held in a church, it was assumed that Buddhism, which was now treated as a religion, had a similar tradition. The American desire for a Buddhist wedding ceremony demonstrates the extent to which the Christian notion that marriage is properly a religious rather than a secular undertaking is embedded in the national consciousness, and this in turn explains why clergy rather than lawyers are most vocal in their opposition to same-sex unions.

Let us return now to our main discussion. Having learnt about the central importance of relationship in Buddhism we can see something positive in the negative view of sex and the absence of wedding ceremonies in traditional Buddhism. It has been suggested that many marriages fail in the United States not because the institution of marriage is undervalued but because it is overvalued. Schooled in the ideals of romantic love the partners expect to live happily ever after, and having been told that their union is a symbol of the mystical union between Christ and his church (as the Episcopalian Prayer Book neatly summarizes the theology of marriage), they may expect each other to be saints; when the honeymoon is over, these romantic and idealistic expectations may be fatally challenged and divorce is seen as the only solution.

Buddhism brings us back to earth. A satisfying and long-lasting relationship is not mystical, but rather the work of the partners as whole and dynamically changing persons. Each partner has a responsibility for the quality of the relationship, maintaining awareness of how it is from moment to moment and adapting to the changes that, as Buddhism makes us keenly aware, are inevitable. Buddhist meditation and the attempt to live according to the pure abidings assist this constant openness to the moment.

Further, because the reality of total interdependence is stressed in Buddhist teaching, the partners are enabled to see themselves in each other. In effect, every committed relationship, whether homosexual or heterosexual, is, from a Buddhist perspective, a same-sex union.

Again, because Buddhism has no clear boundaries, these observations are not only applicable to those who call themselves Buddhists. They can be material for reflection by those of any religion or of none.

NOTES

This article is a significant revision of "Towards a Queer Dharmology of Sex," presented at the conference on Queer Visions in the Americas at the University of California, Santa Barbara, May 24–26, 2002, and adapted for publication in *Culture and Religion* 5, no. 2 (July 2004), 229–43.

1. Pali is one of the major sacred languages of Buddhism. It is the canonical language of Theravada Buddhism (the Buddhism of Southeast Asia), and it has been argued that it may be related to the language that the Buddha himself spoke.

2. Gampopa, *The Jewel Ornament of Liberation: The Wish-fulfilling Gem of the Noble Teachings*, trans. Khenpo Konchog Gyaltsen Rinpoche and ed. Ani K. Trinlay Chödrun (Ithaca, NY: Snow Lion Publications, 1998), 113. Compare the translations of this passage by Herbert Guenther, *The Jewel Ornanament of Liberation* (Berkeley: Shambhala, 1971) 76, with the translation by Ken and Katia Holmes, *Gems of Dharma, Jewels of Freedom* (Forres, Scotland: Altea Publishing, 1995), 76.

3. This is suggested by Leonard Zwilling, "Homosexuality as Seen in Indian Buddhist Texts," in *Buddhism, Sexuality, and Gender*, ed. José Ignacio Cabezón (Albany: State University of New York Press, 1992), 203–214. However, more research needs to be done to clarify the issue. "Hermaphrodite" is a guess at the meaning of *pandaka*, a word that is not fully understood but seems to mean someone whose sexuality is regarded as ambiguous physically, mentally, or in terms of practice.

4. Peter A. Jackson, "Male Homosexuality and Transgenderism in the Thai Buddhist Tradition," in *Queer Dharma: Voices of Gay Buddhists*, ed. Winston Leyland (San Francisco: Gay Sunshine Press, 1998), 60.

5. Hinayana is a Mahayanist technical term referring to Buddhist teachings and practices that need to be given up as the practitioner matures. It should not be confused with, or used for, Theravada, which is a living Buddhist tradition with some structural similarities to Hinayana. See my article "The Hermeneutics of Polemic: The Creation of *Hinayana* and *Old Testament*," *Buddhist-Christian Studies* 11 (1991): 59–74.

6. See Jeffrey Hopkins, *The Tantric Distinction: An Introduction to Tibetan Buddhism* (London: Wisdom Publications, 1984), 155–164, on Deity Yoga.

7. Reports of tantric sex with a human partner on the physical plane are difficult to substantiate. If they can be proved, they have been observed or reported in violation of the Tantric Secret. They may indeed be practical jokes played by Tibetans on gullible researchers.

8. During a teaching on the union of sutra and tantra in Madison, Wisconsin, in 1980, the women, who comprised fully half the number of students present, were told that they should "reverse" the symbolism, but they were given no instruction on how to understand the recommendation to "retain the [energy of the] semen."

9. See note 1.

10. Pe Maung Tin, *The Path of Purity, Being a Translation of Buddhaghosa's Visuddhimagga* (London: Pali Text Society, 1971), 340. Translation modified by the author. For the full discussion of the practice of the Pure Abidings, which Pe Maung Tin calls the Divine States, see pages 340–75.

11. Thomas Cleary, trans., *The Flower Ornament Scripture*, 3 vols. (Boulder and London: Shambhala, 1984–1987).

12. For a translation and discussion see Fung Yu-lan, *A History of Chinese Philosophy*, vol. 2, trans. Derk Bodde (Princeton University Press, 1952–53), 339–59.

13. William H. Masters and Virginia E. Johnson, *Human Sexual Response* (Boston: Little, Brown and Company, 1966).

14. The literature on feminism and how it affects our view of the world is extensive. The classic work on a feminist approach to Buddhism is Rita M. Gross, *Buddhism after Patriarchy: A Feminist History, Analysis, and Reconstruction of Buddhism* (Albany: State University of New York Press, 1993).

15. Stuart Timmons, *The Trouble with Harry Hay: Founder of the Modern Gay Movement* (Boston: Alyson Publications, 1990).

16. Hay only speaks of gay men but his remarks would seem to apply, *mutatis mutandis*, across the spectrum of LGBTI persons.

17. Harry Hay, *Radically Gay: Gay Liberation in the Words of Its Founder*, ed. Will Roscoe (Boston: Beacon Press, 1996), 210. Italics and small capitals in original.

18. Ibid., 260.

19. Ibid. "Fairy" (sometimes spelled faerie) is a word sometimes used by gay men to emphasize their difference from "hetero" men and women.

20. Mitch Walker, quoted by Mark Thompson in "This Gay Tribe: A Brief History of Fairies," in *Gay Spirit: Myth and Meaning*, ed. Mark Thompson (New York: St Martin's, 1987), 272.

21. Hay, *Radically Gay*, 260 (see note 17).

22. A column ran for some time in *Tricycle: The Buddhist Review* in which readers were asked to share how they responded to the question "Are you Buddhist?": did they answer "yes" straightforwardly or did they prevaricate in some way? The assumption that the question is meaningful and is therefore capable of being answered straightforwardly was not challenged.

9

A METHODIST SUPPORTS HOMOSEXUAL MARRIAGE: A STUDY OF SCRIPTURE AND TRADITION

———————————— • ————————————

Tex Sample

———————

The United Methodist Church declares that, although homosexual persons are "of sacred worth," it does "not condone the practice of homosexuality" and "consider[s] this practice incompatible with Christian teaching."[1] This chapter challenges this position by defending the place of homosexual marriage in the church. The first part of the chapter examines scripture and its teaching to see what is taught there about the practice of homosexuality. Because scripture does not address homosexuality as such, the focus is on same-sex practices to see how these may be understood by the church today. The second part of the chapter provides an overview of marriage in the tradition of the church to determine what this teaching has to say about the question of homosexual marriage.

SCRIPTURE AND SAME-SEX PRACTICES

The term "homosexuality" as we understand it today appears nowhere in scripture. In fact, the word was not coined until the nineteenth century. Moreover, there is no evidence that scripture addresses the matter of sexual orientation as that character-istic is now understood. In an examination of homoeroticism in Mesopotamia Martti Nissinen urges caution when discussing "homoeroticism in the ancient Near East": his appraisal of the sources "demonstrate that same-sex erotic interaction was not unheard of, and that moral reservations could be expressed about it.... It is questionable, however, whether the modern concept of 'homosexuality' is appli-cable in this context."[2]

In scripture, little attention is given to same-sex practices. It is a minor concern and appears in only five passages. (I exclude two passages on same-sex rape that are not under consideration here. Rape of any kind is wrong.) Biblical scholars hotly contest all of these passages.

Purity

Leviticus 18:22 and 20:13 are two passages in the Hebrew scriptures that prohibit same-sex practices. These passages are part of the Holiness Code, found in Chapters 17–26 of Leviticus, and it is crucial to see these two passages in terms of two major concerns. The first is the concern of purity, which in the Holiness Code has to do with being unblemished. Impurity involves any defacement or mixture with any other material or specimen; for example, mixing two kinds of cloth or breeding animals of different kinds. Thus, defilement in these terms is a physical mixture of different ingredients or species. Concern for this kind of purity provides the cultural framework for the condemnation of same-sex activity between males. The reason is that one of these men must "lie the lyings of a woman." In this cultural framework, the "purity" of being a male has been compromised by assuming the role of the woman. In doing so, both males are impure by virtue of engaging in this defiling mixture of male and female practices.

In addition, Sarah Melcher suggests that the central concern of the Holiness Code is the land. Although the Holiness Code is a complex document with a great variety of interwoven "concepts, symbols, and signs," its overriding interest is in "the protection of land, of the system of patrilineal land tenure, purity of descent, the special status of the priests, and dwelling securely in the land."[3] Melcher argues that, while the complex Leviticus texts should not be reduced to one factor of influence alone, nevertheless "It seems that the rules of inappropriate sexual intercourse serve to protect pure patrilineal descent."[4]

Thus, purity and the keeping of the land are central to the Holiness Code and key to the prohibition of same-sex male activity. It is a far stretch to maintain that such a cultural framework and its subsequent prohibitions are authoritative for the church today. There is little question that a good deal of the Holiness Code, including its purity codes and certain drastic punishments not in the spirit of Christ, has been surpassed and transformed by the teaching of Jesus and the New Testament church. For example Leviticus 20:13 states that "if a man lies with a male as with a woman, both of them have committed an abomination; they shall be put to death." This requirement to impose the death penalty is not regarded as authoritative for the church in its deliberations today, as a great many of the Leviticus teachings are no longer morally compelling, especially those around purity and the patriarchal inheritance of land. To make a case against same-sex practices and certainly against homosexual marriage one must go beyond these texts.

Exploitation and Femininity

In the New Testament three passages cast same-sex practices in a negative light. In this section I address two of them—I Corinthians 6:9 and I Timothy 1:10—saving the third for the next section. I Corinthians 6:9 names two groups who will not inherit the Kingdom of God, the *malakoi* and *arsenokoitai*;[5] I Timothy 1:10 also uses the term *arsenokoitai*. The translation of these two Greek words is a matter of contention among New Testament scholars.

Arsenokoitai

The word *arsenokoitai* is translated in several ways. Some claim that it involves an active and superior man (the penetrator) and a passive and inferior one (the penetrated) in a sexual act. Others suggest that it is the use of a younger boy or man by an older man (pederasty). Yet others maintain that it is a reference to same-sex prostitution. Still other studies suggest that the sex acts referred to in these passages involve some kind of economic exploitation.

Dale Martin argues that "the etymology of a word is its history, not its meaning."[6] That is, we know what a word means on the basis of how it is used, how it functions. Therefore, "the only reliable way to define a word is to analyze its use in as many different contexts as possible."[7]

Hence Martin traces the history of the use of the word *arsenokoites* in Greco-Roman culture and in various translations of scripture. In Greco-Roman culture *arsenokoites* is used in two contexts: in (1) lists of vices related to economic injustice and exploitation and in (2) two texts in which one might reasonably argue its use to describe same-sex activity. Thus the word is variously used in the Greco-Roman world.[8]

In different translations of scripture the word has been translated in different ways, such as "thei that don leccherie with men," "abusers of them selves with the mankynde," "the liers vvith mankinde," "sodomites," "sexual perverts," "homosexuals," "homosexual offenders," and "homosexual perversion."

Between the end of the nineteenth and the middle of the twentieth century, therefore, the meaning of *arsenokoites* shifted from being the reference to an action that any man might well perform, regardless of orientation or disorientation, to refer to a "perversion," either an action or a propensity taken to be self-evidently abnormal and diseased. The shift in meaning thus reflected the invention of the category of "homosexuality as an abnormal orientation, an invention that occurred in the nineteenth century but gained popular currency only gradually in the twentieth."[9]

The modern translation has been broadened to include both men and women, whereas before it had correctly referred only to men. Martin states that these "interpretations were prompted not by criteria of historical criticism but by shifts in modern sexual ideology."[10] From this study of translations of the word *arsenokoites* Martin concludes that

> I freely admit that it could have been taken as a reference to homosexual sex. But given the scarcity of evidence and the several contexts just analyzed, in which *arsenokoites* appears to refer to some particular kind of economic exploitation, no one should be allowed to get away with claiming that "of course" the term refers to "men who have sex with other men."[11]

Although Martin believes that *arsenokoites* probably refers to the use of sex to exploit others and "perhaps but not necessarily, by homosexual sex," he contends that "the more important question" is why scholars have such certainty that "it refers to simple male-male sex in the face of evidence to the contrary." Martin suggests, "Perhaps ideology has been more important then philology."[12]

Malakos

The evidence from the ancient world on the use of the word *malakos* is abundant and clear. It referred to the softness of a garment, the savory and sumptuous quality of fine food, and the soft comfort of gentle winds and mild breezes. When used in the context of moral disapproval and condemnation *malakos* referred to sloth, degeneracy, corruption, and cowardice.[13] It also referred in the ancient world to the feminine. In the ancient texts, which were produced by men, the relationship between the feminine and *malakos* was clear: women are weak, fearful, vulnerable, and tender. They stay indoors and protect their soft skin and nature: their flesh is moister, more flaccid, and more porous than male flesh, which is why their bodies retain all that excess fluid that must be expelled every month. The female is quintessentially penetrable; her pores are looser than those of a man. One might even say that in the ancient male ideology women exist to be penetrated. It is their purpose (*telos*), and their "softness" or "porousness" is nature's way of inscribing on and within their bodies this reason for their existence.[14]

In this connection Martin points out that a man who allows himself to be penetrated is a *malakos*, but *malakos* does not itself mean a man who is penetrated. Penetration is, rather, a sign that he is *malakos*, which refers to "the entire complex of femininity."[15] The term has a host of meanings as applied to feminine men: those who (1) cannot do hard physical work and take life easy, (2) are lazy, (3) are cowards, (4) live in luxury and decadence, and (5) have too much sex, wine, and fine food, among other designations. Even heterosexual men can be *malakoi*. Martin's point is that *malakos* is very broad in its application and cannot be limited only to those who engage in same-sex activities.

Even though in the ancient world *malakos* meant effeminate, its usage cannot be reduced to any single act or role, such as penetration of a male by a male, male prostitution, or even a male with homoerotic desires for other males. This issue, moreover, is complicated by the fact that "effeminate" in the ancient world did not mean the same thing that it does in the modern world. For example, a man who loved women too much in the ancient world could be seen as effeminate, hardly its meaning today.[16]

What is basic to *malakos*, especially in the context of moral condemnation, is that it is feminine and involves "a rank misogyny" and a "devaluation of the feminine." Martin explains that "at issue here is the ancient horror of the feminine."[17] Furthermore, if we are to translate these terms in light of their usage in the ancient world, we must condemn the effeminate. But do we do this in terms of what the ancients understood effeminate to mean or the way we mean it today? Are we prepared to condemn effeminate men, whether they are gay or not? Are we also prepared to endorse this misogyny and devaluation of the feminine in its historical usage? These are unavoidable issues for those who draw moral guidance from passages in which *malakos* is used in vice lists.[18]

Paul and Greco-Roman Society

The most important biblical text debated by Christians is Romans 1:24–27. It states

> Therefore God gave them up in the lusts of their hearts to impurity, to the degrading of their bodies among themselves, because they exchanged the truth about God for a lie and worshiped and served the creature rather than the Creator, who is blessed forever! Amen. For this reason God gave them up to degrading passions. Their women exchanged natural intercourse for unnatural, and in the same way also the men, giving up natural intercourse with women, were consumed

with passion for one another. Men committed shameless acts with men and received in their own persons the due penalty for their error.

This passage deserves a more extended treatment than we can give it here, but several points need to be stated. First, this passage must be understood in terms of the rhetorical strategy Paul uses in Romans 1:18–3:20. In 1:18–32 he begins with a discussion of how God's wrath will be revealed within the Gentile world; his comments about same-sex practices occur in this section. But he soon turns his attention to others who "have no excuse, whoever you are" because "you are doing the very same things" (2:1). Then in the third chapter he turns to the Jews and the Law, especially. Thus in 1:18–32 he is "setting up" his hearers. That is, he begins with the sin of the Gentiles, but then moves to the sin of all and then to the sin of the Jews. He is making the point that all have fallen short—Gentile and Jew (i.e., everyone)—and therefore all need God's saving grace.

Second, an adequate reading of this text must take into account the huge gulf between how this text was understood in the ancient world and the context in which we address these issues in our own time. Victor Furnish describes four characteristics of the understanding of same-sex practices in the Greco-Roman world, which is quite different from our own.

1. A person who pursued same-sex intercourse was seen as "willfully overriding his or her own 'natural' desire for the opposite sex." No notion of homosexual orientation existed in the ancient world, so that same-sex lust is simply a more intense form of heterosexual desire. That is, same-sex desire is not a different sexual orientation in Paul, but rather the expression of an inordinate and excessive desire. It is the same desire that attracts a man to a woman, except that it has been allowed to get out of control. So, because of their idolatry God gives up the Gentiles to this excessive desire and same-sex practices.

2. Same-sex acts are lustful in themselves, and engaging in them is yielding to excessive and insatiable sexual craving. Examples of this are pederasty and a master's use of slaves. Such practices involve exploitation, willful and lustful. It is important to note, however, that given Paul's understanding as above, even consensual and hence nonexploitative same-sex practices are lustful and degraded.

3. Sexual coitus requires an active (the male) and a passive (the female) role. The problem with same-sex intercourse is that it confuses these roles and distorts the "natural" way things are supposed to be. In sex between two men, it places one of them in the female role, which is not only an "unnatural" posture but also a profoundly demeaning one for a man, though it is a "natural" place for a woman. In the case of same-sex practices by women, one of these women or both usurp the role of a man and hence defies and defiles the natural order.

4. The Greco-Roman world believed that same-sex intercourse rendered a man sterile. Subsequent fears of the extinction of human life were a real concern. Along with this was the view that same-sex practices were a temptation for everyone and hence dangerous to the sustainability of the race.[19]

Returning to the passage in Romans, the third issue is that of the cause and sequence in Paul's thought. Paul, in the first three chapters of Romans, sets up the sharp contrast between the righteousness of God manifest in Jesus Christ and the unrighteousness of all of humanity. Because of this unrighteousness, God's wrath is released on all ungodliness, as expressed in idolatry and a refusal to honor God and to give God gratitude for all God has done. Another manifestation of this ungodliness, though not the only one by any means, is that of homoerotic practice. Paul, reflecting the thought of many in the Greco-Roman world found same-sex practices intrinsically lustful and degrading and therefore in the same category with other "things that should not be done" (1:28–31). Homoerotic practices are one of a group of "obvious" evils he discusses that display the wrath of God against idolatry.[20]

This means, of course, that all of "the things that should not be done," including same-sex practices, result from God's wrath against this idolatrous rebellion. God's wrath "gave them up to degrading passions." As Ernst Kasemann states, "Paul paradoxically reverses the cause and consequence; moral perversion is the result of God's wrath, not the reason for it."[21]

This approach raises important questions for the church in its interpretation of scripture. Can Paul's teaching about homoeroticism be generalized to mean that it is always intrinsically depraved and degrading? Are same-sex practices, indeed, an obviously evil behavior? Moreover, are we to understand that all same-sex acts grow from God's wrath? Paul is clearly speaking to same-sex practices in the Greco-Roman world he knew.[22] For the sake of argument, let us say that the same-sex practices Paul knew without exception did grow from God's wrath over the idolatry of Gentiles. Can such a condition be generalized to all social, cultural, and historical settings surrounding same-sex practices from that time forth? Can Paul's understanding of causation in this setting be generalized to any same-sex couple, no matter the moral nature of their relationship? Is the causation of same-sex practices always and in all circumstances related to God's wrath without exception? If sexual acts occur between people who are, in fact, as profoundly committed exclusively to one another as are persons who regard themselves as married, do they still evoke God's anger? What about faithful Christian people who live in committed relationships with persons of the same sex and who genuinely love Christ and the church and bear witness to this throughout their lives? Are their expressions of love for each other and their mutual commitment to Christ and the church expressions of God's wrath? If one answers "yes" to all these questions, one goes considerably beyond what is in the text. Moreover, sexual orientation is not condemned. Can the expression of homosexual orientation be reduced to lustful, excessive, insatiable, heterosexual desire? Questions like these cannot be borne by the Romans passage.

Creation and Marriage

One last group of biblical texts require our attention: those involving the creation accounts in Genesis and references or possible allusions to these with respect to marriage in the New Testament (Genesis 1:26–28, 2:24–25, Mark 10, and Matthew 19). We look first at Genesis 1:26–28:

> 26 Then God said, "Let us make humankind [Hebrew, "adam"] in our image, according to our likeness; and let them have dominion over the fish of the sea, and over

the birds of the air, and over the cattle, and over all the wild animals of the earth, [Syriac: Hebrew, "and over all the earth"] and over every creeping thing that creeps upon the earth.

27 So God created humankind [Hebrew, "adam"] in his image, in the image of God he created them; [Hebrew, "him"] *male* and *female* he created them.

28 God blessed them, and God said to them, "Be fruitful and multiply, and fill the earth and subdue it; and have dominion over the fish of the sea and over the birds of the air and over every living thing that moves upon the earth.

This priestly account of creation is interpreted by some to mean that the creation of male and female is intrinsic to God's image and that the command that follows to "be fruitful and multiply," when considered together, suggest that heterosexuality is basic to God's created order. Such an interpretation is mistaken for a number of reasons.[23] First, humans share with many species the binary sexual character of male and female. If this male and female sexual characteristic was all that is intrinsic to the image of God humanity reflects, then one would have to understand, for example, gorillas and chimps, to be so made. Surely this is too close to Darwin for our fundamentalist brothers and sisters.

Second, the Hebrew word *adam* is a reference to all of humanity. The translation is rightly *humankind* in the New Revised Standard Version. Hence, it includes both male and female. The passage does not use more specific cultural or social terms like man and woman or any other specific, sociohistorically located, cultural or social references; it does not address ethical issues either. The focus here is expressly on "God's creation of the natural order and what is typical of the human condition."[24] Phyllis Bird observes that "the Hebrew terms for 'male' and 'female' are biological, not sociological terms."[25] These same terms are used later for the pairs of animals Noah is to bring on the ark (Gen 6:19; cf. 7:9). The concern here, writes Bird, is to have "a reproductive pair in order to assure the survival of the species.... It is the same language used in Genesis 1, and it expresses the same concern."[26]

Third, this passage explains why things are the way they are. It is not a prescription for what people ought to be and do, except when God makes certain commands. (It is notable, however, that the command to be fruitful and multiply does itself have limits in terms of its fulfillment; that is, to fill the earth.) But the wider import of this account is a priestly one: to explain why the species and kinds are different and separate and to establish the basis for ritual purity through an account of creation. Note, too, that the Sabbath is also set apart and made "holy" because in this account of creation God rested on this day.

We turn now to Genesis 2:24 where the text states, "Therefore a man leaves his father and his mother and clings to his wife, and they become one flesh." Some interpretations find in this statement the key characteristics of marriage. Moreover, I find that conservative scholars, increasingly pressed by the ambiguous character of the five biblical references and allusions to same-sex acts in the Bible, turn increasingly to this passage and another in Mark to bolster a failing argument.

First, it interesting here that we have a reversal from Genesis 1. This account is not about the creation of male and female (biological words) with its command for procreation, but of man and woman (social and cultural terms). As Genesis 1 is focused on the natural order, Genesis 2 is occupied with the social order. The plot is that of finding a suitable companion for the man (it is man-centered or patriarchal).

Further, this story accounts for why men and women have different roles and responsibilities in the social world.[27]

Second, note that those who would find here the pattern for normative marriage set up serious problems for themselves. First, there is nothing here that speaks of monogamy. It is neither named nor presumed, and although there is the reference to a wife, no mention is made of marriage in any other way. Why? Because the focus is on understanding why a man will leave his mother and father to become one flesh in sexual congress with a woman; hence, to account for the way things are.[28]

Third, the passage is decidedly patriarchal, as I suggested above. It takes for granted that male desire is universally directed to women, but the desires of women are not mentioned. Also, there seems to be no place here for singleness, or for people who may be incapable of sexual relationships or otherwise incapacitated, or those with same-sex desires.[29] It does not, interestingly enough, allow a place for the singleness of Jesus, who left mother and father to pursue his vocation as Christ, or the singleness of Paul (1 Corinthians 7:8; cf. 9:5) who presumably left his parents first to be "as to the law a Pharisee" (Philippians 3:5) and later to pursue his calling as apostle.

In sum, Genesis 1 and 2 do not provide a basis for heterosexual monogamous marriage. Those who see that basis in these texts bring that interpretation to them. Maleness and femaleness are not part of God's image in Genesis 1, and neither marriage nor monogamy is taught or commanded in Genesis 2.

Genesis 1 and 2 are often linked to Mark 10:6–9 and Matthew 19:4–6. Although same-sex practices are not mentioned in the Gospels, Jesus does speak of Genesis 1:27 about God's creation of "male and female" and also of Genesis of 2:24 regarding man and woman "becoming one flesh." The subject matter of this episode, however, is divorce, not same-sex practices. Moreover, in Mark 10 Jesus teaches that divorce is a violation of the created order and is disobedience to God's will. Matthew allows for the one exception of divorcing a wife who is unfaithful. Today the church, rightly or wrongly, does not regard these teachings as substantively authoritative, although Matthew and Mark report them from the mouth of our Lord himself. Further, Jesus does not speak of same-sex practices anywhere in the Gospels. Even his comment about Sodom mentions their failure to practice hospitality, not their engagement in "homosexuality" (Matthew 10:14–15).

Furthermore, as Walter Wink reports, "Polygamy...and concubinage (a woman living with a man to whom she is not married) were regularly practiced in the Old Testament."[30] In the New Testament bishops, deacons, and elders are to be married only once (I Timothy 3:2 and 12 and Titus 1:6), but neither polygamy nor concubinage "is ever condemned by the New Testament."[31] Wink observes that Jesus's quotation of Genesis 2:24 in Mark 10:6–8 does not challenge a marriage with more than one wife because this text was never understood by Israel in biblical times to exclude polygamy. In fact, polygamy continued to be practiced within Judaism several centuries after New Testament times.[32]

Summary

Let me summarize the ideas that are most important for Christians to remember about homosexuality and the biblical text. First, homosexuality, as contemporary society understands it, is not addressed anywhere in scripture. The concept of homosexual orientation as we now know it is not found in scripture, though there is awareness of homoeroticism. What scripture addresses are same-sex practices, and there are seven references or allusions to same-sex practices in scripture. Two have to do with same-sex rape, and the other five are all negative about same-sex activity. It is not condoned anywhere in the Bible.

Second, in the two Leviticus texts same-sex activity between two males is clearly prohibited and is punished by death. The cultural context of this teaching is one of purity based in practices of ritual cleanliness and separation that have been surpassed and transformed in the New Testament. Moreover, the misogynistic and patriarchal view of male defilement through assuming the role of a woman is no longer acceptable. Further, the notion of pure patrilineal descent that frames these prohibitions no longer has authoritative status. Finally, no one operating in the spirit of Christ can argue that the death penalty applies to these cases or arguably in any circumstance. In these terms neither of the Leviticus teachings is morally authoritative for the church today.

Third, the brief references to *malakoi* and *arsenokoitai* in I Corinthians and to *arsenokoitai* in I Timothy are ambiguous and unclear. They are no basis for an authoritative position of the church.

Fourth, Romans 1 cannot provide an adequate basis for a universal condemnation of homosexual practice. The causal sequence resulting in same-sex acts portrayed there cannot account for the full range of homosexual life and practice in all times and places, especially in its faithful and moral expressions.

Fifth, moving beyond those passages that refer or allude to same-sex practices, Genesis 1–3 does not explicitly address marriage, and these passages are clearly not concerned with monogamy. Moreover, Jesus's teachings in Mark 10 and Matthew 19 are directed to divorce and must not be applied as some implicit condemnation of homosexuality. To do so is to bring content to the text that is not there. Moreover, these teachings occurred in a context that accepted both polygamy and concubinage. To bring contemporary understandings of Christian marriage to these texts is a work of anachronistic imposition. It is a violation of the biblical text.[33]

HOMOSEXUAL MARRIAGE AND THE TRADITION OF THE CHURCH

Where does this leave us? A good case can be made that scripture does not provide an explicit and adequate basis for a theology of Christian marriage. In the Hebrew scriptures marriage is profoundly conditioned by patriarchy, polygamy, concubinage, and Levirate marriage. Moreover, the New Testament never condemns these practices and nowhere offers a description or teaching of marriage that is not influenced by these same conditions unless, as we have seen, one generalizes to the entire church the teaching that bishops, deacons, and elders are to have one wife. This is not to say that scripture cannot inform a Christian theology of marriage; it is only to say that one cannot be developed from the texts examined here, taken alone.

In a very real sense we should not be surprised that our contemporary questions and biblical answers do not always line up. Phyllis Bird speaks to the noncorrespondence of the biblical world and our own. The reason is "not solely the result of our more complex understanding of homosexuality. It is the result of the historico-cultural shaping of all our questions—and of all of the Bible's answers."[34] There is always "a disparity" between "the biblical world and our world." This is not, however, a defect but "a condition of all cross-cultural communication, and to some extent of all communication."[35] The reason is that communication "always requires an effort to move beyond the particularity of one's own experience to encounter another in her or his own particularity."[36] As we engage the Bible with new questions, we are both allowed and required to hear the text in new ways. This leads to new understandings of the ancient contexts and to new connections between the text and contemporary experience.[37]

One way to look at the tradition of the church is to see it as the attempt to connect biblical teaching to the cultural settings in which the church finds itself across time and space. This is particularly so with regard to marriage. Without a full understanding of Christian marriage displayed in scripture the church has continually struggled with this issue, and, as we shall see, has come up with a variety of ways of understanding it.

Furthermore, I believe that marriage is the basic way the church must address the issue of homosexuality. The main reason is that marriage is the richer tradition in Christian life and thought and also because I find modern notions of "sexuality" in America so very deeply flawed—not only because of rampant individualism but also because the commitments to expressivity are so often barren of the central importance of daily, loving practices in the formation of our desires and of marital life together. In addition, our notions of sexuality are so flawed because capitalist consumerism plays such an important role in their shaping, with its commodification of everything, especially our "choices." Finally, but by no means exhaustively these notions are distorted by the role played by television as the "pimp for the exceedingly profitable 'sexual revolution,'" as Wendell Berry has stated it so perceptively.[38]

I turn to the tradition of the church to make a "conservative" argument for homosexual marriage. Such an argument places "sexuality" in a different context than our modern one and provides for a greater range of life and thought. To be sure, Christian tradition has been stained by patriarchy and sexism. As we shall see, however, ongoing Christian tradition can challenge and correct this wicked and sinful influence in the life of the church.

We begin with St. Augustine, who is the first major theologian to deal comprehensively with marriage. His work in this regard has played an influential role in church teaching. Augustine addresses the question of marriage in terms of its ends or aims or goods.[39] For Augustine marriage is an office, a duty in which one serves the church and the Kingdom of God. This office serves three goods. First is that of *proles* or offspring, the procreative end, which is understood by Augustine as nurture: "Offspring means that a child is accepted in love, is nurtured in affection, is brought up in religion."[40]

This quote is eye opening in that for Augustine procreation is not simply defined as having children biologically. In fact, there is "an implicit distancing," as Dan Bell characterizes it, between the biological reproduction of children and the procreative end. For example, Augustine makes a distinction between "the blessing of nature" (related to the event of birth) and the marriage blessing. He writes, "Let spouses have their blessing, not because they beget children, but because they beget them honorably and lawfully and chastely and for society, and bring up their off-spring rightly, wholesomely, and with perseverance."[41] Further, in "*The Good of Marriage*," Augustine discusses three marriages he believes to be legitimate in which the couples do not have any biological children.[42] Although wedded couples are to be open to being parents, fulfilling the duty of procreation is not limited to having children of one's own, in a biological sense.

Augustine makes clear two important concepts related to the first aim of marriage. One is the utter centrality of procreation in marriage. The second is that procreation is most prominently concerned with raising children through Christian nurture—raising children for the Kingdom of God—and that biological reproduction is not necessary for legitimate marriage.

The second aim of the office of marriage is the fidelity (*fides*) in which couples learn faithfulness to each other and to God and become thereby witnesses to an "order of charity." Moreover, "fidelity means that one avoids all sexual activity apart from one's marriage"[43] and that "a wife has not authority over her body but her husband has it; as likewise a husband has not authority over his body but his wife has it."[44] Augustine is, of course, here quoting I Corinthians 7:4.

The third aim is that of sacrament, which for Augustine relates to the enduring and unbreakable character of marriage. He writes, "Sacrament means that the marriage is not severed nor the spouse abandoned, not even so that the abandoner or the abandoned may remarry for the sake of children. This is a kind of rule set for marriage, by which nature's fruitfulness is honored and vicious sexual vagrancy is restrained."[45]

These three aims of marriage became foundational for the church's understanding from the time of Augustine until the later Middle Ages, when one important change in the conception of marriage occurred. Although Augustine saw marriage as a grace basically serving to restrain lust, in the later Middle Ages a more positive view developed in which marriage contributes to a growth in holiness.[46]

In the Christian period of the Reformation, these three aims of marriage were basically accepted, but with modifications. The view of marriage as an official sacrament of the church is rejected, but it continues to be sacramental; that is, it can point to God, especially in the mutuality and companionship of couples as a reflection of the faithfulness of God. With this new conception also came a rejection of the immense body of canonical legislation that had developed to implement the church's increasing control of marriage.[47]

Further, the sacramental sense of marriage in the Reformation relates not so much to the indissolubility and restraint of sin, issues that are now taken up in the unitive or fidelity function, but rather to that of mutual support and companionship.

Finally, the procreative end loses its central importance, and other functions such as marriage as a mutual society take center stage. For example, the first edition of *The Book of Common Prayer* (1549) delineates the aims of marriage as procreation, remedy of sin, and mutual society. Further, the aim of mutual society came to be of primary importance to the English Puritans, for whom this aim of marriage corresponded to their rising sense of democracy and the diffusion of notions of romantic love.[48]

Among Methodists, John Wesley edited *The Book of Common Prayer* and sent it to the United States in 1784. He retained the section that lays out the three traditional ends of marriage as found in *The Book of Common Prayer*, but in a 1792 revision of the marriage liturgy U.S. Methodists dropped these three ends. Since that time marriage as loving companionship is central, though fidelity and the indissolubility of marriage are not absent. The procreative end is either seldom or never used.[49]

This is, of course, a brief overview of marriage and its aims or goods in the tradition of the church, but it is quite pertinent to my argument. The point is that marriage in the Christian tradition serves a number of ends: procreation, fidelity, sacramental, mutual support and companionship, mutual society, and loving companionship. Although Augustine laid the foundation for church tradition, the aims or goods of marriage have changed and varied across time. But what is striking here is that all of these ends can be met by homosexual marriages, even the procreative end when understood as Christian nurture and raising children for the Kingdom of God and not primarily as a function of nature. In any case, as indicated above, we do not disqualify couples for Christian marriage because they are not able to have biological children of their own. And the procreative function simply does not have the place in the church's life it once did, which is regrettable when it is understood as a function not limited only to a married couple but as one involving the entire church in the nurture of children for the Reign of God.

Furthermore, all of the teachings of scripture with regard to same-sex practices are profoundly intertwined with the patriarchy of the ancient world and the sinful oppression of women. This historical and cultural context also characterizes Christian marriage throughout the history of the church. But what makes the tradition of the goods of marriage so important is the way in which it can lead to a more profound understanding and practice in which in Christ there is neither male nor female, but all are one in Christ Jesus (Galatians 3:28). Although I do understand that the specific formulations of these goods often occurred in patriarchal and what we would call sexist frameworks today, nevertheless a critical analysis of these aims or goods offers new ways for women and men to be faithfully married. Moreover, as tied to sexism as heterosexism is, faithful critique of the former could bode well for a more welcoming stance of the church toward homosexuals.

CONCLUSION

The scripture never addresses either homosexuality, homosexual marriage, homosexual orientation, or same-sex marriage. In fact, in some cases we do not know exactly what practices are being condemned; for example, with the mention of *malakoi* and *arsenkoitai*. It seems that same-sex practices are the concern, but this kind of indefinite reference is no basis for an absolutist prohibition, especially in the face of the traditional goods of Christian marriage.

Leviticus 18 and 20 state in absolute terms the condemnation of homosexuality, and the latter chapter even imposes the death penalty for violators. But both of these passages are found in teachings focusing on impurity as blemish and as a mingling of species and materials, a view rejected by both Jesus and Paul and one the church no longer holds.[50] Moreover, the cultural contexts of patrilineal land descent and survival concerns over wasting male seed are clearly of another time and place. Further, it is a good question whether such teaching can ever be understood or applied apart from the misogyny and the demeaning roles accorded to women in these patriarchal forms of life. Therefore, these two Levitical texts cannot carry the absolute prohibition against same-sex practices.

The Romans passage is the most important of all of these passages. But the assumption that same-sex desire is an excessive and lustful overreaching of heterosexual desire limits the application of this passage. Likewise limiting is the causal sequence of the passage in which the inflamed passions of these Gentiles are deemed to be a result of God's wrath evoked by their idolatry.

It is clear that the church's absolute prohibition of homosexual practices is based on readings of the five texts we have reviewed, which cannot sustain such an absolute across all times and places and across the entire historic and cultural range of same-sex acts and orientations. Moreover, a reading of Genesis 1 and 2 and Mark 10 and Matthew 19 appear in a context of marriage as including polygamy and concubinage. To apply them directly to Christian marriage as we know it in the tradition of the church and to use them as an absolute prohibition of all same-sex practices and of Christian homosexual marriage are misuses of these texts.

On these grounds, I believe that homosexual marriage can be supported by the United Methodist Church, provided it meets the aims or goods of Christian marriage. Homosexual marriage is not in violation of scripture, nor does it violate the tradition of the church when understood in terms of the goods of Christian marriage.

NOTES

1. United Methodist Church, *The Book of Discipline of the United Methodist Church* (Nashville: Abingdon Press, 2004), paragraph 65.

2. Martti Nissinen, *Homoeroticism in the Biblical World: A Historical Perspective* (Minneapolis: Fortress Press, 1998), 36.

3. Susan F. Melcher, "The Holiness Code and Human Sexuality," in *Biblical Ethics & Homosexuality: Listening to Scripture*, ed. Robert L. Brawley (Louisville: Westminster John Knox Press, 1996), 98.

4. Ibid., 98.

5. Note that *malakos* and *arsenokoites* are the singular forms of these words and *malakoi* and *arsenokoitai* are the plural forms.

6. Dale B. Martin, "*Arsenokoites* and *Malakos*: Meanings and Consequences," in *Biblical Ethics & Homosexuality: Listening to Scripture*, 119.

7. Ibid.

8. Ibid.

9. Ibid.

10. Ibid.

11. Ibid., 123.

12. Ibid.

13. Ibid.

14. Ibid., 124–25.

15. Ibid., 125.

16. Ibid., 128.

17. Ibid., 127.

18. Ibid., 129.

19. Victor Furnish, "The Bible and Homosexuality: Reading the Texts in Context," in *Homosexuality in the Church: Both Sides of the Debate*, ed. Jeffrey S. Siker (Louisville, KY:

Westminster John Knox, 1994), 26–28. I am indebted to Furnish for his reading of my discussion of his points and for his helpful suggestions. For a "conservative" reading of Romans 1 and the other four references and allusions to same-sex practices see Richard Hays, *The Moral Vision of the New Testament: A Contemporary Introduction to New Testament Ethics* (San Francisco: HarperSanFrancisco, 1996), 379–406.

20. I am indebted to Victor Furnish for assistance in this paragraph. I am, of course, responsible for its final form.

21. Ernst Kasemann, *Commentary on Romans*, trans. Geofffey W. Bromiley (Grand Rapids, MI: Eerdmans, 1980), 47. I am indebted to Richard Hays for this Kasemann quote. See Hays, *The Moral Vision of the New Testament*, 385 (see note 19).

22. Furnish states that "it is apparent from both the wording and the content of Paul's remark in Romans that he shared the common Hellenistic-Jewish view of 'homosexuality.' There is nothing distinctively Pauline, or even Christian, about that remark." Furnish, "The Bible and Homosexuality: Reading the Texts in Context," 28 (see note 19).

23. I am indebted in this discussion of Genesis 1:26–28 to Furnish, "The Bible and Homosexuality: Reading the Texts in Context," , 21–22 (see note 19), and Phyllis Bird, "Genesis 1–3 as a Source for a Contemporary Theology of Sexuality," *Ex Auditu* 3 (1987): 31–44.

24. Victor Furnish, "The Bible and Homosexuality: Reading the Texts in Context," 21 (see note 19).

25. Bird, "Genesis 1–3 as a Source for a Contemporary Theology of Sexuality," 33–34 (see note 23).

26. Ibid.

27. Furnish, "The Bible and Homosexuality: Reading the Texts in Context," 22 (see note 19).

28. Ibid.

29. Ibid.

30. Walter Wink, "Homosexuality and the Bible," *The Other Journal.com: An Intersection of Theology and Culture*, 4 (2004), http://theotherjournal.com (accessed October 31, 2006)

31. Ibid.

32. It is interesting in this connection that some African delegates have made impassioned pleas against the practice of homosexuality at the General Conference of the United Methodist Church yet do not also protest against the practice of polygamy that is permitted under the rules that govern United Methodist Churches in Africa, an issue too controversial to handle I presume.

33. Let me be clear that it is not my intent here to disparage holy scripture. They are basic to the identity of the church and foundational to its life and work. My aim here is to attempt to read scripture as one in the church and to read it with as much care and exactness as I can.

34. Phyllis Bird, as quoted in "Memorandum II. The OT as a Resource for a Christian Approach to Homosexuality," A Report to the Homosexuality Study Committee of the United Methodist Church, 1.

35. Ibid.

36. Ibid.

37. Ibid.

38. Wendell Berry, *Sex, Economy, Freedom, and Community* (New York: Pantheon Books, 1992), 124. He states, "Television is the greatest disrespecter and exploiter of sexuality that the world has ever seen."

39. For the entirety of this discussion of the tradition of marriage in the church I am indebted to the work of Daniel M. Bell, Jr. His paper, "The Mysterious Difference of Times:

The Church Studies Homosexuality" (February 1997, unpublished paper) addresses the study of homosexuality by the United Methodist Church and is a fine treatment of biblical and traditional sources, as well as other dimensions of this issue.

40. St. Augustine, *Commentary on the Literal Meaning of Genesis* (bk. 9, chap. 7 n. 12). See also *The Good of Marriage* (chap. 24 n. 30), quoted in Theodore Mackin, *What Is Marriage?* (New York: Paulist Press, 1982), 129. Although other church thinkers like Origin, Gregory of Nyssa, and John Chrysostom viewed marriage as a result of the Fall and as a remedy for sin in keeping with Paul's dictum that it is better to marry than to burn with passion and although they saw propagation of the human species as important, it was Augustine who made procreation a matter of first importance. In his "On Adulterous Marriages," he states that "the propagation of children is the first and natural and legitimate end [causa] of marriage" (bk. 2, chap. 12). Quoted in Mackin, *What Is Marriage?*, 36 n. 11.

41. Augustine, *Holy Virginity*, chap. 3. But see chaps. 10 and 12. I am indebted to Daniel M. Bell, Jr., whose paper, "The Mysterious Difference of Times," 25 n. 81 (see note 39), pointed this out to me.

42. Augustine, *The Good of Marriage*, chaps. 3, 5, 15 (see note 40).

43. Augustine, *Commentary on the Literal Meaning of Genesis*, bk. 9 (see note 40).

44. Augustine, *On Original Sin*, bk. 2, chap. 39.

45. Augustine, *Commentary on the Literal Meaning of Genesis*, bk. 9 (see note 40).

46. See Bell, "The Mysterious Difference of Times," 23 (see note 39); and Mackin, *What Is Marriage?*, 6–8 (see note 40).

47. Bell points out, "For much of its early history, Christian marriages were a family service. Only occasionally were clergy present or did they participate in the service. Clerical supervision grew very slowly. It was not until the eleventh century that an official marriage ceremony appeared and only by the twelfth century was ecclesiastical jurisdiction widespread." Bell, "The Mysterious Difference of Times," 23 (see note 39).

48. Again, I am indebted to Dan Bell for his sum of these events. See Bell, "The Mysterious Difference of Times" (see note 39).

49. Ibid.

50. I do realize that Paul may have coined the word *arsenkoitai* from the Leviticus passages, and he certainly opposes the kind of same-sex practices he knew. However, his charge in Romans is not one of impurity as displayed in the Holiness Code but of being "unnatural" and this as the result of God's wrath against idolatry in which God gives them up "to degrading passions" (Romans, 1:26–27).

10

A Christian Apologetic for Same-Sex Marriage

Mel White

Let's face it. There is no "Christian apologetic for same-sex marriage," at least no Bible-based apologetic that a fundamentalist Christian would find convincing. There are days I long to join my fundamentalist friends in their certainty that "if the Bible says it, I believe it and that settles it." But I just can't accept the fundamentalist bias that those sixty-six books have been passed down to us over the centuries without error or alteration or that they must be read literally to be understood.

However, if I could believe the inerrancy premise that is so basic to fundamentalism, I would at least have to admit that the Bible is silent on the subject of same-sex marriage and that Jesus didn't say one word for or against it. That reality may not help persuade a fundamentalist to join me in my quest for justice, mercy, and truth on an issue that is wasting lives, destroying families, and dividing churches and nations alike, but I have to admit that the Bible's wonderful silence encourages me to accept what my heart makes known to me.

There is not one word in the Old or New Testaments that comments on the subject of homosexuality, either positively or negatively. Biblical authors knew nothing of sexual orientation as we understand it today and therefore had no way to condemn or support homosexuals in our quest for marriage equality. In addition, the six verses ("clobber passages") cited by fundamentalists to condemn homosexuality and homosexuals are misused so egregiously (without consideration of historic, linguistic, or cultural context) that no one who takes the Bible seriously (instead of literally) will be convinced that the biblical authors say anything about homosexuality, let alone condemn gay or lesbian people or our loving relationships.

More than five hundred years ago, Thomas á Kempis began his *Of the Imitation of Christ* with these words:

"He that followeth Me shall not walk in darkness," saith the Lord. These are the words of Christ, by which we are reminded that we must copy His life and conduct, if we wish to be truly enlightened and to be delivered from blindness of heart. To meditate on the life of Jesus should therefore be our chief study.[1]

In the spirit of Thomas á Kempis's classic devotional, the apologetic for same-sex marriage that follows is constructed around a series of questions that I would ask Jesus about homosexuality and same-sex marriage. I confess at the outset that I begin with a bias. I am determined to justify what I already know in my heart to be true. I believe that Jesus would support same-sex marriage, and I also believe that he would have been delighted to preside at my wedding to Gary Nixon, my same-sex partner of almost twenty-five years (after insisting that he give us at least a few sessions of premarital counseling, of course).

QUESTION 1

In making His decision about same-sex marriage, would Jesus ignore my personal experience and the experience of millions of lesbian, gay, bisexual, and transgender (LGBT) people whose experiences are so like my own?

I begin with a brief summary of my own experience. I spent roughly thirty-five years believing that my homosexual thoughts (and, if lucky, an occasional furtive encounter with another closeted gay outcast) were both "sick" and "sinful." From earliest adolescence I was tormented daily by longings that I could not understand, let alone accept. Walled in by silence, pursued by guilt, trembling with fear, I lived my lonely life cut off from my family and friends by ancient superstition and fundamentalist Christian ignorance and biblical misuse. Looking back, however, I realize I was never alone, that Jesus was with me every step of the way. But in this chapter, as I review the lessons I have learned during those thirty-five years in the wilderness, I realize that they are jumbled lessons, not logically ordered or listed by priority, but presented just as I experienced them.

I never dreamed that one day I would even consider same-sex marriage as a possibility. I couldn't even hope for a loving, committed relationship with another gay man. Instead, I married a beautiful woman, had two amazing children, established myself as a heterosexual of worth, and did everything society expected of me, including wasting almost thirty years and at least one hundred thousand dollars on Christian counselors (now called ex-gay therapists) who said that I was a victim of "a sin that can and must be forgiven" and "a sickness that can and must be cured."

After endless conversion therapies, electric shock treatments, and exorcism, I just gave up. There was no blinding light, no moment of truth, and no sudden revelation that God loved me as I am. I just fell back into the arms of grace. I was a gay man who after all that counseling continued to be fearful, wounded, guilty, sad, angry, and confused. After decades of desperation, I sliced my wrists (not very convincingly I might add) and gave up trying to give back to God the gift God had given me.

About that time I had my first counseling session with Dr. Phyllis Hart, the umpteenth counselor I had put to the test with my never-ending story. She heard the first few halting words of my confession that "I liked men" before interrupting me with these words: "You're gay, right?"

I didn't know that *being* gay was an option. I thought "gay" was something you "got over," rebuked, and condemned. I had no idea that "gay" was something so basic to my humanity that it could never be, should never be changed. I didn't know what I know now: that trying to fight my sexual orientation, let alone convert it, was the real sin. I had no idea that refusing to accept my same-sex longings as natural, right, and beautiful was the real sickness, but when she asked if I was gay I nodded a hesitant yes while blowing my nose into another Kleenex tissue, feeling hopeless one more time.

"Then go find a man you can love," she said, "and quit fighting it."

That counselor knew I was married with children. She knew that I was a kind of celebrity in the evangelical world with best-selling books and prize-winning films (all produced, in part, I might add, in my frantic attempts to outrun my "temptations" and to prove to God that I really was a good guy in spite of my need for sexual intimacy with a man).

"How can you say that," I responded, as unable to accept her advice as I was unable to accept the counsel of my ex-gay friends.

"Because, Mel," she said quietly, "you're a gay man and you need to take steps to accept yourself as God created you."

I sat there in dumb silence feeling like the children of C. S. Lewis who emerged from their closet into Narnia, a world that both terrified and delighted them. But too desperate to look back, to start over, to try again to "conquer" my sexuality, I took her advice to heart.

Trembling, and feeling oh so guilty, I walked into my first gay bar in Chicago, met a young lawyer there whose smile took my breath away and whose first kiss set my heart on fire. I tore down the walls that I had built around my sexuality and opened my arms to his embrace.

I was almost forty years old. Be warned. Infatuation looks silly on a middle-aged man. Retarded adolescence is an experience one should avoid by being adolescent, having crushes, dating, and learning about relationships during the appropriate years of youth and young adulthood. I had missed my chance at being young and had postponed too many maturation tasks to save that relationship with Thomas. I bungled one more relationship with David before meeting Gary Nixon, a baritone in the Canterbury Choir of All Saints Episcopal Church in Pasadena, California.

Once again I fell hopelessly in love, and thanks to Gary's endless patience and his amazing ability to forgive and forget, our love has lasted almost a quarter century. And it is with that reality that I begin this "Christian Apologetic for Same-Sex Marriage." I confess that I ground this apologetic in personal experience. That's why I began with the story I know best, my own story, the story of a gay Christian who struggled for decades to overcome his sexuality and found peace only when he gave up that struggle, quit trying to give back the gift that God had given him, and let himself love and be loved as God intended. Now he struggles to see that love recognized officially through same-sex marriage by his church and by his government alike.

In the Gospel of John (9:1–41) Jesus heals a blind man on the Sabbath and in the process of breaking the fourth commandment infuriates the Pharisees. When those self-appointed keepers of the law condemned the man born blind for giving Jesus the credit for his healing, the blind man answered, "Whether he is a sinner or not, I do not know. What I know is this. I was born blind and now I can see."[2]

When someone condemns Dr. Phyllis Hart for suggesting that I fall in love with a man and end this silly struggle, I respond in the spirit of the blind man: "Whether she is a sinner or not, I do not know. What I know is this. When I finally followed her advice and accepted my sexual orientation as a gift from God, the struggle ended and a new life began. For thirty-five years I was blind and now I can see."

Simply put, the work that Jesus did in my life to overcome decades of biblical abuse is the basis of everything that follows and the heart of my "Christian apologetic for same-sex marriage." I refuse to believe that a few Bible verses trump the truth that dawned in my heart when I allowed myself to love and be loved as God intended. I am constantly surprised by the religious people who ignore my experience and the experience of millions of other LGBT people like me and at the same time misuse a handful of biblical proof texts to support their ignorance.

I am dumbfounded every time I hear another story of a Christian parent who has discarded a gay or lesbian child on the basis of a few misused biblical texts. How can they let those verses in Leviticus or Romans (verses they've never even studied seriously) outweigh what their heart tells them about their own children as they watch them grow into adolescence and adulthood?

QUESTION 2

In making His decision about same-sex marriage, would Jesus tolerate the half-truths, hyperbole, and lies told about homosexuality and homosexuals by religious leaders, Catholic and Protestant alike?

Church leaders have not been willing to simply quote those six biblical passages or be content to call homosexuality a "sickness" and a "sin." They have embellished the Greek and Hebrew texts with false and inflammatory rhetoric that leads to suffering and even death. For example, the Roman Catholic Church (with an estimated billion adherents worldwide) calls my love for Gary "intrinsically evil," "objectively disordered," and "deplorably dangerous to children, the family and the nations."

Most of the conservative, fundamentalist, evangelical, charismatic denominations agree with the Southern Baptist Convention (with an estimated twenty-five million members) that "even the desire to engage in a homosexual relationship is always sinful, impure, degrading, shameful, unnatural, indecent and perverted."

Even the more liberal mainline Protestant denominations (Methodist, Presbyterian, and Lutheran) consider the love that Gary and I share as "incompatible with Christian teaching," and they refuse to recognize LGBT people's loving, committed, same-sex relationships with the rites of marriage or to recognize our call to ministry with the rites of ordination.

And the media extremists (Pat Robertson, James Dobson, Jerry Falwell, D. James Kennedy, and the others), who have millions in their media congregations, go even further in caricaturing and condemning LGBT people. Here is just one paragraph illustrating the half-truths, hyperbole, and lies basic to fundamentalist propaganda from a fundraising letter sent by James Dobson to millions of people in his *Focus on the Family* radio audience.

> For more than forty years, the homosexual activist movement has sought to implement a master plan that has had as its centerpiece the utter destruction of the family…. Those goals include universal acceptance of the gay lifestyle, discrediting of Scriptures that condemn homosexuality, muzzling of the clergy and Christian media, granting of special privileges and rights in the law, overturning laws prohibiting pedophilia, indoctrinating children and future generations through public education, and securing all the legal benefits of marriage for any two or more people who claim to have homosexual tendencies…. They don't just want marriage. They want to destroy marriage and the family as we know it…. Barring a miracle, the family as it has been know for more than five millennia will crumble, presaging the fall of Western civilization itself.[3]

QUESTION 3

In making His decision about same-sex marriage, would Jesus condemn the religious leaders who are leading political campaigns to deny us our civil rights?

What are the effects of these false and inflammatory messages described above? At the outset, they are unjust and designed to deny an entire population the rights and protections guaranteed us by the U.S. Constitution. What's Christian about that? During our almost twenty-five years together, Gary and I have cared for each other in sickness and in health, in rich and in poor, in good times and in bad.

Together, we've loved my two children and grandchildren, bought and renovated homes in three different states, voted, paid taxes, obeyed the laws, been faithful members of a local church in every town we've lived in, started and maintained a national organization seeking justice for sexual and gender minorities, and generally done our best to be good citizens of this nation. And yet, we are denied the more than one thousand rights and protections that go automatically with heterosexual marriage. Here is just a small sample of those rights:[4]

- Automatic inheritance
- Assumption of spouse's pension
- Bereavement leave
- Burial determination
- Child custody
- Divorce protections
- Domestic violence protection
- Exemption from property tax on partner's death
- Immigration rights for foreign spouse
- Insurance discounts
- Joint adoption and foster care
- Joint bankruptcy
- Joint parenting (insurance coverage, school records)
- Medical decision making on behalf of the partner
- Various property rights

- Reduced-rate memberships
- Sick leave to care for partner
- Social Security survivor benefits
- Tax breaks
- Visitation of partner's children
- Visitation of partner in hospital or prison
- Wrongful death benefits

And it's getting worse. Fundamentalist Christians will not be satisfied with denying us the rights of same-sex marriage. They will not be content until we have no rights at all. For example, the Virginia State Legislature recently passed and the governor signed into law an initiative that was launched by fundamentalist Christians that denies gay and lesbian couples in the state the right to have any agreements, contracts, or even powers of attorney that might protect the few rights we have.[5] Without even these basic protections, gay and lesbian Virginians with businesses are leaving the state.

And consider the intensity of the war that fundamentalist Christians are waging against us. Jerry Falwell, James Dobson, and Pat Robertson have all promised their followers that they will give the next years of their lives full time to the cause of passing the Federal Marriage Amendment. By superimposing their fundamentalist values on the U.S. Constitution they will make second-class citizens of all lesbian and gay Americans and threaten to undo all the advances we have made toward equality and full inclusion. These extremists will not be satisfied until all our rights are denied and we are driven back into our closets or worse.

QUESTION 4

In making His decision about same-sex marriage, would Jesus condemn the physical, emotional, and spiritual violence that flows out of religion-based, antigay rhetoric?

The results of this "Christian campaign" against same-sex marriage cannot be measured simply by the rights and protections we are denied. Since the publication of my autobiography, *Stranger at the Gate: To be Gay and Christian in America*,[6] I have received tens of thousands of letters (no exaggeration) from LGBT Christians, their families, and friends who are victims of this "Christian" campaign against homosexuality and homosexuals.

A seventeen-year-old boy began his five-page, hand-written letter with these words: "I am so scared and so confused. I don't know what to do or who to believe anymore. I sometimes I wish that I wasn't gay at all. Life would be so much easier then. I wish that I could just give up on God and religion but I can't. I live to please God. I've run out of answers and the next step I take will be a gigantic (fearful) leap. Sometimes I wish that I could just die or be castrated. Then this nightmare would end."[7]

Almost daily, we receive letters, e-mails, or phone calls like this one. And people ask me why gay teenagers are seven times more likely to commit or attempt suicide than their heterosexual peers. It has become painfully obvious that this kind of suffering flows directly out of the antihomosexual teachings and actions of our churches, Catholic and Protestant alike. Here's another tragic example:

> It is with a great sense of anger, frustration, and sadness that I write to let you know of a death in our Christian family…. Cindy received word earlier this week that her twenty-eight-year-old nephew, Mark, hung himself. He was a gay man. He accepted his sexuality until he became a Christian a few months ago. Understanding from the Bible and the Church that he could not be both a Christian and a gay man, Mark's suicide note addressed to God read, "I don't know how else to fix this."[8]

For the past five years volunteers from Soulforce—an organization committed to freedom for lesbian, gay, bisexual, and transgender people from religious and political oppression through the practice of nonviolent resistance—have monitored this religion-based campaign against same-sex marriage. We have collected a mountain of evidence that antigay Christian rhetoric is the primary source of the fear and loathing of homosexuals in this country. Is there any way for followers of Jesus to justify false and inflammatory rhetoric against their enemies that leads to physical and spiritual abuse and even murder?

Fundamentalist Christians who are currently leading this war against same-sex marriage refuse to believe that they are in any way responsible for the intolerance and discrimination that flow out of their antigay rhetoric. The televangelists, preachers, and priests who have launched this campaign to "save marriage and the family" by denying lesbian and gay couples the rights and protections of marriage repudiate the evidence that their condemnation of our loving relationships leads to suffering and even death.

Reread James Dobson's ugly quote above and then hear his response when we accuse him of being a primary source of false and inflammatory rhetoric against God's LGBT people. "In twenty-seven years I have never said anything hateful about homosexuals on our broadcasts, and I do not condone violence or disrespect for anyone."[9] Now read the jail confession below and see how the words of Matthew Williams duplicate exactly the antihomosexual rhetoric of Dobson, Robertson, Falwell, and the others.

On September 22, 1999, in the Shasta County, California, jail, Matthew Williams told his mother why he and his brother Tyler murdered Gary Matson and Winfield Mowder, a gay couple living in Happy Valley, California. "I had to obey God's law rather than man's law," Williams said. "I didn't want to do this. I felt I was supposed to…. I followed a higher law…. I see a lot of parallels between this and a lot of other incidents in the Old Testament…. They threw our Savior in jail…. Our forefathers have been in prison a lot. Prophets…Christ…. My brother and I are incarcerated for our work in cleansing a sick society. I just plan to defend myself from the Scriptures."[10]

QUESTION 5

In making His decision about same-sex marriage, would Jesus support the laws that demean and dehumanize God's gay children?

The Massachusetts Supreme Court rejected an attempt by the Massachusetts State Legislature to grant same-sex couples a civil union in place of marriage on two grounds: first, because the law was unjust and denied gays and lesbians the rights and protections guaranteed them by the State Constitution. But second, and more important, the Court condemned the law because it demeaned and dehumanized gay and lesbian people.

The Court declared the following: "For no rational reason, the marriage laws of the Commonwealth discriminate against a defined class; no amount of tinkering with language will eradicate that stain. The bill would have the effect of maintaining and fostering a stigma of exclusion that the Constitution prohibits."[11]

In June 2005, Canada voted to allow same-sex marriage after the Ontario Court of Appeals declared prohibitions against homosexual marriage unconstitutional.[12] And at the heart of their declaration was the same truth stated by the Massachusetts Supreme Court: "The restriction against same-sex marriage is an offense to the dignity of lesbians and gays."

"Stain," "stigma," and "offense to the dignity" are legal words and phrases, but they have terrible personal consequences in the lives of my sisters and brothers. Even if we defeat the various local, state, and national initiatives against same-sex marriage, the antihomosexual rhetoric (heard on the radio, seen on TV and billboards, and read in flyers, brochures, and newspaper ads) leads to more suffering for LGBT people.

When church and state both demean and dehumanize our relationships, when they refuse to recognize same-sex couples as worthy of the rites and rights of marriage, they make outcasts of every LGBT citizen in this country, and almost immediately these religion-made outcasts become the victims of psychological, physical, and spiritual abuse. "Speech has power," said the Jewish theologian Abraham Heschel. "Words do not fade. What starts as a sound ends in a deed."[13]

QUESTION 6

In making His decision about same-sex marriage, would Jesus ignore the latest scientific, psychological, psychiatric, and medical evidence that homosexuality is not a sickness and therefore does not need treatment?

Those Christians who insist that homosexuality is a sickness that can be cured and a sin that must be forgiven are supported in this heresy by the two primary myths perpetuated by the ex-gay movement: "reparative therapy" and "transformational ministries."

"Reparative therapists" believe that various psychotherapeutic techniques can eliminate or minimize a lesbian or gay person's need for same-sex intimacy and even help the homosexual person enter into a heterosexual marriage.

"Transformational ministries" are based on the notion that "freedom from homosexuality is possible through repentance and faith in Jesus Christ as Savior and Lord."[14] Most transformational ministries do not promise a total reorientation from homosexual to heterosexual, but all believe that various spiritual exercises or disciplines can be introduced into a gay or lesbian life that will eventually, over a long, slow process, eliminate the desire for same-gender contact or minimize those desires to the extent that the gay or lesbian person can be celibate or even enter into heterosexual marriage.

Concerned by "the recent upsurge in aggressive promotion" of these two "solutions" to the "problem of homosexuality"[15] (primarily by fundamentalist Christian and Roman Catholic leaders in the press, in conferences targeting educators, and in television and newspaper ads), organizations representing four hundred and seventy-seven thousand professional American counselors developed and endorsed a document titled "Just the Facts about Homosexual Orientation and Youth."[16] This concise, heavily footnoted, twelve-page document summarizes decades of psychological research in these fifteen words: "Homosexuality is not a mental disorder and thus there is no need for a 'cure.'"[17] The document also includes statements made by the endorsing organizations. Here is a brief summary of those statements:

The American Academy of Pediatrics: "Therapy directed specifically at changing sexual orientation is contraindicated, since it can provoke guilt and anxiety while having little or no potential for achieving changes in orientation."[18]

The American Counseling Association: This organization "opposes portrayals of lesbian, gay, and bisexual youth and adults as mentally ill due to their sexual orientation…and opposes the promotion of 'reparative therapy' as a 'cure' or individuals who are homosexual."[19]

The American Psychiatric Association: "The potential risks of 'reparative therapy' are great, including depression, anxiety and self-destructive behavior, since therapist alignment with societal prejudices against homosexuality may reinforce self-hatred already experienced by the patient."[20]

The American Psychological Association: This organization "opposes portrayals of lesbian, gay, and bisexual youth and adults as mentally ill due to their sexual orientation and supports the dissemination of accurate information about sexual orientation, and mental health, and appropriate interventions in order to counteract bias that is based in ignorance or unfounded beliefs about sexual orientation."[21]

The National Association of Social Workers: "Sexual orientation conversion therapies assume that homosexual orientation is both pathological and freely chosen. No data demonstrate that reparative or conversion therapies are effective, and in fact they may be harmful…. NASW discourages social workers from providing treatments designed to change sexual orientation or from referring practitioners or programs that claim to do so."[22]

"Just the Facts about Homosexual Orientation and Youth" concludes with these significant words: "As these statements make clear, health and mental health professional organizations do not support efforts to change young people's sexual orientation through 'reparative therapy' and have raised serious concerns about its potential to do harm."[23]

QUESTION 7

In making His decision about same-sex marriage, would Jesus consider the stories of same-sex relationships in the Jewish and Christian testaments?

In her book, *Our Tribe*, the Reverend Dr. Nancy Wilson, now Moderator of the Metropolitan Community Church, suggests another fascinating idea to explore in any Christian apologetic for same-sex marriage.[24] She demonstrates how various stories in the Hebrew and Greek Testaments may be read as stories of same-sex relationships. Her work supports an understanding of how, over the centuries, redactors (those who edit or revise writings in preparation for their publication) have shown heterosexual prejudice in rewriting these stories to make them acceptable to their own culture. For example, Dr. Wilson sees in the story of David's relationship with Jonathan a same-sex love story.[25] At the very least it is the account of Jonathan's unrequited same-sex attraction to David.[26] Consider the evidence in the words of I and II Samuel:

> Jonathan, Saul's son, delighted much in David (I Samuel 19:2)...the soul of Jonathan was knit with the soul of David, and Jonathan loved him as his own soul (I Samuel 18:1).... Then said Jonathan unto David 'Whatsoever thy soul desires, I will even do it for thee' (I Samuel 20:4).... And Jonathan caused David to swear again, because he loved him, for he loved him as he loved his own soul (I Samuel 20:17).

The angry words of Saul to his son Jonathan sound so much like a modern father who has discovered that his son is "queer" and badly needs to attend a local chapter of PFLAG (Parents, Family, Friends of Lesbians and Gays). "Thou son of the perverse rebellious woman," Saul screams at Jonathan, "do not I know that thou hast chosen [David] the son of Jesse to thine own confusion, and unto the confusion of they mother's nakedness. For as long as the son of Jesse liveth upon the ground, thou shalt not be established, nor thy kingdom. Send and fetch him unto me, for he shall surely die" (I Samuel 20:30–31).

In one more attempt to save David's life again at the risk of losing his own, Jonathan and a servant boy rush into the fields to find David to warn him that once again Saul was determined to kill him. That reunion of Jonathan with his friend David demonstrates the intensity of their relationship.

> As soon as the lad was gone, David arose out of a place toward the South, and fell on his face to the ground, and bowed himself three times: and they kissed one another, and wept one with another until David exceeded.... And Jonathan said, "The Lord be between me and thee, and between my seed and thy seed for ever" (I Samuel 20:41).

The commentaries I consulted agreed that the meaning of the Hebrew word translated as "exceeded" in the King James Version (by homophobes who hated their patron for his homosexual dalliances) is an unknown Hebrew word. Two modern translations suggest that it indicates that they wept until David's grief exceeded the grief of his friend. And Jonathan's comment on the vow they took that day is translated by modern scholars as "And as regard the oath that both of us have sworn in the name of Yahweh, may Yahweh be witness between you and me, between your descendants and mine for ever" (I Samuel 20.42). This seems very much like the nearest Jonathan could come to an impromptu same-sex marriage ceremony.

When Jonathan was killed in battle, David says clearly that Jonathan's love was different from the love of a brother or a close friend. In David's words I hear a heterosexual man mourning the loss of a gay friend whose love he could not return in kind: "I am distressed for thee, my brother Jonathan: very pleasant hast thou been unto me: thy love to me was wonderful, passing the love of women " (II Samuel 1: 26).

The loving and deeply committed friendship that Ruth showed her mother-in-law Naomi, after her son's death, has become another biblical example of an exemplary same-sex friendship. That Naomi asks Ruth to marry Boaz does not in any way detract from their lifelong commitment. Marriage to Boaz was simply a means of survival for the two women. In fact, when Ruth offered herself to Boaz at the suggestion of Naomi, Boaz responds, "May you be blessed by the Lord my daughter; this last instance of your loyalty [to Naomi] is better than the first; you have not gone after young men, whether poor or rich" (Ruth 3:10).

The vow Ruth makes to Naomi demonstrates a rare bonding of these two women. Whether it has a sexual element or not, it has become one of the most-quoted marriage vows of all time, within both heterosexual and homosexual weddings alike, and there is no reason for lesbian couples not to claim the story as their own.

> Entreat me not to leave thee, or to return from following after thee:
> For whither thou goest, I will go; and where thou lodgest, I will lodge:
> Thy people shall be my people, and thy God, my God.
> Where thou diest, will I die, and there will I be buried:
> The Lord do so to me, and more also, if ought but death part thee and me.
> (Ruth 1:16–17)

My favorite example of a same-sex love story in the Christian Testament is Luke's account of the Roman centurion who "had a servant who was dear to him, who was sick and ready to die" (Luke 7:2–10). There is so much going on beneath the surface of this story. The Greek word normally used for "servant" is qualified by the phrase "who was dear to him" (KJV) or "whom he valued highly" (New RSV) or "a favorite of his" (Jerusalem Bible) or "who was held in honor and highly valued" (Amplified NT).

Luke, the beloved physician, seems to be sending a signal about the relationship between the Centurion and his "servant" in a phrase that would be understood immediately by homosexual readers and yet missed entirely by those who might be turned off by the story if they even suspected a same-sex relationship is involved.

The historical record is clear. From John Boswell's much praised and equally damned *Same-Sex Unions in Premodern Europe*, especially the chapter "The History of Same-Sex Unions in Medieval Europe," we learn, "The Roman custom of forming a union with another male by the legal expedient of declaring him a 'brother' appears to have persisted into the early Middle Ages."[27] Same-sex couples, though not tolerated by the Pharisees, were common to the Roman Empire that this Centurion served. Centurions with gay lovers would be as likely to include that "highly valued" person in his entourage as a heterosexual Centurion would be to invite his wife to join him in the city or area of his command.

The encounter between Jesus and this closeted gay Centurion is also fascinating in what is suggested by their dialogue. First, the Centurion sends Jewish elders to ask Jesus to heal his beloved servant. Jesus agrees and on his way to the Centurion's home he encounters friends of the Centurion, who bring him this message from the Roman ruler: "I am not worthy for you to enter my home, but say in a word and my servant shall be healed" (Luke 7: 6b, 7b). Jesus is amazed by the man's faith and performs a long-distance healing of the Centurion's servant.

Although the central message of this encounter is the faith the Centurion had in Jesus's authority over sickness, there is also an underlying theme that closeted gay and lesbian couples recognize immediately. Think of the film *Bird Cage*. Before "straight" visitors could come to dinner, suggestive statues were placed in storage. Paintings and other sexually charged knickknacks were hidden away. Even photos that revealed their loving relationship were locked up or turned toward the wall.

I believe the Centurion was a man of great faith, but I think he was also playing it safe, not knowing how Jesus might respond to his same-sex relationship with a beloved servant. Of course knowing the story of the special relationship of Jesus with his disciple John might have helped ease the Centurion's fears.

QUESTION 8

In making His decision about same-sex marriage, would Jesus consider His own experience with John, "the disciple He loved"?

There are those who doubt that Jesus loved John more than he loved the other disciples because that intimate history is told only in John's own Gospel. However, John's writings are firmly within the canon and have survived the test of time, even with their five references to the author as "the disciple Jesus loved."

The first time we read the phrase "the disciple Jesus loved" is that amazing moment (especially for gay men) during the Last Supper when one disciple is lying against Jesus's chest during his final sermon before his crucifixion: "Now there was leaning on Jesus' bosom one of his disciples, whom Jesus loved" (John 13:23). Most modern translations have gutted that moment (at least for gay men) by describing John as the disciple "reclining nearby."

The second time the phrase is used is during the crucifixion: "When Jesus saw his mother and the disciple standing by whom he loved, he said unto his mother 'Woman behold thy son!'"(John 19:26).

There are three Greek words used to describe different ways of loving: *philia* (the love of friends), *eros* (sexual love), and *agape* (the love God feels toward humankind that we are asked to emulate). The Greek word *eros* is not used in any of the five references to John as the disciple Jesus loved. Therefore, one might assume that there was no erotic or sexual component in John's relationship with Jesus.

According to John Boswell, however, the Greek word for erotic love "although among the most common subjects of Greek literature" does not appear in any form in the Christian Testament, whereas *agapan* (from *agape*, God's love) appears 136 times and is used to express a variety of ordinary emotions and relationships.[28] Therefore the Greek words John uses do not help define what happened between Jesus and "the disciple he loved."

The third time John is described as "the disciple Jesus loved" is just after Mary Magdalene discovers that the stone has been rolled away from the tomb: "Immediately she ran to Simon Peter and to the other disciple whom Jesus loved and said unto them, 'They have taken away the Lord'" (John 20:1–2). In this third reference the author uses a conjugation of *phileo* to describe their relationship as special friends.

There are just two more uses of the phrase "the disciple Jesus loved" in the entire Christian Testament. After Jesus's resurrection, the disciples are fishing. A man orders them to cast their net on the other side of the boat. At that moment, "The disciple whom Jesus loved said to Peter, 'It is the Lord!'" (John 21:7). Then again during the last meal they had with Jesus on the beach at Tiberias just before he ascended into heaven, we hear the phrase a fifth and final time: "And Peter, turning about, seeth the disciple whom Jesus loved following which also leaned on his breast at Supper" (John 21:20). Both times John uses *agapan* to describe their special relationship, and once again we don't have a clue about what actually happened between them when John and Jesus were together in private.

We just don't know if Jesus and John were same-sex lovers. We don't know if John was gay, but was content to enter into an intimate but celibate relationship with his Lord. We don't know if Jesus was sexually intimate with anyone during his short lifetime. But we do know that he and John had a special, intimate friendship, and I'm content to leave that special, intimate friendship undefined.

Knowing the details doesn't matter to a gay man who finds a certain kind of relief in the fact that John cuddled with Jesus at a public dinner and that no one, including Jesus, seemed to be angered or offended. Who knows what happened between Jesus and John during their three years together on the road? Who cares if their relationship had a sexual component or not? Like David and Jonathan, Ruth and Naomi, and the Centurion and his beloved servant, Jesus and John had a special, same-sex friendship. Their story and the stories like them, in Hebrew and Greek alike, have survived several thousand years with enough detail to give comfort and support to same-sex couples seeking recognition of their own relationships.

QUESTION 9

In making His decision about same-sex marriage, would Jesus consider the tradition of loving, committed, same-sex relationships in the distant past?

According to John Boswell, church history also tells the story of same-sex relationships that are recognized and honored by Christian tradition as far back as the fourth century CE. One of the earliest examples Boswell cites is the same-sex relationship of Perpetua, a Christian noble woman, and Felicitas, a female slave. Martyred in Carthage about 203 CE, these two women were sentenced to death for refusing to denounce their Christian faith. And though several men were martyred with them, only Perpetua and Felicitas refused to wear the pagan costumes laid out for them that would amuse the emperor and his cronies. Tradition says the women kissed each other before being struck down and killed by a mad cow in a public arena. Boswell says their relationship was a model for other paired saints in centuries to come. There is a fascinating subtheme to the story of these two women. Boswell says that Perpetua became a man in her own vision, and "both were lauded at the end as the 'most manly' of 'soldiers.'"[29]

Boswell also tells the story of two Roman soldiers of Greek ancestry, Polyeuct and Nearchos, who were martyred approximately a half-century later. A fourth-century biographer described the two men as "brothers, not by birth, but by affection." He adds, "They enjoyed the closest possible friendship, being both comrades and fellow-soldiers."[30]

In this fascinating story of another same-sex relationship, Polyeuct even though he knew he would be martyred for his act of faith, converted to Christianity primarily to die with his lover, Nearchos, rather than be separated from him. "Even if we were to be separated by death," Plyeuct is supposed to have said, "no one would be able to diminish the devotion and love we have for each other."[31]

Perhaps the most famous of the martyred same-sex pairs are Serge and Bacchus, whose relationship the historian Tertullian compares to a Christian heterosexual married couple. They were, he explained, "united not in the way of nature, but in the manner of faith always singing and saying, 'Behold how good and how pleasant it is for brothers to abide in oneness.'"[32]

Although the two young warriors gained favor with the emperor and were appointed to important positions in the royal court, when they insisted on honoring Christ above all worldly rulers, Bacchus was flogged to death. The emperor, frustrated by the firmness of Bacchus's faith, refused to bury his former friend and instead threw his body outside the city walls to be consumed by wild animals. Tradition says a flock of birds stood guard over Bacchus's body, driving other wild animals away until the dawn.[33]

In his attempt to get Serge to give up his faith, the emperor forced him to run nearly ten miles in shoes into which nails had been driven through the souls, pointing into his bloody feet. When torture failed, Serge too was executed. Tradition has it that just before he died, Serge heard Bacchus in a vision say, "Hurry then, yourself, brother…to pursue and obtain me, when you have finished the course. For the crown of justice for me is to be with you."[34]

Although Boswell's years of research have been praised and vilified equally, he has been able to document Christian same-sex marriage ceremonies all the way back to the eighth century CE. He believes that Barberini 336 (a manuscript he discovered in the Vatican Library before he was no longer welcome there) is the earliest collection of Greek liturgies. The document contains four ceremonies for sacramental union: one for heterosexual betrothal, two separate ceremonies (called simply "prayers") for heterosexual marriage, and a comparable "prayer" for uniting two men. In addition to Barberini 336, Boswell discovered at least seven other known versions of such a same-sex marriage ceremony before the twelfth century.[35]

As we face the challenges of today's society Christians must also ask themselves these questions:

- In making his decision about same-sex marriage, would Jesus consider the tragic state of heterosexual marriage and the role that same-sex marriage could play in strengthening that institution?
- In making his decision about same-sex marriage, would Jesus realize how desperately gay and lesbian couples need the kind of support legal marriage can give to bind their relationships together in ways they have never known?
- In making his decision about same-sex marriage, would Jesus consider the benefits that marriage would provide to the adopted children of same-sex couples?

- In making his decision about same-sex marriage, would Jesus ask religious leaders to end their policies that refuse pastors or priests the rights to perform same-sex weddings in the church or to honor those marriages or the children of those marriages?
- In making his decision about same-sex marriage, would Jesus take into consideration the terrible cost the church is paying as more and more LGBT Christians, their friends, and families are leaving the church because of the bias against homosexuality and homosexuals?

I must add one more personal word. Gary and I have been waiting to be married legally for almost twenty-five years. With the current rise to power by fundamentalist Christians in church and state alike we are afraid that things could get much worse for our community (and for the nation) before they get better. It is possible that we may have to wait another twenty-five years to be legally married and that in the meantime the few civil rights we have gained will be withdrawn by courts and legislatures dominated by antigay fundamentalists. What will we do then?

However, if a miracle happens and the people of this nation discover what fundamentalists have planned for our country and vote them out of political office in time, there is a good chance that same-sex couples will be granted the civil rights and responsibilities of marriage while Gary and I can still enjoy them.

And if another miracle happens and America's Christians discover what fundamentalists have planned for the churches of our country and vote them out of religious office in time, there is a good chance that same-sex couples will be granted the religious rites of marriage as well.

These "miracles" can only happen when we the people decide to resist the fundamentalists' attempt to superimpose their fundamentalist values on the rest of us and volunteer our time, money, and talent to that task. I suppose that's the next question we should ask: In making our decision about same-sex marriage, will we be smart enough to see the consequences for gay and lesbian Americans if the fundamentalists and their unwitting allies prevail? And if we see and understand those consequences not just for sexual minorities but also for the nation, will we have the wisdom and the courage to resist?

NOTES

1. Thomas á Kempis, *Of the Imitation of Christ* (Westwood, NJ: Fleming H. Revell, 1963).

2. King James Version.

3. Dr. James Dobson, *Focus on the Family Newsletter*, April 2004; this newsletter was mailed to over two million people and read on his March 24, 2004, radio broadcast to millions that surround public more.

4. General Accounting Office of the U.S. government, http://www.gao.gov.

5. See Para. 20-45.3, "Affirmation of Marriage Act for the Commonwealth of Virginia," HB 751; CH. 983, http://legis.state.va.us; Debbie Messina, "State's New Law Takes Effect Today/Gay Rights: More Restrictive Measure Meets with Protests," *Virginia-Pilot* (Norfolk, VA), July 1, 2004; Justin Bergman, "New Virginia Law Alarms Gay Activists," *Associated*

Press Online, http://www.ap.org May 25, 2004; Chris L. Jenkins, "New Virginia Law Spurs Gays to Activism Prohibition on Contracts Energizes Community" *Washington Post*, July 28, 2004.

6. Mel White, *Stranger at the Gate: To be Gay and Christian in America* (New York: Plume Books, 1995); also available online at http://www.soulforce.org.

7. Personal correspondence to author.

8. Personal correspondence to author.

9. James Dobson, "Marriage Under Fire," *A Focus on the Family Publication*, 68.

10. Gary Delsohn, "Apparent Confession to Gay Murders," *Sacramento Bee*, September 22, 1999.

11. Commonwealth of Massachusetts, Supreme Judicial Court, No. SJC-09163, request for an Advisory Opinion A-107.

12. *Halpern v. Toronto* (city), CarswellOnt 2159 (2003).

13. Rabbi Abraham Heschel, "On Improving Catholic-Jewish Relations," memorandum on behalf of the American Jewish Committee to Vatican Council II, 1962, quoted in *A Prophet for Our Time: An Anthology of the Writings of Rabbi Marc H. Tanenbaum*, ed. Judith H. Banki and Eugene J. Fisher, 301 (New York: Fordham University Press, 2002).

14. Exodus International Ministries, quoted in American Psychological Association, "Just the Facts: Homosexual Orientation and Youth: A Primer for Principals, Educators & School Personnel," http://www.apa.org/pi/lgbc/facts.pdf (accessed October 11, 2006), 7.

15. Ibid.

16. Ibid. American Psychological Association, "Just the Facts: Homosexual Orientation and Youth" (see note 14).

17. Ibid., 5.

18. American Academy of Pediatrics, "Homosexuality and Adolescence," Policy Statement, 1993, quoted in American Psychological Association, "Just the Facts: Homosexual Orientation and Youth," 6 (see note 14).

19. Resolution adopted by American Counseling Association Governing Council, March 1998, quoted in American Psychological Association, "Just the Facts: Homosexual Orientation and Youth," 6–7 (see note 14).

20. American Psychiatric Association, "Psychiatric Treatment and Sexual Orientation," 1998, quoted in American Psychological Association, "Just the Facts: Homosexual Orientation and Youth," 7 (see note 14).

21. American Psychological Association, "Resolution on Appropriate Therapeutic Responses to Sexual Orientation," 1997, quoted in American Psychological Association, "Just the Facts: Homosexual Orientation and Youth," 7 (see note 14).

22. American Psychological Association, "Just the Facts: Homosexual Orientation and Youth," 6 (see note 14).

23. Ibid.

24. Nancy Wilson, *Our Tribe: Queer Folks, God, Jesus and the Bible* (San Francisco: HarperSanFrancisco, 1995).

25. Ibid., 148–53.

26. Ibid. 151.

27. John Boswell, *Same Sex Unions in Premodern Europe*, (New York: Villard Books, 1994), 221.

28. Ibid., 8.

29. Ibid., 139–61. The stories of each of the same-sex couples who were martyred for their faith are covered in these pages.

30. Ibid., 141.

31. Ibid., 143.

32. Ibid., 147–48.
33. Ibid., 149–50.
34. Ibid., 150.
35. Ibid., 178–79.

11

EACH MUSLIM HAS THE RIGHT TO FIND A MATE WHO IS A "COMFORT AND CLOAK"

Sheikh Daayiee Abdullah

Bismillahi Ar-Rahman Ar-Raheem

During the past five years there has been a marked increase in the visibility of gay Muslims around the world on lesbian, gay, bisexual, transgender, and queer (LGBTQ) political and religious fronts. LGBTQ Muslims find themselves in a quandary because traditional teachings of Islam hold that homosexuality is *haraam* (forbidden). How then can one be Muslim and live a gay lifestyle?

Allah is our Creator, and Allah's message is inclusive—not exclusive. The Holy Quran's message clearly states that Allah's mercy is for all who submit/ surrender their hearts by developing their personal relationship with Allah. Allah does not ask us as gay Muslims to stop being Muslim. Allah asks all Muslims to follow certain nondiscriminatory values that promote the highest regard for human relationships within Muslim society. It is a shame that not all Muslims agree with me.

As a gay Muslim and religious scholar in the Islamic faith, I have been engaged in a search for a gay identity in Islam that is fraught with dead ends and myths. Islamic theological history and Islam's theological dogma are not the same. For those who know little to nothing about Islam, it is a common misinterpretation that homosexuality is condemned in the Holy Quran. I believe LGBTQ Muslims are not denied Allah's blessings even to wed.

What is frequently used as a legal support for the social shaming and, in some Muslim societies, even the murder of gays and lesbians is the story of Lut and Sodom. Based on Islamic scholarship on homosexuality and lesbianism that has grown over the past fifteen years, I offer in this chapter a gay-positive interpretation of the Lut story to show why we need homosexual marriage in Islam.

A misconception within the Muslim community is the condemnation of a "caricature" based upon sexual acts. It is through this misplaced proscription that all formulations of same-sex acts, and not sexual orientation, are summarily condemned. This is like saying that all sexual acts by heterosexuals are condemned because the only correct sexual act is coitus in the missionary position. It is generally accepted in the Abraheemic faiths that in the story of Lut, men who turned from their mates (women) participated in forced rape, torture, and the oppression of the weak. When a Muslim participates in the general gay culture in which alcohol, drugs, and promiscuous/anonymous sex are prevalent, some are likely to succumb to their appeal and fall into the sin of fornication, which is forbidden in Islam.

When the Holy Quran is read in historical context, one should note that Prophet Lut lived during the same time as Abraheem, and therefore at a time where paganism was the norm. Thus we can better understand the crimes of the men of Sodom, who were condemned for their pagan beliefs and oppressive control over innocents. The Holy Quran condemns oppressive governmental states that utilize rape and terror as a form of societal control. These heterosexual men of Sodom, who turned from their spouses, were using homosexual acts as a source of rape and torture. These sexual acts and the reasoning behind them are clearly not the source of love, respect, and comfort that the Holy Quran states is for all of humankind for all time.

Again, traditional Islamic religious teachings have supported this general misunderstanding and continue to harm the well-being of same-gender-loving Muslims in Muslim societies and the West. Prophet Mohammed's (Sallu Alayhi Wa Salaam or SAWS, Peace Be Upon Him) "dislike" for homosexuality is a legal fiction created after the death of Prophet Mohammed (SAWS) by companions of Prophet Mohammed (SAWS). Many Islamic legal scholars clearly state the Prophet Mohammed (SAWS) never dealt with a legal case concerning homosexuality.

Thus these *hadith* (stories written about Prophet Mohammed, SAWS),concerning homosexuality are not based on historical facts and are fabrications to support "*ta'zeer*" (punishment) for political reasons. Additionally, Prophet Mohammed's (SAWS) wives had *Mukhanniths* (effeminate men) and he never expressed any displeasure with having them present in his or their households. At that time, many *Mukhanniths* were considered to be homosexual.

Because Prophet Mohammed (SAWS) exemplifies the Quran and its teachings, Prophet Mohammed's (SAWS) actions reveal to us how the Holy Quran views homosexuality in our day-to-day lives. Human interpretation and intervention have caused such destructive behavior toward homosexuality generally and homosexual marriage specifically.

The Holy Quran speaks to human sexuality and holds that human sexuality is a positive attribute for all Muslims. The Holy Quran states that *nikah*, traditionally a legally binding contract between two consenting adults to wed, is a benefit and blessing from Allah. According to Abdullah Muhammad Khouj's *Handbook of Marriage in Islam*, marriage is the way "to meet one's most basic physical, emotional, mental, social and spiritual needs." How then can heterosexual Muslims deny gay Muslims access to *nikah*?

In the West, same-sex Muslim couples are able to perform a *nikah*. In those countries where same-sex marriages are performed, it is my belief that gay Muslims should utilize these laws to support their "marriage," even though such a marriage may not be openly accepted by the larger Muslim community. As a Sunni Muslim who is homosexual, my personal experience of two long-term relationships/ marriages in my thirty-three years of adulthood strongly supports the value of same-sex marriage. Same-sex marriage supports the concept of family and diversity within our society. From a purely legal perspective, Western societies that have laws that support equal treatment under the "law" have the right idea in putting all marriages on the same level and holding heterosexual and same-sex marriages to the same standard. Property rights or spousal benefits are still upheld as the secular standard, though most of these rights are derived from religious teachings. As for the outcomes of marriage, the positives definitely outweigh the negatives.

Allah's message speaks to us as homosexuals, assuring us that we are a part of Creation and our lives are worth living to their fullest as loving, caring, and nurturing Muslims and particularly as gay Muslims, in loving relationships or not. The Holy Quran speaks in general and specific themes. Each Muslim has the right to find a mate who is a "comfort and cloak"; that is, a sexual mate and caregiver. The Holy Quran supports healthy sexual relations, so much so that there are themes that speak specifically to how a Muslim spouse should be treated and the rights owed to the spouse and themselves. With such clear mandates that Muslims should marry, and the development of same-sex marriage that is based upon the concept of "comfort and cloak," why wouldn't a committed same-sex couple do as heterosexual couples do and get married? Marriage is one of society's elements of maturity in Islam, and gay marriages, in my humble opinion, continue to strengthen the Islamic meaning of a religious family.

Marriage in Islam remains one of the methods of attaining a personal standard as a member of society. Single gay Muslims, I believe, are in the most difficult position. When Muslims participate in the general gay culture in which alcohol, drugs and promiscuous/anonymous sex are prevalent, some are likely to succumb to their appeal and fall into the sin of fornication, which is forbidden in Islam. To combat this possibility and to strengthen the resolve of all gay Muslims, it is important to have a clear understanding of one's faith as a Muslim and how our faith protects us from the social ills of promiscuous sex, the results of which erode the spiritual relationship a Muslim has with his Creator.

It is important that same-sex couples marry and that single Muslims seek a long-term partner/mate so they can be brought within Quranic teachings that marriage is good for you. I know that for those who are not in the West, having a same-sex marriage is a legal impossibility, and in some countries, such public disclosure could mean one's death. There are many Muslims around the world who seek such freedom to be gay and Muslim and live in a society where their sexual orientation does not preclude them from fulfilling their dream of marrying their same-sex partner. I urge those same-sex Muslim couples who are living in the West and have the opportunity to marry legally to have a traditional *nikah* and a civil ceremony to substantiate their marriage in religious and secular ways.

NOTE

Reprinted with permission from Sheikh Daayiee Abdullah, *White Crane: A Journal of Gay Spirit, Wisdom, and Culture*, no. 61, 2004, http://www.whitecranejournal.com/61/art6108.asp (accessed November 1, 2006).

Part III

FAITHFUL STRUGGLE

12

MARRIAGE IN A NEW KEY: A PRESBYTERIAN MAPS THE TERRAIN OF A PROGRESSIVE CHRISTIANITY

Marvin M. Ellison

A shift of perspective is not unfamiliar in Christian history; it is called conversion.[1]
—Robert McAfee Brown

To date religion has played a pivotal role in the North American debate about same-sex marriage, but in a manner that has intensified rather than helped resolve this controversy. Given the Christian Right's fixation on homosexuality and its aggressive "traditional values" campaign,[2] it is not surprising that appeals to religious belief and the Bible are frequently cited as grounds for resisting changes in civil law and religious practice that would accommodate nonheterosexual couples and their families. At the same time, not all religious authorities and traditions condemn homosexuality or reject same-sex marriage. Because advocates for marriage equality include leaders and activists within a wide range of faith traditions,[3] it would be a mistake to consign religion to the forces of reaction. It would also be politically counterproductive because opportunities might be overlooked for entering into alliances with progressive religionists, thereby further impeding efforts to reorder social, economic, and cultural conditions so that all persons may experience security and justice, including those who identify as lesbian, gay, bisexual, and transgender (LGBT).

In analyzing the conflict about marriage policies and practices within North Atlantic, white Reformed Protestantism, the tradition within which I stand, I find good news in Daniel Maguire's observation that "from the beginning, there has never been just one Christianity."[4] No monolithic or fixed Christian tradition exists. Instead, there is a plurality of dynamic, often conflicting Christianities that are deeply divided over sexuality, economic justice, and other concerns. Religion should, therefore, be approached with care and discernment as a complex, ideologically divided force that either promotes justice or legitimates injustice.

This religion divide is vividly illustrated by the wildly divergent responses to the 2003 election of V. Gene Robinson as the Episcopal bishop of New Hampshire. The controversy has been sparked by the fact that Bishop Robinson is not only a divorced father of two adult children but also an "out"—that is, a self-respecting and publicly self-identifying gay man who lives openly with his male life-partner. Christian traditionalists are distressed that a church body would fail to underscore the incompatibility of Christian identity with what they rhetorically invoke as "the gay lifestyle," much less give explicit approval to what they regard as blatant immorality. They are equally alarmed by the heightened visibility of families headed by same-sex couples, the legalization of same-sex marriage in other countries (Canada, Belgium, the Netherlands, and Spain), as well as in parts of the United States (civil marriage in Massachusetts, civil unions in Vermont and Connecticut), and the movement within various religious traditions to bless same-sex partnerships.[5] They contend that homosexuality is intrinsically sinful, that homo-sex threatens personal health and social well-being, that only monogamous heterosexual marriage is biblically authorized, and that the marital family, the cornerstone of society and Western civilization, is undermined whenever church or state adopts a neutral stance toward nonnormative sexualities and "endorses" nontraditional families. In contrast, Christian progressives welcome nonheterosexuals into the life and leadership of the church and support their full civil, human, and ecclesiastical rights, including the freedom to marry. They also press for a reformation of Christian theology and sexual ethics in light of the biblical mandate to pursue justice for those marginalized and oppressed in every community and context.[6]

This split over sexuality and sexual justice within Christianity and other religious traditions[7] has been characterized in terms of a traditionalist-progressive dichotomy. In *Christianity and the Making of the Modern Family*, historian and theologian Rosemary Ruether proposes that "no reconciliation is possible" between the two sides of this religious divide because "their outlooks are based on irreconcilably different presuppositions."[8] Christian fundamentalists, operating with an absolutist worldview "of fixed certainties that support patriarchal hierarchy, militarism, and free-market capitalism," regard gay sex as morally objectionable "regardless of how loving or how committed is the relationship in which it takes place."[9] In contrast, Christian progressives acknowledge and show regard for a range of human sexualities, place the pursuit of an egalitarian justice at the heart of the moral-spiritual life, and, as Ruether notes, "have accepted the diversity of cultures and religious perspectives" as rich assets for community life, rather than threats to religious identity or problems that require fixing.

Because those of us who are progressive Christians increasingly find that we have more in common—in terms of shared faith and values—with our liberal counterparts in other denominations and traditions than we have with our conservative coreligionists, a massive realignment is taking place within the religious landscape. This realignment, which Ruether describes as a "new ecumenism," seeks to link the progressive wings of various denominations so that, among other things, they might pursue justice making more effectively throughout the social order.[10]

Although the distinction between traditionalist and progressive is commonplace in popular discourse and may be useful for grassroots organizing, the dichotomy can be overdrawn and misleading. In particular, framing the debate between only these two poles does not readily draw attention to the limitations of a centrist notion of justice as equal opportunity or equal access. In my judgment, progressives need a richer, more comprehensive notion of justice that emphasizes the restructuring of social power and reconstruction of moral norms, in this case norms regulating sexuality and sexual difference. Otherwise, liberals seeking the inclusion of the disenfranchised may leave unaltered the norms and power dynamics that create the divisive, exclusionary practices in the first place.

To make a case for a broader notion of sexual justice on which to ground religious responses to sexual difference, I begin by comparing church resolutions on same-sex marriage from the Southern Baptist Convention and the United Church of Christ. After drawing the contrast, I suggest that, although progressive commitments in favor of marriage equality move in the right direction by validating same-sex love, actualizing a comprehensive notion of justice requires more. To dismantle entrenched social patterns of privilege and exclusion, progressives must stop privileging not only heterosexuality but marriage as well. The *marital* family must be decentered in order to give recognition and support to a diversity of family and relational options. In rethinking marriage in a postmodern key, I conclude by considering a set of challenges to the liberal Christian marriage paradigm and offer a constructive proposal for moving toward sexual and relational justice. Shifting in this direction resonates well, I argue, with a Reformed Protestant affirmation of justice in intimate, as well as wider, social relations. It may also allow us to appreciate that, while heterosexuality and marriage are vocations to be undertaken by those with these particular gifts, they are not divinely willed or naturally mandated obligations to be expected of all. Further, making this shift may foster the awareness that the moral evil of which Christians are called to repent is not "the sin of homosexuality," but rather its own sex-negativity, the idolatry of heterosexual supremacy, and the refusal to enter into community as coequals with the sexualized Other.

MARRIAGE TRADITIONALISTS: THE VIEW FROM ABOVE

Opponents of same-sex marriage, idealizing a nineteenth-century, middle-class (and typically white) nuclear family as the Christian norm, argue against extending the right to marry to same-sex couples because of what they believe about marriage and about homosexuality. A Southern Baptist Convention (SBC) statement on sexuality defines marriage as an exclusively heterosexual institution, the union of "one man, and one woman, for life."[11] In 1998 the SBC amended its "Baptist Faith and Message" by adding a section on "The Family," which notes three purposes for marriage: to provide a framework for intimate companionship between a husband and wife, to control sex by channeling sexuality "according to biblical standards," and to provide "the means for procreation of the human race."[12] Because the presumption is no longer unassailable that marriage requires gender difference to be valid, the SBC has offered additional reasons for opposing same-sex marriage by declaring that homosexuality is not a "valid alternative lifestyle," but rather, biblically speaking, a sin.[13] According to this viewpoint, for the church to grant religious affirmation or the state to offer legal standing to same-sex unions would be to "sanction immorality." In a 1996 resolution opposing the legalizing of same-sex unions in

Hawaii, the SBC elaborated on its objections by describing homoerotic relationships as "always a gross abomination…in all circumstances, without exception," as "pathological," and as "always sinful, impure, degrading, shameful, unnatural, indecent, and perverted." Leaving no doubt about its opposition to marriage equality, the SBC resolution concluded by stating that the movement to legalize same-sex unions "is and must be completely and thoroughly wicked."[14]

These opponents of same-sex marriage claim to speak from the center of Christian life and culture. As the SBC puts it, the church must protect the integrity of the Christian tradition, and therefore, marriage should be defended as a divinely mandated "order of creation" and "therefore first and foremost [as] a divine institution (Matthew 19:6) and only secondarily a cultural and civil institution."[15] However, in claiming the authority to speak for all, these Christians speak not from the center, but "from above," from a position of social power and privilege, and they intend to deploy their power to forestall changes they fear will erode their cultural dominance.[16]

In opposing same-sex marriage, these traditionalists are not seeking to preserve marriage but rather a certain model of marriage (patriarchal marriage) and, by extension, a certain model of social relations organized in terms of presumably natural hierarchies of power and control. Although affirming that husband and wife are "of equal worth before God," the SBC describes marriage as an unequal power relation in which the two parties have different roles and expectations. The husband must be the leader; he is to "provide for, to protect, and to lead his family." A wife is expected "to submit herself graciously" to her husband "as the church willingly submits to the headship of Christ."[17] This hierarchical marriage paradigm is defended as natural, "pre-political," and divinely mandated, presumably for the benefit of all the parties affected, including the broader social order.

As historian Mark Jordan observes, traditionalists seek to enshrine a definition of marriage as "always and only" one man and one woman by invoking the Jewish and Christian traditions as its chief warrant, but "of course, they are plainly wrong." Polygamy was a sanctioned practice among the Hebrew patriarchs, and Augustine, Aquinas, and the Protestant Reformers all wrestled with the question of holiness and nonmonogamy, including how the New Testament's affirmation of "new life in the Spirit" and an inclusive Christian love seem to justify polyamorous affiliations. "The most urgent challenge for Christian marital theology," Jordan argues, "has been to prevent the universality of the agapic [love] feast from reaching erotic relationships —how to prevent agapic community from enactment as erotic community."[18] Christianity in his proposal "is latent polyamory," insofar as it encourages an inclusive "love of many," even all, and does not fixate on more restrictive pair bonding.[19]

The heterosexual marriage paradigm that the SBC and other traditionalists seek to reinforce as the only legally (and religiously) recognized household pattern resonates with, and gains cultural weight from, modernist assumptions about gender, sexuality, and family. A prevailing sexological paradigm emphasizes biological factors ("anatomy is destiny"), views sexuality as naturally determined and unchanging, and operates within a binary sex/gender schema, in which biological or anatomical sex is presumed, first, to give rise to "proper" masculine or feminine gender identity and social roles, then, to generate "normal" heterosexual desires and interest in the "opposite sex," and finally, to lead steadily to procreation in the context of marriage.

The notions that there are two (and only two) naturally complementary sexes, that "opposites attract," that sexuality is primarily procreative, and that homosexuality signals deviance from the heterosexual norm are unquestioned assumptions among traditionalists.

The prevailing cultural sex/gender paradigm seems commonsensical to conservative Christians because it fits with and helps reinforce two familiar and problematic dynamics within the Christian tradition: first, a devaluing of body and a deep ambivalence, if not outright negativity, toward sexuality, passion, and women; and second, a patriarchal bias that legitimates male control of women's lives, including their reproductive and other labor. Because sex has long been viewed with suspicion as a dangerous energy that threatens to overwhelm and disrupt the established order, marriage has been latched onto as the appropriate "safe container" for keeping this energy within check, in particular by allowing male control of wives and daughters and the orderly transmission of property, including children. In this framework, marriage is as much if not more about gender hierarchy, gender control, and the regulation of sex and property as it is about love and affection.

According to the logic of patriarchal Christianity, moral order is equated with sexism, white racial supremacy, class elitism, and so forth. To maintain good order, all must play their proper roles and, in this instance, fulfill the obligations of compulsory heterosexual monogamy. Failure to conform to patriarchal norms and role expectations places individuals and communities in jeopardy, including risking, as the SBC points out, "God's swift judgment."[20] Given their fear of social anarchy and invocation of divine wrath, traditionalists have become deeply agitated by efforts to "normalize" gay people and grant legitimacy to same-sex partnerships and families, precisely because homosexuality is lifted up as the preeminent example of willful departure from "traditional values." By upending the sex/gender rules, same-sex marriage threatens to disrupt and dismantle not only "the" family but also the entire social edifice constructed on the basis of the heterosexual (and racist, masculinist) social contract.

ADVOCATES FOR EQUALITY: TRANSFORMING A PATRIARCHAL, SEX-NEGATIVE CHRISTIAN PARADIGM

On July 4, 2005, the United Church of Christ (UCC) became the first mainline Christian denomination to give official support for same-sex marriage by adopting a resolution at its General Synod that affirms "equal marriage rights for couples regardless of gender." In keeping with its long-standing advocacy for justice and social equality, including advocacy for LGBT persons, the UCC has identified the marriage exclusion as yet another form of discrimination that violates the principle of equal protection under the law. However, this denomination's stance in favor of marriage equality is rooted more fundamentally in theological and biblical affirmations. "The message of the Gospel," its resolution reads, "is the lens through which the whole of scripture is to be interpreted," and it is a message that "always bends toward inclusion."[21]

In recognition of the fact that marriage is a changing, ever evolving institution and, therefore, subject to greater humanization or dehumanization, the UCC emphasizes its commitment to marriage as a covenant of equals and contends that the biblical call to justice and compassion "provides the mandate for marriage equality" (1–2). Justice, a value to be embodied in interpersonal relationships as well as institutional structures, should seek the elimination of "marginalization for reasons of race, gender, sexual orientation or economic status" (2) and work to create the conditions for social equality. From this justice perspective, the mandate to pursue marriage equality expresses two interrelated notions of equality. First, marriage is defined as a covenantal relationship based on the "full humanity of each partner, lived out in mutual care and respect for one another" (1). The UCC is, therefore, affirming equality of partnership within marriage. Second, equality refers to an affirmation of the full humanity of persons with differing sexual orientations. "We also recognize and affirm that all humans are made in the image and likeness of God," the marriage pronouncement states, "including people of all sexual orientations." The key implication is that, "as created in God's image and gifted by God with human sexuality, all people have the right to lead lives that express love, justice, mutuality, commitment, consent, and pleasure" (2). Equality in this second sense means equal access to marriage, including the moral freedom of same-sex couples to marry, legally and religiously, as well as the freedom not to marry.

Importantly, the UCC statement affirms marriage, but also acknowledges that there are other ways that responsible people live and love. In fact, there are "many biblical models for blessed relationships beyond one man and one woman." Marriage is not the only place in which people "can live fully the gift of love in responsible, faithful, just, committed, covenantal relationships." To underscore this point, the resolution states that "indeed, scripture neither commends a single marriage model nor commands all to marry, but rather calls for love and justice in all relationships" (2). In keeping with these commitments, the UCC calls on its congregations to adopt marriage policies and rituals that do not discriminate against same-sex couples and asks its membership to "prayerfully consider and support" local, state, and national legislation that grant "equal marriage rights to couples regardless of gender," and to work against legislation, including constitutional amendments, that would deny civil marriage rights to gay and lesbian couples (5).

The strength of the UCC resolution is its refusal to privilege heterosexual coupling. Same-sex and different-sex partnerships are affirmed as covenantal relationships having comparable worth. Such covenants should be given equal regard within the church and be eligible to receive equal benefits and protection under civil law. At the same time, by calling for full equality between marriage partners, the UCC statement challenges the legacy of patriarchal Christian marriage in which the spiritual equality of spouses has been asserted, but men have remained in charge and enjoyed advantages of unequal power and status. Finally, the UCC position paper makes room for covenantal relationships outside the institution of marriage. While doing so, it encourages a single ethical standard for all intimate (and other) relationships: that relationships are ethical only when they are loving, just, and based on mutual respect and care for all persons.

The UCC affirmation of marriage equality moves in the right direction, first, by decentering heterosexuality and making room for sexual diversity (in this case, gay and lesbian couples in committed, covenantal relationships), and, second, by decentering marriage insofar as this resolution approaches marriage as a valued, though not exclusive, place for organizing intimate life. Other options have integrity. There are those who love and express their love sexually but do not marry. The church's justice-and-love standard sets an expectation for egalitarian, intimate relationships whether these are marital or not.

These emphases are important correctives to the sex-negativity and marriage exclusivism that characterize the Southern Baptist Convention's approach. Traditionalists espouse the notion that the only acceptable sexual expression is heterosexual, marital, and procreative. Those abiding by this standard are given permission to police others and keep them under control. According to conventional Christian mores, respectable people marry and restrain their sexuality by "settling down," thereby establishing themselves as responsible adults. In this schema, sexually active singles and especially gay men and lesbians are defined as "out of control" because they live and love outside the marriage zone. Gayness has become cultural code language for a generalized immorality that signals both social immaturity and sexual laxity, all because gayness departs from compulsory heterosexuality and because gay sex is neither marital nor procreatively driven and, therefore, not properly constrained.

Given what Gayle Rubin has described as the "dangerously crazy" attitudes about sexuality that typically emerge during times of heightened social and cultural stress,[22] some advocates of same-sex marriage choose to dodge the sex question and avoid dealing forthrightly with the sexual ethics question, including what makes sex ethical or blessed. Instead, they have tried to make a case for equal marriage rights by downplaying sex and "mainstreaming" gay men and lesbians by desexualizing homosexuality. Their message is that gayness should be viewed as a nonthreatening difference similar to left-handedness or eye color. Moreover, they insist that same-sex couples are not interested in altering the institution of marriage, but only in joining the ranks of the "happily conjoined," thereby reinforcing rather than upsetting the status quo.

Downplaying sexual difference and sanitizing gay sex are efforts to reduce the threat that gay identity and culture pose to dominant norms. According to this strategy, safety and access to basic rights, including the right to marry, depend on making "queerness" invisible. In the process, the prevailing norm of compulsory heterosexuality goes unchallenged. The moral problem is mystified, once more, as the "problem" of homosexuality (or of gender and sexual nonconformity). Furthermore, once again the debate is skewed to center on whether a minoritized group of outsiders can ever qualify for access to the majority-insiders' privileges through assimilation or by hiding difference and becoming "like them." Defined this way, the solution to injustice is for gay men and lesbians to conform, to the degree possible, to heterosexist values and practices.

William Eskridge, a gay legal scholar, in defending the legal right to marry for same-sex couples, buttresses his case by putting forward sex-negative and homophobic arguments. His book, subtitled *From Sexual Liberty to Civilized Commitment*, proposes that in the midst of an AIDS pandemic, gay men, especially the "more sexually venturesome," are "in need of civilizing." His argument for extending marriage rights to same-sex couples is that "same-sex marriage could be a particularly useful commitment device for gay and bisexual men."[23] If marriage were the normative expectation among gay men, he suggests, gay male cruising and experimentation with multiple anonymous sex partners would give way "to a more lesbian-like interest in commitment. Since 1981 and probably earlier, gays were civilizing themselves," he continues. "Part of our self-civilization has been an insistence on the right to marry."[24]

To argue that marriage is necessary as a social control mechanism to tame men's sexuality only reinforces the sex-negativity that is so much in evidence among Christian and other social conservatives. To argue, as Eskridge does, that "same-sex marriage civilizes gay men by making them more like lesbians" presumes, first of all, that women are not interested in sex or sexual pleasure but concerned only with intimacy and making relational commitments.[25] Moreover, marriage's purpose becomes sexual discipline and control, this time of gay men. In the process, sexual fundamentalism is not critiqued with its sex-negative control ethic and presumption that only marital heterosexuality is morally sound.

In seeking to legitimate the extension of marriage eligibility to same-sex couples, some advocates have adopted a problematic strategy of "containing" eroticism, including homoeroticism, within marriage. An alternative, more risky, but in the long term more effective strategy, one that the UCC resolution begins to map out, is to launch a nonapologetic defense of healthy eroticism, inclusive of gay sex; to spell out a principled critique of heterosexist norms and values; and to reformulate a sexual ethic no longer based on either the heterosexual or marital assumption.

A *nonreconstructed* Christian tradition will hardly be helpful in moving toward sexual and relational justice. The conventional Christian approach is not sex-positive. Rather, it promulgates a fear-based, reactive, and restrictive moral code aimed at restraining sex within rigidly defined marital boundaries. However, the prevailing Christian code—celibacy for singles, sex only in marriage—is no longer adequate, if it ever was, for at least three reasons. First, this code is fear-based, punitive, and aimed at control rather than empowerment of persons. Second, the Christian marriage ethic has not been sufficiently discerning of the varieties of responsible sexuality. Third, it has not been sufficiently discriminating in naming the ethical violations of persons even within marriage. A reframing of Christian ethics is needed that realistically addresses the diversity of human sexualities while focusing not on the "sin of sex" but on the use and misuse of power and on enhancing the dignity of persons and the moral quality of their interaction. What matters is not the sex or gender expression of the partners or their marital status but whether the relationship exhibits mutual respect and care, a fair sharing of power and pleasure, ongoing efforts to maintain health and prevent transmission of disease, and, in those cases where it applies, avoiding unintended pregnancy. This justice-centered ethical framework also gives pride of place to the mutual giving-and-receiving of pleasure as a moral resource for enhancing intimate communication.

REVISING PUBLIC POLICY BY BREAKING
THE MARRIAGE MONOPOLY

If the strengths of the UCC statement are its conception of marriage as a *human* rather than an exclusively heterosexual institution and its movement toward revising Christian sexual ethics, its weakness is its failure to address more critically the role of the state with respect to marital (and other) families. Civil marriage always involves a third party in addition to the couple: the state with its considerable powers not only to grant privileges and material benefits but also to enforce its notion of sexual morality and public order. A state-sponsored marriage system not only distributes material benefits to some and withholds them from others; it also dispenses cultural legitimation by authorizing some relationships but not others.

Breaking the state-sanctioned marriage monopoly may require several different strategies. One strategy would be to disconnect civil marriage from a wide range of legal rights and economic benefits that the state currently distributes exclusively on the basis of marital status. Instead, those benefits, including Social Security and access to health care, would be made available to persons on the basis of their citizenship status or membership in the community. If basic rights were guaranteed regardless of marital status, people would be less likely to marry solely or primarily for reasons of economic security. They would also be less likely to stay within unsatisfactory partnerships. Individual freedom, as well as personal dignity and well-being, would be enhanced.

A second strategy would be for the state to disestablish the *marital* family as the singular state-sanctioned associational pattern. The state should instead be neutral toward the diverse family and intimacy patterns that people create to meet their relational needs. Disestablishment of civil marriage would also mean the disestablishment of heterosexuality as the normative sexuality in much the same way that the disestablishment of a state-church has encouraged religious pluralism to flourish.[26] This would mean, among other things, that the state would no longer seek to regulate sexual affiliations between consenting adults. The one exception would be laws and procedures for protecting vulnerable adults and children from violence, harassment, exploitation, and abuse.

Along these lines, legal scholar Martha Fineman favors replacing the marital family, with its core sexual (and reproductive) affiliation, with what she calls the caretaking family with its core relationships of dependency and care, such as parents' care of children and adults caring for ill or aging family members.[27] Abolishing civil marriage as a state-subsidized institution would not mean abolishing marriage or family. Family is not coterminous with marriage. As many LGBT families demonstrate, nonmarried persons are able to bond together successfully and fulfill basic family functions. Fineman writes, "We do not need *legal* marriage to accomplish many societal objectives," such as nurturing children, caring for dependent adults, and sustaining domestic partners economically. By no longer privileging the *marital* family above other families, it would be possible to "transfer the social and economic subsidies and privilege that marriage now receives" and distribute these communal resources more equitably to what she identifies as "a new family core connection—that of the caretaker-dependent."[28] The state's constructive role would be to guarantee the social and economic conditions so that all families would have adequate resources and the tools necessary to raise children and do the other functions that society depends on for the well-being of its members and for its own future.

Even if marriage no longer conveyed a legal status, the institution would retain importance as a cultural institution because of its symbolic and expressive power. However, if marriage were no longer privileged and regulated by the power of the state, then a couple's decision to marry (or not) would be determined on other grounds, most likely on the basis of their desire to have their covenant witnessed, celebrated, and supported by their faith community if they belong to a religious tradition. At the same time, civil marriage would no longer serve as the exclusive conduit for distributing state-conferred benefits and protections. Instead, distribution would be made on the basis of the needs of caretaker-dependent family units, some of which would certainly be marital families, but not all. All families would be treated equally, and justice would be enhanced across social and cultural differences.

CONTINUING THE REFORMATION

Protestant Christianity, born as a reform movement in the sixteenth century, is in need of further reformation in keeping with what theologian Robert McAfee Brown calls the adaptable "spirit of Protestantism." Protestantism is a tradition that, at its best, understands itself as "reformed but always to be reforming."[29] The reformation needed this time concerns sexual difference and sexual ethics because Protestantism has fostered sexual injustice. Its relational ethic has been constructed on the basis of heterosexual exclusivism, the presumption that the only acceptable sexual expression is heterosexual, marital, and procreative. Countering religiously sanctioned sexual oppression requires critiquing the prevailing heterosexist sex/gender paradigm and developing an ethical paradigm that respects a diversity of human sexualities and places the focus not on identity but on conduct and the character of relationships.

In this regard, my conviction is that the theo-ethical conversation must be redirected away from a preoccupation with the gender (and gender roles) of persons in partnership and toward an emphasis on the character of the relationship. Moreover, rather than promoting marriage per se, the church should promote only egalitarian marriages, in which the parties are each honored and protected as persons in their own right, share power and resources in a mutual give-and-take, and are committed over the long haul not only to their mutual well-being but also to the building up of the common good. In other words, the church's educational and pastoral focus should be on helping people, regardless of gender, to figure out—and live out—a genuinely holy and blessed relationship.

No one should be naïve about the difficulty of eradicating sex and gender oppression or about how deep the ideological divide runs within religious traditions about these matters. Feminist philosopher Mary Daly noted some years ago that the very categories that frame the debate, namely heterosexuality and homosexuality, are patriarchal classifications and that they mystify rather than clarify what makes genuinely life-enhancing relationships possible. "In a nonsexist society," Daly has argued, "the categories of homosexuality and heterosexuality would be unimportant."[30] However, because we live "between the times," we must stretch our moral imaginations to envision what a nonsexist, nonheterosexist church and society would look like, along with how to shape an inclusive, woman-friendly, and gay-affirming model of Christian marriage.

What is abundantly clear is that for religionists, the affirmation of the full humanity of gay persons, along with advocacy for securing their human rights, marks a dividing line between progressives and those who would bifurcate the human community according to sexual difference and grant heterosexuality a priv- ileged status. Arguments against same-sex marriage pivot on the disapproval of gay sex and the denial that same-sex love is morally comparable to heterosexual love. Viewing heterosexuality and homosexuality as binary opposites reinforces hetero- sexual supremacy and gives credence to the notion that heterosexuality alone is an authentic basis on which to develop intimate relations and family life.

In contrast, once the patriarchal construction of male supremacy and female inferiority is discredited, and once marriage is valued primarily as a protective, sta- bilizing context for intimacy and ongoing care between partners, then justifications for excluding same-sex couples and keeping marriage a "heterosexuals only" club melt away. When the assumptions of "gender complementarity" (coded language for male superiority, female inferiority) and of "opposites attracting" hold no longer, it becomes possible to affirm the goodness of a variety of sexual and social relations based on mutual respect and care. In addition, a progressive Christian ethic honors eroticism, both gay and nongay, as a divinely gifted source of power and energy—of zest for life—that suffuses not only sexual activity but also life pursuits more broadly. Humans in their sexual and social diversity share a remarkably sim- ilar desire (and capacity) for intimate connection, communication, and communion with other persons, the earth, and God. Although this desire for connection does not mean that either marriage or sex is necessary for human fulfillment, it does mean that it is wrong, arbitrary, and cruel to exclude an entire class of persons from these routes to intimacy and shared pleasure.

As the battle rages within Protestant Christianity about granting the freedom to marry to same-sex couples, it is necessary to make a compelling religious case for marriage equality.[31] In doing so, advocates have certain Protestant emphases and commitments on which to draw: first, the primacy of the unitive rather than procre- ative purpose of marriage; second, the defining of marriage as a covenantal relation- ship between coequals; and, third, the moral obligation to deepen respect for the personhood of women and LGBT persons, as well as to protect their human rights.

Although extending the freedom to marry to same-sex couples would be good, in my judgment it would be an ambiguous good. Positively speaking, marriage equality rightly affirms that gay and lesbian people share the human capacity to enter into and sustain loving, morally principled intimate relationships. Accordingly, they too merit full religious and legal standing. Negatively speaking, same-sex marriage may only reinforce compulsory coupling, a dynamic that Protestant Christianity has helped fuel by expecting all (at least able-bodied, nomi- nally heterosexual) adults to marry. As ethicist Beverly W. Harrison observes, "The Reformers, none more passionately than Calvin, embraced marriage almost as a duty." In fact, marriage had to be compelled within a patriarchal religious system because "if men must marry women, whom they view as deficient in humanity, the external role of 'duty' necessarily must be invoked."[32] Because of its marriage exclu- sivism, Protestant Christianity has not only condoned women's second-class status in the family and other arenas but also has failed consistently to celebrate other ways in which people make families and engage in meaningful intimate association.

From a progressive religious perspective, the trouble with marriage lies far beyond the exclusion of same-sex couples, although that too is an injustice that must be corrected. There is a larger problem: how the Christian tradition has fostered fear of sexuality, legitimated male control of women's lives, promulgated compulsory (patriarchal) marriage, and castigated nonconformists as particularly sinful. This *nonreformed* Christian marriage paradigm has caused great damage, first, by reinforcing gender oppression and legitimating male authority and control over women; second, by making alternatives to sexist (and heterosexist) relationships seem unimaginable; and, third, by demonizing sexual nonconformists as "enemies of God" whose bodies and lives could be excoriated with impunity.[33]

In contrast, a progressive Christianity, in promoting sexual justice as an indispensable component of a more comprehensive social justice, advances a larger change agenda than the freedom to marry for gay men and lesbian women or even the restructuring of marriage on egalitarian terms, as necessary and important as these changes would be. Relational justice also requires a positive revaluation of sexuality, including appreciation for the goodness of gay sex; the dismantling of the prevailing sex/gender paradigm that privileges heterosexuality; and conscientious efforts to provide the social, economic, and cultural/religious conditions so that all persons, whether partnered or not and whether heterosexual or not, may flourish and be honored within their communities, including their faith communities.

The church's educational and pastoral responsibilities, along with its justice advocacy, require an expansive moral vision along these lines. In addition, greater candor is needed about how much contemporary Christian moral wisdom about sexuality, marriage, and family stands forthrightly in *discontinuity* with the received tradition. Progressive Christians must insist that good sex is not necessarily procreative, but should be mutually pleasurable for the partners and ethically principled. So, too, good marriages are not male dominant but rather exhibit flexibility about gender roles, power sharing, and ongoing negotiation so that the well-being and integrity of each person are enhanced. Finally, good families do not fit a single pattern, but rather take a variety of forms, including marital families, those headed by single parents, blended families, and families of choice.

Even these postmodern affirmations, however, when viewed through a Christian justice-love lens, resonate quite deeply with the central vocational commitment that resides at the heart of the Christian moral life: the double commandment to love God and neighbor as self. Supporting the freedom of same-sex couples to marry is grounded in a commitment to learn, together, how to live more gracefully with difference, including sexual difference, in an increasingly multicultural, religiously pluralistic society. In doing so, the church may find itself shifting—undergoing conversion is not too strong a word—to be able to stand more solidly within, and add its blessing to, the long-term historical movement toward a comprehensive social justice that delights in the equal status of marriage (and other intimate) partners, shows full regard for the humanity of nonheterosexual persons, and gives abundant thanks to God for wherever holy love is found.

NOTES

1. Robert McAfee Brown, *Theology in a New Key: Responding to Liberation Themes* (Philadelphia: Westminster Press, 1978), 51.

2. See Suzanne Pharr, *In the Time of the Right: Reflections on Liberation* (Berkeley, CA: Chardon Press, 1996); and Susan Brooks Thistlethwaite, "Enemy Mine: Why the Religious Right Needs Homophobia," *Chicago Theological Seminary Register* 91, no. 3 (2001): 33–40.

3. For a progressive interfaith statement in support of marriage equality, see the 2004 "Open Letter to Religious Leaders on Marriage Equality" on the Web site of the Religious Institute for Sexual Morality, Justice, and Healing, http://www.religiousinstitute.org/ Marriage_Open_Letter.pdf (accessed October 11, 2006). For suggestions on how religious leaders can promote marriage equality, see the Action Kit prepared by the Freedom to Marry Project, http://www.freedomtomarry.org/take_action.asp (accessed October 11, 2006).

4. Daniel C. Maguire, *A Moral Creed for All Christians* (Minneapolis: Fortress Press, 2005), 216.

5. The Central Conference of American Rabbis (Reform Judaism), the Ecumenical Catholic Church, Ohalah, Alliance for Jewish Renewal, and the Reconstructionist Rabbinical Association have endorsed their clergy performing commitment ceremonies for same-sex couples. In addition, the United Church of Christ, the United Church of Canada, the American Baptist Churches, the Christian Church (Disciples of Christ), and various Religious Society of Friends (Quaker) meetings leave it to their clergy, congregations, or local governing bodies to decide whether to perform same-sex unions. The Presbyterian Church (U.S.A.) and the Episcopal Church in the United States of America allow clergy to bless same-sex unions if these unions are not called marriages.

6. Two journals in religious studies have addressed religious perspectives on same-sex marriage. For a "sample" debate between progressives and traditionalists, see *Philosophia Christi* 7, no. 1 (2005) with an exchange of point-counterpoint presentations about same-sex marriage by Marvin M. Ellison ("Should the Traditional Understanding of Marriage as the One-Flesh Union of a Man and a Woman Be Abandoned?"), Francis J. Beckwith ("Legal Neutrality and Same-Sex Marriage"), Ronald E. Long ("In Support of Same-Sex Marriage"), and J. Budziszewski ("The Illusion of Gay Marriage"). In particular, see the responses to the presentations, including Ellison's "Heterosexism Is the Moral Scandal: A Response to Francis J. Beckwith" and Long's "Of Argument and Aesthetic Distaste: A Response to J. Budziszewski." In contrast, for a feminist roundtable discussion on same-sex marriage, see the *Journal of Feminist Studies in Religion* 20, no. 2 (Fall 2004), with essays by Mary E. Hunt, Marvin M. Ellison, Emilie M. Townes, Patrick S. Cheng, Martha Ackelsberg and Judith Plaskow, and Angela Bauer-Levesque.

7. See Marvin M. Ellison and Sylvia Thorson-Smith, eds., *Body and Soul: Rethinking Sexuality as Justice-Love* (Cleveland: The Pilgrim Press, 2003); Janet R. Jakobsen and Ann Pellegrini, *Love the Sin: Sexual Regulation and the Limits of Religious Tolerance* (New York: New York University Press, 2003); Patricia Beattie Jung and Ralph F. Smith, *Heterosexism: An Ethical Challenge* (Albany: State University of New York Press, 1993); and Christel Manning and Phil Zuckerman, eds., *Sex and Religion* (Belmont, CA: Thomson Wadsworth, 2005); and Arlene Swidler, ed., *Homosexuality and World Religions* (Valley Forge, PA: Trinity Press International, 1993).

8. Rosemary Radford Ruether, *Christianity and the Making of the Modern Family* (Boston: Beacon Press, 2000), 224.

9. Ibid., 223, 173.

10. Ibid., 224.

11. Southern Baptist Convention, "Sexuality," About Us: Position Statements, http://www.sbc.net/aboutus/pssexuality.asp (accessed October 11, 2006).

12. Southern Baptist Convention, "Family," in "The Baptist Faith and Message," http://www.sbc.net/bfm/bfm2000.asp#xviii (accessed October 11, 2006).

13. Southern Baptist Convention, "Sexuality" (see note 11).

14. Southern Baptist Convention, "Resolution on Homosexual Marriage," June 1996, http://www.sbc.net/resolutions/amResolution.asp?ID=614 (accessed October 11, 2006).

15. Ibid.

16. On this, see Beverly Wildung Harrison, "Agendas for a New Theological Ethic," in *Churches in Struggle: Liberation Theologies and Social Change in North America*, ed. William K. Tabb (New York: Monthly Review Press, 1986), 89–98. See also Thistlethwaite, "Enemy Mine," 33–40 (see note 2).

17. Southern Baptist Convention, "Family" (see note 12).

18. Mark D. Jordan, *Blessing Same-Sex Unions: The Perils of Queer Romance and the Confusions of Christian Marriage* (Chicago: University of Chicago Press, 2005), 165.

19. Ibid.

20. Southern Baptist Convention, "Resolution on Homosexual Marriage" (see note 14).

21. United Church of Christ Synod 25, "In Support of Equal Marriage Rights for All," 2005, 2, http://www.ucc.org/synod/resolutions/gsrev25-7.pdf (accessed October 11, 2006). Subsequent page references are to this document.

22. Gayle S. Rubin, "Thinking Sex: Notes for a Radical Theory of the Politics of Sexuality," in *The Lesbian and Gay Studies Reader*, ed. Henry Abelove, Michele Aina Barale, and David M. Halperin (New York: Routledge and Kegan Paul, 1993), 3–4.

23. William N. Eskridge, Jr., *The Case for Same-Sex Marriage: From Sexual Liberty to Civilized Commitment* (New York: Free Press, 1996), 9.

24. Ibid., 58.

25. Ibid., 84.

26. See Nancy F. Cott, *Public Vows: A History of Marriage and the Nation* (Cambridge, MA: Harvard University Press, 2000).

27. Martha A. Fineman, *The Autonomy Myth: A Theory of Dependency* (New York: Free Press, 2004), 132.

28. Ibid., 152.

29. Robert McAfee Brown, *The Spirit of Protestantism* (New York: Oxford University Press, 1965), especially chapter 4, "The Spirit of Protestantism."

30. Mary Daly, *Beyond God the Father: Toward a Philosophy of Women's Liberation* (Boston: Beacon Press, 1963), 126.

31. For progressive yet divergent perspectives, see Marvin M. Ellison, *Same-Sex Marriage? A Christian Ethical Analysis* (Cleveland: Pilgrim Press, 2004); Mark D. Jordan, *Blessing Same-Sex Unions* (see note 18); and David G. Myers and Letha Dawson Scanzoni, *What God Has Joined Together? A Christian Case for Gay Marriage* (New York: HarperCollins, 2005).

32. Beverly Wildung Harrison, *Justice in the Making: Feminist Social Ethics*, ed. Elizabeth M. Bounds, et al. (Louisville: Westminster John Knox Press, 2004), 55.

33. Kelly Brown Douglas, using the term "platonized Christianity" to describe the dualistic distortions that have plagued western Christianity, analyzes how an oppressive Christian tradition, in demonizing sexuality, has entered into alliance with state power to punish non-normative people as "sexual deviants" and, therefore, enemies of God. See her *What's Faith Got to Do With It? Black Bodies/Christian Souls* (Maryknoll, NY: Orbis Books, 2005), especially part 1.

13

Naming the Problem: Black Clergy, U.S. Politics, and Marriage Equality

Traci C. West

A segment of the PBS television series *Religion and Ethics* that was broadcast during the summer of the 2004 presidential campaign was titled "Black Churches and Gay Marriage." It included the following statements from two local church black pastors[1] in Washington, D.C.

> *Reverend Dennis Wiley, Pastor of Convent Baptist Church (During Sermon)*: A lot of people will say God made Adam and Eve, not Adam and Steve. Have you ever heard that? If God didn't make Steve, who made Steve? Somebody had to make Steve. Why would God create someone of that orientation and then not allow them to have the same kind of opportunity for love, for relationships, for a healthy life as heterosexuals enjoy?
>
> *Reverend Cheryl Sanders, Pastor of Third Street Church of God (During Sermon)*: We do not have any place in the scripture or in our tradition that we would consecrate, or affirm or acknowledge, marriage between two persons of the same sex. Homosexual practice in my understanding of scripture is a sin. And it's not the only sin, and it may not be the worst sin, but it's certainly a sin.
>
> (Later in the program:)
>
> *Rev. Wiley*: To me, it's a bit hypocritical for us—as African Americans who have been the victims of so much hatred, racism, bias, prejudice—for us then to turn around and to deny the opportunity for equal rights to any other oppressed community.
>
> *Rev. Sanders*: Any sexual activity involves some level of choice. What African Americans have faced historically has been on a whole different level from what people have faced historically because of their homosexual practices.[2]

The spectacle of Christian black clergy debating issues related to marriage equality has become a familiar component of national news coverage of this topic. The comments by Reverends Wiley and Sanders that aired on public television are fairly representative of the spectrum of views repeatedly expressed by black religious leaders within a variety of media forums. These two pastors, like others who appear in the media, offer conflicting perspectives on how the relationship between marriage equality and Christian faith and African American history ought to be assessed.

However, neither response can be understood adequately without situating them within the contemporary cultural landscape. A grasp of current Christian beliefs and practices in the United States is needed in conjunction with analysis of the dominant social and political climate that grants marriage equality its status as controversial. We must comprehend how "Christian faith" is defined within the politics of religion and race that surround public debates of marriage equality. More specifically, why are *black* Christians singled out so frequently by media outlets and conservative politicians (and strategists) for their perspectives on "gay marriage"?

These concerns do not arise out of some idle curiosity about U.S. culture. Instead, I raise them in hopes of identifying the pernicious merger of racism, Christian spiritual abuse, and political opportunism in the current opposition to marriage equality. For those Christians committed to developing liberative Christianity (faith that opposes human oppression), marriage equality is a struggle for justice in church and society. It is a struggle for faith-filled, communal support of the intimate, covenantal relationships of black lesbian, gay, bisexual, and transgender (LGBT) Christian couples, as well as support for all other variations of family life across religious, racial/ethnic, and sex/gender identity groups.

When focusing on the need to sustain this struggle, we must not lose sight of the affront to black LGBT Christians embodied in the television debates and newspaper articles that purportedly provide news coverage of how issues of marriage equality are relevant to blacks. Opposition to marriage equality is often attributed misleadingly to "the" black church and "the" black community. Moreover, certain historical, antiblack racist views parallel contemporary antigay views. Such similarities demand analysis but also have anguishing consequences. It can be especially difficult for Christian black lesbians and gay men to be treated purely as sexual objects in statements by homophobic black Christian leaders who seek to deny them equality. This sexual objectification reduces the humanity of black lesbians and gay men to genital sexual practices and labels the expression of their sexuality as innately sinful.

Compounding the viciousness of being attacked for reasons related to their sexual/gender identity, black LGBT persons may experience homophobic sexual objectification by black ministers as racial/ethnic betrayal. Historically, white racist ideas and practices reduced blacks to sexual objects. Note, for example, the practice of breeding slaves for economic gain and white justifications of lynching and segregation.[3] The humanity of blacks was reductively understood in terms of their genital sexual practices; for example, black women were seen as embodying sexual wantonness, and black men were referred to as embodying an insatiable "walking phallus."[4] Their expression of sexuality was identified as innately lascivious and ungodly.[5]

It should be mentioned that, in their condemnations of homosexuals, contemporary white religious and political leaders who oppose marriage equality also sometimes use sexually objectifying and stigmatizing tactics similar to these racist tactics. Such behavior on the part of whites is undoubtedly emotionally and spiritually costly to LGBT members of black communities, though it may not evoke the same sense of betrayal as when black leaders employ these tactics.

Frustratingly, black LGBT churches that are thriving all over the country are not included in the conception of "the" black church that is articulated most often in public discussions of African Americans and marriage equality. These black faith communities can be found in local churches within established denominations, such as the United Church of Christ, small independent Pentecostal ministries, as well as the new national black Protestant denomination, the Unity Fellowship movement.[6] Moreover, sometimes when *supportive* public pronouncements about the importance of "even including gays in our church" are made by black heterosexual allies, these contemporary, vital, black Christian LGBT communities of faith can be hidden from view. Their self-sufficient, multifaceted ministries can be rendered invisible because this claim perpetuates the false perception that all churches are controlled by and made up solely of heterosexuals (who speak for God?), and the full participation of openly LGBT Christians in church life relies on the benevolent invitation of heterosexual church members. Similarly, the current ministries of black LGBT Christian communities of faith are ignored when the heralding of black activist Christians of past eras is the only constructive public reference to black faith communities mentioned by white allies.

Furthermore when black religious leaders express arguments in the media (for and against marriage equality) positing African Americans and homosexuals as two distinct groups, this formulation deletes the existence of black LGBT persons from the group called African Americans. Rhetorically representing these two groupings as mutually exclusive teaches the public a lie. This rhetoric makes it appear as if black LGBT people are not part of African American families, religious groups, and communities.

Like black heterosexuals, black LGBT individuals, couples, and families are subjected to random, daily, antiblack racist insults, such as cabs that will not stop for them or store detectives who follow them around the shops. Like heterosexual black parents, LGBT parents must learn to soothe the damaged psyche of their teenage children who are automatically assumed to be criminals in public places.[7] Black LGBT individuals face compounding emotional and spiritual costs when they have to simultaneously endure public statements by black religious leaders that refer to them as homosexual outsiders who exist somewhere other than within "the" African American experience. They are treated as outsiders who are somehow divorced from or immune to the debilitating social and psychological impacts of being black in a racist society. In the public rhetoric of homophobic black Christian leaders, black LGBT persons are denied their authenticity as black.

As a Christian, I claim a liberative Christian faith tradition that does not simply accommodate itself to racist and heterosexist hierarchies. I claim a religious faith that instead identifies the sinfulness of all arrangements in church and society intent on creating hierarchies of human worth and reinforcing them with exclusive practices. Faithful Christianity ought to be concerned with fervently resisting the desire to separate valuable human beings deserving of basic protections and civil rights from those deemed less valuable because their identities supposedly deserve community-wide shaming and rejection. Christianity ought to engender a revolt against dividing the families to be honored by church and society from the families to be undermined by church and society. But to achieve this kind of resistance in behalf of marriage equality, certain forms of Christian idolatry—worship of social superiority and political power—would have to end. It also requires some decoding of cultural messages communicated to the public. In this white- and Christian-dominated society, what issues of power and status underlie public assertions about race, Christian faith, and opposition to marriage equality by black Christian leaders? When such assertions are publicized in the media, who is named as the problem and who is not? To begin to answer these questions, a few basic assumptions about the characteristics of a Christian family need to be underscored.

CHRISTIAN FAMILY VALUES

Christian theology based on the Bible teaches Christians that, in the beginning, God created humanity. God created intimate family relationships as a central dimension of how human individuals are connected to one another—spiritually, physically, and emotionally. In a Christian interpretation of the Hebrew story of human origins, this form of intimate relationship—family—both supports and hampers the full realization of each individual's inherent moral worth. Murder, deception, and disobedience of God are ensuing consequences of intimacy in those original family relationships, as they sought meaning and order in their world. At the same time, they exhibited a capacity to develop maturity and faithfulness to God. The lesson for Christians in these stories is not that any particular way of structuring human family relationships is intrinsically sacred or even intrinsically good. That is, one is not meant to worship the relationship of Adam to Eve, or of Cain to Abel. Rather, the point of these stories is the importance of tracing human origins to God's gracious act of creation—of endowing sacred worth in human creation—and about the necessary though complicated development of the human relationship to God.

Marriage is but one expression of an intimate, family relationship that exists among varied understandings of family in Christian scriptures, traditions, and practices. Family units, which sometimes include marriage (several forms of it, including polygamy) and sometimes exclude marriage, are part of Christian understandings of the Hebraic and early Christian traditions claimed as scripture. These families include Isaac and his two wives Leah and Rachel; Abraham, his wife Sarah, and his concubine Hagar; two sisters—Mary and Martha; husband and wife, Priscilla and Aquila; Tryphaena and Tryphosa, two women partners in mission[8]; and Paul and Silas, two men partners in mission.

According to Christian scriptural tradition, a Christian marriage between a man and a woman must be characterized by a patriarchal structure requiring wives to be subordinate to the authority of their husbands (Colossians 3:18; 1 Peter 3:1; Ephesians 5:22). This scriptural understanding of patriarchal heterosexual marriage must be rejected because it has been very costly to the physical and emotional health of women. Too many Christian wives are battered by their Christian husbands who feel justified in their spousal abuse because of this biblical teaching about their right to exercise authority over their households.

Nonetheless, for Christians, Jesus is the Word of God (John 1:1–5, 14). Jesus was an unmarried, itinerant Jewish evangelist. When starting out in his ministry, he immediately chose disciples for his intimate, emotional, and spiritual support, forming a crucial family unit for himself. When asked to respond to his traditional family (mother, sisters, and brothers) who desired to speak with him, Jesus declared his conception of family values. He replied with the strident question and assertion: "Who are my mother and sisters and brothers?... [W]hoever does the will of God is my brother and sister and mother" (Mark 3:33, 35). And in the Gospel, the will of God is fundamentally concerned with loving God and loving one's neighbor.

For Christians, Jesus models this love ethic in the Gospels, and implementing it demands certain practices. Although Christians have imitated this model over the past nineteen centuries with widely divergent lifestyles, essential practices include the following: prayer and study with time for thoughtful reflection, humble cognizance of God's grace-filled responses to and presence in one's own life and in the world, and active listening to and support for systemically marginalized and oppressed persons. Neither marriage nor any other intimate, covenantal relationship with another person is ever the goal of Christian life; rather, marriage is just one form of interpersonal intimate bonding that may be chosen. In the Christian religion, Jesus teaches that allegiance to conventional understandings of family is not what matters. Instead, family is to be understood as a component of a more primary faith commitment to manifest an active, loving response to God.

THE POLITICAL SPECTACLE OF BLACK CHRISTIAN OPPOSITION

In most of the current public discussions of marriage equality, distinctively Christian notions of marriage and family have been represented not as supportive of justice and equality but rather as supportive of discrimination and prejudice. Heterosexist interpretations of Christian beliefs and values concerning marriage and family have been injected into twenty-first-century electoral and legislative politics. The assertion of heterosexist interpretations of Christianity in public forums has helped some individuals attain power and status in our Christian- and heterosexual-dominated society. Starting in the late twentieth century, making public claims about possessing Christian faith became an extremely useful political tool for those seeking election to national, higher offices of government. Several U.S. presidents of this era, such as Jimmy Carter, Bill Clinton, and George W. Bush, are examples of high-level politicians who openly used claims about their Christian faith to advance their political careers. The opportunistic use of Christianity in national politics and public life has become standard practice. The significance of all early twenty-first-century claims about race and same-gender marriage by religious leaders and politicians (from varied racial/ethnic backgrounds) is best understood by remembering this fact about public life. The public conversation about marriage equality takes place within a broader cultural context in which the opportunistic merging of Christianity and politics is flourishing.

In media coverage of debates about marriage equality that involve elected officials or candidates for elected office (statewide and higher), the opinions of black clergy and black churches have received considerable attention. For instance, during the presidential election year of 2004, newspaper headlines, such as the following, appeared frequently: "Trouble for Gays in Black Churches" (*Pittsburgh Post-Gazette*),[9]

"Black Clergy Gathering to Fight Gay Matrimony" (*San Francisco Chronicle*),[10] "Gay Debate Splits Black Community" (*Chicago Tribune*),[11] "Local Black Ministers Condemn Gay Marriage" (*The Ledger*, Lakeland, FL),[12] "Blacks, Gays in Struggle of Values, Same-Sex Marriage Issue Challenges Religious, Political Ties" (*Washington Post*),[13] and "Both Sides Court Black Churches in the Battle Over Gay Marriage" (*New York Times*).[14] CNN's *Sunday Morning* show broadcasted a segment titled "African American Leaders debate whether the same-sex marriage issue should be equated with the struggle for civil rights."[15]

In a *New York Times* article on the historic 2005 United Church of Christ vote officially affirming marriage equality, a black pastor at "a predominantly black" congregation is the only opponent to the resolution whose name is included.[16] In justifying her opposition, she is described as explaining "that many blacks were more 'orthodox' in the interpretation of Scripture."[17] After that the *Times* story immediately goes on to include a quotation from another black delegate who voted in favor of the marriage equality resolution but apparently also agreed with some of the views of this black opponent.

Why is there so much nationwide interest in the views of black leaders on same-gender marriage? Why do black leaders in several parts of the nation appear to be taking so much interest in addressing this issue publicly?

When glancing at these headlines and news stories, I wonder why there seems to be disproportionate attention to the views of blacks without at least equal references to the views of the white majority. In other words, I wonder why I do not read "white churches" or "whites, gays" at least as many times as I read similar phrases about blacks in stories about battles over same-sex marriage. Isn't there "trouble for gays" in white churches? Don't white United Methodist or white Catholic clergy gather for meetings to fight "gay matrimony"? Where are the headlines about that? In a *New York Times* story about the United Church of Christ, a denomination that is well over 90 percent white, why are the differing votes of two black delegates racially identified? Why don't the similarly opposing votes of two whites receive the same attention?

Rarely are there headlines or quotations of sources in news stories that racially mark the attitudes and actions of white Christian clergy and laity on the issue of same-gender marriage.[18] Apparently, for both political leaders and reporters, the whiteness of Christian leaders who come mostly from predominantly white churches and communities is considered a nonissue in their opposition[19] to marriage equality.

When compared to the national media coverage of black views on marriage equality, there is less coverage of the views of Latino/a Christians, even less coverage of the views of Asians and Pacific Islanders, and still lesser coverage of the views of Native Americans. But even if the coverage of these groups equaled the coverage of African American church leaders, my question would nonetheless remain as to why the racial identity of white church leaders is not similarly named and highlighted, especially because whites are the politically dominant racial group in this society.

The presentation of race in typical news coverage is symptomatic of white dominance in U.S. society. It offers one of many examples of the ways that the mass media reinforce certain attitudes about race to the public; racial issues seem to be relevant (worth naming) only when people of color are present. When only blacks are discussed, they are almost always identified racially. The message conveyed to whites by this consistent pattern is that their white racial identity is the normal way of being human and that racial identity is primarily associated with nonwhites. Questions about the racial interests being pursued by whites or the racial legacies that whites are trying to extend remain unexamined. For instance, how might the history of white leaders defending their "traditional Christian way of life" against minority populations whom they viewed as threatening relate to similar arguments in defense of tradition now being circulated by contemporary white Christian opponents of marriage equality?

If the blackness of blacks is mentioned, in part, because of the particular history that they share, should not the whiteness of whites also be mentioned? This concern could also be raised about the current realities of racism. If the blackness of blacks is mentioned because of their current, common experience of being victimized by racism, should not the common experience that whites share of benefiting from racism also bring their whiteness into view for discussion?

In terms of history, several racial topics relevant to whites could be examined in public investigations of the opposition to marriage equality. African Americans have a historical legacy of being victimized by and resisting racial discrimination, segregation, and the way that the Bible was used to justify their enslavement. If that U.S. historical legacy is relevant to current public discussions of marriage equality with black Christian leaders, why is it not also relevant to white Christian leaders? Don't whites also share this history? What are the long-term implications of this neglect in current public conversations of their past assertions of white dominance?

Actions upholding the interests of whites by leaders from this dominant, majority racial group have deeply shaped the morality of this nation. White Christians have a historical legacy of crafting Christian biblical arguments in support of slavery and the stealing of Indian and Mexican land,[20] of legislating and maintaining de facto racial discrimination against Asian Americans[21] and other communities of color, and enforcing segregation with Christian terrorism (for instance, KKK lynchings and bombings). Could this legacy be relevant for understanding the white Christian crafting of biblical arguments asserting heterosexual superiority and legislating discrimination based on sexual orientation? Might it be relevant for understanding acts of terrorism like those of the whites who so brutally murdered Matthew Shepard? Why couldn't these possible connections be examined in public discussions of marriage equality with white Christians?

Historical precedents related to race, blackness, and public spectacles may also provide insight when considering why there is so much nationwide interest in the views of black leaders on same-gender marriage. It can be argued that public spectacles featuring blacks that generate interest, curiosity, or amusement for the white majority in the United States and abroad[22] have deep historical roots starting from slavery and continuing to the present in today's entertainment industry.

At the slave auction block, for instance, under the threat of a lashing, black slaves were required to perform songs. Some were "set to dancing even when their cheeks were wet with tears" so that "all the hollering and bawling" provided fun for whites at the marketplace.[23] In the late nineteenth and early twentieth century, lynchings and public burnings were so common in the South that they were sometimes referred to by whites as a "negro barbecue." Entire white families and communities often attended these events. White newspaper reporters and photographers captured the "carnival-like atmosphere" for their papers and even for postcards that were sent later to white family members.[24]

When exploring how the notion of blacks as popular spectacle provides an important context for the disproportionate attention to black views of same-gender marriage, one could also consider the role of the entertainment industry. One could trace the popularity of Negro performers as a source of entertainment for the masses in nineteenth- and early twentieth-century minstrel shows (perhaps even including white entertainers in black face)[25] up to the late twentieth-century consumption of black rap music by a majority of white teenagers.[26]

In sum, black entertainers as well as the real-life horrific treatment of blacks have routinely been a source of popular amusement and curiosity in American culture. Fascination with observing the actions of blacks is a mainstream cultural habit developed over centuries. In the current U.S. political economy, the boundaries between mass news media and entertainment media are quite often blurred. The profit-driven, primary concern of the news media is to sell the public familiar images that they will readily consume. Hence, it makes sense that images of blacks opposing same-gender marriage regularly attract public curiosity and that the marketplace mentality of the news media maintains its dedication to feeding that curiosity. The avoidance of racially identifying mainstream white Christian behavior is also understandable because it fits comfortably with familiar racial assumptions. Asking white Christian leaders about their views and naming their white social status and identity in conjunction with historically based understandings of that status and identity is risky. It would not be as comfortably consumed by most of the news audience, the majority of whom are white. And on such a painfully, politically polarizing issue as this one, observing blacks fits effortlessly with established societal habits of linking issues of race and the regulation of sexual morality.

Yet, why are so many black Christian leaders so eager to participate in this public conversation, especially to express their disapproval? More explanation is needed for why Rev. Gregory Daniels, for instance, not only takes the time to organize a press conference of black Baptist ministers in Chicago to announce their opposition to marriage equality but also makes the extremist statement that "If the K.K.K. opposes gay marriage, I would ride with them" (*New York Times*).[27] His Chicago clergy group gathered to applaud President Bush's call for a constitutional amendment defining marriage as an exclusively heterosexual prerogative. In another example, it is not clear why California television evangelist Frederick K. C. Price, who presides over the twenty-seven thousand member Crenshaw Christian Center, gathered together with many other well-known black evangelists in Washington, D.C., to point out the urgency of opposing marriage equality. In fact, "Price said the prospect of same-gender marriage has inspired his first foray into political activism."[28]

POWER POLITICS

I suppose that the simplest response to my question about why black Christian leaders are spearheading initiatives to oppose marriage equality could be the conclusion that they just want access to an enticing public stage. If, as I have argued, it is especially politically advantageous in this historical moment to make claims about Christianity in public forums, black Christian clergy are religiously equipped for this opportunity. Why shouldn't they try to reap some of those benefits of status and prominence associated with Christian advocacy in public forums? These ministers are repeatedly invited by the media to speak for the views of "the black church" and "the black community." Moreover, they are rarely, if ever, challenged when they proclaim themselves spokespersons, particularly when expressing opposition to marriage equality. Even inexperienced spokespersons can recognize in this trend a recipe for how to become a succeessful profesisonal; one becomes a black clergy expert on which media outlets will rely. Pastors know well that congregations can grow larger as a result of such media exposure!

If the political leaders who have exercised such dominant control over the White House, the Congress, the Supreme Court, and many state legislatures in the nation are adamantly opposed to marriage equality, it certainly appears to be a politically savvy strategy to do likewise. For, if one aspires to be a local community leader who works smoothly with the major political leaders and there is no great cost to bear from one's own community for attacking gays and lesbians, it makes sense to align oneself with those in power by publicly opposing marriage equality. Why would one assume that black Christian leaders would be any less ambitious for power, status, and influence in the broader society than any other leader whose profession draws him or her into the public arena?

I must point out that not all black Christian leaders have publicly opposed marriage equality. I am reproducing the very problem about which I have complained if I fail to acknowledge the presence of local and national black Christian leaders who have offered strong support for marriage equality within public venues. Sometimes, black Christian gay couples, such as Saundra Heath-Toby and Alicia Toby-Heath, declare their faith and share details of their personal lives in news stories.[29] Sylvia Rhue and other leaders of the National Black Justice Coalition (a national black gay rights organization) have tirelessly offered rebuttals to antigay biblical and political rhetoric.[30] Retired activist pastors and veterans of the civil rights movement, such as Rev. Cecil Williams, former pastor of Glide Memorial United Methodist Church (San Francisco), and Rev. Gilbert Caldwell, former pastor of Denver's Park Hill United Methodist Church, have lent their personal credibility to public statements about the validity of comparing the struggle for gay rights with the civil rights movement.[31] Rev. Al Sharpton declared his support for marriage equality repeatedly and publicly when he sought the Democratic Party nomination for the U.S. presidency (2004 election). Before her final illness, Coretta Scott King gave her fervent support to the families of lesbians and gay men, commenting that "a constitutional amendment banning same-sex marriage is a form of gay bashing."[32] Though fewer than the voices of opposition, these kinds of supportive voices are also included in several news stories.

The opposition to marriage equality expressed by most of the black Christians who are interviewed in the media reflects certain patterns within some historically black faith traditions. The preaching and teaching ministries of pastors in black churches have often included sexist understandings of gender, sexuality, and clergy power. The practice of black clergy using their power to sexually shame and condemn community members is neither a recent phenomenon nor one that is restricted to issues of homosexuality and marriage equality. As I have argued elsewhere, many black clergy and black churches have traditionally discussed women's sexuality in a punitive and disciplinary manner.[33] It is not unusual to hear a black male preacher describe the sinfulness of women who dress in pants, wear skirts that he considers too short, or behave in ways that he asserts are sexually tempting men to be sinful. The shaming of unwed pregnant girls in front of the entire congregation has also been a tradition in certain black churches.[34] Sexist church practices are supportively intertwined with homophobic ones.

Opposition to marriage equality by black clergy is directly related to the shame associated with the infrequency and instability of heterosexual marriages in black communities. Rev. Walter Fauntroy, former civil rights movement activist and member of Congress and currently a pastor in Washington, D.C., expressed a typical version of this anxiety to the *Washington Post*. Calling same-sex marriage an abomination, he said, "We have not yet recovered from the cruelties of slavery, which was based on the destruction of the family."[35]

Blacks have disproportionately higher rates of single-parent homes than other racial/ethnic groups. This fact has been publicly labeled as a problem and been featured in the national spotlight most prominently within discussions of welfare reform. An emphasis on marriage constituted the moral lynchpin of the historic 1996 welfare reform legislation, the Personal Responsibility and Work Opportunity Reconciliation Act. This legislation, ushered in by Newt Gingrich and Bill Clinton, constitutes the most draconian public policy assault on the poor in recent times.[36] Black women were featured in the castigation of poor, single-parent-led families by politicians and media pundits when this legislation was passed. Several black Christian leaders have a singular concern with increasing the number of heterosexual marriages; this preoccupation often focuses on pressuring women.

Participating in a newly launched national event, Black Marriage Day, Rev. Herbert Daughtry's House of the Lord Church (New York City) sponsored "Marry Your Baby Daddy Day" during which he conducted a mass wedding of ten black heterosexual couples.[37] The title of this event reveals its goal of shaming and disciplining black single mothers. In the same interview referred to above, Fauntroy also exemplifies the paternalistic and dictatorial use of power by black male clergy that is so often directed at black women. In stating his reasons for opposing same-sex marriage he explains, "Don't tell my young women they don't need a man."[38]

Opponents like Fauntroy repeatedly describe marriage equality as antithetical to the proliferation of black heterosexual marital relationships. It remains unclear how preventing all gay people from being allowed to get married will result in more black heterosexual people choosing to get married. Unfortunately, the news media rarely demand that black Christian opponents of marriage equality explain this supposed benefit of banning same-gender marriage.

Numerous black Christian leaders complain bitterly about the comparison of the 1950s and 1960s civil rights movement with the struggle for marriage equality and for gay rights in general. White gay rights activists may make statements that erroneously claim or appear to be claiming that the racism blacks faced in the past is comparable to the heterosexism that white LGBT people now face. Of course, the state-sanctioned enslavement, rapes, lynchings, disenfranchisement from voting, and daily humiliations of segregation are not the same as the heterosexism faced now by white LGBT people. Such self-serving and ridiculous claims, even when only implied by white gay rights activists, provide handy excuses for the expression of homophobia by black Christian heterosexuals. It does not, however, cause that homophobia.

More than merely an excuse to express homophobia, the black Christian alignment with the powerful white Christian right and Republican Party leaders becomes an opportunity to exercise a degree of power over white men and women, albeit gay ones. I suspect that it may even be true that for many socioeconomically advantaged, white gay men, the maintenance of all of the benefits of marriage exclusively for heterosexuals could represent a unique experience of disadvantage. It could be one of the very few instances when they experience a denial of basic rights and entitlements in society that is unfairly based solely upon their identity. One black clergy opponent revealed to me in the midst of our argument about gay rights that he relished the idea of helping keep a few whites from getting some of the power that they want "just like they have always done to us."[39]

Ironically, in this grab for power and status, the lives of black (and Latino/a, Asian, and Native American) LGBT people and their families are eclipsed. Whites (albeit only LGBT whites) are the only ones who matter in this scenario. The costs to the rights of LGBT persons of color do not count as these black Christian heterosexuals take the opportunity to experience some measure of societally conferred superiority. In other words, based upon their "God-given" identity, they have the chance to enjoy the legal entitlement to certain societal advantages that are denied to (some) whites. Perhaps it is because Christian rhetoric can be used as a moral justification that they seem to have no qualms about sacrificing the rights and needs of low-status members of black communities and their children to maintain this superior status.

In their opposition to marriage equality, homophobic black Christian leaders (and others) use language about Christian faith and scripture in public forums as a tool to exert a degree of power and control over others and to gain influence, status, and social acceptance. Christian rhetoric helps create a pretense that black Christian leaders are concerned with building moral communities while actually immorally solidifying injustice, inequality, and suffering for LGBT spouses and families across all racial/ethnic groups. Homophobic black Christian leaders are hardly the first ones in U.S. history to use rhetoric about Christian scriptures and traditions to justify a notion of their inherent superiority, their right to treat others as inferior, sexualized objects, and their right to have the rules governing church and society uphold their superiority. In our contemporary society, homophobic black Christian leaders are definitely not the only ones engaged in this endeavor. If they were the only ones, their efforts would probably not be mentioned in national newspapers or have very much political efficacy. In fact, blacks are vastly outnumbered by homophobic white Christian leaders in this attempt to maintain inequality and discrimination.

The struggle for marriage equality requires Christians to break out of the familiar patterns of repression that our white, Christian, heterosexual-dominated society has taught so well.

NOTES

1. It should be noted that these two individuals are not typical local church pastors of any racial/ethnic background, in that both are Harvard University educated, with PhDs in theology and ethics.

2. "Black Churches and Gay Marriage," *Religion and Ethics Newsweekly*, episode no. 746, July 16, 2004, http://www.pbs.org/wnet/religionandethics/week746/p-feature.html (accessed July 2004).

3. For examples, see discussions of breeding and sexual violation in Dorothy Roberts, *Killing the Black Body: Race, Reproduction, and the Meaning of Liberty* (New York: Vintage Books, 1997), 24–31; the common accusation of sexual threatening of white women as a reason for lynching is documented in Jacqueline Jones Royster, ed., *Southern Horrors and Other Writings: The Anti-Lynching Campaign of Ida B. Wells, 1892–1900* (Boston: Bedford Books, 1997).

4. See documentation of this problem that ranges from seventeenth-century white observers of Africans to 1968 pop culture U.S. postcards in Jan Nederveen Pieterse, *White on Black: Images of Africa and Blacks in Western Popular Culture* (New Haven: Yale University Press, 1992), 175 and chapter 6, "Libido in Colour."

5. For examples, see Patricia Morton, *Disfigured Images: The Historical Assault on Afro-American Women* (New York: Greenwood Press, 1991); and John D'Emilio and Estelle B. Freedman, *Intimate Matters: A History of Sexuality in America* (New York: Harper and Row, 1988), especially chapter 5, "Race and Sexuality."

6. For examples, see my interviews with leaders and activists in *Disruptive Christian Ethics: When Racism and Women's Lives Matter* (Louisville: John Knox Westminster Press, 2006); see chapter 17 in this volume.

7. See Audre Lorde, "Man Child: A Black Lesbian Feminist's Response," in *Sister Outsider* (Trumansburg, NY: The Crossing Press, 1984); and Lani Guinier and Gerald Torres, *The Miner's Canary: Enlisting Race, Resisting Power, Transforming Democracy* (Cambridge, MA: Harvard University Press, 2002), 254–74.

8. See Mary Rose D'Angelo, "Women Partners in the New Testament," *Journal of Feminist Studies in Religion* 6 (Spring 1990): 65–86.

9. Frank Reeves, "Trouble for Gays in Black Churches," *Pittsburgh Post-Gazette*, April 15, 2004.

10. Don Lattin, "Black Clergy Gathering to Fight Gay Matrimony," *San Francisco Chronicle*, May 15, 2004.

11. Ron DePasquale, "Gay Debate Splits Black Community," *Chicago Tribune*, March 14, 2004.

12. Cary McMullen, "Local Black Ministers Condemn Gay Marriage," *The Ledger* (Lakeland, FL), March 13, 2004.

13. Phuong Ly and Hamil R. Harris, "Blacks, Gays in Struggle of Values, Same-Sex Marriage Issue Challenges Religious, Political Ties," *Washington Post*, March 15, 2004.

14. Lynette Clemetson, "Both Sides Court Black Churches in the Battle Over Gay Marriage," *New York Times*, March 1, 2004.

15. Kelli Arena, Renay San Miguel, Kathleen Koch, and Ray D'Alessio, *CNN Sunday Morning*, March 7, 2004, Transcript No. 030702CN.V46.

16. Shaila Dewan, "United Church of Christ Backs Same-Sex Marriage," *New York Times*, July 5, 2005.

17. Ibid.

18. Some news stories have identified white evangelicals or white conservatives, such as Bob Dart, "Black Preachers and White Conservatives Join to Oppose Gay Marriage," *Cox News Service*, June 1, 2004; One story states, "White Evangelical Protestants were the most firmly opposed…opposition among blacks also remained," Robin Toner, "Opposition to Gay Marriage is Declining, Study Finds," *New York Times*, July 25, 2003.

19. Stories about religious opposition to marriage equality are reported in the news media more frequently than stories about religious support for this issue.

20. See Reginald Horsman, *Race and Manifest Destiny: The Origins of American Racial Anglo-Saxonism* (Cambridge: Harvard University Press, 1981).

21. See Ian F. Haney López, *White by Law: The Legal Construction of Race* (New York: New York University Press, 1996).

22. Pieterse, *White on Black: Images of Africa and Blacks in Western Popular Culture* (see note 4), describes popular images of blacks throughout Europe.

23. As quoted in Saidiya V. Hartman, *Scenes of Subjection: Terror, Slavery, and Self-Making in Nineteenth-Century America* (New York: Oxford University Press, 1997), 37 and chapter 1, "Innocent Amusements: The Stage of Sufferance."

24. Leon Litvack, "Hellhounds," in *Without Sanctuary: Lynching Photography in America* (Santa Fe: Twin Palms Publishers, 2000), 10. This is excerpted from a longer chapter by the same name in Leon F. Litwack, *Trouble in Mind: Black Southerners in the Age of Jim Crow* (New York: Alfred A. Knopf, 1998). In *Southern Horrors*, Wells describes white children being let out of school to watch the burning of Negroes.

25. For discussion of minstrelsy and white audiences see Eric Lott, *Love and Theft: Blackface Minstrelsy and the American Working Class* (New York: Oxford University Press, 1995).

26. See Bakari Kitwana, *Why White Kids Love Hip Hop: Wankstas, Wiggas, Wannabes, and the New Realty of Race in America* (New York: Basic Civitas Books, 2005).

27. Clemetson, "Both Sides Court Black Churches in the Battle Over Gay Marriage" (see note 14); Chinta Strausberg, "Rev. Daniels: 'I'd Rather Ride with KKK,'" *Chicago Defender* 207 (February 25, 2004), 1. For a similar effort by black clergy in Boston, see Michael Paulson, "Black Clergy Rejection Stirs Gay Marriage Backers," *The Boston Globe*, February 10, 2004, http://www.boston.com/news/local/articles/2004/02/10/black_clergy _rejection_stirs_gay_marriage_backers/ (accessed October 11, 2006).

28. Lattin, "Black Clergy Gathering to Fight Gay Matrimony" (see note 10).

29. See Alfred Doblin, "Teen's Death Moves Couple; Joined Lawsuit to Push for Tolerance," *Herald News*, February 13, 2006. Also see Joe Guy Collier, "Black, Christian and Gay: Couple Fight Religious Hurdles," *Detroit Free Press*, May 4, 2004; "Black Churches and Gay Marriage" (see note 2).

30. For an example of Rhue's work before she joined National Black Justice Coalition, see Charlette Adams, "LA's Black Gay/Lesbian Community Speaks Out Against Same-Sex Opposition," *Los Angeles Sentinel*, vol. 70, issue 2, April 1–April 7, 2004. Also see http:/www.nbjcoalition.org (accessed October 11, 2006).

31. See Lattin, "Black Clergy Gathering to Fight Gay Matrimony" (see note 10); and references to Caldwell's letter to the editor in Mary Mitchell, "Gay Marriage Stance Puts Pastors in Unholy Union," *Chicago Sun-Times*, March 14, 2004.

32. Adrian Walker, "Musing King's Legacy," *Boston Globe*, April 29, 2004.

33. See my articles, "Mind, Body, Spirit: Sexism and the Role of Religious Intellectuals," in *The Crisis of the Negro Intellectual Reconsidered*, ed. Jerry G. Watts (New York: Routledge, 2004), 203–23; "A Space for Faith, Sexual Desire, and Ethical Black Ministerial Practices," in *Loving the Body: Black Religious Studies and the Erotic*, ed. Anthony Pinn and Dwight Hopkins (New York: Palgrave, 2005), 31–50.

34. Ibid.

35. Ly and Harris, "Blacks, Gays in Struggle of Values, Same-Sex Marriage Issue Challenges Religious, Political Ties" (see note 13).

36. See my extensive discussion of the birth of this policy in *Disruptive Christian Ethics*, chapter 3 (see note 6).

37. Jabari Asim, "Black Marriage Day," *Washington Post*, March 21, 2005.

38. Phuong Ly and Hamil R. Harris, "Blacks, Gays in Struggle of Values, Same-Sex Marriage Issue Challenges Religious, Political Ties" (see note 13).

39. Personal communication with a black clergy member at the General Conference 2004 of the United Methodist Church in Pittsburgh.

14

THE REFORMED CHURCH IN AMERICA: ONE DENOMINATION'S RESPONSE TO SAME-SEX MARRIAGE

— • —

Norman J. Kansfield

Your discipline comes to me as a crushing blow. I assured this body that I would accept its judgment, and I intend to do precisely that. But I assure you that it will not be easy for me to live with the memory of this moment. This denomination has been the context of my entire ministry, now almost forty years in length. But even before I was ordained, this church formed the cradle of my faith. It was in the First Reformed Church of Mt. Greenwood, Chicago, that I was baptized, immediately following my birth. It was in the First Reformed Church of South Holland, Illinois, that I learned the meaning of faith, and learned how to pray. It was in the institutions of this church that I prepared myself for ministry, and to two of those institutions I have contributed a total of twenty-five years of educational leadership. I have invested my whole self for the welfare of the Reformed Church, and I confess to being very frustrated that it was not possible for me to convince you that even the acts about which we have so much talked today—even those acts were carried out by me with the intention of contributing to the proclamation of the Gospel of our Lord Jesus Christ and the welfare of the Reformed Church in America.

You may depose and suspend me, but the terrible plight of the children of the Reformed Church who are gay and lesbian will remain before you. It is your own children and their children who are gay and lesbian that you have really deposed and suspended—left again with no place within the church. In Jesus' day, the Samaritans were just like that. The Samaritans had no place within the religious conversations of those who considered themselves the people of God, because hundreds of years earlier their forebears had intermarried with the nation which then had taken them captive. Their "sin" was merely a genetic one. And that kept them from being accepted in the circles of "God's people." But Jesus gave Samaritans a prime place in several of his parables. He talked with a Samaritan woman at Jacob's well. In the eighth chapter of the Gospel according to St. John, our Lord finds himself in the middle of a long and violent argument with the religious leaders of his day. It is the toughest verbal fight that the gospels portray for us. As it moves toward its end, the pious, faithful Jews said to Jesus: "Are we not justified in saying that you are a Samaritan and have a demon." Jesus answered, "I do not have a demon." He wanted them to be clear about the kind of person they were arguing with. So he insisted, "I am not going to allow you to think of me as out of my mind—as having a demon." But he did not say, "I am not a Samaritan—you cannot call or think me a Samaritan." Jesus, even though he was not a Samaritan, was willing to bear their name—a name more often spat out by Jews than said with any sense of kindness. In just the same way, Jesus in our time, I am sure, would bear the name of "lesbian" or "gay." He wouldn't even flinch if he were called "Queer," or "Dyke," or "Faggot."

That is, dear friends, exactly what we have to learn to do. You all have continued to say that you regard it as important that the numbers of Reformed Churches increase. You have said that church revitalization and multiplication are the efforts to which you want to give all your attention. Well, you may, but until you learn to accept people—especially people whom you think are not clean and pure enough for you to welcome—the growth of the church is not going to happen. You are concerned about the constantly diminishing number of members within the RCA. But until our denomination is prepared to welcome all the persons for whom Christ died, our numbers will continue to shrink until we are no more. We cannot be concerned with the purity of the church and the growth of the church at the same time. Evangelization only begins to happen when our hands and our feet are muddy with the reality of everyday life all around us.

And so I leave you now. Be assured that I will continue to pray for this Synod, and for the work that yet lies before you. Good Night.

—June 17, 2005, Farewell to the Synod[1] by the Reverend Dr. Norman J. Kansfield following his removal from the office of professor of theology at New Brunswick Theological Seminary and suspension of his ordination by the General Synod of the Reformed Church in America because he presided at the wedding of his daughter Ann and her partner Jennifer.

PART I

Introduction to the Main Characters in the Story

This chapter details a confrontation I had with the Reformed Church in America (RCA) when I held two offices within its structure—the offices of Minister of Word and Sacrament and General Synod professor of theology. The RCA is a small North American denomination with 935 congregations spread thinly across the United States and Canada. The largest concentrations of congregations are found in New York, New Jersey, Michigan, and Iowa. In 2004, its membership numbered just over 282,000. The denomination's theology is Calvinistic, shaped mostly by the Protestantism of the Netherlands, and it is officially spelled out within the "Belgic Confession" (1561), the "Heidelberg Catechism" (1563), and the "Canons of the Synod of Dort" (1618–1619). These three confessions together comprise the *Standards of Unity*, which form one part of the RCA's "Constitution." The other two parts are its *Liturgy* and its *Book of Church Order*.

The denomination recognizes four ecclesiastical offices: Minister of Word and Sacrament, Professor of Theology, Elder, and Deacon.

The Church's life is organized into four assemblies. A local church is governed by a "consistory" made up of the pastor (or pastors) together with the elders and deacons elected by that congregation. The area assembly is called a "classis" (from the Latin word for "fleet") and comprises at least one pastor and one elder from each congregation in its membership. There are forty-five classes, and they range in size from six to forty-one congregations. There are eight regional synods, each comprising from three to eight classes. The General Synod is the binational annual meeting of delegates from all forty-five classes.

I was baptized into the membership of the RCA soon after my birth on Easter Sunday, March 24, 1940. I grew up within the Dutch-immigrant farming community of South Holland, Illinois, twenty miles south of Chicago. I graduated from Hope College (an RCA-related college in Holland, Michigan) and from Western Theological Seminary, also in Holland, Michigan, one of the RCA's two seminaries. In addition to those degrees, I earned the degree of STM from Union Theological Seminary in New York City and the degrees of AM and PhD from the University of Chicago. I served as pastor of the Second Reformed Church of Astoria in Queens, New York; interim pastor of the First Reformed Church of Berwyn, Illinois; and Associate Pastor of the Ivanhoe Reformed Church of Riverdale, Illinois. In 1970, I joined the faculty of Western Theological Seminary, serving as associate librarian until 1974 and from that date to 1983 as librarian of the John Walter Beardslee Library.

In 1982, the General Synod elected me to the office of Professor of Theology, but I had to resign that ecclesiastical office in 1983, when I became the director of the Ambrose Swasey Library, serving the Colgate-Rochester Divinity School/Bexley Hall/Crozer Theological Seminary and the St. Bernard's Institute, in Rochester, New York. In 1993, I was elected the twelfth president of the RCA's New Brunswick Theological Seminary in New Brunswick, New Jersey. The General Synod of 1993 reelected me to the office of Professor of Theology. From my ordination to the ministry in 1965 until my deposition (removal) from the office of Professor of Theology and suspension from the office of Minister of Word and Sacrament by the General Synod of 2005, I had also served the denomination as a member of several committees and commissions and as a trustee for the Ministerial Formation Coordinating Agency, in addition to my work within its congregations and seminaries. This much is introduction to the General Synod and to me, who would later run afoul of the Synod's understanding of propriety.

The Reformed Church in America and Homosexuality: The Facts of the Case

I remain convinced that there is no explicit prohibition against same-sex marriage in scripture or within the Constitution of the Reformed Church in America, which comprises the *Standards of Unity*, the *Liturgy*, and the *Book of Church Order*. That remains a "fact" for me. Others draw radically different conclusions. Three times—in 1978, 1979, and 1994—the General Synod received reports from its Commission on Theology concerning the place within the church of persons who are homosexual. That is a fact about which all agree. But about the meaning of those reports, differences of opinion abound.

Theology That Is "Reassuring and Fraught with Danger": The Report of the Commission on Theology, 1978

In 1978 the stance taken by the Reformed Church in America on homosexuality was a brave one. In that year, the General Synod received and approved a report on homosexuality from its Commission on Theology.[2] This report thoroughly reevaluated all scriptural and theological passages of import, as well as what the commission called "the contribution of the human sciences." On the basis of biblical and theological grounds, the report concluded, "Heterosexuality is not only normal: it is normative. Homosexual acts are contrary to the will of God for human sexuality."[3] There was nothing new or brave in that conclusion. But the commission on Theology described this particular conclusion as "both reassuring and fraught with danger."[4] I, as well as many other leaders within the denomination, believe that the RCA has, since 1978, rested too comfortably in the reassurance of that conclusion and has never squarely faced the danger about which the commission warned. That danger is defined in this sentence from the report: "Despite the compulsive fear and loathing which homosexuality arouses in our society, there are no theological grounds on which a homosexual may be singled out for a greater measure of judgment."[5] That was written in 1978!

Further, when conclusions were drawn from "the human sciences," the commission made a distinction between those persons whose homosexual orientation is a matter of choice (the report called this "perversion") and those persons whose homosexual orientation is a matter beyond their choosing (the report called this "inversion"). The 1978 report may have used very quaint (and now unacceptable) language to describe this difference, and it may have radically misjudged the percentage of persons for whom sexual orientation is not a matter of choice (it accepted, on the basis of the Kinsey Report,[6] an estimate that 4 percent of all homosexual persons were homosexual innately or without their choosing), but the commission and its report carefully pointed the church toward a huge truth with which it has never come to terms: "The church must learn to deal differently with persons who are homosexual by constitution and not by choice."[7] The commission then went on to draw the most amazing conclusion from this insight: "Scripture does not refer to the problem of homosexual acts which emerge in accord with one's conscious, sexual orientation and not against it."[8]

"Christian Pastoral Care for the Homosexual": The 1979 Report of the Commission on Theology and Subsequent Developments

The Commission on Theology followed its 1978 report with a report to the Synod of 1979,[9] focused entirely on "Christian Pastoral Care for the Homosexual." The 1979 report failed to take aggressive advantage of the new ground broken by the 1978 Report. It failed to make clear the obligation of the church to offer pastoral care to those persons who were innately homosexual that was very different from the kind of pastoral care it offered to those who freely chose homosexual behavior. Nevertheless, the 1979 report did powerfully urge the Reformed Church in America toward four "reasonable expectations" of its relationship with all homosexuals:

1. "Toward the elimination of the double standard of morality applied to the homosexual."[10]
2. Toward a moment when the Church would acknowledge "its sins against the homosexual."[11]
3. Toward a reality within which the church would systematically make a "genuine effort to understand homosexuality."[12]
4. Toward the provision of a context within which "the homosexual should reasonably expect personal acceptance and an understanding of the process of sanctification."[13]

The reports of the Commission on Theology, submitted to the General Synod in 1978 and 1979, are very clearly committee documents. They set out powerful new insights and then draw back into old preconceptions. But, at the very least, it must be said that they set an aggressive agenda for the RCA in its ministry to and with homosexual persons. However, that agenda lost priority almost as soon as it was presented. The Synod of 1980 gave some evidence of wanting to continue the trajectory of the Synods of 1978 and 1979.[14] But, in truth, the issue of how the church should welcome and include homosexual persons was no longer the center of the Synod's focus. The next several synods focused their attention on two other equally demanding social issues: racial injustice in the United States and the need to convince the independent but related Reformed Churches in South Africa to commit to the dismantling of apartheid. In ensuing years the concern of Synod after Synod focused on much more internal issues, such as the denomination's liturgy and worship, the shape of its administrative and missional structures, and the means by which the denomination was going to obtain sufficient funding to enable it to continue its ordinary operations.

The Cultural Context of Church Decision Making: The Reagan Revolution

By 1990, when the General Synod next turned its deliberative attention to the character of the church's welcome of gay and lesbian persons, a vast transformation had occurred within the culture of the United States. That transformation has been called the "Reagan Revolution." President Reagan himself, speaking from the Oval Office on January 11, 1989, in his last Presidential Address to the American people, accepted the term "Reagan Revolution" as a correct characterization of his presidency. Those eight years had, indeed, turned much of U.S. culture—especially regarding social sensibilities—on its head. Analyst and presidential biographer Stephen E. Ambrose, participating in a symposium on the question, "How Great Was Ronald Reagan?,"[15] observed that one mark of the revolution was Reagan's reversal of the decades-old flow of power to Washington. Ambrose went on to say:

> By dismantling some federal programs, and reducing others, he forced the states and the cities to assume more responsibilities for running their own shows. If he failed to break the Democratic hold on Congress, he did force the Democratic Party to move to the right. When Reagan entered politics...virtually every Democrat outside Dixie identified himself, proudly, as a liberal; today...almost every Democrat in the nation tries to call himself [sic] a conservative.[16]

Another participant in that same symposium, James Nuechterlein, professor of political thought at Valpariaso University, measured the Reagan Revolution's impact as nothing less than "a fundamental change in the terms of debate of American politics." In a favorable appraisal of Reagan, he concluded that "on all major social issues—abortion, quotas, gay rights, feminism, crime and punishment, the family, moral and religious values—the Reagan administration has been conservative and correct."[17] This fundamental change altered something that was much more than "decades-old." Liberalism had, up until 1981, been regarded as intrinsic to and characteristic of the very spirit of the United States. "Being liberal" was once regarded so highly as an American virtue that people proudly named their hometowns and cities "Liberal"—Liberal, Indiana; Liberal, Kansas; Liberal, Missouri; and Liberal, Oregon—just as communities proudly called themselves "Freedom" or "Independence" or "Federal." No one has yet named a hometown "Conservative."

At first, the RCA resisted these massive social shifts. In 1982, for example, the General Synod received a report from its Christian Action Commission documenting the impact of President Reagan's damaging cuts in social welfare programs and his shifting of that funding to the military budget. The Synod acted to convey to the Republican Administration its feeling of "abandonment" because of the government's apparent refusal to be concerned for the poor and the oppressed.[18] But, by 1990, it is clear that the RCA had chosen to follow the lead of the Reagan administration on most of the social agenda, including the issue of homosexuality. From 1990 on, the denomination's thinking was shaped much more by the culture of the day—the Reagan Revolution—than by its biblical or theological heritage.

Introducing the Concept of "Practicing" Homosexuality: Acts of Synod, 1990–1995

It was in this radically changed environment that the issue of the church's relationship to homosexual persons next arose. In 1990, the Classis of Cascades (State of Washington and Provinces of British Columbia, Alberta, and Saskatchewan) sent an overture to the General Synod requesting that the report of the commission on Theology to the 1978 General Synod be defined as "the official position of the Reformed Church in America."[19] In response to this overture, the Advisory Committee on Theology recommended that the General Synod "adopt as the position of the Reformed Church in America that the practicing homosexual lifestyle is contrary to scripture, while at the same time encouraging love and sensitivity towards such persons as fellow human beings." The advisory committee further recommended that the General Synod instruct the Commission on Theology to prepare a new study on homosexuality for presentation to the Synod of 1992. Finally, the advisory committee recommended that the 1978 and 1979 Commission on Theology papers be commended to the church "as pastoral advice until such time as a subsequent study by the commission is approved by General Synod." The Synod adopted all three recommendations.[20]

These actions, for the first time, introduced the concept of "practicing" homosexuality into the church's conversation. The differentiation that was so important to the 1978 document—making a distinction between homosexual acts by choice and innate homosexual orientation—now was replaced by the differentiation between the "practicing" homosexual individual and the nonpracticing or, presumably, celibate homosexual. The recommendations also, for the first time, described homosexuality as a "lifestyle"—with the clear suggestion that homosexuality was something that one could choose or seek out, in the manner of the television show *Lifestyles of the Rich and Famous*, which had premiered August 1, 1983, and aired for nine seasons.

The report that the Commission on Theology was instructed by the 1990 General Synod to present to the Synod of 1992 finally arrived before the Synod of 1994 after being crafted by a task force that had held "listening sessions" during the 1993 General Synod. These sessions, and other experiences of intentional listening to the church, had led the task group and the entire Commission on Theology to report to the Synod of 1994 as follows:

> [The members of the commission] do not think the most helpful response at this moment is another position paper. What they have learned cannot effectively be shared in such a format. In addition, the RCA has already reaffirmed its earlier position in sending this mandate to the Commission. What is needed is a pastoral response.[21]

The task force and the commission proposed a five-part "season of discovery and discernment." Part 1 was to introduce members of the denomination to the wide diversity of opinion regarding homosexuality within the RCA and to provide an opportunity for members to tell the stories of their experience of persons who are gay or lesbian, as well as to reflect on how that experience had shaped their attitudes and response. This part and all subsequent parts were to include the opportunity for persons to identify "serious questions" that would need exploration and answering in future sessions. Part 2 dealt with matters of biblical witness and interpretation. Explicitly, it called for an exploration of how we in the RCA understand the authority of the Bible, as well as questions regarding what the texts *do* say and what are the key points at which Christians interpret these texts differently. Part 3 was to be a review of what the scientific community had discovered subsequent to 1978. The church would be asked to "consider the relationship between scientific findings (what is) and moral norms (what ought to be)."[22] Part 4 was to involve the development of ministry responses to the conclusions drawn on the basis of Parts 1 through 3. In Part 5 the commission would gather feedback to form the basis of its final report.

This five-part process of discovery was not to be. It was far too open ended. The previous studies of 1978 and 1979 were seen as being given too little status. The proposal of the Commission on Theology seemed to offer far too much chance for the presentation of new data. The Advisory Committee on Theology recommended to the Synod that the report of the Commission on Theology not be approved. The Synod's final vote on the commission's proposed "Season of Discovery and Discernment" was delayed to the following day, at which point a substitute motion—developed overnight by delegates both for and against the commission's proposal—passed unanimously. The substitute motion called on the General Synod to recognize and confess that the RCA had "failed to live up to its own statements regarding homosexuality" and that many of the congregations within the RCA had failed to provide "an environment where persons have felt the acceptance and freedom to struggle with the hard issues involving sexual orientation." Finally, it called the RCA to a process of "repentance, prayer, learning and growth in ministry" to be guided by "the basic biblical-theological framework presented in the previous statements of the General Synod in 1978, 1979, and 1990."[23] This action also instructed the Commission on Theology, with the assistance of the denomination's education professionals, to develop three resources to assist congregations in this process:

1. A study guide for use in RCA congregations, which will assist Christians in reading and understanding the 1978 and 1979 statements…. This study guide will include updating of these reports only with respect to factual information.
2. A process of reflection for RCA congregations who are seeking to increase their sensitivity and awareness of the ways in which persons of homosexual orientation have suffered in our churches and in our society.
3. A collection of models for ministry to persons of homosexual orientation. This collection of models will serve to demonstrate ways of implementing ministry to persons of homosexual orientation that are in harmony with the RCA's stated theological positions.[24]

By the Synod of 1995, the Commission on Theology had clearly become a little gun-shy. Instead of proceeding directly to the development of the materials it had been instructed by the Synod of 1994 to present to the Synod of 1995, the commission presented a "Prospectus Outline" for the mandated study materials that it would then develop only after it had received the encouragement of the Synod. This proved to be a provident approach. The Synod's Advisory Committee on Theology failed to find the "Prospectus Outline" at all appropriate and refused to recommend it to the Synod. The Synod did not approve the commission's proposal.[25]

PART II

Change is not always easy for us to deal with. And, it seems, change is particularly difficult for the church to navigate. Old truths and understandings, long hallowed by the church's practice, and given voice in liturgy and hymn, become worn into habits and traditions that rise above the level of evaluation, critique, and change. But our lessons, this afternoon, tell us that God changes God's mind precisely about the way that the Community of the Faithful—the Assembly of the LORD— is expected to live out its faith. In Deuteronomy 23, God's instructions to God's people were that: "No Ammonite or Moabite shall be admitted to the Assembly of the LORD. Even to the tenth generation, none of their descendants shall be admitted to the Assembly of the LORD."

I do not doubt God said that. At the time it must have been important, in order to insure the purity of the Assembly of the LORD, for persons from these other ethnic traditions to be excluded. And Nehemiah 3:1–3 makes clear that this instruction from God was actually enforced. Those verses in Nehemiah describe just how exactingly some puritans within the Assembly of the LORD committed themselves to enforce this law; destroying marriages, splitting up families, and causing incalculable misery.

And then, along came another word from the LORD. We all read and heard this other word from the LORD on this very subject in the Gospel according to Isaiah. There it is written: Do not let the foreigner joined to the LORD say, "The LORD will surely separate me from the people of God." For thus says the LORD:

The foreigners who join themselves to the LORD, To minister to God, to love the name of the LORD, And to be God's servants, All who keep the Sabbath and do not profane it, And hold fast my covenant—These I will bring to my Holy Mountain, And make them joyful in my house of prayer; Their burnt offerings and their sacrifices will be accepted upon my altar; For my house shall be called a House of Prayer for all peoples.

The sole purpose of this combination of these texts is to assure us—with no room for misunderstanding or uncertainty—that when it comes to loving people, God's mind is always changing in order to be more wonderfully inclusive. And God calls all of us to keep up with the eternal expansiveness of God's love. So, God gives us examples. Just two books away from Deuteronomy is the book of Ruth. In that text it is clear the Ruth is a Moabite. And, not only is Ruth accepted into the Assembly of the LORD, but by the end of the book we have been told that she became the Grandmother of David, King of God's people. And it was into the House of David that Jesus was born.

——Excerpt from the sermon by Norman Kansfield at the marriage of Jennifer Susanne Aull and Ann Margaret Kansfield, Northampton, Massachusetts, June 19, 2004.

Homosexuality and the Seminary: Rescinding a Lesbian Faculty Member's Contract

In the spring of 1998, New Brunswick Theological Seminary, one of the two theological seminaries of the RCA, faced the sudden resignation of its professors of both Old and New Testament. They had been offered wonderful positions in other seminaries. At the New Brunswick Seminary, the president has the prerogative to appoint a person to a one-year faculty term. And so, after careful deliberation with the dean of the seminary and with the moderator of the board of trustees, I appointed the Reverend Dr. Judith Hoch Wray to a one-year term as professor of New Testament. At the time of the appointment, I was well aware that Dr. Wray is a lesbian living in a committed relationship with another woman. Dr. Wray had taught within the seminary as an adjunct member of the faculty for six years, had in no way hidden her sexuality, and yet had also not made her sexuality an issue in any way. No one had ever raised an issue in regard to her serving as an adjunct professor, and her teaching was praised unanimously. But within one day of her appointment to the one-year position, objections and controversy had arisen throughout the denomination.

One Reformed Church minister immediately suggested that he would take the matter to the General Synod. He was dissuaded from this action by leaders of the denomination and was urged, instead, to appeal to the board of trustees. These same denominational leaders, in turn, began to put pressure on me, as president, to withdraw the contract. I refused to do so. The great concern of these denominational executives and officers was that the General Synod of 1998 was to meet in Holland, Michigan. They feared that, if the contract with Dr. Wray were still in effect, there would be a "firestorm" of protest against the seminary at the General Synod because it was their perception that Western Michigan was a "tinderbox" on issues of sexuality, in light of the heresy trial of the Reverend Dr. Richard Rhem, pastor of RCA's Christ Community Church in Spring Lake, Michigan.

In reality, Rhem had been charged at that heresy trial with "universalism." These charges against him had nothing to do with homosexuality. However, the officers of the Synod recognized that, even if initiated on theological grounds, the charges against Dr. Rhem may really have been in response to the fact that he and Christ Community Church held an open and welcoming stance toward gay and lesbian persons and that they were allowing the Christ Community Church building to be used by a congregation of the Metropolitan Community Church (a denomination founded to create a welcoming and affirming Christian community for LGBT Christians). Pastor Rhem was ultimately found guilty of the theological charges. He and the Christ Community Church (with almost all of its three thousand members) chose to leave the denomination, rather than appeal the verdict to the General Synod.

When I took no steps to withdraw Dr. Wray's contract, the Reverend Wesley Granberg-Michaelson, general secretary of the RCA, who is an *ex officio* member of the New Brunswick Theological Seminary board of trustees, chose to come to the board and attempt to convince the trustees to rescind the contract. In doing so, he was quite appropriately exercising his office. It is his responsibility to safeguard the welfare of all of the church's institutions and to do all he can to maintain the unity of the faith in the bond of peace. He very effectively arm wrestled the board into rescinding the contract, although it took this action most reluctantly and only after attaching four conditions: (1) They were committed to paying Dr. Wray for the entire value of her contract, so that she was in every way financially whole, in spite of the rescinding of the contract; (2) they wanted their action to be seen as taken solely for the peace and unity of the church; (3) they called on the general secretary and all other responsible persons within the RCA to immediately facilitate the conversation on the role of homosexual persons within the church that the Synod of 1994 had called for and that had never happened; and (4) they called for the general secretary and others to assure homosexual persons within the church a safe participation within that conversation. They also committed themselves and the seminary to a program of self-education about the issues that have prevented homosexual persons from open participation within the life of the church.[26]

Dr. Wray was, of course, profoundly hurt by this action.

In spite of the fact that the contract was rescinded, and in spite of the best efforts of the leaders of the Synod, the Wray appointment was nevertheless interjected into the meeting of the 1998 General Synod when the Reverend Douglas VanBronkhorst, a delegate from South Grand Rapids Classis (Michigan), introduced it as a matter of new business. The Synod ultimately took no direct action on that matter, but General Secretary Granberg-Michaelson included the matter in his address to the Synod. He stated the fact that "a woman, trained, qualified, an excellent teacher, who is living in a committed relationship with another woman" had been appointed to a one-year position within the Synod's New Brunswick Theological Seminary. He continued, "In my judgment, this action was a mistake. It threatened to create a breach in trust between the denomination and New Brunswick Theological Seminary." General Secretary Granberg-Michaelson noted for the delegates that the seminary trustees, just the week prior to Synod, had

> thoughtfully and prayerfully reviewed this matter and made the decision to rescind the appointment.... This action prevents a potentially divisive conflict from erupting right now in the denomination. But it still leaves us as a church with a crucial and important question: how will we...choose to address this issue, not only in this situation, but in the future?[27]

The general secretary went on to propose a course of action for the denomination. His plan was, in essence, forwarded to the Synod by the Committee of Reference with the following guidelines.

> To instruct this General Synod to refrain from deliberative debate and policy decisions specifically relating to homosexuality, as these matters have already been thoroughly addressed by previous synods, and to urge this same action upon the 1999 and 2000 General Synods; and further, to request all commissions, agencies, assemblies, and institutions related to the General Synod to refrain from taking any action that would be in obvious contradiction of our stated positions, as expressed in 1978, 1979, 1990, and 1994; and further, to instruct the General Synod Council, through its Congregational Services Committee, to help enable congregations and classes to enter a process of intentional discernment over the next two years concerning the pastoral challenges raised by the existence within our churches and within the communities in which we are called to minister, utilizing the study guide and other resources, in order to fulfill the actions called for on this matter by the 1994 General Synod.[28]

Before this motion was passed by the Synod, a motion was made from the floor to amend the text to meet one of the four conditions to which the seminary trustees and General Secretary Granberg-Michaelson had agreed when deciding to rescind the contract with Professor Wray—that the conversation should explicitly include gay and lesbian persons and should guarantee to them a "secure venue" for their participation. That amendment failed.[29]

I was then given a few minutes to address the Synod on this matter. I reminded the delegates that New Brunswick Seminary had a long record of concern for persons at the margins of the church. I indicated that, when one is at the margins of acceptability, it is easy to step over the line. That is what my actions had caused New Brunswick Seminary to do, and I apologized for having caused pain by doing so.

In the course of the next ten months, I met with a total of nine classes, some of whom wanted to hear the rationale for my actions and others to berate me for those acts. A total of about thirty congregations made use of the Synod's print resource, *Homosexuality: Seeking the Guidance of the Church*.[30] Except for these minimal commitments, the long-promised, denomination-wide conversation regarding homosexuality—or the much-heralded "process of intentional discernment"—never became, in any way, a reality.

PART III

> Any reading of Ruth's story or, for that matter, of David's story, immediately begins to make clear just how risky it is for the will of the LORD and the character of the Assembly of the LORD to change and include Moabites. For Ruth and David are barely in the door, when they—Ruth and David—begin to sing a kind of song such as had never been heard before within the Assembly of the LORD—songs that comprised powerful statements regarding same-sex love.
> They may not have had sexual passion in mind, but they gave powerful voice to what a woman-woman relationship might mean. Ruth said to her mother-in-law

Naomi: "Do not press me to leave you, or to turn back from following you! Where you go, I will go; where you lodge, I will lodge; Your people shall be my people and your God my God. Where you die, I shall die—There I will be buried. May the LORD do thus and so to me, and more as well, If even death parts me from you" Ruth 1.16–17.

This kind of song could also show how intensive a man-man relationship could be. David, after Jonathan's death in battle, sang a dirge that concluded: "How the mighty have fallen in the midst of battle! Jonathan lies slain upon your high places. I grieve for you my brother Jonathan; Greatly beloved were you to me; Your love to me was wonderful, Surpassing the love of women" II Samuel 1.25–26.

The lesson from Acts makes the very same point in a way with which no Christian can argue. The church, under the leadership of Peter, was finding its way into defining the character of membership. It began as a Jewish fellowship, accepting all of the definitions that Judaism had used for centuries. But here we meet a man named Cornelius, a Roman army officer. Cornelius didn't fit the Jewish prescription for admission to the Assembly of the LORD. God sent Peter a vision of unclean animals and instructed Peter to kill and eat them. Peter responds that he has not (and will not) "ever eaten anything that is forbidden by our Jewish laws." It is God's response to Peter's affirmation that we have to hear: "Do not call anything unclean that God has called clean." Those whom God has already determined to be clean, have to be regarded as clean enough for us. In other words, it is God who chooses! God had already determined that Cornelius was to be included in the membership of the church. Peter need not hesitate to baptize him. Likewise, all we need to understand, relative to who is included within the Assembly of the LORD and who is not, is to understand just whom it is that God Almighty, in Jesus Christ our Lord, has made clean. When God has determined that a person is to be included, that's that. Everything we do—in word or action—ought to proclaim that person to be clean and worthy of inclusion within the Assembly of the LORD. To separate ourselves from such a person is to be guilty of sundering the body of Christ.

—Excerpt from the sermon by Norman Kansfield at the marriage of
Jennifer Susanne Aull and Ann Margaret Kansfield, Northampton,
Massachusetts, June 19, 2004.

My Dismissal: 2004 and All That

On May 17, 2004, same-sex marriages became legal in the Commonwealth of Massachusetts. On the June 7, 2004, the General Synod of the Reformed Church in America solemnly voted as follows:

- To affirm that marriage is properly defined as the union of one man and one woman, to the exclusion of all others
- To direct the Commission on Church Order to consider an amendment to the *Book of Church Order*, which places this affirmation into our church order, for report to the 2005 General Synod[31]

For the first time in thirteen years, it was impossible for me to be present as a corresponding delegate to the General Synod.[32]

In December 2003, my daughter, Ann Kansfield, and Jennifer Aull determined that they loved each other and wanted to spend the rest of their lives together. They had first met as members of the Middle Collegiate Church, an RCA congregation in the East Village in New York City. Their relationship had grown during their time as students in New Brunswick Theological Seminary, each preparing for what she hoped would be helpful, faithful pastoral service within the Reformed Church. By Christmas, 2003, it was clear to both of them that they wanted to make a binding commitment to each other. They watched intently all of the legal maneuvering regarding equal marriage in Massachusetts, and as soon as it was possible for them to do so, Ann and Jennifer applied for and received a marriage license. On June 19, 2004, they were married in the sanctuary of the First Churches in Northampton, Massachusetts, a united American Baptist and United Church of Christ congregation. As Ann's father, I presided over the ceremony, solemnizing the marriage according to the liturgy of the Reformed Church in America, adapting it appropriately.[33] Jennifer and Ann were radiant, the day was perfect, and the joy was overflowing.

On June 9, 2004, concurrent with my application to the Commonwealth of Massachusetts for legal standing to perform the marriage, I sent a personal and confidential letter to each member of the board of trustees. The letter indicated my intention to preside at the ceremony, but, because I had not yet been legally authorized to do so, it was worded in this way: "If I preside at this wedding."[34] The letter did not ask explicitly for the advice or the permission of the board. It was my intent to provide the board and the seminary as much insulation as possible from my intended act in an attempt to protect against any later negative fallout. My intention was to provide the trustees with the capacity, for themselves and for the seminary, to deny any involvement. The board nevertheless understood my decision to preside at the wedding ceremony as having acted without regard for the welfare of the seminary. Ultimately, the board publicly coupled the issue of the wedding with the difficulties the seminary's administration was having in accurately and promptly reporting its financial condition. And so the wedding became the occasion, even if not entirely the cause, of my dismissal.

At that time, I was working under the terms of a five-year appointment that was to expire on June 30, 2005. During the October 2004 board meeting, the trustees had voted to offer me a new two-year appointment. After the meeting, it was determined that the appointment needed to be approved by a majority of all the trustees, rather than just those who were present and voting. When the matter was taken up again, during the January 2005 meeting, the board voted to allow my appointment to expire at its regular date of June 30, 2005. On March 7, 2005, in a telephone conference meeting, the board voted to end my tenure as of midnight March 27, 2005—Easter Sunday. Because I held the ecclesiastical office of General Synod Professor of Theology, I had the right to appeal dismissal from any position within the seminary to the General Synod. I chose to exercise that right, but the General Synod Council dismissed the appeal even before it had been filed fully.[35]

My last official act was presiding at the seminary's 219th commencement, at the invitation of the interim president, the Reverend Dr. Edwin G. Mulder. At the conclusion of that service, I formally handed over the ceremonial presidential seal to Dr. Carolyn Jones-Assini, moderator of the board of trustees, signaling the end of my official service to New Brunswick Theological Seminary.

PART IV

So, Ann and Jen, the rest of the sermon is for you.

> By hearing and responding to God's call to ministry within the Church, the two of
> you are already powerfully signaling your commitment to imitate the eternal
> expansiveness of God's love for persons. But this day you are making different
> kinds of promises and commitments. You are promising to live with and to love
> each other. And that will require a constant expansion of your love. Each day of life
> together will bring new insights into each other and new challenges to the love you
> thought you knew. Love will, each day, have to be stretched and expanded for each
> of you to continue comfortably to include the other fully within your heart. Earlier
> this week, in an email, I wrote to Ann that she had always been easy to love. She
> quickly wrote back with the suggestion that my memory must be going. Didn't I
> remember adolescence? I responded by pointing out that I had said "easy to love"
> not "easy to live with." It will be the work of your marriage to continue to change
> your mind in order that, each day, more wonderfully to include the other.
>
> —Excerpt from the sermon by Norman Kansfield at the marriage of
>   Jennifer Susanne Aull and Ann Margaret Kansfield, Northampton,
>   Massachusetts, June 19, 2004.

The Trial

The first public objection to the Kansfield-Aull marriage (as well as to the possibility
of Ann being ordained) occurred on September 1, 2004, when the Reverend Thomas
Stark, retired pastor of the University Reformed Church in East Lansing, Michigan,
submitted a posting to the Yahoo Group called Reformed Evangelical Network
(RENew). That act very quickly engendered gossip throughout the denomination—
gossip and not discussion because only one person actually made any attempt to contact me to ascertain the facts of the matter. On the basis of this widespread gossip, two
classes—Illiana (the states of Illinois and Indiana) and South Grand Rapids
(Michigan)—sent letters of concern to the General Synod Council. Neither letter asked
for a specific response from the Council (one did not even mention either my daughter
or me by name). Nevertheless, on the basis of these two letters and other rumors
"expressed…to us in our capacity as officers of the General Synod," the General Synod
Council (GSC), in its October 2004 meeting, "came unanimously to these decisions":

1. To send a delegation from the GSC to visit with me in a pastoral
   manner, sharing the concerns discussed by the GSC, listening to me,
   and expressing a desire to seek the unity of the church
2. To send this pastoral letter to all ministers of Word and Sacrament
3. To inform the board of New Brunswick Theological Seminary of the
   GSC's actions in this matter
4. To designate the members of the General Synod Commission on
   Judicial Business to serve as the investigative committee in the event
   that a charge is filed in this matter (see the *Book of Church Order*
   [*BCO*], Chapter 2, Part 1, Article 4, Section 4)[36]

The GSC, in the letter it sent to all pastors, stated that it had "taken special care both to clarify procedures for any potential exercise of discipline in this matter and to exercise the pastoral concern that should always be a mark of our life together in Christ."[37] In point of fact it did neither of these things. Its delegation did not meet with me until December 6, 2004, five weeks after the GSC letter was sent to pastors. By sending the letter to all pastors within the denomination without contacting me in any way, the GSC had spread rumors, totally unsubstantiated, to every part of the denomination. Pastors who did not even know me thus received inflammatory information about me on the authority of the GSC. Although neither of the letters from the two classes had actually constituted formal charges against me, the letter from the GSC fairly begged for such charges to be submitted. Their fourth decision indicated that the GSC was ready for charges!

The wait for a charge was not long. A charge, from the Reverend Ronald Kelly and five elders of the Calvary Reformed Church of South Holland, Illinois (the "Six Charger Charge"), was received in the Office of the General Secretary on January 25, 2005. The formal charge placed against me read as follows: "Dr. Kansfield's actions were contrary to our faith and beliefs as affirmed by the holy scriptures and the decisions of General Synod concerning relationships of active homosexuality."[38]

The following day thirty-five persons—eight elders and twenty-seven pastors— brought these additional charges:[39]

1. In performing, and thereby supporting, the "marriage" of two women, Dr. Kansfield contradicted the affirmations in the RCA "Declaration for Licensed Candidates," "Declaration for Ministers of Word and Sacrament," and "Declaration for General Synod Professors of Theology," all of which say, "I accept the Scriptures as the only rule for faith and life."
2. In his actions Dr. Kansfield has contradicted his affirmations in the three Declarations mentioned above, all of which say: "I believe the gospel of the grace of God in Jesus Christ as revealed in the Holy Scriptures of the Old and New Testaments."
3. In his actions Dr. Kansfield has contradicted his affirmations in the three Declarations mentioned above, all of which say, "I promise to walk in the Spirit of Christ, in love and fellowship within the church, seeking the things that make for unity, purity, and peace."
4. By Dr. Kansfield's actions he has violated his promise, in the Declaration for General Synod Professors of Theology": "I will submit myself to the counsel and admonition of the General Synod, always ready, with gentleness and reverence, to give an account of my understanding of the Christian faith."[40]

The Commission on Judicial Business was formally constituted as the General Synod Investigative Committee. On February 16, 2005, Daniel VandeZande, chair of the committee, wrote to me, urging me to make no public statements regarding the case. Informally, I was also advised to prepare for a trial at the General Synod and to obtain legal counsel. I named Elder William F. Rupp to serve as lead counsel, with the assistance of Rev. Beverly Bell, Rev. J. Karel Boersma, and Elder Mary

L. Kansfield. The Investigative Committee requested a meeting with me and my entire defense team on Thursday, April 14, 2005, in the Interchurch Center in New York City. The Committee requested that Elder Rupp and I return for additional conversation the next morning, April 15, 2005.

In its report to the General Synod, the Investigative Committee indicated that it had concluded that there was not sufficient merit to proceed with Consolidated Charges One and Two: my acceptance of the scriptures as the only rule for faith and life and my belief in the Gospel of Jesus Christ. The trial would therefore proceed with three charges: Charges Three and Four, in the Consolidated Charges, and the charge in the Calvary Church accusation (the "Six Charger Charge").

By June 16 and 17, 2005, when the General Synod declared itself in judicial session—transforming itself from an assembly of the church into an ecclesiastical judicatory—my defense was extremely well planned and carried out. Before testifying in my own defense, two witnesses were called. Ann Kansfield explained how she had come to understand the character of her sexuality, how aggressively she had sought to deny or "overcome" it, and how she had come to be convinced about the integrity of both her sexuality and her call to ministry in the name of Jesus. Dr. David Myers, professor of psychology in Hope College, Holland, Michigan, a noted researcher and author on the subject of homosexuality, presented a detailed summary of current scientific perspectives on the genetic factors involved in homosexuality and summarized his support for same-sex marriage by asking all to recognize that everyone in society benefits when love, sex, and marriage are kept together.[41]

In spite of the very skilled legal presentation of my case, and in spite of the compelling testimony offered by Ann Kansfield and David Myers, when, at the end of a long afternoon, the Synod finally voted, it voted overwhelming that the charges against me had been proved "with a high degree of probability."[42] After dinner, the Synod reconvened to determine what discipline was appropriate. The Judiciary voted to exercise discipline by deposing "Rev. Dr. Norman Kansfield from the office of General Synod Professor of Theology and suspending him from the office of Minister of Word and Sacrament."[43]

My wife Mary and I returned to New Brunswick the morning after the trial. We immediately began preparing to move out of the President's House and into our much-loved "cottage" on Spring Lake, east of East Stroudsburg, Pennsylvania. The packing of books, furniture, and clothing had a certain healing value. No one has to the date of this writing ever spelled out exactly what suspension from the office of Minister of Word and Sacrament actually entails, so I have not celebrated sacraments but have preached in several congregations, upon the explicit invitation of a consistory, session, or vestry. I had also, before the trial, accepted an invitation to present a lecture series on issues of homosexuality and the church titled *Justice for All*. St. Margaret's Episcopal Church in Staatsburg, New York, sponsored this program in affiliation with the Presbyterian Church and the Reformed Dutch Church of Hyde Park, New York. St. Margaret's Church was filled to capacity, and I received a wonderfully warm welcome and a standing ovation.

I take special pride in two honors that I have received because of the public attention given to my case. On June 11, 2005, Gay Pride Day in Boston, I was awarded the Boston Pride Interfaith Coalition Award for 2005. The plaque is inscribed, "You have donned the mantle of a prophet, courageously risking your career to promote equal marriage for all in both church and state." The previous year the award had been presented to Bishop Gene Robinson of the Episcopal Diocese. On October 11, 2005, National Coming Out Day, the Human Rights Campaign named me one of the Ten Straight Advocates for Gay and Transgender Rights. Among the other nine advocates were such figures as the Reverend Al Sharpton, actresses Kristin Chenoweth and Felicity Huffman, Salt Lake City Mayor Rocky Anderson, and Spanish Prime Minister José Luis Zapatero.

In a very real way, concerned members of the RCA were given a glimpse of the denomination's future even before the trial actually happened. Shortly after the beginning of 2005, even before the seminary board had acted to end my presidency on March 27, 2005, a Web site called Friends of Norm (friendsofnorm.com) was created by friends of my children. This Web site enabled people to send messages to the general secretary of the RCA, to sign a petition in support of me, and in a variety of other ways to express their support for the inclusion of gay and lesbian persons within the church and its offices. It was a beginning.

One of several powerful events that further signal a better hope for the future of the RCA's relationship with gays and lesbians is the "Hold Us Accountable Petition." During the spring of 2005, when it became clear that my trial was likely to occur, the Reverend Seth Kaper-Dale, copastor of the Reformed Church in Highland Park, New Jersey, began to circulate a petition to be introduced into the business of the General Synod at the opportunity for new business. This petition listed six convictions:

- We believe that the vast majority of persons in the world are heterosexual in orientation, and that it is God's desire that heterosexual persons live in lifelong covenant relationships, one man and one woman, or that they live lives of celibacy.
- We believe that God has created some persons with an orientation toward persons of the same sex, and that it is God's desire that homosexual persons live in lifelong monogamous relationships, or that they live lives of celibacy. We believe that God has created some persons with a bi-sexual orientation, and that it is God's desire that bi-sexual persons live in lifelong covenant relationships, or that they live lives of celibacy.
- We believe that the Spirit baptizes persons of all sexual orientations, and that the Spirit works in and through persons of all sexual orientations, and that the Spirit calls some persons of all sexual orientations to be ministers and deacons and elders—leaders for the Spirit-filled church.
- We believe that the Church of Jesus Christ, full of the Spirit, should bless covenantal same-sex relationships, as it does heterosexual relationships.
- We believe that committed same-sex relationships are not sinful, but rather a blessing from God.
- We believe that the Reformed Church in America ought to confess its sinfulness in adhering for too long to an oppressive position on homosexuality and ought to seek the forgiveness of its lesbian, gay, bi-sexual and transgendered brothers and sisters.[44]

The petition went on to state: "We, the undersigned, want to begin anew, speaking with honesty and integrity about this issue. We call on the General Synod of the Reformed Church to commit to a process of honest engagement and intentional dialogue...recognizing from the start that there are many who share the convictions of Rev. Dr. Kansfield."[45] The names of 167 individual RCA office-bearers, plus the Consistory of the Reformed Dutch Church of the Town of Brooklyn (Old First), were then read into the record of Synod as in support of this matter. The Synod was encouraged by the advisory committee to vote against the recommendation. It did so vote. However, the powerful witness of these persons and the direction in which they would have the denomination move are now clearly part of the Church's record.

> And the rest of us, as we seek to encourage the church to move toward the gracious inclusion of as many persons within the Assembly of the LORD as God in Christ Jesus is prepared to include, will pray for the two of you, as we pray for ourselves, that we may all learn to love as we know ourselves to have been loved by God.
> —Excerpt from the sermon by Norman Kansfield at the marriage of Jennifer Susanne Aull and Ann Margaret Kansfield, Northampton, Massachusetts, June 19, 2004.

NOTES

1. I have reconstructed these comments from this July 17, 2005, meeting.

2. The official text of this report can be found in the Acts and Proceedings of the 172nd Regular Session of the General Synod, Reformed Church in America (1978, vol. LVIII), 229–240. Hereinafter all references to the Acts and Proceedings will be referred to as *MGS* (*Minutes of General Synod*), followed by the year of the meeting, and the page number or numbers. The text of the Theological Commission's report was republished in James I. Cook, ed., *The Church Speaks* (Grand Rapids, MI: W. B. Eerdmans, 1985), 243–58.

3. *MGS* (1978), 235; Cook, ed., *The Church Speaks*, 251 (see note 2).

4. Ibid.

5. *MGS* (1978), 238. Cook, ed., *The Church Speaks*, 252 (see note 2).

6. Alfred C. Kinsey et al., *Sexual Behavior in the Human Male* (Philadelphia: W. B. Saunders, 1948).

7. *MGS* (1978), 238; Cook, ed., *The Church Speaks*, 255 (see note 2).

8. *MGS* (1978), 155.

9. The official text of this report can be found in the *MGS* (1979), 128–35. As with the 1978 Report, the text also appears in Cook, ed., *The Church Speaks*, 258–66 (see note 2).

10. *MGS* (1979), 130; Cook, ed., *The Church Speaks*, 260 (see note 2).

11. Ibid.

12. Cook, ed., *The Church Speaks*, 261 (see note 2).

13. Ibid.

14. The 1980 General Synod received two overtures regarding homosexuality. The Classis of Schoharie (New York) asked that Synod act to deny ordination to any of the church offices to "practicing Homosexuals and Lesbians." The Synod voted to deny the overture (*MGS* [1980], 285). The Classis of Wisconsin presented an overture to the Synod to include "Homosexuality" among the offenses subject to ecclesiastical discipline. The Synod voted to deny this overture as well (*MGS* [1980], 284). An "overture within the RCA is a letter to the General Synod from a classis (an area assembly of congregations like a presbytery within the

Presbyterian Church) in which the classis asks the General Synod for advice or action.

15. "The Reagan Years," *Policy Review,* Spring 1989, http://www.policyreview.org/spring89/symposium.html (accessed October 11, 2006).

16. Ibid.

17. Ibid.

18. *MGS* (1982), 70–82.

19. This concern arose from the fact that the Synod of 1978 had forwarded the report of the Theological Commission to the churches "for study." The report, therefore, had never been given the status of the RCA's "official position" on the matter.

20. *MGS* (1990), 461.

21. *MGS* (1994), 373.

22. *MGS* (1994), 374.

23. *MGS* (1994), 375–6.

24. *MGS* (1994), 376.

25. *MGS* (1995), 381–9.

26. Minutes of the Meeting of the Board of Trustees, May 28–30, 1998.

27. *MGS* (1998), 60.

28. *MGS* (1998), 511.

29. *MGS* (1998), 510.

30. *Homosexuality: Seeking the Guidance of the Church* (Grand Rapids, MI: Reformed Church Press, 2005).

31. *MGS* (2004), 333. An urgent request to take some action to define marriage came from the Classis of the Canadian Prairies in response to the legalization of same-sex marriage for all of Canada. In 2004, the Classis of the Canadian Prairies had a total of six congregations in the provinces of Alberta and Manitoba, with a combined membership of 643 persons (*MGS* [2004], 362).

32. The president of each RCA seminary is present at the Synod as a corresponding delegate. Corresponding delegates have the privilege of speaking to issues on the floor but have no vote. I was unable to attend this synod because my wife, Mary, was faced with a potentially life-threatening condition that ultimately required thoracic surgery.

33. The complete text of the liturgy and sermon is available in the Appendix.

34. Authorization finally arrived on June 15, 2004.

35. Wesley Granberg-Michaelson to William F. Rupp, April 2, 2005. But see William F. Rupp to Wesley Granberg-Michaelson, April 11, 2005.

36. General Synod Council to all RCA pastors, October 28, 2004. This letter was signed by the Reverend David Schutt, Moderator, General Synod Council; the Reverend Steve VanderMolen, President, General Synod; the Reverend Irving Rivera, Vice President, General Synod; and Wes Granberg-Michaelson, general secretary.

37. Ibid.

38. "Charge" forwarded by the office of the general secretary "pursuant to *Book of Church Order*, Chap 2, Article 4, Section 1" on January 25, 2005.

39. Twenty-five of these persons live or then lived in the state of Michigan, three in Illinois, two in the province of Ontario, two in the province of Alberta, and one each in California, New Jersey, and the province of Ontario.

40. "Charge," forwarded by the office of the general secretary, January 26, 2005. This charge, slightly modified but in substance identical, was resubmitted on February 28, 2005, with only five chargers, and signed by the Reverend Todd Krygsheld, and forwarded by the Office of the General Secretary to me on March 10, 2005. Other versions of these charges were submitted by different groups of signers at almost the same date. These charges became known as the "Consolidated Charges."

41. David Myers's credentials are available at http://www.davidmyers.org (accessed October 11, 2006). He and Letha Dawson Scanzoni have authored a book titled *What God Has Joined Together: A Christian Case for Gay Marriage* (San Francisco: HarperSan Francisco, 2005).

42. The *BCO* (2.1.5.11.e) only requires a "high degree of probability" and not "beyond a reasonable doubt." The votes were as follows: On the first charge—"that Rev. Kansfield's actions were contrary to our faith and beliefs as affirmed by the Holy Scriptures and the decisions of the General Synod"—182 yes/65 no; on the second charge—"that in his actions Dr. Kansfield [his affirmation] to walk in the spirit of Christ and to seek the things that make for unity, purity, and peace"—164 yes/83 no; and on the third charge—that "Dr. Kansfield has violated his promise...[to submit himself] to the counsel and admonition of the General Synod"—167 yes/80 no. The formal report of the trial is published in *MGS* (2005), 43–52.

43. *MGS* (2005), 44. I was given a few minutes to address the Synod after the imposition of discipline. Unfortunately, I had no written notes, and my address was not recorded.

44. *MGS* (2005), 379.

45. Ibid.

15

MAKING JUSTICE/SHOWING LOVE: THE EPISCOPAL CHURCH AND SAME-SEX MARRIAGE

Renee L. Hill

Early in my life as an ordained priest in the Episcopal Church I was asked to officiate at the wedding/commitment ceremony for a lesbian couple. The two women were women of color, one Latina and one African American. As an African American lesbian I was delighted that the first wedding that I performed would be a celebration for Christian lesbians of color who wanted to express their love for one another publicly while seeking the support and blessings of God and of their family and community. Officiating at this service was also a way for me to live out my theology, to live out God's radically inclusive love, calling us to acts of justice.

What I didn't realize at the time (now over thirteen years ago) was how deeply I had already waded into the streams of resistance and struggle that are churning in the Episcopal Church and indeed the entire Anglican Communion today. That ceremony signified something very deep in the life of the church. What does a lesbian of color commitment ceremony officiated by a lesbian of color priest mean for the Episcopal Church, whose popular image and power base still rest in the normative appearance of white, presumably heterosexual men? For some it signifies a deep fear of the visibility, autonomy, and authority of women, lesbians, and people of color and a consequent fear of displacement and lack of control. For others it symbolizes a deep uncertainty about where they should stand as people who are marginalized in some ways (according to gender, for example) but not in others (according to race). For still others what we did together in the name of God symbolized everything that is potentially freeing in the life and teaching of Jesus—love, solidarity, action, and justice making in community.

The presence of such conflicting responses to same-sex marriage in the church is reflected in the "Pastoral and Liturgical Guidelines for the Blessing of Holy Unions" of the Episcopal Diocese of Massachusetts:

> At present time, the worldwide Anglican Communion remains sharply divided over the matter of the blessing of same-sex marriage. In accordance with the dictates of the Book of Common Prayer and Canon 18, the Presiding Bishop and Archbishop of Canterbury have asked our bishops to instruct clergy to hold back from officiating at the marriage of gays/lesbians while those primates continue the hard work of maintaining unity within the world wide Anglican Communion and within our own country where the dialogue about the nature of Christian marriage is on-going.[1]

The legalization of same-sex marriage in Massachusetts brought the conflicts even more to the fore as bishops could no longer ignore or pretend not to know that the blessing of same-sex relationships was taking place. If the state was recognizing these relationships, the secret was out, and the reality of same-sex marriage would need to be addressed. Same-sex marriage is just one site of struggle in the multifaceted struggle for power and authority within the Episcopal Church (locally) and the Anglican Communion (internationally). Other sites of struggle include gender equality (woman's ordination to all orders) and global economic justice (Third World debt, global North/South issues). In spite of the fact that this struggle is made manifest in a variety of ways and on many different levels it is issues surrounding homosexuality, including same-sex marriage and the ordination of lesbians and gay men, that have become the focal point of debate in both the Episcopal Church and the Anglican Communion.

The debates surrounding homosexuality play an interesting dual role in the life of the church. They both highlight and mask the depth and complexity of the struggle for power and authority in the church. These debates have brought lingering racism, sexism, homophobia, ethnocentrism, and residual neocolonial attitudes to the surface of church life in the words and actions of some on all sides. For example, at a gathering of so-called church progressives, post-Lambeth (post-1998 international meeting of Anglican Bishops that included historic debates about LGBT rights), I was appalled by the suggestion of a white woman priest, who self-identified as a lesbian, that the solution to the "African problem" was to feed "their" children poisoned KoolAid, a clear reference to the Jonestown suicide/massacre. Rejection, name-calling, and even violent rhetoric have come from all sides.

At the same time, the focus on homosexuality has served as a vehicle for pushing discussion and action on economic justice (national and international), gender equity, and domestic racism to the back burner. Racism and sexism are both highlighted in words and actions *and* ignored in the same atmosphere of contention, thus demonstrating the impossibility of disconnecting these forms of oppression from sexual oppression or from each other. Although challenging, this interconnection also provides a tremendous opportunity for the Episcopal Church and indeed the global Anglican Communion to build a church whose transformed foundation is truly love and justice for all.

The debate around the possibilities for same-sex marriage in the Episcopal Church, and around homosexuality in general has roots in the increased access to power by those who had previously been on the margins of decision-making authority in the church. The increase in the number of people of color in congregations and within the priesthood and the ordination of women and the consecration of women as bishops have played a significant role in shaping the atmosphere in which the church is debating same-sex marriage.

This growth in access to power is the result of an active stream of protest and antioppression activism that have a long history in the Episcopal Church. This legacy is made manifest in the challenges to oppressive power in all of its forms. It serves to remind the Episcopal Church of the history and traditions of inclusion, justice, and love. It consists of the everyday protests, rebellions, and actions of Episcopal women and men who seek to live out these freedom traditions often over and against the tactics of disempowerment and despair that are rooted so deeply in the church.

This legacy of freedom is seen in the actions of Absalom Jones who, along with Richard Allen, in 1786 walked out of the St. George's Episcopal Methodist Church in Philadelphia rather than endure the injustice of segregation in their faith community. Jones went on to found the St. Thomas African Episcopal Church and was eventually ordained as the first African American Episcopal priest. Likewise, this stream of activism includes the Episcopal women and men of color who have insisted on their places, voices, and vision as both laity and clergy in a predominantly white institution.

The struggle for women's ordination further highlighted the church's impulse toward inclusion and transformation, as well as its resistance to liberating change. The "irregular" ordination of women to the priesthood took place in 1974. Eleven women were ordained as priests without the consent of the majority in power either nationally or internationally in the Anglican Communion. "Regular" (canonically legal) ordinations of women happened for the first time in the Episcopal Church USA (ECUSA) in 1976. Even today there remain a few Episcopal dioceses in the United States that do not allow the ordination of women. There are also a number of places in the global Anglican Communion that are just beginning or that continue to refuse ordination to women.

The liberative stream that allowed for women's ordination to the priesthood pushed even further through institutional sexism (and racism) to the moment in 1989 in which the first woman (an African American woman), the Right. Reverend Barbara Harris, was consecrated a bishop in the Episcopal Church and in the Anglican Communion internationally. This consecration caused a great deal of turmoil and contention in the entire church. Schism was threatened, and tensions remain today over women's ecclesiastical power and authority.

Any shift in the number, voice, visibility, and real authority of white women and for all people of color threatens the racist patriarchal "norms" of the Episcopal Church. Granting visibility, voice, and real authority to gay men and lesbians of all colors (not to mention bisexual, transgendered, and intersexed people) in the form of marriage equality, ordination to the priesthood, and open representation in the episcopacy further challenges racist hetero-patriarchy. For many, this extension of rights to its openly gay and lesbian members was the final straw in the struggle for power and authority in the national Episcopal Church.

The ordination of gay men (and later, with women's ordination, lesbians) as well as bisexual people has most certainly occurred throughout the history of the American Episcopal church. Likewise, same-sex couples in the Episcopal Church have almost certainly been ritually celebrating their relationships long before the push for official rites. However, the ordinations of openly gay and lesbian people in the late 1980s and beyond, along with proposals for rites of blessing for same-sex couples, have pushed gay and lesbian issues to the forefront of church power struggles, both nationally and internationally. In 1979 the first open lesbian, the Reverend Ellen Barett, was ordained a priest in the ECUSA. In 1990 controversy arose when the Right. Reverend Walter Righter (who had been authorized to do so by the Right. Reverend John Spong) ordained an openly gay man to the deaconate in the Episcopal Diocese of Newark, New Jersey. Bishop Righter was later tried in a church court for his actions, and the trial drew a great deal of media attention. Eventually all of the charges against Bishop Righter were dropped, and the man he had ordained was ordained to the priesthood. Other controversies related to gay and lesbian ordination were bubbling up in other places in the church during the 1990s. As lesbians and gay men became more visible as authority figures in the church and as they became unwilling to stay silent and invisible with regard to their marginalized identities, tensions mounted.

Added to this shift was the movement for the creation of marriage rites for same-sex couples to be used officially in the church. At the 1997 General Convention of the ECUSA a resolution to approve the development of a rite for same-sex blessings failed by only one vote in the House of Deputies.[2] Two more critical moments in the response to these tensions were the 1998 Lambeth Conference of Bishops and the 2003 General Convention of the ECUSA.

LAMBETH 1998: RISING VOICES, GLOBAL STRUGGLES

In 1998, over seven hundred Anglican bishops from all over the world met in England for the Lambeth Conference of Bishops. The Lambeth Conference is an international gathering of bishops that meets once every ten years. A number of dynamics were especially significant at this meeting, as for the first time it included female bishops and the majority of bishops came from the southern hemisphere of the globe. American and European bishops no longer constituted the majority. This new majority was in some ways finding its voice and speaking up in response to decades of marginalization by the dominant European and American branches of the Church. As religious scholar Mary-Jane Rubenstein explains:

> In the last two decades, as the Anglican Communion has begun officially to ordain women, and as individual bishops in the United Kingdom, Canada, and America have begun ordaining and blessing the unions of lesbian and gay-identified people, the dioceses of the southern hemisphere—and the African dioceses in particular— have come to consider themselves the true bearers of the light of the gospel, their task the reconversion of the "fallen" British and North American Churches.[3]

These churches of the global south raised their voices in harmony with conservative Anglicans in the United States to oppose full inclusion for lesbian and gay Anglicans, including ordination and the sanctioning of same-sex marriage. At the Lambeth meeting the debate over homosexuality was contentious and divisive. The struggle even included the highly publicized attempted exorcism of a British gay Anglican priest by an African bishop.[4]

Meanwhile women's ordination, the other contentious issue that had been festering and threatening division in the Anglican Communion, was addressed at

Lambeth through a resolution that maintained the status quo. The resolution titled "The Unity of the Anglican Communion" (Lambeth Resolution III.2), allowed individual bishops to decide on the question of women's ordination and the recognition of women's authority in the church. "According to the logic of this particular resolution, then, the all important unity of the Anglican Communion not only permits but depends on the disunity [of opinion and practice] concerning women's religious authority," Rubenstein explains.[5] It remains to be seen whether even an agreement to respect a diversity of opinions on issues surrounding homosexuality would result in the continued unity of the Anglican Communion.

It is important to note that several important issues were overshadowed by the intense focus on homosexuality and to a lesser extent on women's ordination. The critical issues of global poverty and debt relief for the world's most impoverished countries were not at center stage. This situation certainly worked to support the ideals and concerns of economic conservatives, especially those in the northern hemisphere. It also weakened the ability of the Anglican Communion to engage issues of global economic justice from a religious perspective with the depth of focus that they deserve.

GENERAL CONVENTION ECUSA 2003: BREAKTHROUGHS AND LAST STRAWS

The General Convention of the ECUSA is a decision-making body of the church comprised of lay deputies, clergy, and bishops. It meets triennially to consider a variety of issues and vote on resolutions through a parliamentary process.[6] When the national church gathered at its convention in the summer of 2003 it had more than 250 resolutions to consider. However, the major focus was on two resolutions. One supported local churches in exploring liturgies for the blessing of same-sex unions. The other controversial resolution was one that affirmed the election of Gene Robinson as the bishop of New Hampshire. This election marked the first time in the Anglican Communion that an openly gay priest who was living with his same-sex partner was elected to the episcopate. Both resolutions passed.

The reaction to their passage by conservatives in the church was powerful. As Ethan Vesely-Flad writes, "For the outvoted community of church conservatives, these decisions were seen as the culmination of decades of 'oppression' of conservative theology and tantamount to a declaration of war."[7]

Because the ECUSA is part of a global communion already at odds over homosexuality, this "declaration of war" was not limited to the national church. Within days of the confirmation of Bishop Robinson, the Archbishop of Canterbury, Rowan Williams, called for an "extraordinary meeting" of the Anglican primates for later that fall. He called this meeting also in response to the decision by a diocese in Canada to authorize a public rite of same-sex unions. Out of that meeting came the formation of the Lambeth Commission on Communion to discuss the state of the Anglican Communion, especially in light of its current controversies. The Commission released its report, the Windsor Report, to mixed response from different factions in the church.[8] The struggle for authority and for the power to define boundaries of inclusion and exclusion in the church is ongoing and complex and will most likely remain for some time to come.

SAME-SEX MARRIAGE, JUSTICE, AND THE POWER OF LOVE

The legacy of movements for transformation and justice with regard to race, gender, and sexual orientation serves as the context for the church's consideration of same-sex marriage. The history noted above reflects the interrelated power struggles that pushed the Episcopal Church to openness and, in response to that push, created a strong reaction and new rigidity. This process is ongoing, and although painful, it is a sign of life and hope within both the ECUSA and the Anglican Communion.

The question of same-sex marriage in the Episcopal Church symbolizes far more than the acceptance and sanctioning of same-sex relationships and certainly something beyond the mistaken hope that lesbian, gay, bisexual, and transgender (LGBT) people can be seen as the same as heterosexuals. More exciting, it symbolizes another potential force for positive change that can bring about true wholeness, justice, and power sharing in the church. This potential force for change and for overall transformation of the church has been undermined by the inability or resistance to understanding and addressing the interconnections of oppressive forms of power. The determination of the left, right, and center factions that addressing more than one form of oppression at a time is "too much" limits freedom and interrupts the possibility of real alliances.

Heterosexism, racism, sexism, and class boundaries—to name a few forms of oppressive power—are certainly interrelated/interconnected and addressing them simultaneously, however difficult, is more effective in the long run than doing so one by one. In fact a multipronged approach to counter multidimensional oppression is the only way to build a church transformed and ever open to embracing all that is necessary to make God's inclusive love and justice manifest in the world. It is only this comprehensive approach that will allow the movement for same-sex marriage in the church to have a deep and meaningful impact beyond individual relationships, individual congregations, or single dioceses. Understanding and reflecting on questions surrounding same-sex marriage in the context of the complexity of individual and communal identity and the corresponding multidimensional reality of oppression makes the issue that much more powerful as a vehicle for transforming the church.

Marriage has never been only or simply between two people. The institution of marriage has its roots in the desire for economic, political, and social alliances. Even in contemporary times when many people indeed marry for love, a marriage is not just the concern of two individuals alone. It involves families and communities. In the case of the church, marriage also involves a covenant with the community of faith and with God. Because marriage has such a broad impact in terms of socioeconomic life in general and communal/theological questions in the life of the church, it needs to be considered in terms of justice and love for all of creation.

MAKING JUSTICE

The debate over same-sex marriage both inside and outside of the church has given Christians an opportunity to examine issues around sexuality in general. Homosexuality and issues related to lesbian, gay, bisexual, transgender, and queer (LGBTQ) individuals and communities are only a small part of the vast subject of human sexuality. We have the opportunity to engage the subject broadly, and if we choose we can end silences in the church and society that have been kept too long about sex, gender identity, gender roles, pleasure, and desire. Engaging human sexuality more broadly also allows us to see the community's greatest needs, bringing to our consciousness and actions the necessity to end sexual violence, domestic abuse, sex trafficking, and exploitation. When our focus is solely on same-sex marriage we risk ignoring aspects of human sexuality that are in desperate need of theological reflection and decisive action on the part of the church as well as individual Christians.

Human sexuality is a topic that also invites us to examine and reexamine our ideas and fears about maintaining masculine stereotypes and patriarchal hierarchies both inside and outside of the church. If a traditional heterosexual structure of marriage is challenged, what impact will it have on male/female power differences in couples, communities, and in the church? It is not a coincidence that the struggle around homosexuality in the ECUSA has intensified just as women are increasing in numbers in the clergy, especially in the episcopate. Women's power and the insistence on equal rights for self-identified lesbian and gay members of the church challenge both subtle and overt patriarchal power. An even deeper shock wave will be heard when bisexual and transgendered members of the church become more vocal and visible, insisting on recognition and rights in their faith communities.

As long as the clergy remain agents of the state every time we sign a marriage license, the church needs to take seriously the economic and social inequities that result from marriage inequality in the church and in civil society. Civil marriage gives heterosexual couples over one thousand federal benefits to which nonmarried couples are not entitled.[9] These benefits include assumption of the spouse's pension after his or her death, the ability to file joint tax returns (and receive tax breaks), and the ability to invoke spousal privilege in a court of law.

There are at least two ways of approaching this inequality as members of faith communities. First, knowing that civil marriage and religious marriage are (or should be) separate questions, one approach is to work to make certain that all who are consenting adults and wish to marry will have access to this institution that would benefit them and enhance the well-being of their families. The second perspective, and one that I believe is closer to a Gospel value of love and justice for all, is to insist on a society in which access to health care, financial security, and property rights is not tied to marital status. Universal access to these human needs will move us all closer to ensuring the well-being of all.

SHOWING LOVE

In my experiences in the church as a black lesbian priest and as an organizer working to build support for marriage equality for lesbians and gay men, I have too often witnessed and experienced the misuse and distortion of "love" to justify oppression and exclusion. "Love the sinner but hate the sin" is nothing but a twisted lie and justification for bigotry and hatred, too often in the name of God.

The opposite also distorts—the notion that we need to accept bigotry and abuse in the name of loving our neighbors. My argument with unexamined and amorphous understandings of love is that too often it masks truth and enforces silence with regard to what needs to be changed, whether in relationships between people in committed relationships or within communities like the church.

It can be hard to imagine that in the places of deepest conflict love could emerge as a healing force that points to and indeed insists on true justice for everyone. The good news is that conflict can be fertile ground for building a community of faith that continues to grow in its commitment to the Gospel of love and justice. The key is that the conflict must be grounded in Christ's *transforming* love.

The Gospel has a great deal to say about love. None of it is simple, easy, or shallow. The idea of love that is invoked in the Bible has its grounding in the life, death, and resurrection of Jesus Christ. Love is the source of justice, true inclusion, and real respect. Without this kind of love centering us, our actions, our gifts, and our knowledge are without their deepest meaning and strongest potential. As Paul writes in the opening verses of the "Hymn to Love":

> If I speak in the tongues of mortals and of angels, but do not have love, I am a noisy gong or a clanging cymbal. And if I have prophetic powers, and understand all mysteries and all knowledge, and if I have all faith, so as to remove mountains, but do not have love, I am nothing. If I give away all my possessions, and if I hand over my body so that I may boast, but do not have love, I gain nothing. (I Cor. 13:1–3)

This kind of love is not about "you and me against the world," nor is it about a narrow definition of marriage as between one man and one woman. It is about the justice-making love that is at the heart of Christian community. It is the love that nurtures and supports all committed relationships and keeps each of us conscious of our commitments to Christ, to the Church, and to the wider world.

There is no Christian person in a committed relationship (LGBTQ or straight) who is not also in a committed relationship with a larger community, including the church, as well as in a committed relationship with God through Christ. For Christians the covenant entered into in a committed relationship is set in the context of our relationship with Jesus our healer and teacher, with Christ's earthly body, with the church, and with all the beloved creation of God. Our commitments are not just about ourselves alone; they are about an ever-widening circle of community and creation—local and global. We, therefore, do not enter into commitments outside of the necessity of justice, peace, and well-being for all.

Love is not a concept floating in the clouds. Love is a concrete, on-the-ground aspect of discipleship. Love is why Christians need to care about and work for equal rights and human rights for LGBTQ people and our families, not only in this country but also around the world. Love is why Christians need to insist on continued struggles to dismantle racism, sexism, and classism both in the church and in the wider society. Our commitment to truly hearing and acting on the wisdom of love forms the basis for why we who call ourselves disciples of Christ need to be willing to continually challenge all forms of oppression and injustice in ourselves as well as in our communities.

NOTES

1. "Pastoral and Liturgical Guidelines for the Blessing of Holy Unions," The Task Force on the Blessing of Holy Unions, Episcopal Diocese of Massachusetts, http://www.diomass .org/Documents/PastoralLiturgicalGuidelines.pdf (accessed October 11, 2006).

2. The General Convention of the Episcopal Church USA is the national gathering of the church. It meets every three years. The General Convention has two voting bodies, the House of Deputies (lay people) and the House of Bishops.

3. Mary-Jane Rubenstein, "An Anglican Crisis of Comparison: Intersections of Race, Gender, and Religious Authority, with Particular Reference to the Church of Nigeria," *Journal of the American Academy of Religion* 72, no. 2 (June 2004): 343.

4. Ibid.

5. Ibid.

6. Individual dioceses gather lay and clergy leaders at annual diocesan conventions.

7. Ethan Veseley-Flad, "For the Soul of the Church: Why the New War in the Episcopal Church is Over Race and Sex," *Color-lines*, Spring 2005, 14.

8. The full history and contents of the Windsor Report are well beyond the scope of this chapter. For more detailed information see the report on the official Web site of the Anglican Communion (http://www.anglicancommunion.org [accessed November 3, 2006]) or for a summary and discussion see Ian T. Douglas and Paul F. M. Zahl, *Understanding the Windsor Report: Two Leaders in the American Church Speak Across the Divide* (New York: Church Publishing, 2005).

9. For more information see http://www.lambdalegal.org (accessed November 3, 2006), the official Web site of the Lambda Legal Defense and Education Fund.

16

LOVE WINS: AN EASY GOSPEL FOR UNITARIAN UNIVERSALISM

Keith Kron

In 2004, the first same-sex couple in the state of Massachusetts to receive a marriage license were Unitarian Universalists. The city clerk who issued that license was a Unitarian Universalist. Later that day, four of the seven couples who were plaintiffs in the lawsuit for equal marriage were married by Unitarian Universalist ministers—which made sense considering they were Unitarian Universalists themselves. The lead plaintiff couple, Hillary and Julie Goodridge, were married at the Unitarian Universalist Association, by the Reverend William Sinkford, the first African American to be elected president of the Unitarian Universalist Association (UUA). The event made news around the world, from China to *People* magazine. And Unitarian Universalism celebrated. We had come a long way.

Unitarians believe in one God, not three; at least that is the short history. Unitarians have always highly valued the intellectual nature of their tradition. Many of the oldest churches in the United States were founded as Unitarian (now Unitarian Universalist) churches. Many of those historic churches are on the town greens of Massachusetts. Both John Adams and John Quincy Adams are buried in the basement of First Parish, United, which is a Unitarian Universalist congregation in Quincy, Massachusetts. Although there were individuals who held Unitarian theological beliefs in the earlier colonial period, it was not until 1825 that the American Unitarian Association was formed in Boston. Nineteenth-century writers Ralph Waldo Emerson and Henry David Thoreau were both Unitarians.

The Universalist tradition originated in the United States when John Murray landed on the shores of New Jersey and founded a church for people who believed that all would be saved. However, many early on believed that salvation might only come after a person spent thousands of years in purgatory. Universalism, unlike the Unitarian tradition that attracted New England elites, was more of a working-class religion that thrived in many parts of the country. By the turn of the twentieth century, however, the popularity of Universalism had peaked, and the numbers in congregations began to decrease. In the late 1930s, the youth ministries of the Unitarians and the Universalists were combined, and in 1961 the denominations merged into one religious movement, Unitarian Universalism.

Both Unitarians and Universalists have often been at the leading edge of a quest for justice in society, motivated by a desire for all people to be treated with respect. Today, many Unitarian Universalists rely on a multitude of sources for inspiration about their connectedness to the Divine. Although we acknowledge our Judeo-Christian roots, we also honor other religious traditions and today include members from a wide variety of backgrounds and beliefs. We are home to many interfaith families. We have Unitarian Universalists who identify as Buddhist, Christian, pagan, or Humanist, along with people with many other beliefs and traditions.

Our differences have united and instilled in us a deep respect for each person and his or her spiritual journey. Unitarian Universalists know there are many paths to truth and the Divine, and we honor the seeker who chooses to embark on this quest for truth. This foundation of our tradition has also cultivated a deep desire for justice. The first woman Universalist minister, Olympia Brown, was ordained in 1863. Unitarian Universalists have been at the forefront of movements that called for the end of slavery, the rights of women, ending of wars, and preserving the planet's resources. We have always tried to do "the right thing"—to work for what is just and respectful of human dignity and of our environment—though we have not always been successful.

In 1942, when the Unitarians voted to work against racism, Italians were included in the group of people identified as most affected by racism. However, there seems to be no historical record of any actions to support this commitment except for passing this resolution. In the 1960s, if a Unitarian Universalist minister was discovered to be gay he was ousted from his position (the vast majority of clergy were male). In one case, the congregation rehired the minister as its congregational janitor, at significantly less pay. At national general assemblies of the denomination, gay and lesbian people would exchange knowing glances and initiate conversations about whether there could ever be a day when gay and lesbian people would be accepted in our faith.

In 1968, Unitarian Universalism (approximately 92 percent white in membership) tried again to address the need for racial justice, committing a million dollars to work toward ending racism. In 1969, this commitment was revoked. In protest, people of color walked out of the General Assembly. Because this protest had such a dramatic effect on the church's understanding of itself as having reneged on its commitment to justice, this may have been one of the most crucial moments that led to the acceptance of equal marriage in Unitarian Universalism.

Later that year, after the Stonewall Riots (attacks on gays and lesbians in New York City), Rev. James Stoll, a Unitarian Universalist minister serving a congregation in Washington state, came out (announced his gay sexual orientation) at a youth conference. He never served a congregation again. After coming out and believing he would not be called to a congregation, he moved on to work as a hospital chaplain in San Francisco. No one discouraged this move.

In 1970, at the next general assembly in Seattle, Washington, a resolution was introduced to support equal rights for lesbian, gay, bisexual, and transgender (LGBT) people. It passed, but only because members of the assembly were fearful of another walkout. Bisexual, gay, and lesbian Unitarian Universalists began to gather openly and strategize together. They wanted an institutional office with a structure modeled after the Black Affairs Council in the UUA. In 1973, they introduced a resolution to create such an office. Though the administration of the UUA opposed it, a fear of another walkout helped the resolution to be passed by the narrowest of margins. A year later, in a similarly close vote, funding was approved for the office. In 1975, Arlie Scott was hired part time to be the director. She was a lesbian, but not a Unitarian Universalist. It was eighteen months before a congregation invited her to speak. She stayed in the position for two years.

Perhaps just as importantly, in the early 1970s the religious education department of the UUA created a sexuality education curriculum titled "About Your Sexuality." Unlike other curricula, "About Your Sexuality" talked openly and frankly about sexuality issues and included a section about sexual orientation, indicating that no one sexual orientation was better or worse than any other one. The curriculum, which would be used for twenty-five years before being replaced by *Our Whole Lives*[1] (which includes an even more in-depth study of sexuality), was intended for junior high students, though many parents and teachers were educated through it as well. Like so many other Protestant denominations, many of these youth left our faith when they went to college, and later, many found their way back.

By the 1970s, many Unitarian Universalist ministers began performing religious weddings, usually called a "ceremony of unions," for same-sex couples, though not without controversy. In fact, several ministers reported that they officiated at their first same-sex wedding ceremonies in the late 1960s, and the minister of my church at the time, Rev. Harry Scholefield, reports conducting his first same-sex wedding in 1958. In 1980, the first openly gay and lesbian ministers were called to congregations.

Many congregants were upset that their ministers were performing these ceremonies; some congregations asked their ministers not to perform them or at least not to do so within the church building because they were afraid that Unitarian Universalism would be seen as a gay church, even though it is still about 95 percent heterosexual. Some congregations did allow their ministers to perform these unions in the church, but not in the sanctuary. Ministers who wanted to perform these ceremonies and faced resistance from congregations asked the UUA for support, and in 1984 a resolution passed at general assembly supporting the duty of its ministers to perform a ceremony of union for same-sex couples.

Although Unitarian Universalism was seen by others outside of the denomination as being a liberal community and tradition, and this was also an important aspect of its own self-identification, many barriers and inequalities related to issues of sexual orientation still remained. In 1985, LGBT Unitarian Universalists gathered for the first time from across the continent in Houston. The following year, this group met with the newly elected president, Rev. William Schulz, to discuss how to help Unitarian Universalism become more accepting of LGBT church and community members. A committee was formed, called "Common Vision," to look more closely at the inequalities related to sexual orientation. Many congregations held focus groups, and a questionnaire on attitudes toward LGBT people was included in the national magazine of Unitarian Universalism. The responses varied along a wide spectrum. Many were positive, many were cautious, and some were very negative. The very negative responses surprised many Unitarian Universalists, who thought the church was liberal enough and needed to do no work to address issues of sexual orientation. Negative comments included the following: "Hitler had the right idea. Homosexuals should be exterminated." "I don't want them around my kids." "We don't want too many of those people."

In 1988, a group of LGBT leaders gathered to strategize in Boston about how to broaden people's understandings and views. This group created guidelines for congregations to follow to become "Welcoming Congregations." A resolution creating this program passed overwhelmingly at the 1989 General Assembly. In 1991, First Parish in Brewster, Massachusetts, was designated as the first Welcoming Congregation. Over the next five years, more than fifty UUA congregations (with one thousand or more members in each) would join in this effort.

In 1992, the UUA passed, for the third time, a resolution in support of antiracism initiatives in the denomination. In large part, the successful efforts in behalf of the rights of LGBT people within Unitarian Universalism had given people of color some hope that institutional change related to racism might also be possible. Unlike the majority white population of Unitarian Universalism, which was overwhelmingly heterosexual, there were disproportionate numbers of LGBT people of color within the overall population of people of color within Unitarian Universalism. But within the whole denomination there also seemed to be evidence of a genuine and renewed commitment to doing antioppression work, even if it sometimes felt like these two areas of concern competed against one another.

In 1996, the Central Conference of American Rabbis, the rabbinical organization for Reform Judaism, announced its support for equal marriage for same-sex couples. With almost no controversy attached to it, at the 1996 UUA General Assembly, 97 percent of the delegates voted to support equal marriage for same-sex couples. This vote garnered national attention and ignited a more intentional focus on public witness to our faith within our denomination.

By this time, the UUA office was staffed by two full-time people. This amount of staffing was historic for the denomination. It is now called the UUA's Office of Bisexual, Gay, Lesbian, and Transgender Concerns. The office had gone through several name changes—from the original Office of Gay Affairs to the Office of Gay Concerns to the Office of Gay and Lesbian Concerns to the Office of Lesbian, Gay, and Bisexual Concerns to its new name, which listed the constituencies in alphabetical order. In many of our Welcoming Congregations, the focus seemed to shift from the anxiety of "Will we be known as a gay church?" to a positive commitment to "Why aren't we living our values?" In the late 1990s the average growth of this movement went from ten new Welcoming Congregations per year to nearly fifty per year. Additionally, Unitarian Universalist congregations increasingly had more than a token population of bisexual, gay, and lesbian people, and transgendered people were common enough to be visible in attendance.

In 1998, on a cold Wyoming evening, Matthew Shepard was left to die on a fence row. The harrowing media images of this young man and a renewed consciousness of the reality of violence that LGBT people live with in the back of their minds on a daily basis brought the issues of homophobia and inequality to the fore-front for much of the general public. No longer could many Unitarian Universalists who lived in relative ignorance and denial of the reality of homophobia and violence think that there was no real oppression suffered by sexual minorities. Matthew Shepard reminded Unitarian Universalist adults of so many of our own children—who were more often liberal than not, and therefore more likely to talk about these issues of homophobia, including their encounters with it in their own lives. Many of our youth had also already been ostracized for their beliefs and appearance, regard-less of their own sexual orientation. Although never spoken aloud, many of the youth in our churches knew that Matthew could easily have been one of us. In response to the Shepard tragedy, many congregations held vigils or participated in community-wide vigils against hate. The immovable middle of Unitarian Universalism—those who appreciated our liberal stance but have never felt com-pelled to act on it—moved. That next year, our general assembly, in Salt Lake City, furthered this movement. In typical Unitarian Universalist fashion, the general assembly had traditionally been a source of liberal words without necessarily equal effort put into implementing actions.

However, spurred by the passage of the 1996 resolution to support equal mar-riage rights and privileges for same-sex couples, the creation of a Public Witness advisory team, and a desire to do something especially significant, the Office of Bisexual, Gay, Lesbian, and Transgender Concerns decided to offer a different form of protest at the Utah General Assembly in 1999.

Instead of protesting against sodomy laws, we decided that we would need to do something different in Utah. The office went to Utah six times that year in preparation. Through the combined efforts of the office, the local Utah congrega-tions, the newly created Family Matters Task Force, and the Public Witness Team of the UUA, the focus of that general assembly was on Unitarian Universalist fam-ily values. In addition to internal programming about the changing nature of the family, the wide variety of families within Unitarian Universalism (including fam-ilies with LGBT children or parents), and gay-straight alliances in Utah, the gen-eral assembly devoted a significant effort to outreach, particularly to the Utah LGBT community.

The office sponsored programming about building gay/straight alliances. In addition, the office sponsored an event that would have more impact than any other public witness in recent general assembly history: "The Prom You Never Had." All general assembly attendees were invited, as were members of the local LGBT com-munity. The minister in Ogden, Utah, took special delight in passing out tickets and in the awe and joy she experienced in watching people's faces, mainly youth, light up as they learned that a church sponsored this prom. More than one thousand people attended. This general assembly received more news coverage than any previous general assembly ever had, and the overwhelming majority of it was quite positive.[2]

It had been disturbing for many Unitarian Universalists to hear inaccurate state-ments by Religious Right spokespersons portraying them as being antifamily and having antifamily values. This general assembly had provided Unitarian Universalists with an alternative, truthful self-understanding. We became more acutely aware of the wide variety of families within Unitarian Universalism and our unique and abundant membership of LGBT families, interfaith families, and multiracial families. Interestingly, the place where Unitarian Universalists felt like they could do the most effective public witness and social justice work was in relation to LGBT families.

A few months later, a few days before Christmas in 1999, the Vermont Supreme Court ruled that there was no compelling reason to deny same-sex couples the benefits of marriage through civil unions. There are twenty-one Unitarian Universalist congregations in Vermont, situated in the center of its towns and representing about 1 percent of the state's population of just over six hundred thousand people. Vermont Unitarian Universalists, elated by the ruling, got busy organizing a religious response to it. A statewide interfaith clergy network was formed, with the majority of its membership and staff being Unitarian Universalist. This network provided a liberal religious voice in the state, reminding the people of Vermont that being religious need not equal being conservative As a result of this leadership by lay people and ministers on this issue, Unitarian Universalism learned it could have an impact on statewide politics. In addition, when the *Rutland Herald* newspaper won a Pulitzer Prize in 2001 for reporting on issues surrounding the civil union ruling, the reporter, David Moats, was a Unitarian Universalist.

During this time period, local and national debates on this issue started to heat up. Media outlets were looking for a religious voice to balance the Christian fundamentalist opponents of equal marriage, and they almost always found a Unitarian Universalist minister available to respond.

For example, in 2002, Rev. Rhett Baird, a minister in Fayetteville, Arkansas, decided to refrain for one year from signing marriage licenses for any couple until all couples, regardless of sexual orientation, could marry. This was not a new idea. Ministers in other places had previously taken the same stand, but there was more media attention given to it at this time.[3] While many ministers had already signed on to support equal marriage, the idea of a protest by ministers who refused to sign any marriage licenses until all couples could get married with the same rights and privileges received considerable public attention, especially in Massachusetts. In 2003, several Unitarian Universalist ministers announced from their pulpits that they would not sign marriage licenses until equal marriage was a reality, and they received standing ovations from their congregations.

That same year, four of the plaintiff couples in the Massachusetts court case were Unitarian Universalist. There are 146 Unitarian Universalist congregations in Massachusetts, again most of which are centrally located on the town green. Most of these congregations have same-sex couples as part of their membership, and many of those couples have children. In addition, many of the heterosexual couples had joined Unitarian Universalist congregations because they were known to be strong supporters of the rights of LGBT persons. Unlike other states, most of the people in Massachusetts were familiar with Unitarian Universalism, if only as "the ones with the oldest building in the center of town."

Both because of our increasing ability and knowledge about what it means to be an articulate public witness to the need to make a difference in the lives of disenfranchised people in our midst, our congregations in Massachusetts responded enthusiastically to the opportunity to support marriage equality. They hung banners, held political forums, and celebrated same-sex families.

Then the court ruling came in the fall of 2003. On a sunny November day, the Massachusetts Supreme Court ruled that same-sex couples had the right to marry. The ruling would take effect in 180 days, on the fiftieth anniversary of the 1954 U.S. Supreme Court desegregation decision, *Brown v. Board of Education*. The language of the Massachusetts ruling even included the phrase "separate is not equal." Unitarian Universalists had been making this same claim about inequality for a long time.

What followed was a flurry of intense and frenetic activity. Much time and energy were spent on gathering liberal religious voices to speak on behalf of equal marriage as the debate ensued in the media. Unlike most other religious bodies in the state, Unitarian Universalists were able to speak unequivocally in favor of marriage without any internal organizational resistance.

Location does mean something. The offices of the Unitarian Universalist Association are next to the Massachusetts Statehouse. As political forces inside the Statehouse tried to figure out whether to vote to amend the state constitution to ban marriage equality, the UUA put up a large sign facing the Statehouse that read, "Civil Marriage is a Right." Legislators noticed it. Liberal legislators who wanted to meet together and avoid the scrutiny of those trying to circumvent the state Supreme Court ruling with a constitutional ban found refuge in the meeting spaces of the UUA headquarters.

The day before the historic ruling, our congregation in Marblehead had consented to be filmed for national television. The service was a celebration of our faith, our belief in the inherent worth and dignity of all people, and an ode to justice. At the conclusion of the service, the congregants, primarily straight, started dancing in the aisles. The minister joined in the celebration. She remembers noticing how profoundly moved one of the cameramen was who was filming the event for a television news station broadcast. He was in tears, and she speculated that he was ready to join in the celebration. He seemed to be moved by this opportunity to witness not only an historic moment for society but also a celebration of what was possible spiritually—a church where straight and LGBT people were seen as equal and whole and where legalization of this just cause (that would take place on the following day) prompted raucous celebration. Perhaps no event is a greater expression of Unitarian Universalism than this one. This worship service celebrated life as a witness to justice that is grounded in the profound Universalist belief that God resides in all people. By creating a society where people can be whole, we strengthen the bond between humans and the Divine.

Just after midnight, the first same-sex couple was issued a marriage license by a city clerk in Cambridge, Massachusetts. As mentioned above, all three—the city clerk as well as both members of the couple—were members of the Unitarian Universalist congregation located right there in Cambridge. Later that day, Hillary and Julie Goodridge were married in the chapel of the UUA building in Cambridge. From Cambridge to China, the picture of an African American president of the UUA marrying two white Unitarian Universalist women was widely broadcast. It was a testimony to faith in action and to the meaning of faith in people's lives that was seen around the planet.

Yet, this was only a beginning. Unitarian Universalists across the nation worked as hard as the Massachusetts Unitarian Universalists had to secure marriage equality. In California, the California Unitarian Universalist Legislative Ministry sprang up. Congregations in Georgia wrapped themselves in a rainbow ribbon to support equal marriage. Congregations in Florida helped same-sex couples who applied and then were denied marriage licenses and held special ceremonies honoring the commitments of long-term couples, both same- and opposite-sex couples. Risking arrest and prosecution, Unitarian Universalist ministers in New Paltz, New York, married same-sex couples. Over four thousand Valentine cards were sent out on Valentine's Day to the California governor's office saying that Unitarian Universalism supported marriage equality.

As one child wrote on her Valentine, "Let's be logical. Love is not a sin." The traditions of freedom, tolerance, and reason continue to inform Unitarian Universalism. The refusal to rely on biblical scriptures as the only source of truth for honoring the human lived experience continues to shape our theology. Years of hard work on education about human sexuality and support for LGBT people in our midst made the work of marriage equality easier. In addition, even if they have never been fully realized, the long-standing commitments of Unitarian Universalists to work on issues of race, ethnicity, and class did pave the way for the work on equal marriage. The historic faith of Unitarian Universalism has carried its activists and leaders to this point and will continue to be an invaluable source of strength in the ongoing struggle for all citizens of the United States to have access to equal marriage, legally as well as religiously. For Unitarian Universalists, our faith must be lived and our gospel is this: love wins. It is an easy gospel for Unitarian Universalism.

NOTES

1. *Our Whole Lives* is a sexuality education curriculum developed by the Unitarian Universalists for children, youth, and adults, available online at http://www.uua.org/owl/ (accessed November 3, 2006).

2. For example, see Karen Brandon, "Unitarians Meet and Mormons Get Quite an Eyeful," *Chicago Tribune*, June 28, 1999.

3. For example, see Dennis McCaslin, "A Voice in the Arkansas Wilderness," *The Advocate*, January 10, 2003.

17

EMBRACING MARRIAGE EQUALITY: A FAITHFUL CALL TO PENTECOSTAL CHRISTIANS

Joseph W. Tolton

At the age of seven, I received the baptism of the Holy Ghost and spoke in unknown tongues for days thereafter. I have a deep respect for the universal truth expressed in all religions, but cannot imagine being tied to any other form of worship than the profound joy of Pentecostalism, which allows for an ecstatic and uncontrollable release. All religions embody an experience with the Divine, but few allow for such a physical demonstration of the Divine touch that is so readily comparable to a sexual experience. The human experience is indescribably complex, but there are primordial experiences that connect us. The transcendent nature and universal appeal of the Pentecostal Christian experience touch us where our sexuality and spirituality meet. The great irony of the Pentecostal Church is that the experience of Pentecost is physically liberating, while the Pentecostal belief system is spiritually binding.

In a recent sermon I gave, some of the listeners were appalled that I proclaimed that the Pentecostal Church would one day bless same-sex unions. As a prophet I rest my case on God's revealed plan. However, in the interest of a more rigorous explanation, let's consider the history of this tradition.

HISTORY

The roots of the Pentecostal Holiness church are found within a Holiness culture defined by a commitment to radical social change and inclusion expressed through its historic involvement in supporting the abolition of slavery and women's rights.

Pentecostalism is widely viewed today as an amalgam of splintered charismatic denominations that identify strongly with the mystical experience of the baptism of the Holy Ghost in fire, recognized through the gift of speaking in tongues (foreign languages that are identifiable but unknown to the speaker). The origin of American Pentecostalism is most often identified with the great revival on Azusa Street in Los Angeles, which began in April of 1906. These worshipers were the first group in America to experience glossolalia and to establish a religious tradition whose process of conversion had three steps: (1) confession and belief in Jesus as savior, (2) baptism by full immersion, and (3) the baptism of the Holy Ghost witnessed by the experience of speaking in tongues.[1] Before the Azusa Street revival, the process of salvation in the Holiness Church was considered complete after the first step of this three-tiered process.

However, an independent Holiness movement had developed in the nineteenth century, which reflected the combination of spiritual rootedness and social change that uniquely characterizes the culture of this tradition. The two major stakeholders who helped create this culture during this period were abolitionist Wesleyan Methodists (1843) and the ethically rigorous Free Methodists (1860).[2]

The founding of the Wesleyan Methodist Church was driven by its unique stance on the moral bankruptcy of slavery. The Wesleyan Methodist Chapel of Seneca Falls, New York, was established on March 27, 1843, as part of a nationwide schism in the Methodist Church over slavery. From the moment of its inception, the residents of Seneca Falls identified the Wesleyan Chapel with radical reform. It came as no surprise to them when the first Women's Rights Convention was held within its walls in July 1848.

The Free Methodist Church was founded in 1860 in western New York's Burned-Over district, a term that refers to religious and reform movements that flourished in this region during the nineteenth century. Free Methodists are so named, in part, because church members believed it was improper to charge for better seats in the pews—those closer to the pulpit.[3] They deeply opposed slavery and advocated "freedom" from secret societies, which had allegedly undermined parts of the Methodist Episcopal Church.

This "higher Christian life" culture would swell throughout the country and crystallize into the Holiness movement. It included a radical commitment to abolitionism. The early editors of the magazine, *A Guide to Holiness*, were abolitionists who even suggested the validity of civil disobedience in the face of fugitive slave laws. Gilbert Haven, a Methodist bishop, also claimed by the Holiness movement, went so far as to advocate interracial marriages.[4]

In addition to its ethical stance on slavery, the Holiness Church was also an incubator for feminist ideas, as best exemplified in the work of Phoebe Palmer. She was a dynamic and determined evangelist from New York City who would become best known as the publisher of the magazine mentioned above, *A Guide to Holiness* (originally titled *A Guide to Christian Perfection*).[5] Phoebe Palmer spoke of a theology rooted in the work of the Holy Spirit. The Holy Spirit is the transformative agent in the Church, working in us a sanctification that establishes the viability of the promise of Pentecost. This promise, she argued, was the fulfillment of the Prophet Joel's prediction that in the last days a new move by God would be welcomed into the Church allowing for "your sons and daughters to prophecy" (Joel 2:28).[6] Seth Cook, a founder of the Pilgrim Holiness Church, was so inspired by her writing that he declared, "nothing but jealousy, prejudice, bigotry, and a stinging love for bossing in men have prevented women's public recognition in the Church."[7]

Another recurring theme in the Holiness Churches was serving as an earnest witness against an ostentatious lifestyle. This belief was expressed through a concern for simplicity and an affirmation of radical equality, prompting believers to replace the appellations, "Mr." with "Brother" and "Miss" with "Sister."[8]

In the shadow of Reconstruction and at the end of a century that saw radical modernization, some members of the Holiness movement began to focus on the further fulfillment of the Prophet Joel's promise for these end times. Specifically, there was increased interest in what would come to be the third step in the process of salvation, the baptism or infilling of the spirit, which would yield a more perfect Christian than those who only experienced step one, confession and belief. This shift led to the birth of American Pentecostalism, which came to subsume the Holiness movement.

In February 1906, a young black Holiness preacher, William Seymour, was invited to a Holiness Church in Los Angeles to tell about his notions of a deeper process of sanctification, which would come through the gift of the Holy Ghost as evidenced by the experience of glossolalia. Seymour had experienced conversion through confession and belief, but at this point he had not yet experienced the baptism of the Holy Ghost, the gift of speaking in tongues. Seymour's early meetings bore the trademarks and aspirations of the Holiness tradition: they were interracial, open to women in ministry, and incorporated the gift of divine healing. The church participants all embraced conversion in the same manner that Seymour had— through confession and belief—but they longed for the baptism of the Holy Ghost. After a month of participating in services and listening to Seymour preaching, several believers began to realize the Pentecostal experience they desired.[9] Their understanding of what defined salvation evolved from conversion through confession and belief to include the baptism of the Holy Ghost as evidenced by speaking in tongues. This Pentecostal experience brought with it ecstatic joy and the evidence of xenoglossolalia, speaking in an identifiable foreign language without understanding.

These early days of the Pentecostal Church were focused on an unusual demonstration of love and equality in the body of Christ based on the experience of the church in the Apostolic age in the aftermath of Pentecost, as recorded in the second chapter of the book of Acts.[10]

The historical ethos of the Holiness movement reflects American revivalism and challenges its contemporary fundamentalist tendencies, rather than affirming it. The Holiness culture is more oriented toward ethics and spiritual life than a defense of orthodoxy. In fact, the Holiness Church historically elevated social ethics to the status that some Christian fundamentalists today attribute to doctrine. This foundational history of spirit-led radical activism compels similar faithfulness in our contemporary period, such as activist support for marriage equality.

The decisive factors determining the Pentecostal Church's contemporary culture are manifold. Unfortunately, they have gutted the Church of its commitment to radical social change that brings about equity and compassionate human relationships. In its contemporary form, it has, in too many instances, become a self-satisfied Church defined solely by its unique spiritual experience of ecstatic joy and focused on selling its message rather than evangelism. Original tenets of "holy" conduct (no drinking, no smoking, no dancing, and no cursing) have become the point of entry into the American Pentecostal Church, creating a literalist dogma that has robbed the Holiness Church of its (socially) ethical base.

The ideals of Christian perfection in the Holiness culture were exemplified by a thirst and quest to experience more of the spirit and an expansive revelation of truth. Seymour and the parishioners at the Azusa Street revival embraced confession and belief in Jesus Christ as Lord as complete salvation. However, they were open to God's evolving revelation and to the concept that salvation could be expanded to include an experience beyond what they had previously known, making these believers open to an organic process of spiritual understanding. At Azusa Street, this new denomination, rooted in progressive activism, was born out of a desire for spiritual expansion in the interests of a higher quality of life with just human relationships.

THE PENTECOSTAL CHURCH AND HOMOSEXUALITY

The coupling of activism and an inquisitive theology supports (in fact demands) that the Pentecostal Church explore what the spirit of God is saying to the Church today about homosexuality and the need for God's gay and lesbian children to be included equally within the Pentecostal communion. Because such a large part of the Pentecostal Church in the United States is black-identified, this analysis must also be discussed within the context of the black church.

As a teenager raised in a deeply Pentecostal home, I was stunned the afternoon I came home from school to find my mother wearing pants. I immediately challenged her because the church taught that women were not to wear pants. My mother defended herself by telling me that God can expand our interpretation of scripture with new revelations that bring us into greater truth. She also vehemently argued that the Bible passages cited to keep her in a skirt had been misused to deprive women of their full equality in the Church. My mother, grandmother, and I lived below the poverty line. My mother was my hero because she somehow found a way for me to be educated in one of New York's most elite preparatory schools. I grew up in amazement of her courage and conviction about who I was, despite how the world sought to define me. My mom's wearing of pants was not the issue that I learned about that day; it was her passionate commitment to truth as an ever-evolving process that was so dynamic. That is the Pentecostal spirit. The Pentecostal Church is governed by the principle that God is free to reveal Himself anew. I cannot imagine more fertile ground in which to plant the seeds of marriage equality.

Unlike other traditions that make room for gay and lesbians at the kid's table and are self-satisfied with their limp idea of inclusion because they have historically been conservative socially and spiritually, the Pentecostal Church must be true to itself by making a bold and decisive step to fully support same-sex unions. Pentecostalism is well positioned to support marriage equality as it is the tradition that has historically focused on God's revealed plan in the context of current realities. Other Protestant traditions may be aligned with one another on many current social issues, such as their opposition to marriage equality. However, finding themselves outside of the collective stance of the greater Christian community has never deterred Pentecostals from maintaining their own convictions. Some congregations in the Holiness Church have led the tradition of black women in ministry, even when women's leadership was not allowed by other denominations. The Pentecostal church with inclusion in its DNA has a unique platform from which to make a declarative spiritual decision like the blessing of same-sex unions.

The possibility for blessing same-sex unions in Pentecostalism is strengthened further by the black identities of so many who are part of this communion. Historically, the black church has so often been an agent of social change, and today it must refuse to become a wholesale pocket of homophobia. As an economically underprivileged youngster, I was emboldened by my faith because of the social activism of the black church. It inspired me to insert myself into New York City's privileged circles—places where I was not invited. It is this spirit of self-loving deviance in the interest of inclusion that drove Phoebe Palmer to take her place in the pulpit, William Seymour to take his place among his white sisters and brothers, and the original and free Methodists to take an aggressive abolitionist stance almost a century before the end of Jim Crow.

In supporting gay marriage, the Pentecostal Church has an historic and redemptive opportunity to rediscover its founding principles of radical inclusion. By taking the lead on marriage equality, the Pentecostal Church can once again distinguish itself by embracing its independent spirit as we prove to the world that, just as God spoke anew on Azusa Street in 1906, God is still speaking now.

The recent politics of homosexuality in the black community have in many ways been shaped by the black power movement of the 1970s, which made black masculinity synonymous with external displays of prowess that are expressed most vividly by some hip-hop artists' glorification of thug life.[11] This construct of masculine identity often impedes gay black men from attaining healthy loving relationships that are the precursor to a loving union. Gender identity within gay relationships is a difficult issue for members of all racial groups, but the dynamics are especially complicated for black men who live in a racist society and within black communities that often celebrate the ideal of manhood as embodied in a hardened persona.

This problem has led me to develop a teaching series in my ministry called "And God called them Adam," which revisits the creation stories. The thesis of the lesson is rooted in Genesis 5:2, which speaks of God calling both male and female beings Adam, after the female component *is taken out of man*. The power of this lesson is that God created Adam in the image of God, whom I contend is equally male and female. I am amused when Pentecostal black parishioners challenge the idea of the Goddess (ironically most black Pentecostal Churches in which many of these wonderful people grew up are about 65 percent female). I usually respond by asking them, "Don't we believe that God is a 'Mother to the motherless and a father to the Fatherless'? If this often-repeated Christian adage is true for us, I suggest to my parishioners then that the theory of the Christian divine articulated as both God and the Goddess also stands up as true. Aha! God named both male and female creatures Adam, which suggests that the independent male and female beings were a reflection of Adam in his or her first incarnation. This is the only logical conclusion because if Adam in the first creation was not equally female and male, then Adam would have only been created somewhat and not fully in God's image.

It is particularly empowering for black gay men to realize that in creation Adam equally embodied both a masculine and feminine identity. This radical understanding of our creation gives Pentecostal gay couples the freedom to decide the balance of masculine and feminine energy that each partner brings to a relationship. It has been marvelous to witness Bible-thumping gay black men come to reject such destructive notions of manhood and instead embrace all of who they are within themselves first and then ultimately in relationship to their husbands.

The idea that the benefits of gay marriage are exclusively for the upper middle class is erroneous. My pulpit is a forum from which I continue to trumpet the importance of gay marriage for the gay community, focusing upon urban, poor members of this community. The value of marriage equality must be articulated as a covenant that has vital implications for the community as a whole. The tremendous growth of the black Pentecostal Church has the potential to be even more meaningful if it chooses to embrace same-sex unions.

Because the black church has the power to help define the social agenda for its community, it can help same-sex unions in the black community reach the potential to be the following:

- A catalyst to redefine marriage as a spiritual union
- A shelter for our communities' abandoned children
- A base from which economic freedom can be obtained
- A partnership that insulates the community from the nihilism of HIV/AIDS

To realize the full potential of our community, I challenge the black Pentecostal Church to be a safe space for same-sex marriages. Given the universal appeal of Pentecostalism and its unprecedented cross-denominational influence, the Pentecostal Church is a sleeping giant. Can you imagine it exporting a new revelation on marriage equality with the same magnitude and depth it had with regard to the experience of speaking in tongues?

Pentecostals Christians, we can do this if we would deeply explore and embrace our provocative heritage and independent culture. In Pentecostalism, we claim a dynamic visitation of the spirit after "we are all on one accord." By embracing marriage equality the Pentecostal Church can experience Pentecost again.

NOTES

1. See Walter J. Hollenweger, *Pentecostalism: Origins and Developments Worldwide* (Peabody, MA: Hendrickson, 1997).

2. See Donald Dayton, *Theological Roots of Pentecostalism* (Peabody, MA: Hendrickson, 1984).

3. See Paul Merritt Bassett, "Exploring the Social Vision of the Wesleyan Movement," *Wesleyan Theological Journal* 25 (Spring 1990): 7–129; and John Wetherwax, "The Secularization of the Methodist Church: An Examination of the 1860 Free Methodist-Methodist Episcopal Schism," *Methodist History* 20 (April 1982): 156–63.

4. Christopher H. Owen, *The Sacred Flame of Love: Methodism and Society in Nineteenth Century Georgia* (Athens, GA: University of Georgia Press, 1998), 128.

5. Ibid., 87–88.

6. Ibid.

7. Charles Edward White, "Phoebe Palmer and the Development of Pentecostal Pneumatology," *Wesleyan Theological Journal* 23 (Spring–Fall, 1998): 198–212.

8. Vinson Synan, *The Holiness-Pentecostal Tradition: Charismatic Movements in the Twentieth Century* (Grand Rapids, MI: Eerdmans, 1997); and Donald Dayton, "Holiness Churches: A Significant Ethical Tradition," *Christian Century* 92 (February 1975): 192–201.

9. William L. Bonner Literary Committee, *And the High Places I'll Bring Down: Bishop William L. Bonner, The Man and His God* (Detroit: Bonner Literary Committee, 1999).

10. Ibid.

11. For example, Nelly, one of the most prominent rappers, has cashed in on this idea by manufacturing and selling pimp juice.

Part IV

FAITHFULLY PRACTICING EQUALITY

18

RECONSTRUCTIONIST JUDAISM AND MARRIAGE EQUALITY

Rebecca T. Alpert

The Reconstructionist movement has long been in the vanguard on the issue of gay and lesbian rights. This stance is in keeping with the basic principles of Reconstructionism, a movement that began in the United States in the 1920s based on the philosophy of Mordecai Kaplan (1881–1983). Reconstructionists affirm the idea that American Jews live in two civilizations, the American and the Jewish, and that those two worlds are quite compatible in their emphasis on democratic principles and other values. Reconstructionists also believe that the customs and traditions of Judaism can be brought to life for every generation of Jews, who must "reconstruct" their Jewish heritage in ways that both incorporate the Jewish past and are in keeping with the best values of contemporary society. Reconstructionist Jews are innovative in their worship practices, tending toward an informal style of prayer while at the same time preserving the traditional Hebraic character of Jewish liturgy. From its inception Reconstructionism supported gender equality and is perhaps known best as the originator of the Bat Mitzvah in 1922. This rite of passage at puberty had been restricted to boys until then.

For these reasons, Jews who began to identify publicly as gay and lesbian found the Reconstructionist movement to be a supportive location in the Jewish world, and the movement has responded positively to their demands for inclusion and equality.[1] The Reconstructionist Rabbinical College (RRC) has ordained openly gay and lesbian clergy since 1984, and the movement adopted a nondiscrimination policy for rabbinic placement in 1991. The Jewish Reconstructionist Federation (JRF), the umbrella organization that represents Reconstructionist congregations, has welcomed congregations that serve primarily gay and lesbian Jews since 1985. Gay and lesbian Jews have been welcomed and accepted in all facets of the Reconstructionist movement, including in key leadership positions. As a small movement, Reconstructionism has been highly visible because of its public support of gay rights, earning the reputation in some circles of being a "gay" movement, although the actual number of openly gay and lesbian people involved in the Reconstructionist movement do not support this conclusion.[2]

THE RECONSTRUCTIONIST POSITION ON MARRIAGE EQUALITY

The Reconstructionist movement has been involved both in performing religious ceremonies for gay and lesbian couples and in providing public support for the legalization of same-sex civil marriage. The movement has created liturgy for rabbis to use in performing same-sex religious ceremonies and has publicly gone on record to support civil marriage. Individual rabbis have invented their own ceremonies, and some have been active in the civil marriage fight through various legislative and judicial initiatives in their cities, states, and provinces throughout the United States and Canada.

These actions are consistent with Reconstructionist values. As I have argued elsewhere, in Reconstructionist Judaism, same-sex marriage is understood as a religious value because it provides economic justice, creates stable committed relationships, and fosters support for childrearing.[3]

Economic Justice

Marriage in Judaism has an economic basis. As witnessed by the text of the Jewish marriage contract, the *ketubah*, marriage in ancient Jewish law and custom was an exchange of property: a man would "give" his daughter in marriage to another man. Her economic value was determined by her sexual status (because virgins were worth more than widows, virginity had to be proven through physical evidence or the contractual terms were open to renegotiation). The husband was contractually obligated to provide the basic necessities of life for his wife, who was then considered his property.[4] Although a notion of women as property is offensive to modern sensibilities, the Jewish marriage contract provided economic protection for women at a time when their choices were limited. Jewish marriage contracts are clearly designed to establish economic well-being for the parties involved. However, the fact that the contract also provided conjugal rights for the wife is considered by many to be an important dimension of the transaction, indicating an understanding of women as sexual beings and recognizing their humanity, eventually leading the way for a change in the understanding of gender relationships in marriage.

The political and economic emancipation of women over the past few centuries has changed the terms of the economics of marriage. With those changes have come a variety of changes in the Jewish marriage contract. Although traditional Jews still use the ancient contract, and some liberal Jews also retain it for symbolic reasons, there are now widely used texts of contemporary contracts, for liberal Jews, that have been recast to omit any economic factors. This is based on the assumptions that women no longer need these ancient protections[5] and that the text of the traditional ketubah as it has been preserved no longer reflects the contemporary sensibilities of gender equality. What remains, however, is the consciousness that marriage had economic consequences for Jews under Jewish law and still does for some, as the traditional ketubah is the only contract valid in Orthodox communities in which the economic consequences of Jewish marriage and divorce are still a serious concern for women.

In contrast, civil marriage has great significance in conferring rights that affect the well-being, economic and emotional, of gay and lesbian couples. For many gay men and lesbians, the fight for same-sex marriage is about gaining these civil rights. Married couples automatically share property and inherit from one another, are defined as next of kin in medical decision making, are allowed to adopt each other's children, receive each other's pension and health benefits, can file joint tax returns, and provide citizenship for immigrant spouses.[6] The lack of benefits has caused severe financial and emotional hardships for gay and lesbian couples. Reconstructionist support of gay marriage is based both on (1) the principle of economic justice as reflected in the traditional Jewish recognition of the economic basis of marriage and on (2) the Reconstructionist principles of gender equality and the reconciliation of new values with old customs.

Public Commitment

Marriage has other purposes in Judaism. Marriage is also about sanctifying a loving relationship. It is an opportunity to give public, communal support to a committed partnership between two individuals. It is a chance to express faith in the relationship through the acknowledgement of the community that supports it. Marriage celebrates the religious values of long-term commitment, faithfulness, and the willingness to share life's joys and sorrows. The nature of the commitment is no longer about a woman's protection by and subservience to a man, but has been "reconstructed" to emphasize equality between the partners, yet the committed nature of the relationship is paramount and enforces deeply held religious values.

From a Reconstructionist perspective there is no difference in the fulfillment of these religious values between heterosexual and same-sex marriage. The partners pledge the same commitment to love and devotion, in the presence of a loving community, and there is no evidence that the intent to make a lasting commitment is different in either case. Same-sex couples seek to be married within the Jewish tradition for the same reasons that heterosexual couples do: they see this public declaration of their commitment in religious terms. Same-sex couples know that the state does not at this time validate their marriages, but they want to be considered married in the eyes of God and the Jewish people. They are looking to invest the ceremony with religious meaning. The principle of religious equality espoused by the Reconstructionist movement requires that these expressions of love be given the same societal validation, regardless of the genders of the partners involved.

Reconstructionist Judaism rejects differences based on gender in the wedding ceremony. Rings and vows are exchanged by equal partners; both parties sign the marriage contract, and they are often "pronounced" life partners, rather than the traditional husband and wife. Often, both parties break a glass at the conclusion of the wedding, a role traditionally assigned only to the groom. This egalitarian approach defines a marriage ceremony that is a transaction of interdependence between equals and removes any assumption that those equals must have different genders.

Pro-natalism

The other main purpose of marriage from a Jewish perspective is to control and encourage procreation. In today's society procreation outside of marriage is not stigmatized as greatly as it once was, although single parents are often not granted social status equivalent to that of a married couple. Married people without children are also more common, and childlessness within marriage is more acceptable. But Jewish communal values are strongly pro-natalist. The shrinking of the Jewish community through the Nazi genocide on the one hand and factors of assimilation on the other produces a strong communal value in support of having and raising children. The Jewish population has remained stable over the past few decades, but Jews still form a very small percentage of the world population. The threat of extinction makes Jewish leaders passionately committed to population growth, despite larger societal concerns about the need for global population control.

Although many people assume that same-sex marriages are childless, this is far from the truth. Stereotypic notions of gay antipathy to children are being eroded. The availability of children for adoption to single parents (and even to gay couples), the growing awareness and acceptance of alternative insemination methods, and the presence of children from previous heterosexual unions make children commonplace in gay and lesbian communities. In the Jewish community in particular, one can speak of a gay and lesbian baby boom.[7] Gay and lesbian Jews are often attracted to involvement in the Jewish community because of their desire for children and for a place for those children to develop Jewish identities and connections. And this desire is often connected to a wish to marry, for legal protection for children if for no other reason.

Reconstructionist Judaism retains a pro-natalist stance. There are no contemporary secular values that would cause Reconstructionist Jews to reevaluate this vital concern of the Jewish people. In emphasizing support for same-sex marriage, Reconstructionists would argue that, because raising children is a paramount value, and research studies have concluded that being raised by gay or lesbian parents has no negative effects on a child, same-sex marriage would strengthen the pro-natalist agenda of the Jewish people.

Same-sex marriage promotes "family values"—pro-natalism, communal involvement, monogamy—and enhances economic justice. These theoretical considerations are the bases upon which Reconstructionist Judaism has built its support for same-sex marriage. The Reconstructionist movement has pioneered in the development and legitimization of ceremonies of commitment for same-sex couples, and those ceremonies in turn form the basis for advocating civil marriage. This support has been manifested through public pronouncements and political activities to argue for legalization of same-sex marriage in the United States and Canada.

RECONSTRUCTIONIST RELIGIOUS CEREMONIES
FOR SAME-SEX COUPLES

The first official step toward a Reconstructionist commitment to performing same-sex wedding or commitment ceremonies took place in 1993 when the Reconstructionist movement published the findings of its Commission on Homosexuality. The document included support for rabbis who officiated at rituals for same-sex couples, although the decision about whether to perform these ceremonies was left up to the conscience of the individual rabbi.[8]

However, the movement did not leave the performance and construction of these ceremonies up to the individual rabbi for very long. The first Reconstructionist Rabbinical Association's (RRA) *Rabbi's Manual*, published in 1997, provided a ceremony to celebrate same-sex relationships. This was the first such ceremony to be incorporated into a standard manual published by any movement in Judaism, which includes the Reform, Conservative, and Orthodox groups. The presence of this ceremony in the standard manual, which provides guidance for rabbis about how to conduct ceremonies for life-cycle events from weddings to housewarmings, made Reconstructionist support of gay and lesbian weddings official. It was an important signal to Reconstructionist rabbis and to the Reconstructionist community that performing such ceremonies was indeed legitimate and in keeping with the movement's policies, not simply a matter of personal preference or individual conscience. In the manual the introduction to the ceremony indicates it is in response to

> a great need to create formulas and procedures whereby this generally marginalized segment of our community can publicly legitimate, formally validate or otherwise rightfully express principles of love and dedication, and so move into the mainstream.[9]

However, the ceremony is not called *kiddushin*, the term for the Jewish marriage ceremony that fulfills the requirements of Jewish law. Instead, it is given the name, *Berit Ahavah*, which means covenant of love. The introduction to the ceremony states that it is meant to be similar to kiddushin but not the same, as "in this ritual elements and forms of the traditional kiddushin interweave with strands of prayer and song."[10] The ceremony includes special readings that come from gay and lesbian sources. It also makes the necessary changes to the language of those parts of the ceremony (in the welcoming blessing and the seven wedding blessings) that refer specifically to heterosexuals or to God exclusively as male.

The ceremony is stunning in its willingness to acknowledge the love between gay men and lesbians as worthy of religious and communal recognition. The ceremony indicates this boldly, as the rabbi is encouraged to say the following:

> For so long in our people's history, the love of two men or two women was not a cause for rejoicing. Today we rejoice—we thank the source of life for giving us life and the capacity to love, for sustaining us in life and for enabling us to reach this joyous moment.[11]

But there is also a substantive change that makes it clear that this ceremony is not a legal Jewish wedding, or kiddushin. This ceremony does not use the traditional marriage vow recited over the exchange of rings ("With this ring, you are consecrated to me according to the law of Moses and Israel"). Rather, it is replaced with a distinct vow for two men, "With you I make this covenant, for I love you as my soul. Journey with me in peace and the Holy One shall be with you and with me," and a different one for two women: "Wherever you go, I will go and wherever you lodge, I will lodge. Your people shall be my people, your God shall be my God. Where you die, I will die, and there I will be buried." These vows are based on biblical verses.

The verse for two men is from the story of David and Jonathan in the book of I Samuel, and the one for women is from the vow uttered by Ruth to her mother-in-law Naomi in the book of Ruth.

This change reflects what the introduction to the ceremony terms "the difficult tension between the halachic [Jewish legal] system and a yearning, felt by many gays and lesbians, to participate as practicing Jews." Yet the heterosexual marriage vows in the Reconstructionist tradition also do not meet halachic standards because they permit the woman to say the same vow as the man and require an exchange of rings.[12] In an Orthodox wedding it is absolutely forbidden for a woman to give a man a ring, although some permit the woman to speak after the conclusion of the legal aspect of the wedding, the reading of the ketubah. According to the Orthodox interpretation of Jewish law, when a woman gives a man a ring and makes the same vow as a man, as is the case in the Reconstructionist kiddushin ceremony, it nullifies the nature of the vow that is made, which is not a contract between equals, but, as noted above, a symbolic acquisition.

In the ceremony in the latest edition of the Conservative rabbi's manual, women are permitted to say a vow and give the man a ring as well, but only the man says the traditional vow, which both men and women are allowed to recite in the Reconstructionist ceremony. It is ironic indeed that the woman's vow in the Conservative ceremony ("I will betroth you to Me forever. I will betroth you to Me with righteousness, with justice, with love, and with compassion. I will betroth you to Me with faithfulness and you shall love Adonai") is an adaptation of a biblical verse from Hosea 2:21–22, just as the Reconstructionist ceremony adapts gay and lesbian vows from other appropriate biblical texts.[13] The unwillingness to permit gay men and lesbians to use the traditional words of the vow indicates that the Reconstructionist liturgy struggles with the issue of identifying gay and lesbian religious ceremonies as equivalent to heterosexual Jewish marriages in a manner that corresponds to the Conservative movement's discomfort with contravening halachah to create parity in the woman's role.

The Reconstructionist rabbinical manual not only includes a same-sex ceremony but also has a "Resources for Marriage" section with a list of questions and answers about the ceremony to be "distributed to congregants, family members and others in need of guidance and instruction."[14] The resource guide avoids the questions raised above about the differences between the Berit Ahavah and kiddushin ceremonies, indicating that the ceremony "generally follows a traditional Jewish wedding format."[15] The resource guide does however explain why the ceremony is given the name "Berit Ahavah":

> We suggest that it be called a *berit ahavah* or "covenant of loving dedication." The Hebrew word *berit* holds much power. It is the word used to signify the special loving…relationship and binding "contractual" connection between God and the Jewish people. And *ahavah* means love. Bringing together these two words—the one which resonates so strongly in Jewish history and tradition, and the other which simply expresses a couple's deepest feelings for each other—seems most appropriate.[16]

This description is consistent with the Reconstructionist aim to honor Jewish law while at the same time acknowledging the needs and wishes of gay and lesbian

Jews, and it maintains the awareness within the Reconstructionist community that these goals are indeed in tension.

The resource guide also instructs the couple that, because this ceremony defines a serious commitment, its ending should be marked by a "formal dissolution ritual,"[17] although no specific ritual other than the traditional Jewish divorce proceedings has been devised for this purpose.

Although not the equivalent of the heterosexual Jewish marriage ceremony, the Berit Ahavah is a valuable tool for gay and lesbian Jews who want to claim the support of a religious movement in Judaism for same-sex marriage. But this ceremony is not the only one that Reconstructionist rabbis use. Many Reconstructionist rabbis had been performing commitment ceremonies for gay and lesbian Jews before the *Rabbi's Manual* was published and so they created their own ceremonies,[18] and others continue to do so, as I discovered in my own survey of Reconstructionist rabbis.[19]

In some cases, the rabbis noted that their gay and lesbian friends and congregants did not want to have ceremonies and instead chose anniversaries of other significant moments in their relationships to celebrate. They indicated that these friends and congregants were uncomfortable with doing a religious ceremony, given its associations with heterosexuality. The rabbis, on the other hand, had little or no hesitation in performing the ceremonies. In keeping with Reconstructionist traditions, almost all of the rabbis indicated that they worked with individual couples to craft ceremonies that would work for them. One rabbi remarked as follows:

> I don't have a personal policy re[garding] which ceremony (or what liturgical elements) I would use. I don't have any objections to using the same liturgical ingredients as in an opposite sex wedding—nor do I have a problem going a different route, if that was what seemed would best serve the couple. My decisions on liturgical/religious elements for a same-sex wedding would be informed by the same things I think about with opposite gender couples—what the couple wants, my own judgment as a rabbi about what is best serving them, my own honoring any issues that are important to my Jewish practice/public representation of Judaism.[20]

Rabbi Linda Holtzman commented that her practice was to use the traditional Jewish ceremony as an outline (for all couples) and "to walk people through the ceremony letting them add/subtract/choose the rituals that they like and that are meaningful to them. As a result, all ceremonies have the same starting point but no two look the same."[21]

Many said they were comfortable using the traditional ceremony and changing only the gender-specific elements in the vows and blessings. Many noted that they also omit the blessing over a wedding that includes a list of forbidden unions (*birkhat erusin*) in both heterosexual and gay ceremonies, although it is standard in Orthodox and Conservative ceremonies and included in the ceremony in the Reconstructionist manual.

Only a few of the respondents specifically mentioned the Berit Ahavah ceremony, although those who did commented mostly about finding the gender-neutral translations of the blessings particularly useful. Only one rabbi indicated her preference for using vows from Berit Ahavah.[22]

Several rabbis mentioned encouraging all couples to look at *The New Jewish Wedding Book* by Anita Diamant to help them make decisions about what to include in the ceremony.[23] Others mention using the ceremony created by Jewish feminist scholar Rachel Adler.[24] Adler invented a new ceremony, B'rit Ahuvim (Covenant of Lovers), that focused on an exchange of objects rather than rings and vows. Although its name bears a strong resemblance to the ceremony in the Reconstructionist *Rabbi's Manual*, the two ceremonies are quite different. The Reconstructionist Berit Ahavah (covenant of love) retains the traditional framework of a Jewish wedding. The goal of Adler's ceremony is to create an entirely different framework in order to circumvent the tensions that arise when contemporary people seek to change Jewish law. Adler created the ceremony as an alternative to the Jewish wedding ceremony because she argued that the inherent structure of the ceremony (symbolic acquisition of a woman by a man, rather than a covenantal relationship between them) could not be changed by making it a double ring ceremony or changing the language of the vows and the ketubah, as is the practice of Reform, Reconstructionist, and many Conservative Jews. Because the ceremony circumvents Jewish laws regarding weddings and substitutes a legal framework related to Jewish contract law, it can be used by both heterosexual and same-sex couples who would not feel comfortable using the traditional ceremony.

Although the idea is a good one, several Reconstructionist rabbis responded that couples generally prefer modifying traditional ceremonies to inventing new ones. They seek out rabbis to marry them in order to avail themselves of Jewish traditions. Many of the elements that are important to rabbis (language and legal status) are not the concern of those who come to a rabbi for a Jewish wedding, which to them usually means standing under a *huppah* (wedding canopy) and breaking a glass.

The commentary in the Reconstructionist *Rabbi's Manual* suggests that lesbian and gay couples may not want to stand under the huppah, "one of the most powerful symbols of a heterosexual Jewish marriage."[25] However, that idea was not reflected in any of the comments of the Reconstructionist rabbis. Some did mention using the occasion of breaking the glass to speak about gay and lesbian oppression as one element of the broken world represented by the broken glass.

Other rabbis mentioned different additions to the traditional ceremony, such as:

> spill[ing] a drop of wine from the 2nd cup after the *Sheva Brachot* [Seven Wedding Blessings] to indicate that our cup is not full. Then we would say a *shehehiyanu* (prayer for special occasions) and give thanks for the joy that the couple shares, thus balancing bitter with sweet.[26]

Others mentioned performing such additional rituals at weddings of heterosexual couples who are sensitive to this issue, often because of family members and friends who would be present at the ceremony.

RECONSTRUCTIONIST EFFORTS ON BEHALF OF CIVIL MARRIAGE EQUALITY

Although the primary focus of the Reconstructionist movement has been to create and support opportunities for same-sex couples to participate in Jewish wedding ceremonies and alternative rituals, the RRA and individual rabbis have also participated in the struggles for civil marriage for same-sex couples in the United States and Canada.

In March 2004, the RRA passed and promulgated a resolution titled "In Support of Civil Marriage for Same-Sex Couples."[27] The resolution reviewed the history of Reconstructionist support for gay and lesbian issues. In it, the authors argue that this resolution is important because gay and lesbian couples are being denied access to the automatic benefits of marriage bestowed on heterosexual couples, and that legal recognition would ensure those benefits and provide respect for these couples. They also suggest that this is a conversation in which religious voices have been misrepresented:

> We deem it imperative that progressive religious voices be raised in support…and in opposition to attempts to present religious traditions in general and Jewish traditions in particular, as being uniformly opposed to equality.[28]

The resolution went on to state that the RRA supports the rights and responsibilities of same-sex couples to marry, opposes all efforts to ban civil marriage, encourages its members to extend benefits to same-sex employees in the institutions in which they work, encourages the giving of *tzedakah* (charitable contributions) to same-sex marriage advocacy organizations, and urges rabbis to educate their constituencies about the importance of these issues through sermons, premarital counseling, and newsletter articles. It also encouraged rabbis to become involved and speak out in public forums, based on a commitment to "religious liberty as well as economic and political justice."[29]

Reconstructionist rabbis have been involved in a variety of efforts that support the ideas presented in this resolution in states and provinces that have legalized same-sex marriage, in those areas where same-sex marriage has been denied through passage of the Defense of Marriage Act, and in those states where the issue is being contested either through constitutional amendments to ban gay marriage or initiatives to legalize civil unions or gay marriage. The majority of respondents mention giving sermons or writing articles for synagogue bulletins and writing letters to editors of local newspapers and to elected officials.

Several rabbis reported activism with such groups as the Freedom to Marry Coalition, organized by the Lambda Legal Defense and Education Fund.[30] In two cases, the rabbis worked on interfaith events on Valentine's Day in support of same-sex marriage, and another was president of the local chapter of the Freedom to Marry Coalition.[31] One reported that he is a founding member of the Colorado Clergy for Equality in Marriage. Another rabbi reported working with the Religious Response Network in Oregon in a failed effort to defeat the constitutional amendment on the November ballot that defined marriage as between a man and a woman. He continues to work to lobby the legislature for change.[32] Another participates in a clergy roundtable for supporters of same-sex civil marriage in New York State, whereas another works in New Jersey with a group called Sacred Unions Network.[33] One rabbi gave testimony to the state legislature in Vermont,[34] and another testified and lobbied in Massachusetts.[35] Another rabbi spoke before the Durham County Council in North Carolina in support of domestic partner benefits.[36] All but one of these eleven rabbis is married to a person of the opposite sex.

Reconstructionist rabbis in Canada and Massachusetts, where civil marriage is an option, report having performed legal same-sex marriages. For most of them, doing so has opened up new dimensions of understanding the difference that legalization of same-sex marriage can make to the well-being of same-sex couples. One rabbi has had to keep his involvement secret, as he believes his congregation would not appreciate his efforts.[37]

Rabbi Michael Luckens, who has done these legal ceremonies now for Jewish couples and non-Jewish couples,[38] described a civil ceremony he performed for a couple planning a Jewish wedding in the future:

> I combined some poetry, selections from Marcia Falk's *Shir Hashirim* (The Song of Songs), birkat hashalom (blessing of peace), and invited the couple to say words to each other. I also invited others present to add a blessing, good wishes, etc. These were relatively small, intimate and informal gatherings, filled with an incredible spirit.[39]

Rabbi Barbara Penzner talked about how her practices in officiating at weddings have changed as a result of the Massachusetts decision to permit civil marriage:

> Now I always include a "pronouncement," something I never included.[40] I use it in straight or gay weddings to point out the legal and economic benefits of marriage, as well as the fact that even with recognition in MA, straight couples still have many more rights, and there's more work to be done.

Rabbi David Dunn Bauer came up with a pronouncement that encapsulates the responses of those who now do gay weddings in jurisdictions where they are, at least at the time of this writing, legal: "I sign the certificate and say 'By the power unaccountably vested in me by the Commonwealth of Massachusetts, I now pronounce you legally married.'"[41]

In addition to legislative initiatives, there are also judicial strategies in which Reconstructionist rabbis have engaged. A 1995 case, *Shahar v. Bowers*, demonstrated how the acceptance of same-sex marriage in Reconstructionist Judaism could be used in judicial as well as legislative battles. Reconstructionist support for same-sex marriage was evoked as a factor in the arguments made by a public employee in Georgia who claimed that she was fired from her position because she participated in a same-sex marriage ceremony performed by Rabbi Sharon Kleinbaum.[42] A religious discrimination argument was part of the argument presented by Shahar's lawyers. Shahar lost the case at the federal Court of Appeals level, and the U.S. Supreme Court decided not to hear the case on appeal.

Elsewhere I have argued that same-sex marriage has been supported by Reconstructionist Judaism as an issue of economic justice and gender equality and that these factors establish a warrant for Reconstructionist Judaism to define same-sex marriage as a deeply held religious belief. On that basis the movement could claim the right to perform same-sex marriages as a dimension of religious liberty based on the First Amendment and initiate a legal case on that basis.[43]

Marriage equality is an issue that the Reconstructionist movement has embraced wholeheartedly as a logical dimension of the agenda of living in two civilizations, the North American and the Jewish. Advocating for gay men and lesbians to participate in religious wedding ceremonies that bestow full civil rights as well has been an important part of the Reconstructionist program for the past decade. The movement's leadership and many of its rabbis and congregations have been in the forefront of challenging the idea that religious groups oppose marriage equality. Reconstructionist Jews are well aware that this issue is far from resolved, either in the Jewish or secular worlds, and that they are in a strategic position to play an important role as the debate over this issue unfolds.

NOTES

1. See the articles by Reconstructionist Rabbis Linda Holtzman, Rebecca Alpert, Leila Gal Berner, Sharon Kleinbaum, and Julie Greenberg in *Lesbian Rabbis: The First Generation*, ed. Rebecca Alpert, Sue Levi Elwell, and Shirley Idelson (New Brunswick, NJ: Rutgers University Press, 2001). The articles tell the stories of the early struggles for equality and acceptance.

2. For example, of the 238 current members of the Reconstructionist Rabbinical Association, 22 identify as lesbian, gay, bisexual or transgender (LGBT). No LGBT congregations are members of the Jewish Reconstructionist Federation, preferring to join the Reform movement. Of 38 faculty members (adjunct and full time) at RRC, 7 identify as LGBT.

3. The next section of this chapter is based on my "Religious Liberty, Same-Sex Marriage and the Case of Reconstructionist Judaism," in *God Forbid: Religion and Sex in American Public Life*, ed. Kathleen Sands (Oxford: Oxford University Press, 2000), 124–32. Reprinted in *The Reconstructionist: A Journal of Contemporary Jewish Thought and Practice* 68, no. 1 (Fall 2003): 33–42.

4. Judith Wegner, *Chattel or Person? The Status of Women in the Mishnah* (New York: Oxford University Press, 1988). See also Rachel Adler's "B'rit Ahuvim: A Marriage Between Subjects," in *Engendering Judaism: An Inclusive Theology and Ethics* (Philadelphia: Jewish Publication Society, 1998).

5. Many Web sites now advertising ketubot (marriage contracts) for purchase also include versions of the document that can be used by same-sex couples. These ketubot are called "Commitment Vows Ketubah" and are described as having "gender neutral text…written to accommodate same-gender unions. They may be used by any couple." They are available, for example, at http://www.judaicconnection.com/ (accessed May 17, 2005).

6. The ability to bring a non-U.S. citizen into the country through marriage is an often overlooked but most significant benefit that has enormous repercussions for gay and lesbian relationships. One of the respondents to my survey of Reconstructionist rabbis about their positions on gay marriage remarked (Rabbi Gail Diamond in a conversation with the author, March 1, 2005),

> As far as marriage equality goes, this subject could not be closer to my heart. As you know, I live outside the United States because my partner of 11 years is not a U.S. citizen and as a citizen I have no rights to get her residence in the United States…. I hope you will include the issue of immigration in whatever you write— as Jews we should be sensitive to this issue since our ancestors were immigrants to the United States, and marriage based immigration rights have been used by Jews in forming connections all over the world. The lack of immigration rights for our partners is one of the greatest injustices to gay people in the United States. BTW [by the way], in contrast, the Supreme Court in Israel recently ruled that a foreign

national who was to be deported could not be deported because he was the partner of an Israeli citizen.

7. See Christie Balka, "Thoughts on Lesbian Parenting and the Challenge to Jewish Communities," *Bridges* 3 (1993): 57–65; and Linda Holtzman, "Jewish Lesbian Parenting," in *Twice Blessed: On Being Lesbian or Gay and Jewish*, ed. Christie Balka and Andy Rose (Boston: Beacon Press, 1989), 133–40.

8. Lenore Meyers and Robert Glück, "Homosexuality and Judaism: The Reconstructionist Position, The Report of the Reconstructionist Commission on Homosexuality," 1993, 40–41.

9. Reconstructionist Rabbinical Association, *Rabbi's Manual* (Wyncote, PA: Reconstructionist Rabbinical Association, 1997), M-15.

10. Ibid.

11. Ibid., M-28.

12. Ibid., M-9: "Behold, with this ring, you are consecrated to me, according to the sacred custom of Moses, Miriam and Israel!"

13. Volume 1 of the new edition of the Rabbinical Assembly *Rabbi's Manual*, C-49 (see note 9), also provides other biblical options: "I am my beloved, and my beloved is mine" (Song of Songs) and "Let me be a seal upon your heart, like the seal upon your hand" (Song of Songs 8:6). It suggests that the bride *may* place a ring on the groom's forefinger, and it may be done before the ketubah reading. (In an older edition, there was no option for the bride to give the groom a ring or to speak in Hebrew.)

14. Reconstructionist Rabbinical Association, *Rabbi's Manual*, M-15 (see note 9).

15. Ibid., R-3.

16. Ibid.

17. Ibid., R-2.

18. Although these ceremonies have been around for many years, it is likely that the first such ceremony performed by a Reconstructionist rabbi (for another Reconstructionist rabbi's ceremony) took place in 1984. See Linda Holtzman, "Struggle, Change and Celebration: My Life as a Reconstructionist Rabbi," in *Lesbian Rabbis: The First Generation*, 43–44 (see note 1).

19. The information about the activities of Reconstructionist rabbis in regard to same-sex marriage is based on responses I received to an e-mail message I sent to my colleagues on February 28, 2005, asking them whether they performed same-sex commitment ceremonies or civil marriages in states, provinces, or countries where these ceremonies are legal. I also asked about what ceremony they used and whether they have been involved in this issue politically. Of the 238 members of the Reconstructionist Rabbinical Association to whom I wrote, 61 responded. (Of the 22 publicly identified gay and lesbian rabbis, I received responses from 11.) Of those, sixty indicated that they were willing to or had performed these ceremonies. Sixty respondents felt comfortable with the survey; but one respondent reminded me that the rest might have preferred anonymity, commenting: "If you really want honest answers from people who are less certain about this issue, you might want to provide some sort of Web site where people could answer while maintaining some measure of anonymity." I agree with this respondent, but my goal was not to discover opposition among Reconstructionist rabbis to the movement's policies, but rather to learn about how the policies are being implemented. This respondent's suggestion (and the results of my inquiry) did point out clearly that those who are opposed to the policy or, as this respondent suggested, "may be unsure, uncomfortable with the way it is being framed, the prominence given the issue, or any of a number of other matters that may fall short of actual opposition" do not feel comfortable to speak out. This suggests that the Reconstructionist movement has made its decision to support lesbian and gay rights and same-sex marriage as a foundational part of its

philosophy and that those who disagree do not always feel that they can do so freely and openly.

20. Rabbi Maurice Harris (Rabbi of Temple Beth Israel, Eugene, Oregon), in a conversation with the author, February 28, 2005.

21. Rabbi Linda Holtzman (Director of Practical Rabbinics, Reconstructionist Rabbinical College), in a conversation with the author, February 9, 2005.

22. Rabbi Yael Ridberg (West End Synagogue, New York), in a conversation with the author, February 15, 2005.

23. New York: Fireside Books, 2001. The revised and updated edition includes a section on same-sex weddings that was not included when the book was first published in 1985.

24. Rachel Adler, *Engendering Judaism: An Inclusive Theology and Ethics* (Philadelphia: Jewish Publication Society, 1998), 169–208.

25. Reconstructionist Rabbinical Association, *Rabbi's Manual*, R-3 (see note 9).

26. Rabbi Barbara Rosman Penzner (Rabbi of Temple Hillel B'nai Torah, Boston, Massachusetts), in a personal conversation with the author, February 15, 2005.

27. The text of the resolution can be found at the RRA Web site, http://www.therra.org/resolution-Mar2004.htm (accessed 2 February 2005).

28. Ibid.

29. Ibid.

30. Rabbi Benjamin Arnold (Rabbi of Temple Sinai, Amherst, New York), in a personal conversation with the author, February 27, 2005.

31. Rabbis Jane Litman (Rabbi of Congregation Beth El, Berkeley, California); Rebecca Lillian (Rabbi of Temple Beth Or, Miami, Florida); and Melissa Klein (Congregation Am Haskalah, Allentown, Pennsylvania), in personal conversations with the author, February 27, 2005.

32. Rabbi Maurice Harris (Rabbi of Temple Beth Israel, Eugene, Oregon), in personal conversation with the author, February 28, 2005.

33. Rabbi Rachel Gartner (Rabbi of B'nai Keshet, Montclair, New Jersey), in personal conversation with the author, May 13, 2005.

34. Rabbi Michael M. Cohen, Senate Committee on the Judiciary, file H-847, State of Vermont, 2000.

35. Rabbi Barbara Rosman Penzner (Rabbi of Temple Hillel B'nai Torah, Boston, Massachusetts), in a personal conversation with the author, February 15, 2005.

36. Rabbi Jennifer Feldman (Rabbi of the Chapel Hill Kehillah, North Carolina), in a personal conversation with the author, February 24, 2005.

37. This rabbi prefers to remain anonymous. Personal communication with the author, May 25, 2005.

38. Note that interfaith weddings are much more highly contested in Reconstructionist circles, and a good number of the rabbis who responded to my inquiry indicated that they will perform same-sex ceremonies only for two Jews or, in the cases where they can perform a civil ceremony, only will do it for two people if neither of them is Jewish as was the case described here.

39. Rabbi Michael Luckens (Rabbi of Congregation Kerem Shalom, Concord, Massachusetts), personal conversation with the author, February 28, 2005.

40. Most states require clergy to incorporate a legal pronouncement, "by the authority vested in me by the State of X, I now pronounce you…" either publicly or at the time of the signing of the certificate.

41. Rabbi David Dunn Bauer (Jewish Community of Amherst, Massachusetts), personal conversation with the author, February 17, 2005.

42. *Shahar v. Bowers*, 70 F.3d 1218, 1223 (11th Cir. 1995).

43. Alpert, "Religious Liberty, Same-Sex Marriage and the Case of Reconstructionist Judaism," 129–30 (see note 3).

19

WHEN COVENANT-MAKING BECOMES JUSTICE-MAKING: A SAN FRANCISCO PASTOR'S STORY

Karen P. Oliveto

The picture appears with surprising regularity on the San Francisco Bay area evening news: a couple in a church, hands joined, and standing before a pastor. At a casual glance, one would assume that a wedding is taking place, until a closer inspection reveals that the couple consists of two white men, dressed in suits with boutonnieres. In San Francisco, this realization does not evoke shock or even a raised eyebrow, because in February 2004, more than four thousand gay and lesbian couples said, "I do," before city officials, deputies, judges, and clergy. Their pictures and stories appeared in newspapers and television newscasts for nearly six weeks when Mayor Gavin Newsom allowed the city to issue marriage certificates to same-gender couples.

That particular couple featured on the evening news, Bill Hinson and Dan Johnson, was the first gay couple ever legally married in a United Methodist Church. I was privileged, as their pastor, to officiate at their wedding, with the entire congregation of Bethany United Methodist Church as their witnesses. Seeing the images on TV, years later, as a backdrop whenever a story on same-gender marriage is aired is startling. Every time it appears, I am reminded of a historical moment that shaped U.S. political and ecclesial debate, as well as affected my own vocational life.

The story actually began several days before Bill and Dan's wedding. Early in the afternoon on February 12, 2004, I received a phone call from Michael Eaton, one of my parishioners, who told me, "The city is issuing marriage licenses to gay and lesbian couples!" A quick check online confirmed the accuracy of Michael's call. Hours earlier, Phyllis Lyon and Del Martin, two long-time lesbian activists, had exchanged vows at City Hall and had been issued a marriage certificate. City Assessor-Recorder Mabel Teng had solemnized the wedding while the mayor, city officials, and leaders of the city's lesbian, gay, bisexual, and transgender (LGBT) community looked on.

An hour or two later Michael called me back, "Sean and I are in line for our license. Will you come marry us?" Without a moment's hesitation, I said, "yes."

I had known Michael and his partner, Sean Higgins, for many years. I officiated at their holy union several years before, provided them with pastoral support as they decided to expand their family through adoption, and walked with them through the emotional valleys and mountaintops as they went through the adoption process. Now, as they sought legal recognition of their relationship, we were about to share in another major milestone as pastor and parishioners.

We rendezvoused at City Hall and found a quiet spot to do the ceremony. We stood and faced each other, and then, taking a deep breath, began the ritual. Tears welled as the familiar words were recited. As we finished the ceremony, and the couple kissed, we stepped back, looked each other in the eye, and realized that we had just stepped into history. The personal act of covenant-making had become a political act of justice-making.

As a pastor of Bethany United Methodist Church, whose demographics were half LGBT and half straight, I found myself at the epicenter of a tectonic social shift. Arriving at City Hall to perform Michael and Sean's wedding, I found it filled with hundreds of lesbian and gay couples of all races and ethnicities, as well as dozens of reporters and camera crews. Clothed in a clergy shirt and clutching *The United Methodist Book of Worship*, I represented to the media the collision of worlds: the secular versus the sacred, the gay versus the straight, the personal versus the public, the legal versus the ecclesial.

Once in City Hall, I found more and more of my parishioners in line to get married. As I officiated at their ceremonies, camera crews and photographers began to record each one, many of which made their way into local and national papers and TV stations. Reporters began to ask me questions. How can you as a Christian minister participate in these ceremonies? Doesn't the Bible say that homosexuality is a sin? Does the United Methodist Church support gay marriage? Will there be any repercussions for doing these marriages?

It was this last question that piqued the interest of the media. But the media, in exchange, provided me, for a short while, with a very public pulpit from which I could provide a theological framework based upon my Christian faith perspective about what was occurring in San Francisco. The tension in the story was whether or not I would be disciplined by my denomination for performing the weddings. Yet, the press afforded me a great deal of latitude to talk—as a pastor, teacher, and theologian—about the historic moment we were experiencing and to offer testimony about how God continues to work in the world.

Mayor Newsom's decision to extend marriage certificates to same-gender couples was an unexpected move. In San Francisco, a politically progressive city, Newsom was considered the conservative candidate, running for mayor opposite a Green Party candidate. Yet, scarcely one month into his term of office, Newsom surprised everyone by using his authority as mayor in a radical way. It is rare that we who are progressives have the opportunity to set the terms of debate regarding controversial social issues. Aware that the Religious Right has all too often framed gay rights, the media were giving me—and all of us in San Francisco—an opportunity to describe what was happening in San Francisco and offer an argument about the social benefits of same-gender marriage before those in other parts of the country (and on another side of the political/theological/ideological spectrum) had the chance to denounce it.

The Bethany congregation where I was serving as pastor has a long history of working for LGBT rights within the United Methodist Church (UMC). Several members of the laity have been leaders nationally within the denomination, seeking the full inclusion of LGBT persons at every level of the church. It was unacceptable to this congregation that the official UMC stance pronounced homosexual practice as "incompatible with Christian teachings." This local congregation—an urban church with a membership diverse in age, race, class, sexual orientation, and gender identity—expected its pastor to treat all members equally. The lay members of the church issued a policy statement on holy unions when the UMC prohibited them. The statement declared that Bethany congregants had the right to ask their pastor to perform their ceremonies, that they expected their pastor to perform them, and that their sanctuary was available for holy unions. The congregation raised funds to send members of the congregation to the General Conference of the United Methodist Church (the denomination's legislative body, which sets policy for the church) every four years to lobby for LGBT rights.

It was together, in partnership with this theologically articulate and politically savvy congregation, that I responded to questions from the press. Whenever possible, I had a member of the congregation present with me when a journalist or camera crew interviewed me (preferably, one of our newly married couples), so that middle America could "meet" the people whose lives were so highly politicized by these events.

Additionally, I informed my district superintendent in the UMC, my immediate supervisor, of any interviews and press releases to keep her informed of what I was saying and to whom I was saying it. I was aware that in performing these marriages, I was walking in murky territory regarding our denominational rules. Technically, I was performing a legal marriage, authorized by the government. However, *The United Methodist Book of Discipline 2000*, our denominational "rule book," prohibited "ceremonies that celebrate homosexual unions."

If you asked any of my parishioners who had had a holy union in the past whether what they experienced when they were married was merely a repeat of their holy union, the response would be an emphatic "no." Even though their holy unions were planned carefully, attended by family and friends, and complete with receptions and gifts, and their wedding ceremonies were, for some, a quick "Let's meet after work and get married" decision, every single couple was amazed at the power of the marriage ceremony to more fully legitimize their relationship, both for the couple as well as for their family and friends. Their marriage licenses are still hung prominently and proudly in homes, long after the city's actions were declared illegal. Parents started calling their child's partner "my daughter-in-law" or "my son-in-law." People went back to work after their wedding to find that their co-workers had transformed the office into an impromptu wedding reception. In fact, the whole city felt like one big wedding reception, as newlyweds returned to their neighborhoods and celebrated with friends.

On February 14, members of the congregation went down to City Hall and handed out Hershey's KISSES to those waiting in line to be married. With each candy that exchanged hands, a simple statement was offered, "A kiss of congratulations on your wedding day from Bethany United Methodist Church." One woman, when she received the candy, fell into my arms sobbing, "I am a United Methodist! I never thought the church would offer someone like me a blessing."

With the help of a cell phone, I managed to keep track of my parishioners' places in line, so that once they had been issued a license, we could determine a place to rendezvous so we could do the ceremony. One couple, Bill and Dan, didn't get their license until late in the afternoon. Unfortunately, I had already entered into a worship retreat and could not meet them. They sorely wanted me to perform their ceremony, but there was simply no way I could join them. Thinking it over, I reminded them that they did not have to immediately solemnize the license. We could do the ceremony at another time. In fact, the next day was our annual Valentine's Day Service of Recommitment, to which we had invited all couples— gay and straight—to come and reaffirm their vows and receive a prayer of blessing. What if Bill and Dan exchanged vows before the congregation and then we invited other couples to come forward to reaffirm their own?

The more we discussed it, the more this seemed right, both for the couple and for the congregation. The congregation had cared for the couple when Dan was sick. The couple had also faithfully served the congregation in numerous ways. On Sunday morning, the congregation could enter into the couple's joy as they wed.

A few minutes later, a realization struck: never before had a gay couple been legally married in a United Methodist Church. Aware that we had one more opportunity to shape public perceptions, we issued a press release, alerting the media about the wedding. An e-mail announcement went out to the congregation, and the leaders of the church began to organize for the worship service.

On Sunday, Bill and Dan walked down the aisle with the entire congregation as witnesses. The Sunday School teachers decided to cancel Sunday School, so that our children could remain in worship. We told them, "Someday, you will tell your children and grandchildren about this day." Our senior citizens all claimed grandparent status, their love of Dan and Bill evident in the tears they shed. Together, we did what congregations around the world do: we praised God through worship. We prayed, read scripture, sang hymns about our faith and commitment, and affirmed the blessedness of love as Dan and Bill exchanged their solemn vows. The media captured it all.

In the days that followed, I continued to perform weddings for members of the congregation. On February 19, I received a phone call from my district superintendent, the Reverend Jane Schlager, informing me that a formal complaint had been filed against me for "disobedience to the Order and Discipline of The United Methodist Church" and that a supervisory process with the bishop would soon begin. The purpose of the supervisory process is to explore whether resolution and reconciliation can occur between the person filing the complaint and the accused. If not, or if the bishop determines that a violation of *The Book of Discipline* has occurred, the complaint can be sent to the Committee on Investigation. This committee collects all the details related to the case and determines whether there is enough evidence to convert the complaint to a charge, which then sets into motion a church trial. A trial, in which fellow clergy serve as judges, can ultimately lead to the removal of one's ordination credentials.

I had tried to prepare myself for the possibility of a complaint. I knew there were those across the denomination who would be outraged by my pastoral actions. As much as I tried to steel myself for the words I feared were inevitable, when I was actually told that a complaint had been filed, it was devastating. I knew I needed to put into place a support network so I could face, emotionally and spiritually, the uncertainties of the complaint process while at the same time continuing to offer a prophetic witness about the weddings.

First, I called my clergy colleagues who had had complaints filed against them to learn about the process they experienced. Second, I called Rev. Barbara Troxell, who became my spiritual director for the next several months. Lastly, I spoke to an old seminary friend, Rev. Ginnie Pearson, who became my advocate, accompanying me at all supervisory sessions with the bishop and serving as an important voice of support for me in those sessions.

With that level of support in place, the leaders of the congregation and I considered ways we could continue to articulate a theological reflection on the weddings for the wider church and society. We decided to hold a press conference and asked United Methodists from around the Bay Area to attend so that the media could capture the fact that Christians outside of San Francisco supported the right of gay men and lesbians to marry. With less than twenty-four hours notice, the sanctuary was filled with supporters for the press conference. With the entire congregation standing behind me and United Methodists from other churches filling the pews, I said these words:

> I have received word from my District Superintendent, the Rev. Jane Schlager, that a complaint was filed against me for "disobedience to the Order and Discipline of The United Methodist Church" for conducting a legal marriage during worship at Bethany Church on February 15, 2004. As a loyal and faithful United Methodist pastor, who is bound by the covenant of my ordination, I respect the process for accountability and review of my ministry. Since this is a confidential personnel matter, I will not be discussing the details of the complaint.
>
> However, in these days when God's justice is ushering in an era of human liberation, I will continue to interpret to the Church the changing cultural context in which we are living, for legal marriage between same-sex couples may have begun in San Francisco, but it is inevitable that it will become a reality throughout America. And I will continue to be a representative of the Church of Jesus Christ in the world.
>
> We who follow Jesus are called to stand against hate, not against love. I pray that faithful Christians everywhere will join us as we celebrate the love that is being deepened and the families that are being strengthened through the institution of marriage.
>
> We at Bethany are very aware of our unique social setting, and we know we have a responsibility to witness to those across the country the miracle of God moving in our midst in San Francisco. And so I have invited representatives from this congregation to share what they have been experiencing as we celebrate the legal marriages of our same-sex couples.[1]

Jeff Friant, the lay leader of the congregation, articulated the congregation's commitment to be in ministry with and for gay and lesbian people. Shannon Horton and

Sean O'Connor spoke about how their relationship as a straight couple was strengthened by seeing the depth of commitment of gay and lesbian couples in the congregation. Gloria Soliz and Julie Williamson movingly talked about the profound impact that being legally wed had on them, and Michael Eaton and Sean Higgins, the first couple I married, joyously displayed their marriage license to the crowd.

The level of support we received from United Methodists in our region was not surprising. The California-Nevada Annual Conference, as well as the entire Western Jurisdiction of the United Methodist Church, was on record as publicly supporting the rights of LGBT persons. In 1999, 150 clergy and lay representatives from seventeen congregations blessed the relationship of Ellie Charlton and Jeanne Barnett, long-time United Methodists in the California-Nevada Annual Conference. Complaints were filed against these clergy, and as a result of the supervisory process, the Committee on Investigation reviewed the complaints against 68 of them. I was a member of the committee that reviewed the complaints. After three days of hearings, the committee declared that the complaints would not be converted to charges, and the case was closed.[2]

Meeting just three months later, the General Conference of the United Methodist Church passed legislation that continued the discriminatory policies toward LGBT persons within the church. In response, the Western Jurisdiction of the United Methodist Church, encompassing annual conferences in the western part of the United States, passed a declaration declaring their commitment to ministries with and for LGBT persons:

> We of the Western Jurisdiction of the United Methodist Church have heard the call of the prophet Micah "to do justice, love mercy, and walk humbly with God." We have heard Jesus's invitation for all to come to the banquet table of God's abundant grace.
>
> Certain actions of General Conference 2000 have caused tremendous pain for individuals and communities and have resulted in an attempt to suppress our prophetic and pastoral ministries among all people, regardless of sexual orientation.
>
> The votes may have been cast but our voices will not be silent. Our jurisdictional vision calls us to be "a home for all God's people, gathered around a table of reconciliation and transformation." Affirming the statement of United Methodists of Color for a Fully Inclusive Church, "We acknowledge that there may be differences of opinion among us, but this does not require that we wait on justice." We cannot accept discrimination against gay, lesbian, bisexual or transgender persons and, therefore, we will work toward their full participation at all levels in the life of the church and society. Valuing the voices of those who disagree, we will continue to be in dialogue as we journey together in creative tension. We will continue to be in ministry with all God's children and celebrate the gifts diversity brings. We will continue to feast at table with all God's children.[3]

Against this backdrop, I informed my district superintendent that my intent was to work collaboratively with her and the bishop as we entered into the supervisory process. I realized we all had to be accountable to our denomination's *Book of Discipline* and that each of us had our own role to fulfill within this process. Because of the social location of our members and the communities where we bear witness to our faith, we United Methodists in the West are provided with a unique perspective on our denominational rules and how they impact our ministries, which I had hoped would inform our task.

Unfortunately, after the first session with Bishop Shamana and Jane, Ginnie and I realized that the process really does not allow for a collaborative approach. Although the purpose of the supervisory process is "pastoral and administrative" with the intent to reach a just resolution that "God's work of justice, reconciliation and healing may be realized in the body of Christ,"[4] the process ultimately is designed to support and maintain the institution. In this case, the world I ministered in had taken a giant step forward into the future regarding the rights of gay men and lesbians while the institution was clinging to a past that did not begin to address the pastoral issues that had emerged with the legalized marriages.

Additionally, a colleague shared a conversation she had had with her district superintendent (DS). When she conferred with her DS about doing a marriage for a gay couple in her congregation, she was told, "Okay, just don't hold a press conference." It became clear to me that one reason why I was facing the supervisory process was because I had talked publicly about doing the weddings.

I remain troubled by this fact. The "don't ask, don't tell" policy around holy unions was fairly easy to follow. In the 1980s and 1990s, holy unions were primarily private affairs, with only one's closest family (if they would come) and friends present. Many gay men and lesbians faced job loss or the possible loss of child custody if they came out. Legal marriage, however, is a very public act. In addition to family and friends, the government has a vested interest in the success of the institution. Unlike holy unions, marriages are formalized in legal public documents, with a pastor's signature clearly affixed to the license. Additionally, recent gains in LGBT civil rights have allowed people to come out of the closet and live their lives openly.

The "press conference" reference also failed to take into account the United Methodist Church's understanding of our theological task. The theological task includes identifying "the needs both of individuals and of society and to address those needs out of the resources of the Christian faith in a way that is clear, convincing, and effective."[5] As pastor of a church in San Francisco that included gay men and lesbians, I had experienced the movement of God during San Francisco's "Winter of Love" in profound ways. God was doing a new thing, and as a pastor, I had a responsibility both to inform the Church about the future God was calling us to and to help those outside the church see how God was at work in the world. Press conferences became a way for the Bethany congregation and me to proclaim the Good News that God was, indeed, with us as we in San Francisco experienced unparalleled unity and goodwill in those days of legal same-gender marriage.

As the supervisory process continued over the next nine months, I became increasingly unsure of my future as a United Methodist clergywoman. Although I remained convinced of the faithfulness of my actions, I was not sure that my bishop or superintendent saw my actions in quite the same way. Questions I raised in supervisory sessions regarding what a just resolution might look like or what I could do to begin the work of reconciliation went unanswered. With no answer, how could resolution and reconciliation be achieved?

In May 2004, the General Conference met in Pittsburgh. My colleagues elected me as a delegate. Debates about homosexuality dominated the conference. Over the course of the two-week meeting, the delegates voted to further marginalize gay men and lesbians from the life of the church. The entire Western Jurisdiction, known for its commitment to LGBT persons, was stunned by the relentless attacks on our ministries of hospitality and justice. I returned to San Francisco with grave questions about how I could continue to be pastor to the Bethany community. If my actions regarding the weddings had resulted in a complaint that was still unresolved, what would happen now that ministries to, with, and for LGBT persons were further limited? Would I face more complaints? How could the congregation and I renegotiate the ministry expectations we had of each other?

On June 1, 2004, a multidenominational seminary, Pacific School of Religion, offered me a position in its office of Academic Affairs. Unsure of where the complaint might ultimately lead and feeling God at work in my life yet again, I agreed to take the position. On July 1, 2004, after twelve years of ministry, I was no longer the pastor of Bethany.

However, although I was no longer appointed to a local church, I was still under the appointment of the bishop and we were still meeting as part of the supervisory process. The bishop called me into her office on September 10, 2004. At that meeting, she and my district superintendent informed me that the complaint had been resolved. I issued one last statement to inform all those who had supported me through prayers, e-mails, and calls that the supervisory process had ended. The statement included a brief review of the historical moment we experienced in San Francisco related to same-gender marriage, our congregation's sense of call to prophetic witness, the subsequent complaint and its process, as well as disappointment in the decisions of General Conference:

> In the spring of 2004, the General Conference of The United Methodist Church voted to define marriage as solely between two persons of the opposite sex, and limited the ministries of the church by refusing to allow clergy to celebrate the marriages of same-sex couples. In spite of these proclamations, we know that God's love and justice are unstoppable. Having glimpsed the future God is unveiling, we know the Church will eventually confess its sin of heterosexism, which has fractured the body of Christ and will affirm the love and commitment of all couples, regardless of sexual orientations or gender identities.
>
> I am grateful for the words and prayers of support from individuals and communities across the country. The notes and calls from clergy and laity from within our United Methodist connection as well as those outside our denomination were overwhelmingly supportive…. It was humbling to have so many people praying for me throughout the complaint process. I remain inspired by the witness of the 4,000 couples who were married in San Francisco during our "Winter of Love." Their love and commitment touched and changed the hearts and minds of people across the country. In spite of the setback of a court decision that annulled the marriages, we know that this is but a temporary delay to the acquisition of the full rights and responsibilities of marriage for gay men and lesbians. In the meantime, I pray that the couples may be forever mindful of the blessings of God that are found in their life together.[6]

I remain convinced that my actions in February 2004 will remain the most faithful of my pastoral career. God's justice is unstoppable. The glimpse of equality we experienced in San Francisco during that time will one day be a reality for all loving couples. The role that many faith communities are currently playing in the struggle for marriage/rites for all loving couples displays the institutional church's sinful reflection of our human failings. How can the church, founded on the teachings of Jesus, seek to limit love in the world? How can the church, as God's arms and legs in the world, be complicit with injustice? How can the church, as the body of Christ, intentionally seek to amputate parts of the body by refusing to provide basic pastoral services to its gay and lesbian members? Just as the church has had to confess its most overt practices of racism and sexism, it will, in the future, confess its sin of homophobia and seek forgiveness.

Although same-gender marriages have been stopped in San Francisco, they continue in Massachusetts, Canada, Spain, and numerous other places. We have a glimpse of an inevitable future: when loving couples, regardless of sexual orientation, will be offered equal rites and rights as they join their lives together. Already, the media images of thousands of happy gay and lesbian couples of all races and ethnicities standing in line to be married at San Francisco's City Hall have left indelible marks on future generations. As five-year-old Amy told her mother, "Last night I had a dream that two girls got married. It was such a happy dream."

NOTES

1. Oliveto Press Conference, Bethany United Methodist Church, San Francisco, California, February 22, 2004.

2. See "Decision of the Committee on Investigation for Clergy Members and Statement by Bishop Melvin Talbert," http://www.umaffirm.org/cornews/calnev13.html (accessed October 11, 2006), for more information.

3. "We Shall Not Be Silent" (declaration, Western Jurisdiction of the United Methodist Church, Casper, Wyoming, July 14, 2000).

4. United Methodist Church, *The Book of Discipline of the United Methodist Church 2004* (Nashville: United Methodist Publishing House, 2004), 75.

5. Ibid.

6. Excerpts from Oliveto resolution statement, Pacific School of Religion, Berkeley, California, September 16, 2004. The statement also included expressions of gratitude to members of the California-Nevada Annual Conference of The United Methodist Church, for their affirmation of my ministry; including: the national staff and constituencies of the Reconciling Ministries Network and the Methodist Federation for Social Action; Sister Bernie Galvin, the steering committee of Religious Witness with Homeless People, and my San Francisco interfaith colleagues for their vocal support of my ministry; the Reverend Barbara Troxell, whose spiritual direction provided care for my soul; the Reverend Linda Snider, who accompanied me to one of the supervisory sessions; especially the Reverend Ginnie Pearson, who was my advocate throughout the duration of the complaint and who provided much guidance and wisdom; my family, whose constant love provided strength for the journey; lastly, I am eternally grateful for the people of Bethany United Methodist Church. Throughout the twelve years I was privileged to be their pastor, we learned that we are most faithful when we are willing to face the cross for the sake of the Gospel. I am grateful for the ways we challenged one another to love God more deeply and to live out that love by radical acts of justice and compassion.

On July 1, 2004, I left Bethany United Methodist Church to become the assistant dean for academic affairs and director of contextual education at Pacific School of Religion (PSR) in Berkeley, California. I welcome this opportunity to serve a seminary committed to training progressive Christian leaders for the sake of Christ's church. Becoming a part of the community at PSR feels like a natural extension of the ministry I began at Bethany.

20

AFFIRMATION OF MARRIAGE EQUALITY IN THE UCC: THE HISTORIC MOMENT AT OUR SYNOD

Ruth Garwood

At the Georgia World Congress Center in Atlanta on July 4, 2005, delegates of the General Synod of the United Church of Christ (UCC) prepared themselves for the upcoming decision on whether to affirm the church and societal rights of people to marry, regardless of gender.

The huge convention space was filled for the UCC meeting, with seven hundred delegates at tables in a cordoned-off area and, surrounding them in folding chairs on three sides, as many as one thousand non-delegate visitors from the UCC, other denominations, and the press. The space was the main meeting area of the denomination over the course of the General Synod, used for worship as well as debate, with adjacent exhibit space, meeting rooms, and dining areas. The vast hall, with row after row of chairs, was oriented to the long platform on one side. On the platform were a podium, a communion table, musical instruments, and colorful banners.

The General Synod is the biennial meeting of the United Church of Christ. Delegates from many U.S. geographic regions, ministries, and a broad range of interest groups meet every two years to consider the business of the church and its relationship with the wider world. Because every UCC congregation is self-governing, General Synod resolutions speak *to* but not *for* each local church. Rather, the Constitution of the UCC calls for local churches to hold "in the highest regard" actions by, and decisions or advice emanating from, the General Synod.

Delegates and visitors waited for the results of months of consideration. The marriage resolution came to the General Synod through a defined process that requires congregations and conferences to discern what actions to bring to the national representative body of the church.

The General Synod is a combination of a business meeting, town hall gathering, information forum, worship celebration, and church family reunion. I love being at General Synod to worship, see friends, meet new people, experience a national expression of the church, and to watch as decisions are made. I sat on one side of the observers' section of the convention hall. The area where I sat was darkened, and though the delegates were hundreds of yards away, I could see them clearly because of the large video screens placed around the hall in the sections designated for the delegates as well as the ones for the visitors. I was sitting with about forty-five members of the Coalition while dozens of other members of our group were scattered around the hall.

The Coalition, shorthand for the United Church of Christ Coalition for Lesbian, Gay, Bisexual and Transgender (LGBT) Concerns, was formed in 1972, after the ordination of William R. Johnson, the first openly gay person ordained by a mainline Protestant denomination. The Coalition is the home of the UCC's Open and Affirming (ONA) program, which shepherds congregations in explicitly welcoming LGBT persons into the lives of their churches. The ONA program, as of July 2005, listed nearly six hundred congregations as Open and Affirming, meaning that the more than one hundred and fifty thousand members of those churches have made a statement of inclusion. The Coalition also has a Youth and Young Adult program, providing pastoral care for people in their teens and twenties, education at youth events, and training on suicide prevention for church people who work with youth and young adults. The Coalition has been increasingly involved in community organizing efforts, expanding its work by joining with other LGBT-supportive groups—both interfaith and secular—to protect and broaden rights for LGBT persons in political as well as religious arenas.

Coalition members prayed for a vote that would affirm the equal rights of LGBT people in the church and in society. Having heard the comments made by delegates during the open forum at the committee hearing and committee deliberations that preceded the floor debate, we were cautiously hopeful for a positive outcome.

The UCC (formed in 1957) and its ancestor denominations have historically acted on justice issues. Notable events include its abolitionists supporting the slaves aboard the *Amistad* (1839), its ordination of the first woman in a mainline denomination (Antoinette Brown, 1853), the founding of colleges and universities for blacks in the south (1862–1877), and the election of the first African American leader of a racially integrated mainline denomination (Joseph Evans, 1976).

The UCC seemed a likely place to affirm equal marriage rights for LGBT people, because the history of supporting LGBT folks has been a strong part of the life of the UCC. In 1985, the General Synod passed a resolution calling for an end to discrimination for lesbian, gay, and bisexual people. This led to the ONA movement. In 2003, the General Synod affirmed the full rights and personhood of transgendered people.

With 5,725 congregations and 1.3 million members, the UCC is located all over the United States, in both rural and urban areas. It is a predominantly white Protestant denomination with approximately seventy-five thousand members who are people of color.

THE FIRST DAYS OF GENERAL SYNOD

At a General Synod, the delegates are assigned randomly to committees to consider various business items, such as budgets and elections of officers, as well as resolutions on a range of topics that are before the General Synod. Resolutions concerning marriage at the 2005 General Synod were assigned to Committee 3. On the first day of the General Synod, however, all committees were asked to consider the meaning of marriage and ministry before considering resolutions about preparation for ministry and same-gender marriage.

Each committee and its visitors participated in facilitated discussions that focused on the following issues:

- Bible study about various relationships described in the scriptures
- What makes a particular relationship eligible to be considered for marriage
- The government's position on marriage
- The history of marriage

During the discussions, lesbian and gay people talked about crucial life events from which they can be excluded as long as marriage is deemed illegal for them. They can be barred from visiting their partners in intensive care units of hospitals, caring for the bodies of their partners after they die, and adopting children. The General Accounting Office of the United States lists more than one thousand legal and financial benefits of marriage.

Marriage equality is important to me because it is a full and legal affirmation of the status and rights of LGBT people. The discussion of same-gender marriage, as well as several states' attempts to specify that marriage is between one man and one woman, is particularly heated because people have fixed ideas that marriage is a heterosexual institution. Even some people who are supportive of LGBT people balk at expanding marriage to include all couples.

Although support for marriage equality came from all geographic regions and ethnicities within the United Church of Christ, some constituencies were more resistant to it than others. I think that many of the heterosexual African Americans who are opposed to same-gender marriage are opposed not necessarily because they resist including LGBT people in the full life of the church but because they question whether white members in the UCC and in the broader society remain committed to justice concerns of all people of color, giving them the same priority as LGBT rights. Those justice concerns include fighting the continuing racism in society as demonstrated most obviously in the criminal justice system, employment practices, and the disproportionate incidence of poverty in the United States among communities of color.

Other resistance to marriage equality came from people across racial/ethnic groups who are likely to be conservative on other issues—white people from the South and the Midwest, from rural churches, and some ethnic constituencies of color, including most of the delegation from Puerto Rico. Proponents of the resolution expected that there would be members of these groups who would not be supportive of marriage equality, but very few groups were uniform in their response. In these groups, some clergy and lay people supported the resolution, and other clergy and lay people did not. There were also delegates from areas generally assumed to be supportive, such as large cities and both U.S. coasts, who were resistant to marriage equality.

COMMITTEE 3

Resolutions reach the General Synod through a defined process in which they are proposed by local congregations or geographic conferences, endorsed by at least one other conference, and presented by an early spring deadline. Three resolutions were assigned to Committee 3: one offered by the California-Nevada Southern Conference that was the main point of discussion; one from the Central Atlantic conference basically affirming marriage equality, but calling for a period of study; and another asserting that marriage is between one man and one woman.

Committee 3 began the day with a hearing on issues of marriage. Much of the testimony was from lesbian and gay people who voiced some of the same concerns that were expressed in the general discussions the day before; they stressed the importance of legal rights and the full affirmation of the personhood of same-gender couples.

Several of the delegates who testified about the resolution expressed not only their personal support of marriage equality but also their anxiety about explaining a favorable decision to the members of their churches once they returned home. In the culture and structure of the UCC, General Synod voters are *delegates* from their respective conferences and boards, who can vote as their personal discernment dictates, rather than *representatives*, who would be expected to vote as their constituents would require.

By the end of the day, the first two resolutions were combined for presentation to the plenary, and it was guaranteed that there would be a plenary vote on marriage equality.

PLENARY DELIBERATIONS

Eric C. Smith, a twenty-eight-year-old gay man and Coalition member and one of the assistant moderators of the General Synod, moderated the session on marriage equality. Afterward, he offered the following reflection on the decision selecting him to be the moderator for this sensitive session.

> The moderators decide who will moderate which session. I was fairly confident that I could moderate the session on marriage equality, but I couldn't be sure that I wouldn't freeze. And eventually I felt I *had* to moderate. If this was to go in a positive direction, maybe there had to be someone to absorb the criticism and potential negativity.... I felt if the floor conversation was going to be as contentious as people thought, there had to be limits, but there also had to be allowance for painful things to be said. I felt I could hold some of that pain so that things wouldn't be felt only by the LGBT people, who were invisible. We know from the ONA process that painful things need to be said.
>
> My fear was that if the moderator were too reactive, too quick to stop things that needed to be said, we wouldn't get where we needed to go. We wouldn't get

things out. Having me up in front forced me to be as transparent as possible: no shortened discussion, no shortcut to a particular vote. If you've spent as much time as I have not only advocating for change but also listening to people [opposed to me], there would not be anything shocking that people could say.[1]

Beth Nordbeck, a professor at Andover-Newton Theological School, a UCC seminary, and chair of the committee that deliberated on the resolution, presented the resolution to the General Synod on behalf of the committee:

Now is the moment for the United Church of Christ gathered in this very public place to make a statement of prophetic witness. At the same time, the committee was aware of and extremely pastorally concerned about the fact that many in our congregations back home will find this resolution troubling and difficult.[2]

After it was presented, Lisa Stedman and Johanna Hattendorf, from Massachusetts, were the first ones to testify in support of the resolution. They talked about the positive difference that legal marriage has meant for them, which occurred eighteen years after their covenant ceremony in a Unitarian-Universalist Church because there was no UCC church that would affirm their union.

Johanna: Legal marriage "has made a huge difference."
Lisa: After twenty-plus years, it's finally clear, we're not just in business together anymore, partner. In naming you and claiming you as my spouse, our love and commitment are more fully expressed in the language and idiom of our day and our society.
Johanna: Even more importantly, we are equally understood, acknowledged, affirmed and respected.... Legal marriage means equal understanding, equal affirmation, equal respect.[3]

One delegate proposed an amendment to replace "marriage" with the words "covenanted relationships," because, he believed, changing the commonly accepted definition of marriage would set back the cause of equal rights. Because of the power of words, he feared that people would fight about the word "marriage" even though they supported equal rights.

As I watched the debate from the gallery, I feared the language of the original resolution presented to the session was going to be watered down, that it would fall short of an affirmation of same-gender marriage. I was afraid that we would have another halfway affirmation of LGBT people, on the order of advocating for legal rights and for the full inclusion of LGBT people but saying, in essence, "We love you, but you are definitely not mainstream; you must remain on the margins."

The moderator, Eric, rather than ruling the amendment out of order, asked the General Synod to decide its appropriateness. As I watched anxiously, I thought he was taking a big risk. Afterward, I saw the value of letting the delegates decide how far they wanted to go. The final decision would be stronger if no one was able to say that his or her ideas had not been heard. Again, Eric reflected on the process later, commenting as follows:

I divested myself of any interest in the outcome, knowing it would come out the way it was supposed to (whatever that was) if the process was good. The process, for all of its flaws, is a spiritually grounded process. If the body is honest and authentic, it's a movement and a process that's beyond anyone.

How was the outcome going to be perceived, based on the process? We have synapses in that process, where we provide a place for the Holy Spirit to be. I have never felt so much a sense of being utilized by the Holy Spirit, as being in the midst of something that was not in anyone's control. You can get to that place only if the process is clear.[4]

Delegates who spoke in favor of changing the language of the resolution from "marriage" to "covenanted relationships" cited how emotionally loaded the term "marriage" is and claimed that affirmation of gays and lesbians would be accepted more readily in their churches and in society at large if less contested language were used. Gregory Morrisse, a young pastor from Massachusetts, spoke to this issue, saying the following:

Covenanted relationships are not under constitutional threat. My constitutional rights to marry are under threat…the President of the United States tells me that I am not worthy, that I am not loved by God, and therefore not having the opportunities that other people will have. The word marriage, the institution of marriage is very important…. I don't need your affirmation for covenanted relationships. I can do that all on my own. What we're talking about are rights.[5]

Delegates are issued voting cards, to distinguish voting members on the floor from those who have voice without vote. To vote, delegates raise their voting cards above their heads so that they are easily seen. On the amendment to change "marriage" to "covenanted relationships," a few scattered cards went up to support the language change, the amendment was defeated, and the delegates continued discussion on the resolution. Hector Lopez, Conference Minister of the Central Pacific Conference, then spoke in favor of the resolution:

I come from a small Latino church in Southern California. Historically, we have had a lot of trouble keeping up with the United Church of Christ. Every time there's a faith and justice issue, we're caught running behind you, but every time, we catch up. And this is another issue that has my small church running behind you, but we are catching up. In March of 2004, Multnomah County in Oregon allowed marriage for gay/lesbian couples. There was a call put out for ministers to come and perform marriage ceremonies for those couples seeking such ceremonies. I experienced a compassionate conversion. I had gone to the auditorium where these weddings were to take place, as a duty, because I am committed to justice and faith. But after performing about a dozen ceremonies, I became passionately converted to the right for gays and lesbians to have marriages. I saw the love and affection. The respect and dignity manifested by the lives and the couples in the thousands that were there to celebrate marriage. Such a longing from these brothers and sisters to have their sacred commitments made holy by a religious and spiritual ceremony of marriage manifested to me God's love. Let us welcome our brothers and sisters from the gay and lesbian community by loving one another as Jesus loved us, by affirming equal marriage rights for all.[6]

Paul Osgood from Kansas City also testified in favor, saying,

I love this denomination. You accepted me when no one else would accept me. Others would accept my money, but no one would accept me. I have finally found a denomination that will accept both me and my money. I didn't wake up one morning and decide to be gay; it's just part of who I am…. My sexuality is a gift of my creation. I have been in a relationship with Jerry for twenty-nine years…. I know that our relationship is a gift from God and that God accepts us as a married couple. I know that it is a gift from God because the closer I grow in my relationship with Jerry, the more I understand the true love and compassion and the wonder of God. We're going to survive, whether this resolution passes or not…. We're going to continue living together and loving each other right up until the end, but pass this resolution for the children. Pass it for those children out there that are growing up gay and who are getting the messages over and over again that God does not love them, they are second-class citizens, and they don't deserve to live. It's no accident that many gay children are committing suicide.[7]

After several testimonies both for and against the resolution, Eric observed that there were long lines of people ready to speak in favor of the resolution and no one to speak against. It was time to vote.

THE VOTE

During the debate, Eric had reminded delegates and observers not to applaud comments or decisions. Coalition members and supporters were careful not to make any audible response to the speakers. Whatever the outcome, we wanted to honor both those whose positions prevailed and those whose did not. We planned to gather outside the plenary space after the vote was taken.

Finally the vote was called. Many of us from the Coalition held hands and prayed. My partner, Adrienne Brockway, a delegate from New York, described the moment this way:

As the vote was being called for I looked at the faces of delegates from all over the country…many had a look of anxiety and anticipation. And I thought to myself, "When we raise our cards, should I look at the other members of my delegation or not? Did I really want to know how others voted?" I was seated among some people I had known for years only through New York Conference Annual Meetings and among other folks that I did not know at all. And then we heard the question…. "All in favor, raise your voting cards." Everything felt as if in slow motion. And as I took a breath and raised my card, and I saw around me hundreds of other hands raising cards in unison with mine. I took one more look around, and what had been anxious faces seconds before was now a host of faces with a look of peace and pride.[8]

From my viewpoint in the gallery, it looked like a forest of voting cards went up in favor of marriage equality. The vote was immediately clear to all who were in the hall. Officially reported as 80 percent in favor of the resolution; the favorable votes looked to me like a much larger majority.

The thrill of the result was nearly impossible to contain. Coalition members and other supporters streamed out of the hall, searching for a place where we could go to celebrate together.

The decision had seemed like too much to hope for. The United Church of Christ had felt welcoming to me, a lesbian, and now I feel that welcoming embrace even stronger, as if the arms of the church had been thrown open wider than ever. It felt like my church was reaching out to me as enthusiastically as God reaches out.

AFTER GENERAL SYNOD

The resolution from that General Synod has received wide publicity and reaction. Individuals and churches have contacted the UCC about joining the denomination. Through December 2005, twenty-three new congregations had affiliated, and another forth-two had expressed interest in joining. I think they are responding to the bold statement for justice and inclusion made by the UCC. The witness that the denomination has made to society and to other churches inspires them. The Rev. David Schoen, of the UCC's Evangelism Ministry, said that, in addition to support-ing the stand on same-gender marriage, people admire a pastoral, prophetic, and compassionate stand—"not just the stand we took, but that we took a stand."

The vote has also cost the UCC. By the end of 2005, about forty-nine churches had voted to disaffiliate, most because of the marriage resolution. Others decided to withhold their financial contributions to the denomination. The General Synod of the United Church of Christ does not dictate anything to local churches. Thus, local churches are not required to support marriage equality or to marry same-gender couples in their own sanctuaries.

I believe that the churches who are protesting do not feel as though the UCC is family. They do not understand why the clan with whom they have covenanted could make a statement so opposed to their own understanding. Where discomfort may have occurred with certain pronouncements of the General Synod in the past, affirmation of same-gender marriage has been the most difficult to date. Some churches that have withdrawn were already unhappy with the denomination because of its progressive positions, and the marriage equality decision was one step more than they could tolerate. I think that some of the decisions to withhold contributions may be temporary and that, after these congregations have time to consider the issues, they may resume their contributions.

In one example of an effort to continue dialogue among members with differ-ing perspectives on the decision, a conference was held within a few months of General Synod titled "Black Church in Crisis." It brought together 125 African American UCC clergy to discuss same-gender marriage. The Coalition was among the groups sponsoring the conference. The participants ranged from those who were strongly opposed to the resolution to those who were actively in favor. Through Bible study, prayer, and open conversation, they engaged in serious and respectful dialogue. Participants do not know whether anyone changed his or her mind because of the conference, but they were grateful for the opportunity to discuss it and asked that the conference be repeated in the following year.

The resolution is provoking many authentic conversations as well as arguments in churches and other settings of the United Church of Christ about marriage, LGBT issues, and the nature of covenant. It is a painful, but important process. I vividly recall the testimony of delegates who were concerned about the reaction of their home churches but who were going to vote in favor of the resolution. Their courage to vote their conscience in the face of controversy inspires me.

The implications of the affirmation of marriage equality will not be known for some time. The joys of inclusion and the sorrow of loss remain. The denomination is challenged by the financial implications of the churches who have left and those who have withheld their money. I feel that the United Church of Christ has continued the prophetic witness that makes the denomination an example of God's loving justice.

Immediately after the General Synod vote on the marriage resolution, John Thomas, President and General Minister of the UCC, offered this prayer:

> Lord Jesus, to you we live, to you we suffer, to you we die. Yours will we be in life and in death. Today, as in ancient Bethlehem, the hopes and fears of all the years are met in you. We give you thanks for these days of prayer and discernment, and especially for your presence this morning. We have felt your warm embrace, stilling us, as we tremble with joy, with hope, with fear, with disappointment. Remind us, that as we are tempted to run from each other, so too, we run from you. We know that every choice confers a cost, so let us attend in the coming hours and days to those for whom this decision confers a particular burden. Let us find words that comfort, rather than congratulate. Let us seek to be a community of grace and forgiveness, rather than organizing constituencies of protest. Let us use our hands, not to clap, but to wipe away every tear, and in all this, may we know in surprising new ways the comfort of belonging to you. This is our prayer. Hear us, Lord Jesus. Amen.[9]

NOTES

1. Eric Smith, in conversation with the author, January 20, 2005.
2. *General Synod 25*, DVD (Plenary on Marriage Equality, United Church of Christ, July 4, 2005).
3. Ibid.
4. Eric Smith, in conversation with the author, January 20, 2005.
5. See note 2.
6. Ibid.
7. Ibid.
8. Adrienne Brockway, in conversation with the author, January 22, 2005.
9. See note 2.

Appendix:
A Sampling of Religious Wedding and Holy Union Ceremonies for Same-Sex Couples

———————————— • ————————————

INTERFAITH CEREMONY (HINDU, JEWISH, CHRISTIAN)

Wedding of Ruth Vanita and Monica Bachmann
Park Avenue Church
New York, NY
June 3, 2000

Wedding processional with music, Monica with mother, preceded by sister as maid of honor. Ruth, with older friend, preceded by friend as maid of honor.

Lighting of lamp (symbolizes Agni, God of Fire, who acts as witness to all major rituals).

Blessing by Rabbi Lippman:

> *Rabbi: Blessed be you who enter here in happiness and in joy.*
>
> *Blessed be each of you, Monica and Ruth*
>
> *Ruth and Monica, we rejoice in life's moments of happiness, and among those moments, none will be greater for the two of you than this hour of marriage, for it will be remembered vividly through the years by each of you as the tangible symbol of your love for one another. So, for all of us gathered here with you who share your happiness, there is gratitude in our hearts. We feel joy in your marriage, as we are uplifted by your devotion to each other. Your hearts become joined, as you speak the words hallowed by history, and in the echo of these words is heard our wish that your marriage will be blessed with health, with happiness and with peace.*

Excerpts from the following (read by friends):

> Plato's *Symposium*,
> The Book of Ruth
> Corinthians 1:13

Conducted in the presence of Shri Ganesh, elephant-headed God, who presides over auspicious beginnings; Shri Lakshmi, Goddess of prosperity; and Shri Saraswati, Goddess of wisdom and the arts. (Images of these three Gods at the altar, near the lamp.)

Also at the altar a *kalash* (brass jar), a coconut, and a red veil, which are auspicious objects.

An arati (worship ritual) by a friend of Ruth's, to welcome Monica into the family.

Jaimala (garlanding of one another by the spouses) signifies acceptance of one another as spouses.

Saptapadi (seven steps or seven words): This Vedic ceremony is considered the essential part of the wedding ceremony. Seven steps are taken, accompanied by seven Sanskrit *shlokas* (verses) from the sacred texts, the Veda Samhitas (these texts are about thirty-five hundred years old). The ceremony is based on the Vedic idea, often repeated in Hindu texts, that seven steps taken together or seven words spoken together constitute friendship.

Recited by a friend (in Sanskrit), invoking Shri Vishnu, the preserver God, as the couple walks seven times around the fire:

> *Om eka misheya Vishnustavaneyatu*
> *Om dveya urjeya Vishnustavaneyatu*
> *Om triniraysposhaaya Vishnustavaneyatu*
> *Om chatvaari maayo bhavaaya Vishnustavaneyatu*
> *Om panch pashubhyo Vishnustavaneyatu*
> *Om shadritubhyo Vishnustavaneyatu*
> *Om sakhey saptapadaa bhava sa mamanuvrataa bhava Vishnustavaneyatu*

> *Translation: The first step is taken for increase of grain, the second step for increase of energy, the third step for increase of wealth, the fourth step for increase of happiness, the fifth step for the happiness of animals, the sixth step for the happiness of the six seasons, and the seventh step for friendship and conjugal virtue.*

Guests throw flower petals on the couple.

Reading of Shakespeare's sonnet 116 and a poem by "Michael Field" (Katherine Bradley and Edith Cooper), 1893, by friends.

Rabbi's address

Hymn sung by Monica's brother and sister-in-law

Exchange of vows, led by Rabbi, under huppah, held by four friends:

I, _____, take you, _____, to have and to hold from this day forward, for better for worse, for richer for poorer, in sickness and in health, to love and to cherish, till death do us part.

Exchange of rings

Rabbi: And now, _____, as you place the ring, the token of marriage, upon _____'s finger, please repeat the words:

With this Ring I you wed, with my body I you worship, and you are now my partner in everlasting love.

As by these rings you symbolize your marriage bond, may their meaning sink into your hearts and bind your lives together by devotion to one another. Truly, then, will these rings celebrate the words of scripture, of the Song of Songs, where it is written, "Wear me as a seal upon your heart, as a seal upon your arm, for love is infinitely strong." In ever-deepening love for one another, may you establish a home filled with the spirit of truth, of righteousness, and of peace, a home filled with true Shalom.

Sharing the wine:

We pray that this covenant will be blessed, that this bond of marriage will be sealed with love as we say:

Blessed are You, O God, Source of all Creation, Creator of the fruit of the vine.

The couple drinks the wine.

Rabbi: As together you have now drunk from this cup, so may you share contentment, peace, and fulfillment from the cup of life, and thereby may you find life's joys doubly gladdened, its bitterness sweetened, and each of its moments hallowed by true companionship and love.

The last six of the seven Hebrew blessings:

Rabbi: And now that you have spoken the words and performed the rites that unite your lives, it gives me great pleasure to pronounce you married in the sight of God and enlightened men and women and to extend to you the best wishes of all those who love and care for you.

I know that I speak for everyone gathered here when I say that it is my hope that the blessings flowing from all of our hearts toward the two of you at this very moment will always be with you, and that you will be satisfied with long life together and with great happiness.

In a few moments, you will break the glass as a symbol of the fact that life is bittersweet and that we are thankful for this time of joy and hope in your lives that you are sharing with us. But before you break we close with a benediction found in scripture, in the Book of Numbers:

May God bless and keep you.

May God's countenance shine upon you and be gracious unto you.

May God's countenance be lifted upon you, and give you peace. Amen.

Breaking of the glass and the kiss.

Exit, accompanied by Hindi film song, sung by Indrani Chatterjee: "*Tum jo huey merey humsafar*" (Now that you are my companion on the journey, all the roads have changed/ Millions of lamps are lighted along the roads of my love).

Signing of Ketubah.

CALVINIST CHRISTIAN CEREMONY

Performed by Rev. Norman J. Kansfield, PhD
Wedding of Jennifer Susanne Aull and Ann Margaret Kansfield
The First Churches of Northampton
Northampton, MA
June 19, 2004

Votum

> *Minister: Our help is in the name of the LORD who made heaven and earth.*
>
> *People: Amen.*
>
> *Minister: I will sing of the LORD's great love forever...*
>
> *People: with my mouth I will make your faithfulness known to all generations.*
>
> *Minister: I will declare that your love stands firm forever...*
>
> *People: that you establish your faithfulness in heaven itself. (Psalm 89:1–2)*
>
> *Minister: Grace and peace be yours in fullest measure. Through the knowledge of God and Jesus our LORD. (II Peter 1:2)*
>
> *People: Amen!*

Processional Hymn

> *Minister: Let all who are able please stand.*

"O, God, you give humanity its name" (Text: Fred Kaan, 1968; tune: "National Hymns," George William Warren, 1892,

Minister: Please be seated

Lessons

Old Testament: Isaiah 56:1–8
Epistle: Acts 10:24–36
Gospel: John 2:1–12

The Sermon

Minister: The opening paragraph in the 1968 Wedding Liturgy—the order of worship from which today's service has been adapted—described the theological foundations of marriage this way: "marriage…is an honorable estate, instituted by God when he said that a man shall leave his father and his mother and shall cleave to his wife; they shall be one flesh." Very clearly that would not work for today. We need some new metaphors and points of origin. Change is necessary.

The 1968 Liturgy, itself, already represented such change. In it, for the first time, a bride no longer had to pledge to obey *her husband. This change, in 1968, was thought to be quite scandalous. I regularly remind Mary that we were married in 1965, when the Liturgy still included that blessed pledge.*

Change is not always easy for us to deal with. And, it seems, change is particularly difficult for the church to navigate. Old truths and understandings, long hallowed by the church's practice and given voice in liturgy and hymn, become worn into habits and traditions that rise above the level of evaluation, critique, and change. But our lessons, this afternoon, tell us that God changes God's mind precisely about the way that the Community of the Faithful—the Assembly of the LORD—is expected to live out its faith. In Deuteronomy 23, God's instructions to God's people were that:

No Ammonite or Moabite shall be admitted to the Assembly of the LORD. Even to the tenth generation, none of their descendants shall be admitted to the Assembly of the LORD.

I do not doubt God said that. At the time it must have been important, in order to ensure the purity of the Assembly of the LORD, for persons from these other ethnic traditions to be excluded. And Nehemiah 3:1–3 makes clear that this instruction from God was actually enforced. Those verses in Nehemiah describe just how exactically some puritans within the Assembly of the LORD committed themselves to enforce this law; destroying marriages, splitting up families, and causing incalculable misery.

And then, along came another word from the LORD. We all read and heard this other word from the LORD on this very subject in the Gospel according to Isaiah. There it is written:

Do not let the foreigner joined to the LORD say,

"The LORD will surely separate me from the people of God."

For thus says the LORD:

The foreigners who join themselves to the LORD

To minister to God, to love the name of the LORD,

And to be God's servants,

All who keep the Sabbath and do not profane it,

And hold fast my covenant—

These I will bring to my Holy Mountain,

And make them joyful in my house of prayer;

Their burnt offerings and their sacrifices will be accepted upon my altar;

For my house shall be called a House of Prayer for all peoples.

The sole purpose of this combination of these texts is to assure us—with no room for misunderstanding or uncertainty—that when it comes to loving people, God's mind is always changing in order to be more wonderfully inclusive. And God calls all of us to keep up with the eternal expansiveness of God's love. So, God gives us examples. Just two books away from Deuteronomy is the book of Ruth. In that text it is clear the Ruth is a Moabite. And, not only is Ruth accepted into the Assembly of the LORD, but by the end of the book we have been told that she became the Grandmother of David, King of God's people. And it was into the House of David that Jesus was born.

Any reading of Ruth's story or, for that matter, of David's story, immediately begins to make clear just how risky it is for the will of the LORD and the character of the Assembly of the LORD to change and include Moabites. For Ruth and David are barely in the door, when they—Ruth and David—begin to sing a kind of song such as had never been heard before within the Assembly of the LORD—songs that comprised powerful statements regarding same-sex love.

They may not have had sexual passion in mind, but they gave powerful voice to what a woman-woman relationship might mean. Ruth said to her mother-in-law Naomi:

Do not press me to leave you, or to turn back from following you!

Where you go, I will go; where you lodge, I will lodge;

Your people shall be my people and your God my God.

Where you die, I shall die—There I will be buried.

May the LORD do thus and so to me, and more as well,

If even death parts me from you. (Ruth 1:16–17)

This kind of song could also show how intensive a man-man relationship could be. David, after Jonathan's death in battle, sang a dirge that concluded:

How the mighty have fallen in the midst of battle!

Jonathan lies slain upon your high places.

I grieve for you my brother Jonathan;

Greatly beloved were you to me;

Your love to me was wonderful,

Surpassing the love of women. (II Samuel 1:25–26)

The lesson from Acts makes the very same point in a way with which no Christian can argue. The church, under the leadership of Peter, was finding its way into defining the character of membership. It began as a Jewish fellowship, accepting all of the definitions that Judaism had used for centuries. But here we meet a man named Cornelius, a Roman army officer. Cornelius didn't fit the Jewish prescription for admission to the Assembly of the LORD. God sent Peter a vision of unclean animals and instructed Peter to kill and eat them. Peter responds that he has not (and will not) "ever eaten anything that is forbidden by our Jewish laws." It is God's response to Peter's affirmation that we have to hear: "Do not call anything unclean that God has called clean." Those whom God has already determined to be clean, have to be regarded as clean enough for us. In other words, it is God who chooses! God had already determined that Cornelius was to be included in the membership of the church. Peter need not hesitate to baptize him. Likewise, all we need to understand, relative to who is included within the Assembly of the LORD and who is not, is to understand just whom it is that God Almighty, in Jesus Christ our Lord, has made clean. When God has determined that a person is to be included, that's that. Everything we do—in word or action—ought to proclaim that person to be clean and worthy of inclusion within the Assembly of the LORD. To separate ourselves from such a person is to be guilty of sundering the body of Christ.

All of this may sound to you like a sermon on the need of the church to find ways by which it can include within its fellowship those groups of persons which certain portions of the Body of Christ want to ban "to the tenth generation." But if that were the point of this sermon, I would truly, as they say, be "preaching to the choir." By your presence here, all of you are confessing that you are prepared to embrace the kinds of changes to which God is, in these days, calling the church. So, Ann and Jen, the rest of the sermon is for you.

By hearing and responding to God's call to ministry within the Church, the two of you are already powerfully signaling your commitment to imitate the eternal expansiveness of God's love for persons. But this day you are making different kinds of promises and commitments. You are promising to live with and to love each other. And that will require a constant expansion of your love. Each day of life together will bring new insights into each other and new challenges to the love you thought you knew. Love will, each day, have to be stretched and expanded for each of you to continue comfortably to include the other fully within your heart. Earlier this week, in an e-mail, I wrote to Ann that she had always been easy to love. She quickly wrote back with the suggestion that my memory must be going. Didn't I remember adolescence? I responded by pointing out that I had said "easy to love" not "easy to live with." It will be the work of your marriage to continue to change your mind in order, each day, more wonderfully to include the other.

And the rest of us, as we seek to encourage the church to move toward the gracious inclusion of as many persons within the Assembly of the LORD as God in Christ Jesus is prepared to include, will pray for the two of you, as we pray for ourselves, that we may all learn to love as we know ourselves to have been loved by God.

Solemn Charges

Minister: (to the congregation) It is into holy matrimony that these two persons have come to be joined. If anyone can show just cause why they may not lawfully be joined together, let that person now declare it, or else hereafter forever keep silent.

Minister: (to those to be married) I charge you, each and both, as you shall answer to the One before whom the secrets of all hearts are open, that if either of you knows of any reason why you may not lawfully be married, declare it now. For be assured that if any persons are joined together contrary to the Word of God, their marriage is not blessed of God, nor is it lawful in God's eyes.

Prayer

Minister: All who are able please stand. Let us pray.

People: Almighty and eternal God, giver of all good gifts, look with favor, we pray, on these your servants who lift up their hearts to you. Enable them to make their vows to one another in all sincerity, as in your sight, and to be faithful hereafter in keeping them, to the glory of your holy name; through Jesus Christ our Lord. Amen.

Vows

Minister: Before you make your vows to each other, in the sight of God and of this company, hear what the Word of God says concerning Christian love:

Love is patient and kind; love is not jealous or boastful; it is not arrogant or rude. Love does not insist on its own way; it is not irritable or resentful; it does not rejoice at wrong, but rejoices in the right. Love bears all things, believes all things, hopes all things, endures all things. (I Corinthians 13.4–7)

In the spirit and hope of such love, I now ask: Do you Ann receive Jennifer as God's true gift to you? Do you commit yourself, before God and these witnesses, to live in covenant and faithfulness with her?

Ann: I do.

Minister: Will you love her, comfort her, honor and sustain her, in sickness and in health, and forsaking every other, continue faithful to her so long as you both shall live?

Ann: I will.

Minister: Do you, Jennifer receive Ann as God's true gift to you? Do you commit yourself, before God and these witnesses, to live in covenant and faithfulness with her?

Jennifer: I do.

Minister: Will you love her, comfort her, honor and sustain her, in sickness and in health, and forsaking every other, continue faithful to her so long as you both shall live?

Jennifer: I will.

Ann: I, Ann commit myself in marriage to you, Jennifer; from this day forward, for better, for worse; for richer, for poorer; in sickness and in health; to love and to cherish until death parts us, according to God's holy ordinance; and thereto I pledge myself truly with all my heart.

Jennifer: I, Jennifer commit myself in marriage to you, Ann; from this day forward, for better, for worse; for richer, for poorer; in sickness and in health; to love and to cherish until death parts us, according to God's holy ordinance; and thereto I pledge myself truly with all my heart.

Minister: What token do you give of this marriage?

Ann and Jennifer will then each say: This ring I give to you in token of the covenant made this day between us; in the name of the Father and of the Son and of the Holy Spirit.

People: Amen!

Declaration

Minister: Forasmuch as you, Ann, and you, Jennifer, have covenanted together according to God's holy ordinance of marriage, and have confirmed the same by making solemn vows and by joining hands and by giving and receiving rings, I pronounce you solemnly and lawfully married in the name of the Father and the Son and the Holy Spirit

People: Amen!

Minister: What therefore God has joined together, let no one attempt to separate.

Prayer

Minister: Let all who are able please stand. Let us pray.

People: O faithful God, you bind yourself in grace and faithfulness with those whom you love, hear in heaven, your dwelling place, the marriage vows which your servants Ann and Jennifer have vowed with you. Grant them the gift of your good Spirit, that with all fidelity they may observe and keep these vows, walking together in your faith and worship, being led by the angel of your presence and strengthened by your hand, until they come to the inheritance of your saints in light; through Jesus Christ our Lord, who has called us always to pray:

Our Father in heaven,
hallowed be your name,
your kingdom come,
your will be done
on earth as in heaven.
Give us today our daily bread.
Forgive us our sins
as we forgive those who sin against us.
Save us from the time of trial,
and deliver us from evil.
For the kingdom, the power,
and the glory are yours,
now and forever. Amen!

Minister: Please remain standing for the singing of the hymn.

Hymn: "Surprised by joy no song can tell" (text: Erik Routley, 1976 [Honoring C. S. Lewis]; tune: "Melcombe," Samuel Webbe, 1782)

Benediction

Minister: May the LORD bless you and keep you;
May the LORD look with favor upon you and be gracious to you;
May the LORD smile upon you and grant you peace.

People: Amen!

Ceremony in the Jewish Reform Tradition
סֶדֶר קִדּוּשִׁין
Seder Kiddushin
Wedding of Sue Levi Elwell and Nurit Shein
June 14, 1998
20 Sivan 5758

This document describes the קִדּוּשִׁין (*Kiddushin*/wedding) celebrated by Rabbi Sue Levi Elwell and Nurit Shein at their home in June 1998. The מְסַדְּרֵי קִידּוּשִׁין (*m'e-sadrei kiddushin*/officiants) for the ceremony included Phyllis Ocean Berman and Rabbis Richard F. Address, Rebecca T. Alpert, and Leonard D. Gordon.

When guests arrived, they received a program that included the texts for the songs and communal readings that were a part of the ceremony. Once they were seated under the אוהל מועד (*ohel moed*/the tent of meeting), guests were wel-comed with the extraordinary music of Deborah Redding and Julie Rosenfeld, friends of Sue and Nurit and the violinists of the acclaimed Colorado Quartet. Their welcome was followed by the music of MIRAJ, a Philadelphia women's a capella group. The members of MIRAJ, Juliet Spitzer and Rabbis Margot L. Stein and Rabbi Gecla Rayzel Raphael, taught a round, *V'Yashan Mipnei Chadash*, crafted from the words of Leviticus 26:10–11 ("You shall clear the old to make room for the new. I will establish my abode in your midst, and I will not spurn you"), with music by Rabbi Raphael with Rosie Peugeros and Shoshana Zonderman. MIRAJ then led the *kahal*/community in singing *Kol HaNeshama* as the huppah holders, the *m'saderet*, Sue and Nurit's parents, and Sue and Nurit entered the yard.[1]

The ceremony began with a ברוכים הבאים (*Bruchim Habaim*/welcome) by the first *m'saderet kiddushin*, Phyllis Ocean Berman, and continued with an *azkara*/memorial. This was followed by a short blessing for the כוס ארוסין (*Erusin*/Bethrothal cup), following the Reform tradition of using an abbreviated wine blessing. The goblet used for the wine was a kiddush cup that had been a wed-ding gift to Sue's great-grandfather, Jacob Krieger, on the occasion of his marriage to Sue's great-grandmother, Ella Lehman, in August 1880. Phyllis noted that this wedding took place in Philadelphia 118 years ago, which represented the sum of Sue and Nurit's ages plus חי (18). After the blessing, the wine was shared by Sue, Nurit, and their parents. The *Brit Ahuvot*/Lovers' Covenant document[2] was then read in Hebrew and in English, followed by a powerful *derash*/sermon delivered by the *m'saderet*.

The next section of the ceremony, the *shutafut*, or partnership section, was introduced by Rabbi Richard F. Address. Drawing on the scholarship of Rachel Adler, he explained that Sue and Nurit, as the two principals to the partnership being proclaimed, had each placed something of value into a shared pouch. In addition, the rings that they were giving as gift to one another were in this pouch, which was fashioned from Nurit's mother's wedding veil. He asked Sue and Nurit to lift the pouch and then to extract the rings, which they placed on one another's forefingers with the words הרי את מקודשת לי בפני קהילת קודש זו ("You are sanctified to me before this sacred community").[3]

The Wedding Blessings were then recited and sung by members of Sue's and Nurit's family and Rabbi Rebecca T. Alpert. The Hebrew alternated between mas-culine and feminine language for the divine (i.e., *Baruch Atah Adonai/Baruch At Yah*). Also, "Soul of the Universe" (*Ruach Ha Olam*) was used in place of "Ring of the Universe (*Melech Ha Olam*).[4]

Blessed are You, our God, Spirit of the world, Creator of fruit of the vine.

Blessed are You, our God, Spirit of the world, whose creation is glorious.

Blessed are You, our God, Spirit of the world, Creator of human beings.

Blessed are You, our God, Spirit of the world, who shapes humanity in her image and likeness and enables us to renew creation by nurturing generations to come. Blessed are You. You created us in your image.[5]

May women rejoice when their daughters gather in joy. Blessed are You, who glad-dens Zion with her children.

May these loving companions rejoice as did God's first creations in the garden of Eden. Blessed are You who enables lovers to rejoice with one another.

Blessed are You, our God, Spirit of the world, Creator of joy and gladness, soulmate and beloved, merriment, song, dance, and delight, love and harmony, peace and companionship. Our God, may all soon hear in the cities of Judah and in the court-yards of Jerusalem the voices of joy and rejoicing, the voices of the lover and her beloved, the sound of lovers' jubilation from their huppah, the celebratory songs of peace. Blessed are You who enables these beloveds to rejoice in one another.

The wedding blessings were followed by final words to seal the covenant. Rabbi Leonard D. Gordon introduced this final portion of the ceremony with words about the binding of two souls and the unbinding of Jewish tradition. He spoke about the power of the concluding words of Jewish life-cycle rituals and reminded the assem-bled community of the importance of their role in scaling this covenant. He asked the rabbis and *m'sadrei kiddushin* to rise and recite the following blessing:

הֲרֵי אַתֶּן מְקוּדָּשׁוֹת אַחַת לַשְּׁנִיָּה בְּעֵינֵי יִשְׂרָאֵל כְּשֵׁם שֶׁנִּכְנַסְתֶּן לְחוּפָּה
וְלִבְרִית אֲהוּבוֹת כֵּן תִּזְכּוּ לִלְמוֹד וּלְלַמֵּד תּוֹרָה וּלְקַיֵּם מִצְוַת תִּיקוּן עוֹלָם:
You have set one another apart from all others in the eyes of the people of Israel.
As you have come under the huppah, and signed this lovers' covenant, may you
continue to study and teach Torah and to fulfill the mitzvah of working toward the
repair of the world.[6]

Rabbi Gordon then invited the entire *kahal*/community to rise and share the three-fold blessing from the Torah, with Hebrew corrected for gender, for Sue and Nurit[7]:

יְבָרְכְכֶן יְיָ וְיִשְׁמְרְכֶן
May God bless you and keep you.

יְיָ יָאֵר פָּנִים אֲלֵיכֶן וְיִחֻנְכֶן
May God's light and grace shine upon you.

יִשָּׂא יְיָ פָּנִים אֲלֵיכֶן וְיָשֵׂם לָכֶן שָׁלוֹם
May God's face be lifted up to you and may you be blessed with peace.

The ceremony concluded with a single shofar blast, celebrating the season of both Sue's and Nurit's fiftieth birthdays, and Israel's jubilee.[8] The shofar was sounded by Noah Harvey Cohen, Sue's thirteen-year-old godson.[9]

אֲהוּבוֹת בְּרִית (*Brit Ahuvot*/Lovers' Covenant)

On the first day of the week, the twentieth day of Sivan 5758, according to Jewish reckoning, June 14, 1998, according to secular reckoning, in the city of Philadelphia, Pennsylvania, Sue Levi Elwell, daughter of Charles and Claire Levi, Elana Beruriah bat Ora v'Ya'akov, and Nurit Shein, daughter of Yusek and Basha

Shein, Nurit Penina bat Batia z'l v'Yosef, confirm in the presence of witnesses a lover's covenant and declare their household as a partnership among the people of Israel.

The agreement into which Sue and Nurit are entering is a holy covenant like the ancient covenants of our people, made in faithfulness and peace to stand forever. It is a covenant of protection and hope like the covenant God swore to Noah and his descendants.[10] It is a covenant of distinction, like the covenant God made with Israel.[11] It is a covenant of devotion, like the covenant David and Jonathan made between them.[12] It is a covenant of mutual lovingkindness, like the wedding covenant between God and Israel.[13]

These are the provisions of the lovers' covenant into which Sue and Nurit now enter: Sue and Nurit declare that they have chosen each other as companions.[14] Sue and Nurit declare that they are setting themselves apart for each other and will take no other lover.

Sue and Nurit hereby assume all the rights and obligations that apply to family members, and to attend, care, and provide for one another, for Sue's daughters Hana Eyre and Mira Levi Elwell, and for our beloved parents, Charles and Claire Levi and Yusek Shein. Sue and Nurit commit themselves to a life of kindness and righteousness as a Jewish family and to continue the sacred work of repairing the world. In celebration of this covenant Nurit is adding the Levi family name to her own and will henceforth be known as Nurit Levi Shein. Sue and Nurit pledge that one will help the other at the time of dying by carrying out her last rational requests, protecting her from indignity or abandonment, and by tender, faithful presence with the beloved until the grave separates them.[15]

To this covenant we affix our signatures on this day during the reading of Parashat Shelach.[16]

BUDDHIST MARRIAGE COMMITMENT CEREMONY

Wedding of Diana Elrod and Nancy Burns
Soka Gakkai International (SGI)-Nichiren Buddhists

5:45 pm–6:15 pm

Play various musical selections until the two to be married have arrived to the front by the altar.

6:15–6:30 pm

Emcee: Thank you all for coming to this celebration of Diana and Nancy's love and commitment to one another. Since many of you are probably new to Buddhism, they've asked me to share with you some basic information about our practice. Diana and Nancy have chosen to express their spirituality through the practice of Nichiren Daishonin's Buddhism, which is a form of Buddhism that originated in thirteenth-century Japan. As part of our practice, we perform morn-

ing and evening prayers, involving the recitation of two sections of the Lotus Sutra. Following the recitation of the sutra, we will start chanting Nam-Myoho-Renge-Kyo, which we believe expresses the fundamental meaning of life. Chanting Nam-Myoho-Renge Kyo helps focus our energy and gives us the wisdom to overcome any challenges. There is more information about Nichiren Daishonin's Buddhism in today's program.

Although we'll probably go too fast for most people to join in the recitation of the sutra, please feel free to chant Nam-Myoho-Renge-Kyo whenever you hear the words.

Minister of Ceremony, Ed Horan, leads chanting and recitation of prayers.

Sake Ceremony Assistant, Lesley Dale, begins setting up the San San Kudo sake ceremony paraphernalia while emcee is talking. Musician begins playing at this time.

The couple move their chairs to face one another.

Emcee: San San Kudo is a traditional ceremony of Japan that is used on occasions of celebration and joy. As used in the Buddhist wedding, the San San Kudo is the act by which two people pledge their commitment before the Gohonzon. The ceremony consists of sipping sake three times from three cups symbolizing the union of body, mind, and spirit—the Three Aspects of Life. It also expresses Diana and Nancy's understanding that they are, and have been, united throughout the past, present, and future. With this commitment, they pledge to create the deepest kind of unity, building a happy and harmonious family, and together overcome all difficulties they may find in the future.

Musician plays while San San Kudo is performed.

Diana, Nancy, and Lesley do the San San Kudo ceremony.

Lesley places the San San Kudo set off to the side. Diana and Nancy turn their chairs around more toward the audience.

Musician concludes playing.

Emcee: In the writings of Nichiren Daishonin, he describes the Three Kinds of Treasures: the treasures of the storehouse, the treasures of the body, and the treasures of the heart. Although the first two treasures are important aspects of our lives, bringing to us material comforts and good health, the treasures of the heart contain our relationships with other people, our capacity for compassionate action, and our spiritual wealth. The treasures of the heart are, more specifically, our Buddha nature. This is the only treasure that brings us unshakable happiness and gives hope and courage to others. Ultimately, the treasures of the heart are our faith.

By giving rings to one another, Diana and Nancy acknowledge and celebrate the "treasures of the heart" in themselves and each other, giving their commitment to advance each other's spiritual growth and happiness. The rings also acknowledge the importance of the other two treasures, symbolized in the beauty of the rings them-selves and the fact that Diana and Nancy are connected physically in wearing them.

Diana and Nancy exchange rings and personal vows with one another.

Readings

Ed Horan reads from the writings of Nichiren Daishonin and adds a few minutes of spiritual guidance:

The men with whom you have exchanged marriage vows over the course of all your previous lifetimes must outnumber even the grains of sand in the ocean. Your vows this time, however, were ones made with your true husband. The reason is that it was due to his encouragement that you became a practitioner of the Lotus Sutra. Thus you should revere him as a Buddha. When he was alive, he was a Buddha in life, and now he is a Buddha in death. He is a Buddha in both life and death. This is what is meant by that most important doctrine called attaining Buddhahood in one's present form. The fourth volume of the Lotus Sutra states, "If one can uphold this [sutra], one will be upholding the Buddha's body."

*Neither the pure land nor hell exists outside oneself; both lie only within one's own heart. Awakened to this, one is called a Buddha; deluded about it, one is called an ordinary person. The Lotus Sutra reveals this truth, and one who embraces the Lotus Sutra will realize that hell is itself the Land of Tranquil Light. ("Hell is the Land of Tranquil Light," written to Ueno-ama Gozen on 11 July 1274 from Mount Minobu, Japan [*The Writings of Nichiren Daishonin, *p. 456])*

*The heart of the Lotus Sutra is the revelation that one may attain supreme enlighten-ment in one's present form without altering one's status as an ordinary person. This means that without casting aside one's karmic impediments one can still attain the Buddha way. Thus T'ien-t'ai said, "The other sutras only predict Buddhahood...for the good, but not for the evil; This [Lotus] sutra predicts Buddhahood for all." ("On Reply to Hakiri Saburo," written to Hakiri Saburo on 3 August 1273 from Sado Island, Japan [*The Writings of Nichiren Daishonin, *p. 410])*

Emcee: We want to thank everyone who came today, and ask that you join us in say-ing Nam-Myoho-Renge-Kyo three times to end the ceremony.

Ed Horan completes the ceremony by leading the chanting.

Musician plays the recessional.

Note: This commitment ceremony took place at the San Francisco Culture Center in November 1995. Earlier that year, Soka Gakkai International-USA, a Buddhist organization of the Nichiren lineage, established a policy to support and conduct same-sex weddings even though they are not legal. Nancy Burns and Diana Elrod were one of the first couples to be married in the United States under this policy. Officiating at this ceremony was Ed Horan, then-San Francisco area Headquarters Leader of the SGI-USA.

CHRISTIAN FEMINIST HOLY UNION AND COMMITMENT CEREMONY*

Performed by Diann L. Neu, WATER, dneu@hers.com

When two people find one another as lifetime companions, they usually want to gather family, friends, and colleagues to celebrate their good fortune. For some women, their life partner is a man; for others it is a woman. The theme of a wedding and a commitment ceremony is the same. Two people promise publicly to love as equal partners, cherish and respect one another, nurture each other's personal and spiritual growth, create community together, and work for a more just society. Some ask, "Do we need a commitment ceremony at all?" Lesbians and gay men often question, "Since secular and religious law in most countries provide us no legal standing, what validity is there in a commitment ceremony? Would we be mimicking heterosexual weddings by choosing to have a liturgy of our own?" Most couples, straight and lesbian, ask, "What power does communal affirmation have for us?"

This liturgy has been adapted for holy unions, for commitment ceremonies, and for weddings. Use it as a model to design the partnership liturgy you want and need.

Preparation

Choose a setting that matches your values and lifestyle, one that will accommodate your guests. Couples have chosen community centers, gardens, backyard settings, churches, homes, parks, a private room in a restaurant or hotel, or outside by the sea or riverbank. Set the chairs in a semicircle. Place a table in the front and cover it with a meaningful cloth. Put candles, flowers, rings, bread, wine, and cups on it. This is a time to use family heirlooms and symbols that can have sentiment for you in the future.

Processional

When the guests have arrived, the processional music begins. Pachelbel's Canon, Handel's Pasacaile, and Clarke's Trumpet Voluntary work well for this entrance. Those who have a part in the ceremony usually process in first, followed by the couple. Some couples prefer to walk in together. Others choose to enter arm in arm with their parents. Some walk in with their children.

Welcome

One of the partners, or a person they designate, welcomes those gathered using words similar to the following:

> *We want to welcome all of you and thank you for joining us today. We are so happy you are here to share in our joy. You are the people in our lives who have helped us arrive at this place on our respective paths. You have helped us to be who we are and to create the relationship we are so delighted to have. Each of you has made some difference in our lives. If it were not for you we would not be who we are now or where we are now.*

Introductions

The other partner, or a designated person, continues:

> *We want you to know one another. You come from different parts of our lives, so a lot of you have not met, although most of you have heard about each other. Take a couple of minutes right now and introduce yourself to anyone who is sitting near you. Tell them your name, where you are from, and how you know us.* (Sharing)

Song: "We Are a Wheel," words by Hildegard of Bingen, music by Betty Wendelborn[17]

Call to Gather

> *This sacred hour we are gathered as a community of friends and family to witness the love and commitment N. and N. have created from the union of their own individual lives. We gather to give thanks for their love and for the new life it has created. Their love for one another, for each of us here, and for the broader community shows that love makes a difference in the world. Proclaiming that love publicly takes an act of courage. Thank you, N. and N., for inviting us to witness your love.*

> *Our presence here for and with you, N. and N., is a sign of our support, of our love, and of our commitment to you as a couple. Our coming together today in the context of this liturgy is a declaration that love is powerful and transforming, that human companionship and love are precious values. We come together, not to mark the start of a relationship, but to recognize a bond that already exists. This union is one expression of the many varieties of loves in this room.*

> *The ceremony today will include three readings, the rite of marriage, an exchange of vows and rings, a eucharist, and a blessing. Feel the power of love this day; know of love's presence as we share with N. and N. Let us ask the Holy One to bless us.*

Opening Prayer

> *God of Love, Spirit of Commitment, Wisdom Sophia,*

> *Thank you for this day!*

> *Bless this occasion that brings us together to celebrate with N. and N. as they join their lives.*

> *Bless what we do and say here to reflect our deepest selves and our sense of the sacredness of life.*

> *Bless all creation through this sign of your love shown in N. and N.'s lives.*

> *God of Love, Spirit of Commitment, Wisdom Sophia,*

> *Thank you for this day!*

Reading 1

The story of Ruth and Naomi reminds us of love's qualities. A reading from the book of Ruth 1:16–18.

> *But Ruth said, "Do not press me to leave you or to turn back from following you! Where you go, I will go; Where you lodge, I will lodge; your people will be my people, and your God my God. Where you die, I will die—there will I be buried. May God do thus and so to me, and more as well, if even death parts me from you!" When Naomi saw she was determined to go with her, she said no more to her.*

> *This is the word of the God of Love.*

> *Response: Thanks be to God.*

Song: "Make Wide the Circle," by Rae E. Whitney[18]

Reading 2

A reading from I Cor. 13:1–13:

> *If I speak in human tongues or the tongues of angels, but have not love, I am a noisy gong or a clanging cymbal. And if I have prophetic powers, and understand all mysteries and all knowledge, and if I have all faith, so as to remove mountains, but have not love, I am nothing. If I give away all I have, and if I deliver my body to be burned, but have not love, I gain nothing.*

> *Love is patient and kind; love is not jealous or boastful; it is not arrogant or rude. Love does not insist on its own way; it is not irritable or resentful; it does not rejoice at wrong, but rejoices in the right. Love bears all things, believes all things, hopes all things, endures all things.*

> *Love never ends; as for prophecies, they will pass away; as for tongues, they will cease; as for knowledge, it will pass away. For our knowledge is imperfect and our prophecy is imperfect; but when the perfect comes, the imperfect will pass away. When I was a child, I spoke like a child, I thought like a child, I reasoned like a child; when I became an adult, I gave up childish ways. For now we see in a mirror dimly, but then face to face. Now I know in part; then I shall understand fully, even as I have been fully understood. So faith, hope, love abide, these three; but the greatest of these is love.*

> *This is the word of Love.*

> *Response: Thanks be to God.*

Song: "Make Wide the Circle," by Rae E. Whitney

Reading 3

A reading of The Beatitudes: choose a version of Matthew 5:1–10 you are familiar with, or a contemporary adaptation of it, such as "The Gospel According to Shug," from *The Temple of My Familiar* by Alice Walker.[19]

Song: "Make Wide the Circle," by Rae E. Whitney

Words of Reflection: "What's Love Got to Do with It?" by Mary E. Hunt

Mary wrote these words for the commitment ceremony of Margaret Sequeira and Donna Jones:

> *Good day to all of you, and warm wishes to you, N. and N., on this festive occasion. On behalf of all of us gathered, let me thank you two for inviting us to share in the goodness of your love. Thank you especially for giving us this opportunity not only to support you in your commitments to one another but also for the chance to meet people from many facets of your lives, and in so doing to be enriched by what I think of as your love-seeking community. That is what makes this day different from every other day. You have decided to mark time in a new way from this day forward, dividing your lives into the time before you proclaimed your love and the time after, in what I, speaking for all of us gathered, hope will be many happy, healthy years.*

> *Thank you for inviting me to express a few thoughts on this special occasion, thoughts which, borrowing boldly from Tina Turner, I have focused around a central question for all of us, "What's Love Got to Do with It?" In all the hoopla of the parties this weekend, and especially in all of the debate which surrounds same-sex marriages, I worry that love may be moved off center stage just when it deserves a solo. Or, that in overusing the word we might miss its power completely.*

> *Getting married is a gutsy thing to do today. Standing before the people you most want to think well of you and promising to keep at this relationship through thick and thin is risky business, human frailty being what it is. I admire you as I catalogue just how frail I am, indeed how frail most of us are, in this regard. But love insists.*

> *In your case, commitment is made even more difficult by loving at a time when the President of the United States [Clinton] doesn't believe in such things for women like us, and can't seem to keep his prejudices to himself. I know you don't need his approval, but it is hard for some people to understand what we're about here today when the President doesn't get it and is ready to sign our rights away before we receive them. Between that attitude and the outcry of the Religious Right, it is amazing that you and other lesbian, gay, bisexual, and transgender friends have the courage to trust your love, live it out, and more so in this climate, to entrust it to the rest of us. Good for you!*

Your efforts are thwarted too by so-called Christian churches, the churches of which you are both a part whose doors are all but closed to you today. History alone will judge those churches that disgrace themselves by offering blessings to animals for the feast of St. Francis but withhold their sacraments from same-sex couples who seek nothing more than to call attention, religious attention, to their love as heterosexual people have done for millennia. I know you don't need institutional approval, but it is important that you know that the People of God are with you today in the persons of your family and friends, despite the recalcitrance of the hierarchies. Given such behaviors, it is a wonder that you want to celebrate your love in the context of a religious community. But you do, and so we are here from a range of backgrounds to offer you our religious support.

Your love and your choice to celebrate it in this way are even controversial in the larger community of lesbian and gay people. No less a theological expert than comedienne Kate Clinton speaks of events like today as cases of "mad vow disease." There may be days down the road when you will think she was right—I must have been mad to do it—but I think that something far more powerful is at play here for which we who are privileged to participate as witnesses can only express our gratitude. That something is love. The answer to Tina Turner's question, "What's love got to do with it?" is everything.

Love is what brought you together for reasons you'll never fully understand and no one has a right to expect you to explain. Love is why you bother to work out the little things like whose turn it is to do the dishes, and the big things, like whether and when to choose children. Love is the excuse for giving each other extra time in a day when there just isn't another minute. Love is the reason why you've decided to enter into one another's families when you each have a family of your own. There is no other good explanation for such things, and love will have to do, and it does just fine.

Love is not a political matter at base, nor only a private one. Rather, love is the very essence of ourselves in community, which some like you have found and touched and hope to deepen together. You have been lucky in love because many people long all their lives for what you have in such abundance today. Guard it, but above all enjoy it to the max. It may not happen again. Love is like that.

Given this very unique but quite abundant experience called love, it is no wonder that love is the name of God, of the Divine, of Sophia. And Her nickname is love and his middle name is love, and its confirmation name is love because there is no other better way to describe what is so palpable this important day when you put us in touch with something so precious. The insights of Alice Walker and Ruth that we have just heard, these sacred texts by two other loving, justice-seeking women, the music, prayers, and vow sharing that make up this ceremony are vivid testimony to the presence of the Divine in all things, and above all, in love. Likewise, our sharing of bread and wine reminds us that love is always very concrete, and that it has consequences that shape the world. It is for this that we can only be grateful for love, just grateful.

Thank you for standing before us today, giving love two beautiful faces, so that we may see it in ourselves, in one another, and in our God forever. That's what love has to do with it, all of it. Amen. Blessed be. Alleluia.

Sharing Memories/Reflections/Blessings

> *Love is revealed to us through the beautiful faces of N. and N. What memories do you have of their love? Let us share these memories now.* (Sharing)

Rite of Partnership

> *We read in the book of Corinthians that "faith, hope, and love abide, but the greatest of these is love." We as a community are here to witness the love of N. and N. Come forward, N. and N., to speak your vows to one another.*

Vows of N. and N.

N. and N. face each other, join hands, and repeat in turn:

> *I take you N. to be my partner*
>
> *and I promise you these things:*
>
> *I will be faithful to you and honest with you,*
>
> *I will respect you, trust you,*
>
> *help you, listen to you, and care for you.*
>
> *I will share my life with you*
>
> *in plenty and in want,*
>
> *in sickness and in health,*
>
> *I will support you and encourage you*
>
> *to share your gifts with family and friends and with the larger community to which we belong.*

Family Vows

> *Families of N. and N., please come forward and form a circle around them. The vows N. and N. have made affect not just each of them but everyone around them. Their union is not just of two individuals but of two families and two communities. We ask now if N. and N.'s families will promise to come together as one and support N. and N. as they build a life together. We also ask N. and N. to commit to their families to continue to grow in love and support their families as they build their lives.*

> *To the families: Families, will you support, celebrate, and witness N. and N.'s relationship? Will you forgive and ask for forgiveness when there is hurt and misunderstanding? Will you strive with them as they strive to live together in mutuality and love, as they work toward making their dreams a reality?*

Response: We will.

To N. and N.: N. and N., will you support and celebrate with your families who have loved you, cared for you, and let you go? Will you forgive and ask for forgiveness when there is hurt and misunderstanding? Will you strive for deeper understanding, love, and mutuality with your families?

Response: We will.

Community Vows

All gathered here, you have come from diverse parts of N. and N.'s lives. You are friends from childhood, college, work, and church, but you all have in common your relationship with each of them. You have been brought together today as one community and are asked to witness, support, and celebrate the commitment N. and N. have made.

To the community: This community of N. and N., will you support, celebrate and witness N. and N.'s relationship? Will you forgive and ask for forgiveness when there is hurt and misunderstanding? Will you strive with them as they strive to live together in mutuality and love, as they work toward making their dreams a reality?

Response: We will.

To N. and N.: N. and N., this is your community, which over the years has grown and will continue to evolve throughout your lives. Do you promise to support and celebrate with your community? Will you forgive and ask forgiveness when there is hurt and misunderstanding? Will you be a source of love and strength to them?

Response: We will.

Exchange of Rings

In partnership ceremonies, the giving and receiving of rings is not simply a perfunctory act; not simply the giving of a piece of jewelry. Rather, rings are a visible sign of the sealing of a promise, an announcement that can be seen for all the days and years to come.

N. and N., rings are made of precious substances and symbolize the treasure that your relationship holds. Fashioned to be worn as a circle, they are a sign of love that is a continuous, strengthening tie. N. and N., as you give and receive rings, may you be attentive to the bond of love that is ever deepening between you.

The couple exchanges rings, and says in turn:

N., I give you this ring as a sign of my love for you,

as a symbol of the communities to which we belong,

and as a reminder of the vows and promises we have made here today.

Pronouncement of Holy Union

Said by all, in unison:

> *We speak for the circle, for the Spirit of love in each heart gathered around us, seen and unseen. With the power of life invested in us, we pronounce you joined together as partners in life, love, and spiritual integrity.*

Blessing the Bread

One partner blesses the bread.

> *Come, extend your hands toward the bread and wine.*

> *Blessed are you, Gracious and Loving Holy One, Wisdom Sophia, for this eucharistic love feast. You call us to the banquet table. We take, bless, break, and eat this bread in thanksgiving for the love we have known, in thanksgiving for the love we have received, in thanksgiving for the love we have given and will give. May our love increase.*

Blessing the Wine

The other partner blesses the wine.

> *Blessed are you, Holy One of Joy, Wisdom Sophia, for creating this fruit of the vine. Young wine reminds us of new love; aged wine, growing richer and fuller, symbolizes long-lasting love. We give thanks for this fruit of the vine and recall the lasting love of beloved partners and dear friends. May our love increase.*

Communion

The couple passes the bread and wine around the circle for all to eat and drink.

Song: "Bring the Feast to Ev'ry Hillside," by Joan Prefontaine[20]

Closing Blessing

> *Let us ask the God of Love, Wisdom Sophia, to bless and keep N. and N. in Her care. I invite each of us to respond "Blessed Be" to the following blessing.*

> *N. and N., may your lives together be joyful and content, and may your love be as bright as the stars, as warm as the sun, as accepting as the ocean, and as enduring as the mountains.*

> *Response: Blessed be.*

> *May you respect, have patience with, and delight in your cultural, spiritual, and personal differences.*

Response: Blessed be.

May you remember that your love, like planet Earth, when nurtured, fertilized, and watered can withstand the most treacherous storms. May you let the roots of your relationship be planted into the solid ground of love so that in the dry season you may drink deeply from its source.

Response: Blessed be.

May your heart hear more than words...listening to each other's silences and exploring each other's processes. May you have the courage to not always agree but always understand.

Response: Blessed be.

May your love for each other pull you beyond yourselves into the hearts and lives of all those calling for justice, dignity, and love.

Response: Blessed be.

May you be blessed with wisdom to find the path upon which you both may walk, and with clear vision to keep sight of the grace that surrounds you.

Response: Blessed be.

May you continue to make your love clearly and truly a reflection of the infinite love that embraces us all.

Response: Blessed be.

And may you, N. and N., be blessed in the name of the Holy One, Wisdom Sophia, who loves us into being, the Beloved who is the way of love, and the Spirit whose burning love sets us free. Amen. Blessed be. Let it be so.

Sending Forth

With this blessing, this part of our celebration is concluded. Let us go forth in the name of the God of Love, filled with the power of love revealed through N. and N.

May we each treasure love this day.

May we give thanks for those we have loved and for those who have loved us.

May love increase so that violence and injustice may cease.

Amen. Blessed be. Let it be so.

Recessional

The music of Handel's Water Music Suite *begins to play. N. and N. walk out, followed by their party and the guests.*

Reception

CATHOLIC DIGNITYUSA HOLY UNION CEREMONY

Provided by Michael and Dennis, Dignity/Washington

Gathering and Entrance Rites

Prelude

Procession (stand)

Trumpet Tune

Greeting

> *Presider: In the name of the God Who Creates us, Who Redeems us and Who makes us Holy.*
>
> *Response: Amen*
>
> *Presider: The grace of our Lord Jesus Christ and the Love of God and the fellowship of the Holy Spirit be with you all.*
>
> *Response: And also with you.*

Penitential Rite

> *Presider: My brothers and sisters, to prepare ourselves to celebrate the Sacred Mysteries, let us call to mind our sins. You were sent to heal the contrite of heart, Lord have mercy*
>
> *Response: Lord have mercy.*
>
> *Presider: You came to call all Sinners, Christ have mercy.*
>
> *Response: Christ have mercy.*
>
> *Presider: You plead for us at the right hand of the Father, Lord have mercy.*
>
> *Response: Lord have mercy.*
>
> *Presider: May almighty God have mercy on us, forgive us our sins, and bring us to everlasting life*
>
> *Response: Amen.*

Opening Prayer

> *Presider: Let us pray. Oh Lord our God, You bestowed all things on us for salvation and commanded us to love one another and to bear with one another's weakness. You yourself were a friend to humankind; therefore grant unashamed devotion and unfeigned love all their days to [first name] and [second name], Your servants, who love each other in a Holy and Blessed love and have come into Your Holy Temple to be blessed by You. We ask this through our Lord Jesus Christ Your Son, who lives and reigns with You and the Holy Spirit, one God, forever and ever.*

> *Response: Amen*

Liturgy of the Word

> *First Reading: A reading from the First Book of Samuel (I Samuel 16:19–23; 18:1–5; 20:35; 20:40–43):*

> *Saul sent messengers to Jesse, saying "Send me David your son who is with the sheep." Jesse took five loaves, a skin of wine and a kid, sent them to Saul by David his son. And so David came to Saul and entered his service; Saul loved him greatly and David became his armor bearer. Then Saul sent to Jesse saying, "Let David enter my service; he has won favor. And whenever the spirit from God troubled Saul, David took the harp and played; then Saul grew calm, and recovered, and the evil spirit left him.*

> *After David had finished talking to Saul, Jonathan's soul became closely bound to David's and Jonathan came to him as his own soul. Saul kept him from that day forward and would not let him go back to his father's house. Jonathan made a pact with David to love him as his own soul; he took off the cloak he was wearing and give it to David, and his armor too, even his sword, his bow and belt. Whenever David went out, on whatever mission Saul sent him, he was successful, and Saul put him in command of the fighting men; he stood well in his people's eyes and in the eyes of Saul's officers.*

> *The next morning Jonathan went out into the fields for the agreed meeting with David, taking a young servant with him.*

> *Jonathan then gave his weapons to his servant and said, "Go and carry them to the town." When the servant went off, David rose from beside the hillock and fell with his face to the ground and bowed three times. Then they kissed each other and shed many tears. Then Jonathan said to David, "Go in peace. And as regards the oath that both of us have sworn in the name of Yahweh be witness between you and me, between your descendants and mine forever.*

> *The Word of the Lord.*

> *Response: Thanks be to God.*

> *Responsorial Psalm: We Have Been Told*

Second Reading: A reading from the First Letter of Paul to the Church at Corinth (I Corinthians 12:31; 13:4–13):

Set your hearts on the greater gifts. I will show you the way, which surpasses all others. If I speak with human tongues and angelic as well, but do not know love, I am a noisy gong, a clanging cymbal. If I have the love of prophecy and, with full knowledge, comprehend all mysteries; if I have the faith great enough to move mountains, but have not love, I am nothing. If I give everything to feed the poor and hand over my body to be burned, but have not love, I gain nothing.

Love is patient, love is kind. Love is not jealous, it does not put on airs, it is not snobbish. Love is never rude, it is not selfish, it is not prone to anger; neither does it brood over injuries. Love does not rejoice in what is wrong but rejoices with the truth. There is no limit to love's forbearance, to its trust, its hope, its power to endure.

Love never fails. Prophecies will cease, tongues will be silent, and knowledge will pass away. Our knowledge is imperfect and our prophesying is imperfect. When the perfect comes, the imperfect will pass away. When I was a child, I used to talk like a child, think like a child, reason like a child. When I became an adult, I put childish ways aside. Now we see indistinctly, as in a mirror; then we shall face to face. My knowledge is imperfect now; then I shall know even as I am known. There are in the end three things that last: faiths, hope, and love, and the greatest of these is love. Love never fails.

The Word of the Lord.

Response: Thanks be to God.

Gospel Acclamation: Celtic Alleluia (stand)

Gospel

Presider: The Lord be with you.

Response: And also with you

Presider: A reading from the Holy Gospel according to Matthew (Matthew 5:13–16). Jesus said to his disciples:

You are the salt of the earth. But what if salt goes flat? How can you restore its flavor? Then it is good for nothing but to be thrown out and trampled under foot.

You are the light of the world. A city set on a hill cannot be hidden. People do not light a lamp and then put it under a basket. They set it on a stand where it gives a light to all in the house. In the same way, your light must shine before all so that they may see your goodness in your acts and give praise to your heavenly Creator.

This is the Gospel of the Lord.

Response: Praise to You, Lord Jesus Christ.

Homily

Holy Union Address and Statement of Intention

Presider: My dear friends, you have come together in this church so that the Lord may seal and strengthen your love in the presence of the Church's minister and this community. In this way you will be strengthened to keep mutual and lasting faith with each other and to carry out the duties of your Most Holy Union. And so, in the presence of the Church, I ask you to state your intentions.

[first person's name], you come here freely and without reservation to affirm your covenant of love and fidelity to [second person's name] and your intention to live together in a committed relationship. Will you love (him/her), comfort (him/her), honor and keep (him/her), forsaking all others, and be faithful to (him/her) as long as you both shall live?

First person: I will.

Presider: [second person's name], you come here freely and without reservation to affirm your covenant of love and fidelity to [first person's name] and your intention to live together in a committed relationship. Will you love (him/her), comfort (him/her), honor and keep (him/her), forsaking all others, and be faithful to (him/her) as long as you both shall live?

Second person: I will.

Presider: Will all of you witnessing these promises do all in your power to uphold these two persons in their covenant?

Witnesses: We will.

Consent and Exchange of Vows

Presider: Since it is your intention to enter into this Holy Union, join your hands and declare your consent before God and the Church.

First person: In the presence of God and our community, I, [first person's name], take you, [second person's name], to be my companion in a covenant of love, comfort, forgiveness, and faithfulness; in times of ease or unease, whether we are rich or poor, in sickness and in health, as long as both shall live. This is my solemn vow.

Second person: In the presence of God and our community, I, [second person's name], take you, [first person's name], to be my companion in a covenant of love, comfort, forgiveness, and faithfulness; in times of ease or unease, whether we are rich or poor, in sickness and in health, as long as both shall live. This is my solemn vow.

Presider: You have declared your consent before the Church. The sweet smell of love is lovely to us and much desired. It was the foundation of our ancestors, the guide of prophetic voices sanctified through the preaching of the Holy Apostles, because love is superior to all beautiful things of earth. Where there is love, enmity cannot harm, demons have no power, and sin has no reality. May the Lord in His goodness strengthen your consent and fill you both with God's blessings. What God has joined, men and women must not divide.

Blessing and Exchange of Rings

Presider: Lord, bless these rings which we bless (sign of the cross) in your name. Grant that those who wear them may always have a deep faith in each other. May they do Your will and always live together in peace, goodwill, and love. We ask this through Jesus Christ our Lord.

Response: Amen.

Exchanging Rings, each person says to the other:

[the other person's name], I give you this ring as a symbol of my love and commitment. In the name of God the Creator, the Redeemer, and the Sanctifier.

General Intercessions

Presider: (petitions) We pray to the Lord.

Response: Amen.

Liturgy of the Eucharist

Presentation of the Gifts

Prayer over the Gifts

Presider: Pray, my brothers and sisters, that our sacrifice may be acceptable to Almighty God.

Response: May the Lord accept the sacrifice at your hands for the praise and glory of God's name and the good of all God's Church.

(Stand)

Presider: Loving God, accept our offering for [first name and second name]. By your love and providence you have brought them together. May the mystery of Christ's unselfish love, which we celebrate in this Eucharist, increase their love for you and for each other. We ask this in the name of Jesus the Lord.

Response: Amen.

Eucharistic Prayer

>*Presider: The Lord be with you.*

>*Response: And also with you.*

>*Presider: Lift up your hearts.*

>*Response: We lift them up to the Lord.*

>*Presider: Let us give thanks to the Lord our God.*

>*Response: It is right to give God thanks and praise.*

Preface

Holy, Holy, Holy

Memorial Acclamation

The Great Amen

Communion Rite

The Lord's Prayer

Nuptial Blessing

Adaptation from a twelfth-century Roman Catholic marriage rite for two persons of the same gender.

>*Presider: My dear friends, let us turn to God and pray that God will bless [first person's name] and [second person's name] and that through the sacrament of the Body and Blood of Christ, God will unite in love the couple joined in this Holy Union. For these two persons joining themselves in the loving union of life.*

>*Response: We pray to the Lord.*

>*Presider: For these servants, [first person's name and second person's name] and for their union in Christ.*

>*Response: We pray to the Lord*

>*Presider: That the Lord our God unites them in perfect love and inseparable life.*

>*Response: We pray to the Lord.*

>*Presider: For the holy gift of the precious Body and Blood of our Lord, Jesus Christ, that they should receive it in holiness and it should preserve their union without jealousy.*

Response: We pray to the Lord.

Presider: Oh Lord Our God, Benefactor and Friend of the human race, these two servants of Yours, who love each other with the sacred and holy love, have come to Your holy temple wishing to receive your sanctification and blessing. Grant them unashamed fidelity and sincere love in all things needed for salvation and eternal life and union for the rest of their lives through God, the Creator, the Redeemer and the Sanctifier.

Response: Amen.

Sign of Peace

Presider: Lord, Jesus Christ, you said to our Apostles: I leave you peace, my peace I give you. Look not on our sins, but on the faith of your Church, and grant us the peace and unity of your kingdom, where you live forever and ever.

Response: Amen.

Presider: The peace of the Lord be with you always.

Response: And also with you.

Presider: Let us offer each other the sign of peace.

Breaking of the Bread

Lamb of God

Communion

Presider: This is the Lamb of God who takes away the sins of the world. Happy are those who are called to this supper.

Response: Lord, I am not worthy to receive you, but only say the word and I shall be healed.

Communion Song: We Remember

Meditation A Nuptial Blessing (Choir)

Prayer after Communion

Presider: Lord, in your love you have given us this Eucharist to unite us with one another and you. We pray for our friends, [first name and second name], whom you have joined together in this Holy Union. May their love for each other proclaim to all the world their faith in you.

Response: Amen.

Concluding Rites

Blessing

> *Presider: The Lord be with you.*
>
> *Response: And also with you.*
>
> *Presider: (Blessing)*
>
> *Response: Amen.*

Dismissal

> *Presider: Go in the peace of Christ.*
>
> *Response: Thanks be to God.*

Closing Hymn: Now Thank We All Our God

NOTES

*Diann L. Neu, "Creating Community." From *Women's Rites: Feminist Liturgies for Life's Journey* (Cleveland: The Pilgrim Press, 2003), 106–20. Copyright © 2003 by Diann L. Neu. Used by permission. All rights reserved.

1. Rabbi Lisa Edwards and Tracy Moore also were ushered under the huppah with this song, which was sung with the tune that has become the signature of Kehillat Kol HaNeshama in Jerusalem.

2. See Rachel Adler, *Engendering Judaism: An Inclusive Theology and Ethics* (Philadelphia: Jewish Publication Society, 1998), especially chap. 5.

3. Both the *brit ahuvot* and the partnership exchange were developed following the research and interpretations of Rachel Adler. The declaration that accompanies the ring exchange focuses on the communal context of the *brit* rather than the object exchanged to consecrate the covenant, as in a traditional *kinyan* ceremony.

4. These blessings draw on the blessings developed by many other couples. Special thanks to the pioneering work of Rabbis Yoel Kahn and Lisa Edwards, and Reena Kling and Miriam Bronstein. These blessings alternate masculine and feminine blessing formulations.

5. Expanding the tradition of naming one's students and followers as בנים, all women are honored as potential teachers, guides, and nurturers of the next generation. In this particular wedding, Sue and Nurit were celebrated as the guides and nurturers of the four young women who held the huppah: Sue's daughters and Sue's and Nurit's nieces.

6. This innovative *hatima* provided an opportunity for all of the rabbis present to serve as officiants at this *brit*. The formulation echoes both the declaration of the partners and the traditional declaration made at the *brit* ceremony of an infant, acknowledging the maturity of these partners: that study and sharing communal responsibility for *tikkun alam* are continuing responsibilities of Jews.

7. The blessing was offered in the feminine plural.

8. Leviticus 25:9ff.

9. For further information about this *kiddushin* ceremony, please contact Rabbi Sue Levi Elwell, UAHC, 1511 Walnut Street, Suite 401, Philadelphia, PA 19102, 215-563-8183.

10. Genesis 9:16–17.

11. Jeremiah 30:22.

12. 1 Samuel 15:1.

13. Hosea 2:21–22.

14. Avot d'Rabbi Natan 8.

15. Song of Songs 5:6.

16. Adapted from the Britot of Rachel Yehudit Adler and David Yitzhak Schulman and Tracy Mika Moore and Lisa Devorah Edwards.

17. Betty Wendelborn (music), "We Are a Wheel" (words by Hildegard of Bingen), *Sing Green: Songs of the Mystics*, 2nd ed. (Aukland, New Zealand: Pyramid Press, 1999), 1.

18. Rae E. Whitney, stanza 1 adapt., music by Donna Kasbohm, *Bring the Feast*, (Cleveland, OH: The Pilgrim Press, 1997), 24.

19. Alice Walker, "The Gospel According to Shug," in *The Temple of My Familiar* (New York: Simon and Schuster, 1989), 288–89.

20. Joan Prefontaine, "Bring the Feast to Ev'ry Hillslide" (music, "Feast" by Jane Ramseyer Miller), *Bring the Feast* (Cleveland: Pilgrim Press, 1997), 7.

SELECTED RESOURCES

—————————— . ——————————

Abelove, Henry, Michele Aina Barale, and David M. Halperin, eds. *The Lesbian and Gay Studies Reader*. New York: Routledge and Kegan Paul, 1993.

Adler, Rachel. *Engendering Judaism: An Inclusive Theology*. Philadelphia: Jewish Publication Society, 1998.

Alpert, Rebecca, Sue Levi Elwell, and Shirley Idelson. *Lesbian Rabbis: The First Generation*. New Brunswick, NJ: Rutgers University Press, 2001.

Balka, Christie and Andy Rose, ed. *Twice Blessed: On Being Lesbian or Gay and Jewish*. Boston: Beacon Press, 1989.

Baum, Gregory. "Homosexuality and the Natural Law." *The Ecumenist,* January–February 1994.

Boswell, John. *Christianity, Social Tolerance and Homosexuality*. Chicago: University of Chicago Press, 1980.

———. *Same Sex Unions in Premodern Europe*. New York: Villard Books, 1994.

Brandt, Eric, ed. *Dangerous Liaisons: Blacks, Gays, and the Struggle for Equality*. New York: The New Press, 1999.

Brawley, Robert L., ed. *Biblical Ethics & Homosexuality: Listening to Scripture*. Louisville, KY: Westminster John Knox Press, 1996.

Brooten, Bernadette J. *Love between Women: Early Christian Responses to Female Homoeroticism*. Chicago: University of Chicago Press, 1996.

Brown, Ruth Murray. *For a "Christian America": A History of the Religious Right*. Amherst, NY: Prometheus Books, 2002.

Cabezón, José Ignacio, ed. *Buddhism, Sexuality, and Gender*. Albany: State University of New York Press, 1992.

Chauncey, George. *Why Marriage? The History Shaping Today's Debate Over Gay Equality*. New York: Basic Books, 2004.

Cherry, Kittredge, and Zalmon Sherwood, eds. *Equal Rites: Lesbian and Gay Worship, Ceremonies, and Celebrations*. Louisville, KY: Westminster John Knox Press, 1995.

Cianciotti, Jason. *Hispanic and Latino Same-Sex Couple Households in the United States, A Report from the 2000 Census.* New York: National Gay and Lesbian Task Force Policy Institute / National Latino/a Coalition for Justice, 2005.

Comstock, Gary David. *Unrepentent, Self-affirming, Practicing: Lesbian/Bisexual/Gay People within Organized Religion.* New York: Continuum, 1996.

————. *A Whosoever Church: Welcoming Lesbians and Gay Men into African American Congregations.* Louisville, KY: Westminster John Knox Press, 2001.

Cott, Nancy F. *Public Vows: A History of Marriage and the Nation.* Cambridge: Harvard University Press, 2000.

Dang, Alain, and Somjen Frazer. *Black Same-Sex Households in the United States, A Report from the 2000 Census, Second Edition.* Washington, DC: National Gay and Lesbian Task Force Policy Institute, 2005.

Diamond, Sara. *Roads to Dominion: Right-wing Movements and Political Power in the United States.* New York: The Guilford Press, 1995.

Douglas, Kelly Brown. *Sexuality and the Black Church: A Womanist Perspective.* Maryknoll, NY: Orbis Books, 1999.

————. *What's Faith Got to Do With It? Black Bodies/Christian Souls.* Maryknoll, NY: Orbis Books, 2006.

Ellison, Marvin M. *Erotic Justice: A Liberating Ethic of Sexuality.* Louisville, KY: Westminster John Knox, 1996.

Ellison, Marvin M., and Sylvia Thorson-Smith, eds. *Body and Soul: Rethinking Sexuality as Justice-Love.* Cleveland: Pilgrim Press, 2003.

————. *Same-Sex Marriage? A Christian Ethical Analysis.* Cleveland: The Pilgrim Press, 2004.

Eskridge, William N. Jr., *The Case For Same-Sex Marriage: From Sexual Liberty to Civilized Commitment.* New York: The Free Press, 1996.

————. *Gay Marriage: For Better or for Worse? What We've Learned from the Evidence.* New York: Oxford University Press, 2006.

Falk, Nancy Auer. *Living Hinduisms: An Explorer's Guide.* Belmont, CA: Thomson Wadsworth, 2005.

Gomes, Peter J. *The Good Book.* New York: William Morrow, 1996.

Greenberg, Steven. *Wrestling with God and Man: Homosexuality and Jewish Tradition.* Madison: University of Wisconsin Press, 2004.

Gross, Rita M. *Buddhism after Patriarchy: A Feminist History, Analysis, and Reconstruction of Buddhism.* Albany: State University of New York Press, 1993.

Hay, Harry. *Radically Gay: Gay Liberation in the Words of Its Founder.* Edited by Will Roscoe. Boston: Beacon Press, 1996.

Herman, Didi. *The Antigay Agenda: Orthodox Vision and the Christian Right.* Chicago: University of Chicago Press, 1997.

Jacob, Walter, and Moshe Zemer, eds. *Gender Issues in Jewish Law.* New York: Berghah Books, 2001.

————. *Marriage and Its Obstacles in Jewish Law.* Pittsburgh: Solomon B. Freehof Institute of Progressive Halacha, 1999.

Jakobsen, Janet R., and Ann Pellegrini. *Love the Sin: Sexual Regulation and the Limits of Religious Tolerance.* New York: New York University Press, 2003.

Jennings, Theodore W. *The Man Jesus Loved: Homoerotic Narratives from the New Testament.* Cleveland: Pilgrim Press, 2003.

Jordan, Mark D. *The Invention of Sodomy in Christian Theology.* Chicago: University of Chicago Press, 1997.

————. *Blessing Same-Sex Unions: The Perils of Queer Romance and the Confusions of Christian Marriage.* Chicago: University of Chicago Press, 2005.

————. *Authorizing Marriage?: Canon, Tradition, and Critique in the Blessing of Same-Sex Unions*. Princeton, NJ: Princeton University Press, 2006.

Jung, Patricia Beattie with Joseph A. Coray, eds. *Sexual Diversity and Catholicism: Toward the Development of Moral Theology*. Collegeville, MN: The Liturgical Press, 2001.

Jung, Patricia Beattie, and Ralph F. Smith. *Heterosexism: An Ethical Challenge*. Albany: State University of New York Press, 1993.

Kennedy, Randall. *Interracial Intimacies: Sex, Marriage, Identity, and Adoption*. New York: Vintage Books, 2004.

Lamm, Maurice. *The Jewish Way in Love and Marriage*. New York: Harper and Row, 1982.

Levitt, Laura. *Jews and Feminism: The Ambivalent Search for Home*. New York: Routledge, 1997.

Lewin, Ellen. *Recognizing Ourselves: Ceremonies of Lesbian and Gay Commitment*. New York: Columbia University Press, 1998.

Leyland, Winston, ed. *Queer Dharma: Voices of Gay Buddhists*. San Francisco: Gay Sunshine Press, 1998.

Lucas, Charles L. *The Lord is My Shepherd and He Knows I'm Gay*. Los Angeles: Nash Publishing, 1972.

Manning, Christel, and Phil Zuckerman, eds. *Sex and Religion*. Belmont, CA: Thomson Wadsworth, 2005.

Myers, David G., and Letha Dawson Scanzoni. *What God Has Joined Together? A Christian Case for Gay Marriage*. New York: HarperCollins, 2005.

Nelson, James B. *Embodiment: An Approach to Sexuality and Christian Theology*. Minneapolis: Augsburg, 1978.

Nissinen, Kristi, and Kirsi Stjerna. *Homoeroticism in the Biblical World: A Historical Perspective*. Minneapolis: Fortress Press, 1998.

Oliveto, Karen P., Kelly Turney, and Traci West. *Holy Conversations: Talking about Homosexuality, A Congregational Resource*. Cleveland: Pilgrim Press, 2004.

Osment, Steven. *When Fathers Ruled: Family Life in Reformation Europe*. Cambridge: Harvard University Press, 2004.

Pinn, Anthony, and Dwight Hopkins. *Loving the Body: Black Religious Studies and the Erotic*. New York: Palgrave, 2005.

Ratti, Rakesh, ed. *A Lotus of Another Color: An Unfolding of the South Asian Gay and Lesbian Experience*. Boston: Alyson Publications, 1993.

Ruether, Rosemary Radford. *Christianity and the Making of the Modern Family*. Boston: Beacon Press, 2000.

Sands, Kathleen, ed. *God Forbid: Religion and Sex in American Public Life*. New York: Oxford University Press, 2000.

Scharen, Christian. *Married in the Sight of God: Theology, Ethics, and Church Debates Over Homosexuality*. Landham, MD: University Press of America, 2000.

Swidler, Arlene, ed. *Homosexuality and World Religions*. Valley Forge, PA: Trinity Press International, 1993.

Thumma, Scott, and Edward R. Gray, eds. *Gay Religion*. Walnut Creek, CA: AltaMira Press, 2005.

Vanita, Ruth. *Love's Rite: Same-Sex Marriage in India and the West*. New York: Palgrave-St. Martin's; New Delhi: Penguin, 2005.

————. "2002: India Considers Abolishing Sodomy Laws." In *GLBT History*. Pasadena, CA: Salem Press, 2005.

————. "Born of Two Vaginas: Love and Reproduction between Co-Wives in Some Medieval Indian Texts." *GLQ* 11, no.4 (2005): 547–77.

Vanita, Ruth, ed. *Queering India: Same-Sex Love and Eroticism in Indian Culture and Society*. New York: Routledge, 2002.

Vanita, Ruth, and Saleem Kidwai. *Same-Sex Love in India: Readings from Literature and History*. New York: Palgrave-St. Martin's, 2000.

Wallenstein, Peter. *Tell the Court I Love My Wife: Race, Marriage and Law, An American History*. New York: Palgrave, 2002.

West, Traci. *Disruptive Christian Ethics: When Racism and Women's Lives Matter*. Louisville, KY: Westminster John Knox Press, 2006.

White, Mel. *Stranger at the Gate: To be Gay and Christian in America*. New York: Plume Books, 1995.

Wilson, Nancy. *Our Tribe: Queer Folks, God, Jesus and the Bible*. San Francisco: HarperSanFrancisco, 1995.

Wolfson, Evan. *Why Marriage Matters: America, Equality, and Gay People's Right to Marry*. New York: Simon and Schuster, 2004.

Wood, Robert W. *Christ and the Homosexual*. New York: Vantage Press, 1960.

CUMULATIVE INDEX

———————————— • ————————————

ABOUT THE EDITOR
AND THE CONTRIBUTORS

─────────────── • ───────────────

Rev. Dr. Traci C. West is Associate Professor of Ethics and African American Studies at Drew University Theological School (Madison, NJ). She is the author of *Disruptive Christian Ethics: When Racism and Women's Lives Matter*, *Wounds of the Spirit: Black Women, Violence, and Resistance Ethics*, coauthor with Kelly Turney and Karen Oliveto of *Holy Conversations: Talking about Homosexuality*, and many articles on clergy ethics, racism, sexuality, and other justice issues in church and society. She is an ordained United Methodist minister who has previously served in parish and campus ministry.

Sheikh Daayiee Abdullah is a scholar of Arabic, Shari'ah sciences, and Quranic interpretation, as well as comparative (Western and Islamic) legal systems. He is the current moderator of Muslim Gay Men, a Yahoo-based discussion group, and a board member of Al-Fatiha Foundation, an organization for LGBTQ Muslims.

Rebecca T. Alpert is chair of the Department of Religion and associate professor of religion and women's studies at Temple University. She was ordained as a rabbi at the Reconstructionist Rabbinical College. She is the coauthor of *Exploring Judaism: A Reconstructionist Approach*, with Jacob Staub; author of *Like Bread on the Seder Plate: Jewish Lesbians and the Transformation of Tradition*; editor of *Voices of the Religious Left: A Contemporary Sourcebook*; and coeditor of *Lesbian Rabbis: The First Generation* with Sue Elwell and Shirley Idelson. She teaches in the areas of religion and contemporary social issues with a focus on sexuality, the politics of race and gender, and medical ethics. She is currently at work on a volume about Jews, race, and baseball.

Rev. Dr. Herbert W. Chilstrom is a graduate of Augsburg College, Lutheran School of Theology at Chicago, and Princeton Seminary. He has a doctor of education degree from New York University. He served as a parish pastor, college professor, and dean and is a retired presiding bishop of the Evangelical Lutheran Church in America.

Roger J. Corless, professor of religion emeritus, Duke University, has published four books and more than sixty articles on Buddhism, Christianity, Buddhist-Christian dialogue, and gay studies, especially in relation to Buddhist practice in the LGBT community. Dr. Corless's primary research interests are in Pure Land Buddhism and Buddhist-Christian studies, a newly developing field that he has helped define. He is a cofounder of the Society for Buddhist-Christian Studies. After retiring from teaching at Duke University for thirty years, he wrote this article as he recuperated from successful cancer treatment. However, he has been diagnosed with irreversible macular degeneration, an affliction of the eye, and his contribution to this volume may well be one of his last full-length articles.

Kelly Brown Douglas is professor of religion at Goucher College in Baltimore Maryland. Her books include *The Black Christ*, *Sexuality and the Black Church*, and *What's Faith Got to Do with It? Black Bodies/Christian Souls*. She is an ordained Episcopal priest.

Marvin M. Ellison teaches Christian social ethics at Bangor Theological Seminary and is an ordained Presbyterian minister. He founded the Religious Coalition Against Discrimination in Maine to support civil rights protections for LGBT people. His publications include *Same-Sex Marriage? A Christian Ethical Analysis* (2004), *Body and Soul: Rethinking Sexuality as Justice-Love* (2003), and *Erotic Justice: A Liberating Ethic of Sexuality* (1996). He lives in Portland, Maine with his partner Frank Brooks, a clinical social worker.

Rev. Ruth Garwood, an ordained minister in the United Church of Christ, is the national coordinator of the United Church of Christ Coalition for Lesbian, Gay, Bisexual and Transgender Concerns, an organization affiliated with but independent of the denomination. The Coalition is based in Cleveland, Ohio.

Renee L. Hill is currently serving as a community organizer and public educator for the Lambda Legal Defense and Education Fund. She is an Episcopal priest who has served parishes in New York and in Southern California. She is a former instructor and program coordinator at the Center for Anti-Violence Education in Brooklyn, New York, and a former member of the faculty at the Episcopal Divinity School in Cambridge, Massachusetts, where she was assistant professor of theology and director of the Feminist Liberation Studies program. Dr. Hill earned both her MDiv. and her PhD in systematic theology at Union Theological Seminary in New York and has published several articles, including "Black Theology and Black Power 1968/1998—Disrupted/Disruptive Movements" in *Black Power and Black Theology: The 30th Anniversary edition* and "Who are We for Each Other?: Sex,

Sexuality, and Womanist Theology" in *Black Theology: A Documentary History*, vol. 2 (1993). Her broad interests include spirituality, ending violence in all of its forms, and the blending of physical and spiritual strategies for empowerment and justice making.

Patricia Beattie Jung is professor of Christian ethics and chair of the Theology Department at Loyola University Chicago. She is the editor of *Sexual Diversity and Catholicism: Toward the Development of Moral Theology* and a coeditor with Mary E. Hunt and Radhika Balakrisnan of *Good Sex: Feminist Perspectives from the World's Religions*. She has been married for thirty-three years; she and her husband, Shannon, have been blessed with three sons, Michael, Robert, and Nathan, and, most recently, with two wonderful daughters-in-law, Heidi and Cara.

Norman J. Kansfield, after graduate education at Union Theological Seminary, New York, and the University of the Chicago, was the director of two very different theological seminary libraries: the John Walter Beardslee Library, serving Western Theological Seminary in Holland, Michigan, and the Ambrose Swasey Library, serving the Colgate Rochester Divinity School/Bexley Hall/Crozer Theological Seminary and the St. Bernard's Institute, in Rochester, New York. In 1992, he was elected as the twelfth president of New Brunswick Theological Seminary. His career in theological education was interrupted after he presided at the wedding of his daughter Ann to Ms. Jennifer Aull. He was terminated as president of the New Brunswick Theological Seminary, and the General Synod of 2005 removed him from the office of Professor of Theology and suspended him from the office of Minister of Word and Sacrament. Since 2006, it has been his delight to serve within the Theological School of Drew University as Senior Scholar in Residence.

Peter S. Knobel is rabbi of Beth Emet the Free Synagogue (Evanston, Ilinois) and has chaired the CCAR Liturgy and Reform Practice Committee. He is also a member of the CCAR Ad Hoc Committee on Human Sexuality and the Taskforce on Same Sex Ceremonies. He is coeditor of *Duties of the Soul:The Role of the Commandments in Liberal Judaism*, as well as several other books.

Rev. Keith Kron is the director of the Office of Bisexual, Gay, Lesbian, and Transgender Concerns for the Unitarian Universalist Association. He revised the Welcoming Congregation manual and wrote an additional curriculum, "Living the Welcoming Congregation," both used by Unitarian Universalist congregations. He advises congregations and individuals on such issues as marriage equality, public witness, antiracism/antioppression, equal opportunity in ministerial settlement, and issues of homophobia, biphobia, and transphobia. He cochairs the UUA's Family Matters Task Force. He also teaches a class for Starr King School for the Ministry, a Unitarian Universalist seminary, on children's literature. He leads training on the enneagram and is an avid tennis player. He lives in the Pacific Northwest with his partner Collin.

Karen P. Oliveto is associate dean for Academic Affairs and adjunct professor of United Methodist Studies at Pacific School of Religion in Berkeley, California. She is a United Methodist clergywoman. She is the coauthor of *Talking about Homosexuality: A Congregational Resource.*

Tex Sample is the Robert B. and Kathleen Rogers Professor Emeritus of Church and Society at the Saint Paul School of Theology. He is a freelance lecturer and workshop leader for church, government, and business groups. Sample is coeditor with Amy E. DeLong of *The Loyal Opposition: Struggling with the Church on Homosexuality.*

Christian Scharen (PhD, Emory University), is director of the Faith as a Way of Life Project at the Yale Center for Faith and Culture and teaches practical theology and congregational studies at Yale Divinity School. He has written several books, including *One Step Closer: Why U2 Matters to Those Seeking God* and *Married in the Sight of God: Theology, Ethics, and Church Debates over Homosexuality.* An ordained pastor in the Evangelical Lutheran Church in America, he has served congregations in California, Georgia, and Connecticut.

J. Terry Todd is associate professor of American religious studies at Drew University in Madison, New Jersey. The author of a number of articles exploring Protestant Christianity in urban American cultures, his research interests focus on Christianity and U.S. nationalism in the twentieth century along with representations of Jesus in America. Todd is a lay leader of New York's Village Church, a progressive United Methodist community in Greenwich Village.

Elder Joseph W. Tolton is the pastor of Rehoboth Temple Christ Conscious Church in New York City. His affirming ministry seeks to empower all people with the transformative power of the Gospel and to nurture disciples of Christ in the progressive Pentecostal tradition. Elder Tolton received his BA in religion from Vassar College and his MBA in management from Columbia Business School.

Ruth Vanita, formerly associate professor at Delhi University, India, is now professor at the University of Montana. She was founding editor of *Manushi*, India's first nationwide feminist magazine, from 1978 to 1990. She is the author of several books, including *Sappho and the Virgin Mary: Same-Sex Love and the English Literary Imagination, Same-Sex Love in India: Readings from Literature and History, Love's Rite: Same-Sex Marriage in India and the West*, and the forthcoming *Chocolate: Stories on Male Homoeroticism* by Pandey Bechan Sharma Ugra, translated with an introduction. She was raised Christian but has now been a Hindu for over two decades.

Rev. Dr. Mel White has been a Christian minister, author, and filmmaker all his adult life. Raised as an evangelical Christian and taught that homosexuality was a sin, he fought to overcome his own homosexual orientation for decades. In 1993, he came out publicly when he was installed as dean at the Dallas Cathedral of Hope of the Universal Fellowship of Metropolitan Community Churches (UFMCC). He announced during his first sermon, "I am gay. I am proud. And God loves me without reservation." His first book *Stranger at the Gate: To Be Gay and Christian in*

America (1994) describes his reconciliation of his homosexuality with his Christian faith. His latest book is *Religion Gone Bad—The Hidden Dangers of Fundamentalism* (2006). Mel White founded Soulforce, Inc. with his partner, Gary Nixon, and since 1993 has devoted himself full time to minister to LGBT persons and to work on their behalf in the media, in the political process, and with fellow religious leaders. In 1997, the Reverend Dr. Mel White was awarded the ACLU's National Civil Liberties Award for his efforts to apply the "soul force" principles of Gandhi and King to the struggle for justice for sexual minorities.